A COMPANION TO
THE MIDDLE ENGLISH LYRIC

To
Douglas Gray

A COMPANION TO
THE MIDDLE ENGLISH LYRIC

Edited by Thomas G. Duncan

D. S. BREWER

The right of the Contributors to be identified as
the authors of this work has been asserted in accordance with
sections 77 and 78 of the Copyright, Designs and Patents Act 1988

First published 2005
D. S. Brewer, Cambridge

Transferred to digital printing

ISBN 978-1-84384-065-7

D. S. Brewer is an imprint of Boydell & Brewer Ltd
PO Box 9, Woodbridge, Suffolk IP12 3DF, UK
and of Boydell & Brewer Inc.
668 Mt Hope Avenue, Rochester, NY 14620, USA
website: www.boydellandbrewer.com

A CiP catalogue record for this book is available
from the British Library

This publication is printed on acid-free paper

Contents

Acknowledgements

For agreeing to participate in this volume and for their gracious response to my queries and suggestions as editor I owe an immense debt of gratitude to all contributors. I gratefully acknowledge generous help and advice from friends and colleagues, especially Margaret Connolly (University of Cork), Jill Gamble (Research Secretary, St Andrews University School of English), Christine Gascoigne (St Andrews University Library), David Gascoigne (University of St Andrews), Ann Hargreaves, Michael Herbert (University of St Andrews), Christopher Jones (University of St Andrews), Julian Luxford (University of St Andrews), Barbara Murray (University of St Andrews), Rhiannon Purdie (University of St Andrews) and Karla Pollmann (University of St Andrews). I also wish to express my gratitude to Caroline Palmer not only for her efforts as in-house editor in bringing this volume to publication but also for the kindly tolerance with which she bore with delays at various stages in its preparation.

The invitation to edit this Boydell & Brewer *Companion* came to me through Ad Putter of the University of Bristol. He has read contributions through chapter by chapter, made many corrections, suggested valuable improvements, and has been a never ending source of support and good cheer. I extend to him above all my heartfelt thanks.

Indebtedness is acknowledged to *Neuphilologische Mitteilungen*, to *The Review of English Studies*, and to *Publications of the Modern Language Association of America* in which journals some material reworked in this volume was first published.

Finally, in the planning of this volume and in bringing it to fruition, I have as ever relied on advice from Douglas Gray. No one has made a greater contribution to the study of Middle English lyrics in recent decades. Mindful of his friendly guidance and ever-generous help over many years, to him I gratefully dedicate this book.

Abbreviations

Benson	Benson, L. D., ed. 1988. *The Riverside Chaucer*. 3rd edn Oxford.
BL	London, British Library.
Bodl.	Oxford, Bodleian Library.
Brook	Brook, G. L., ed. 1968. *The Harley Lyrics*. 4th edn Manchester.
Brown *XIII*	Brown, C., ed. 1932. *English Lyrics of the Thirteenth Century*. Oxford.
Brown *XIV*	Brown, C., ed. 1952. *Religious Lyrics of the Fourteenth Century*. 2nd edn revised by G. V. Smithers. Oxford.
Brown *XV*	Brown, C., ed. 1939. *Religious Lyrics of the Fifteenth Century*. Oxford.
CT	*Canterbury Tales*.
CUL	Cambridge University Library.
Duncan *LMELC*	Duncan, T. G., ed. 2000. *Late Medieval English Lyrics and Carols, 1400–1530*. Harmondsworth.
Duncan *MEL*	Duncan, T. G., ed. 1995. *Medieval English Lyrics, 1200–1400*. Harmondsworth.
EETS	Early English Text Society.
ES	Extra Series.
EUL	Edinburgh University Library.
Gray	Gray, D. 1972. *Themes and Images in the Medieval English Religious Lyric*. London and Boston.
Greene	Greene, R. L., ed. 1977. *The Early English Carols*. 2nd edn, revised and enlarged. Oxford.
IMEV	*The Index of Middle English Verse*. Eds C. Brown and R. H. Robbins. New York. 1943. *Supplement to the Index of Middle English Verse*. Eds R. H. Robbins and J. L. Cutler. Lexington, Kentucky. 1965.
MED	*Middle English Dictionary*.
NLS	Edinburgh, National Library of Scotland.
NS	New Series.
OED	*Oxford English Dictionary*.
OS	Original Series.
PL	*Patrologiae Cursus Completus . . . Series Latina* [*Patrologia Latina*]. Ed. J. P. Migne. 221 vols. Paris 1842–80.
Robbins *Hist.*	Robbins, R. H., ed. 1959a. *Historical Poems of the Fourteenth and Fifteenth Centuries*. New York.
Robbins *Sec.*	Robbins, R. H., ed. 1952. *Secular Lyrics of the Fourteenth and Fifteenth Centuries*. Revised edn. Oxford.

SS   Supplementary Series.
STS   Scottish Text Society.
Woolf   Woolf, R. 1968. *The English Religious Lyric in the Middle Ages*.
                            Oxford.

Editorial Note

One aim of the editorial policy of this volume has been to make this *Companion* accessible to as wide a readership as possible. Accordingly, quotations in Middle English may differ in capitalization, punctuation, word-division and metrical arrangement from the texts as found in the source editions cited. The symbols thorn, eth, wynn and yogh have not been used. Some other spellings have been replaced with Middle English variants which are more transparent to a present-day reader with limited knowledge of Middle English.

References have been made using the author-date form and are keyed to the works cited in the Bibliography at the end of the book.

Introduction

In the history of English literature, the emergence of the Middle English lyric is an event of considerable significance on several counts. One is a matter of poetic form. Readers of short poems in English from Chaucer to the present day might be tempted to think that such poems had always been written in stanza form. This, of course, is not the case. Only in early Middle English, less than two centuries before Chaucer, did poems structured in sequences of verse units each having the same number of lines, matching in length and marked out by a scheme of rhymes, make their appearance in English literature. Prior to the twelfth century, poems in English, short or long, had been written in one and the same verse form, the Old English alliterative line, a line divided into two parts, each of two stresses, with the stressed words of each part linked by alliteration. Rhyme scheme and stanza form alike were unknown to Old English literature.[1] Only in Middle English did stanzaic verse form emerge – a striking innovation derived from and modelled on stanzaic lyrics in Old French and Medieval Latin literature.

Along with this new verse form there appeared an equally novel feature in the content of Middle English secular love lyrics: here, for the first time in English literature, poets write of love in terms of absolute devotion and service to a lady. The poet suffers in his love-longing for his lady; his life is wholly dependent on her; he beseeches her to have mercy on him; he pledges his life-long loyalty to her; her love is the only remedy for his distress. This mode of love-longing was unlike anything hitherto encountered in English poetry. Occasionally a cry of love was heard in Old English, as in the following lines translated from the enigmatic poem *Wulf and Eadwacer*:

> Wulf, O my Wulf, my yearning for you
> Has made me ill, the rareness of your visits,
> My sorrowing spirit, not a lack of food.   (13–15)

Here, however, the speaker is not a man but a woman. In the heroic world of Old English poetry a man's concern centred on his duty to his lord; his ruling values were those of loyalty and courage. Love as devotion to a lady was as yet unknown as an ideal let alone as an all-consuming passion. By the twelfth

---

1   Seeming exceptions in Old English have been noted; see Scattergood (below), 40–1. However, the six sections of the 42-line poem *Deor* (each concluded by the refrain-like line *þæs ofereode, þisses swa mæg*) are at best verse paragraphs; differing in length from the fourth of 3 lines to the sixth of 15, they are certainly not stanzas. Likewise sporadic occurrences of internal rhymes, or of end rhymes in the so-called 'Rhyming Poem', bear little resemblance to the rhyme schemes of stanzaic poetry.

century, however, this had become the creed of the southern French troubadour poets for whom the feudal concept of service to a lord was transformed, in the name of love, to become service to a lady. It is in Middle English lyrics that this troubadour ideal of romantic love first made its appearance in England.

No less striking was an equally new but somewhat different concept of love which emerged in Middle English religious lyrics. In the pre-twelfth-century world of Anglo-Saxon England the Christian doctrine of the Atonement finds expression in one of the finest short poems in the whole of English literature, *The Dream of the Rood*. Christ is here depicted as a young warrior, a hero, strong and steadfast, as he mounts the cross to do battle for mankind. At the end of the poem he is still a hero, a warrior, triumphant, mighty and successful in his final mission, the Harrowing of Hell. In this poem the suffering of the crucifixion is registered not through Christ but through the cross, the personified, speaking cross: it is the cross that is pierced with dark nails, the cross which is drenched with blood. Christ at the conclusion of the crucifixion scene, far from being pictured as a victim suspended in agony, continues to be represented as a hero, described as a warrior now resting, exhausted after a great battle. However, the emotive power of this poem derives not from Christ but from the immediacy with which the experiences and emotions of the dreamer and of the personified rood are presented. Christ the hero here remains a remote figure.

What a contrast emerges in Middle English devotional poetry. Here we encounter the mood and sensibilities of a new age in which the doctrine of salvation, earlier conceived as a heroic battle between Christ and the Devil, now, as in Anselm's *Cur Deus Homo*, focussed on love; Christ, out of love for man, becoming man to suffer death on the cross for man's salvation, a conception superbly expressed in *Love me broughte*, a lyric found in John of Grimestone's late fourteenth-century Commonplace Book.[2]

Love me broughte,	
And love me wroughte,	*created*
Man, to be thi fere;	*companion*
Love me fedde,	*nourished*
And love me ledde,	
And love me letted here.	*kept me here*
Love me slow,	*slew*
And love me drow,	*drew, stretched out*
And love me leyde on bere;	*laid on a bier*
Love is my pes,	*peace*
For love I ches	*chose*
Man to byen dere.	*buy (i.e. redeem) at a cost*
Ne dred thee nought,	
I have thee sought,	
Bothen day and night;	
To haven thee,	

2 See Whitehead (below), 104.

Wél is me,
I have thee wonne in fight.   *won*   (Duncan *MEL*, No. 70)

Love triumphs, but only, paradoxically, through suffering.

In contrast to the rather remote young hero of the Old English *Dream of the Rood*, Christ as man, his suffering vividly depicted, is the immediate subject of several early Middle English lyrics including the following, one of various renderings into Middle English verse of a passage beginning *Candet nudatum pectus* from John of Fecamp's *Liber Meditationum*.

Whyt was hys naked brest   *white*
    and red of blod hys side,   *red with blood*
Bleyk was his fair andled,   *pale, fair face*
    his woundes dep and wide,   *deep*
And hys armes y-streight,   *stretched*
    hey upon the rode;   *high upon the cross*
On fif stedes on his body   *five places*
    the stremes ran o blode.   *the streams of blood ran*
                                       (Duncan *MEL*, No. 85)

Also in early Middle English devotional lyrics is found for the first time a simple vocabulary of affective piety (characteristic of devotional poetry for centuries to come) marked by the repetition of words such as 'love', 'sweet' and 'heart', not to mention the very name of Jesus.

Swete Jhesu, king of blisse,
Min herte love, min herte lisse,   *heart's love, my heart's joy*
Thou art swete mid y-wisse,   *sweet indeed*
Wo is him that thee shal misse.   *who will lose you*
                                       (Duncan *MEL*, No. 67, 1–4)

Important as the formal and thematic innovations first encountered in early Middle English lyrics are, continuities from Old English literature are also amply evident. In its essential features the Old English alliterative line continued to be used in many Middle English lyrics, now frequently (as in several excellent Harley lyrics) within the structure of rhyming stanzas. Likewise, major themes of Old English verse – decay, transience (still often expressed through the 'ubi sunt' topos), death, Judgement Day, aspects of body and soul debates, etc. – remain prominent in Middle English moral and penitential lyrics.

Nevertheless, however significant the place of Middle English lyrics in the history of English literature (whether in terms of innovation or continuity) and however excellent so many of these lyrics undoubtedly are, it is a regrettable fact that they have failed to reach a wide readership even among university students of English.[3] The reasons for this situation are not far to seek: they partly have to do with problems of context and modality.

The most obvious problem is that of linguistic context. Middle English was a

---

3   Even as recently as 1999 *The Cambridge History of Medieval English Literature* (Wallace 1999) failed to offer an account of the lyrics.

period of diverse literary dialects. Each author wrote in his own dialect. Chaucer wrote in the dialect of London which, in his day, was simply one dialect among others. However, since the London dialect was the origin of what was later to become standard English, it is the form of Middle English most familiar to modern readers. Thus while readers of Chaucer have to encounter only one dialect (and a relatively familiar one at that), readers of Middle English lyrics are faced with the many different dialects in which they survive. Yet, this variety of dialects need not, in itself, constitute a serious difficulty; a reader can readily come to terms with the linguistic features of any dialect, even those of Middle Scots, with the aid of on-line glossing to explain unfamiliar words. Happily, on-line glossing has become increasingly available in recent editions of Middle English texts.

Greater difficulties have arisen from the context in which Middle English lyrics survive, a context which involves the vagaries and hazards of medieval scribal transmission. Surviving texts of lyrics seldom if ever have the status of authorial copies. On the contrary, they are all too frequently the seemingly casual productions of careless, unprofessional scribes, versions not only characterized by bizarre spellings but also frequently marred by textual corruption. It was, of course, valuable that such texts, however imperfect, were first printed largely as they survived in the standard collections of Brown and Robbins. These remain a valuable scholarly resource (though one increasingly superseded by the publication in more recent times of excellent facsimiles of major lyric manuscripts) usable by experts in Middle English familiar with the idiosyncratic scribal spellings and alive to the textual corruption so especially prevalent in the lyrics. However, as with any other early writings, the editorial task of attempting to arrive at texts purged of corruptions is of primary importance. Ironically, it is perhaps because of the extent to which corruption presents a challenge in the case of Middle English lyrics that wholehearted and systematic attempts to face up to this all-important editorial duty have for so long been shirked. Happily, this state of affairs is also changing; as a result of recent scholarly and editorial efforts improved and (arguably) restored texts are increasingly becoming available. However, as this volume shows, not all attempts at emendation find favour: the editing of Middle English lyrics is a necessary and ongoing task.

Yet, even presented with intelligible, properly edited texts, a further contextual problem confronts the reader of Middle English lyrics – an absence of authorial context. The great majority of Middle English lyrics are anonymous. In theory, this might hardly seem disadvantageous to readers approaching these poems from the standpoint of New Criticism, rejoicing in the independence of each poem as a stand-alone 'verbal icon' and suspicious of any biographical input into literary appraisal. In practice, however, readers of lyrics and sonnets from Wyatt and Surrey, through Shakespeare, Donne, Herbert, Vaughan, Crashaw and Milton to Wordsworth, Keats, Shelley and beyond, have been accustomed to known authors as one crucial aspect of the context of reading: through the centuries, the grouping of short poems 'belonging' together as the work of one author has allowed such poems to be approached with a supportive sense of familiarity.

The absence of a sense of context stemming from the anonymity of the majority of Middle English lyrics is compounded by their brevity. With longer poems (anonymous or not) comparable problems of context do not arise. *Beowulf, Sir Gawain and the Green Knight*, or *Piers Plowman* can stand alone simply because, to some extent, each in its very length generates its own context, a context recognizable in terms of the genres of these lengthy poems – heroic epic, or romance, or religious allegory. At the other end of the scale, there are short poems among surviving Middle English lyrics which, by contrast, have been characterised, in John Burrow's oft-quoted phrase, as 'poems without context', that is, poems lacking any immediately self-evident context: the question of the appropriate context within which to read them is problematical. One example may be offered from the present volume: within what sociocultural context is the brief lyric *Wer ther outher in this toun* (Robbins *Sec.*, No. 9) to be situated? For John Scattergood (below, 48–9) this is a poem about bereavement and memory, in which context the mention of ale and wine in the opening lines is taken as referring to 'a *myndale*, a memorial drink to a dead person'. John Burrow finds it 'a very enigmatic poem of tragic love', and comments briefly on R. H. Robbins's suggestion that the poem 'might be a drinking song', and Basil Cottle's view that it represents 'the monologue of a deserted drunk' (Burrow 1984, 10–11). Another possibility is that this poem deals with the archetypal reversal of fortune suffered by a jilted lover, here in a popular mode. First we have the joy of confident love which rings out in lines 1–10: this lover would do anything for his beloved, he would buy her any ale or wine to be had in the town, he would protect her from anyone – even from the son of the King of Normandy! But, in Chaucer's words:

> But al to litel, weylaway the whyle,
> Lasteth swich joie, ythonked be Fortune. (*Troilus and Criseyde* IV, 1–2)

Lines 11–18 record the tragic reversal of this lover's lot: his beloved has deserted him. But even though she has taught him the sorrow of rejection nonetheless, like the ever-faithful Troilus, he cannot dismiss her; despite all, even yet he commends her, his former love, to Christ.[4]

---

[4] This interpretation depends partly on an editorial reappraisal of the version of the Rawlinson text as printed by Robbins and on adopting the revised reading of lines 15–16 suggested by Dronke 1961. The text of this poem (printed without division by Robbins) seems to invite a three-part structure: (a) lines 1–4, ending *lemmon myn*; (b) lines 5–10, ending *lemman myn*; and (c) lines 11–18, ending *my lemman*. This division (as printed below) is confirmed to the extent that the second and third sections both begin with *Welle wo*.

Wer ther outher in this toun	*were there either*
Ale or wyn,	*wine*
Ich hit wolde bugge	*I would buy it*
To lemmon myn.	*for my beloved*
Welle wo was so hardy	*accursed was anyone so rash*
For to make my lef al blody!	*as to harm (i.e. make all bloody) my dear one*
Thaugh he were the kynges son	*though*
Of Normaundy,	
Yet Icholde a-wreke boe	*I would be avenged*
For lemman myn.	

One further disadvantageous aspect of the context within which Middle English lyrics have to be read relates to the probable loss of so much of the original corpus. Post-medieval literature by and large offers the 'complete' or 'collected' works of known authors: the reader is thus supported by the confidence derived from the sense that the whole picture is available for the analysis and comparison so essential to the practice of literary criticism, and not least for discussions of genre development. Since, as is generally agreed, many lyrics have failed to survive, such a complete picture is lacking in the case of Middle English. This consideration is not without significance for our response as readers of these lyrics. First, there are several striking but isolated poems, often poems which do not readily fit into any of the usually recognized categories or genres. One such is the lyric beginning:

Swarte smeked smithes	*black smoke-begrimed smiths*
smattered with smoke,	*smutty with smoke*
Drive me to deth	
with din of here dyntes!	*din of their blows*
	(Duncan *MEL*, No. 132, 1–2)

Ostensibly a tirade against blacksmiths who keep the poet awake by their nightly din, here is the work of a poet, the vivacity of whose writing invites comparison with a Gerard Manley Hopkins. Beyond the force of his invective (so magnificently supported by the strong stresses of his alliterative medium) one senses sheer zest for composition, the joy of a wordsmith expertly fashioning in sustained alliteration a vivid and detailed realisation of blacksmiths at work, both in sight and, with skillful onomatopoeia, in sound:

The mayster longeth a litel	*the master smith lengthens a small piece*
and lasheth a lesse,	*and hammers out a smaller bit*
Twyneth hem twayn	*welds the two together*
and toucheth a treble.	*and strikes a treble note*
Tik, tak! Hic, hac!	
tiket, taket! Tik, tak!	
Lus, bus! Lus, das! –	
swych lyf they leden! (17–20)	*such is the life they lead*

Welle wo was me tho!	*accursed was I then*
Wo was me tho!	*cursed was I then*
The man that leseth that he loveth	*the man who loses the one whom he loves*
Hym is also.	*he is likewise cursed*
So she me lerde –	*so much she taught me*
Ne no more I ne can!	*I can do no more!*
But Christ Ich hire biteche	*to Christ I commend her*
That was my lemman.	*who was my beloved*

In the glossing given above, *Welle wo* (5) and its repetition in line 11 (identically beginning the second and then the third section of the poem) are taken, as would seem likely, to have the same meaning, i.e. as forms of *MED* **wei-la-wei** interj. a. (d) 'woe to (sb. or sth.), accursed be (sb. or sth.)'. Likewise the sense of *Wo* (12) is taken as that given under *MED* **wo** n. 7b. (a). It is also to be noted that the past tense *was* with reference to the *lemman* in the final line does not necessarily mean that she is dead; it may simply mean that she is no longer the poet's beloved.

All the sounds are here – the plosive 't's and 'k's with different vowels evoking the anvil's response to various kinds of hammer-strokes, the 's' consonants for the splutter and hiss of red-hot iron plunged into water. Another striking lyric is the inimitable account of the Man in the Moon (*Man in the moone stont and strit*, Duncan *MEL*, No. 114), found in the Harley manuscript. The wit, humour and imagination found here again bespeak a poet of outstanding talent. Other such superb, seemingly 'one-off' poems could be mentioned. Each, however, prompts the same forlorn question: how much of the output of poets of such calibre has perished? Again, it is truly a chilling thought that had BL MS Harley 2253 failed to survive, half the Middle English love lyrics from before Chaucer's time – and those the best – would have been lost. Without this one manuscript who could have guessed the level of achievement already reached in this genre by English lyric poets of the later thirteenth and early fourteenth centuries, for the early love lyrics surviving from other sources do not bear witness to literary talent comparable to that of the Harley lyrics. In addition to the crucial matter of lost evidence, the uncertainty of the chronology of surviving early Middle English lyrics – not least the love lyrics – is to be borne in mind. The dating of manu- script sources can be no better than approximate and, moreover, by how long a lyric may have pre-dated its surviving copy is often far from certain. As far as the early Middle English lyric is concerned, these considerations should make us wary of the discussions of the 'origins' and 'development' of genres to which literary historians are so greatly addicted. Surviving evidence no more allows one to trace any significant development in the love lyric before Chaucer, than it allows for anything more than the most tentative of speculations concerning the origins of the carol genre in English.

The English origins of another genre – the ballad – are likewise controversial. It is perhaps not unreasonable to suppose that of all kinds of literature, popular literature should have been most liable to loss, and the ballad has as good a claim as any to be counted as 'popular'. Prior to the fifteenth-century Robin Hood ballads[5] only two ballad-like poems survive in English, the thirteenth- century *Hit was upon a Shere Thorsday* (Duncan *MEL*, No. 112) and the early fifteenth-century *Seynt Stevene was a clerk* (Duncan *MEL*, No. 126).[6] Both are short narrative poems: the former recounts the betrayal of Judas by his sister and his subsequent betrayal of Christ; the latter relates a pious legend of St Stephen. Stephen, a servant of King Herod, catches sight of the star over Beth- lehem as he leaves the kitchen carrying a boar's head into the king's hall, and thereafter announces that he will forsake King Herod for the child born in Beth- lehem. 'Are you mad?' asks the king; but Stephen is vindicated by the roasted cock on Herod's plate which crows 'Christus natus est'. He is thereafter stoned

---

5   See Gray 1984.
6   A possible third might be *Robyn and Gandelyn* (also, like *Seynt Stevene was a clerk*, found in BL MS Sloane 2593). This brief song is in ballad metre and has other ballad-like features. However, there is no certain evidence for connecting the *Robyn* of this poem with the hero of the Robin Hood ballads. For a recent study of popular poetry in Middle English, including the ballad, see Boklund-Lagopolou 2002. Excellent accounts of medieval English ballads are to be found in Gray 1989 and Green 1997.

to death. In their respective manuscripts each poem is copied in two-line couplets. These lines, however, are long, mainly of seven stresses, and most readily resolve into two lines, one of four, the other of three stresses. Given a four-line arrangement of the manuscript couplets, what emerges is none other than the form which has come to be called the ballad stanza.

He cast adoun the bores hed,
    and went into the halle;
'I forsak thee, Kyng Herowdes
    and thy werkes alle.

'I forsak thee, Kyng Herowdes,
    and thy werkes alle,
Ther is a child in Bedlem born
    is better than we alle.'

'What aileth thee, Stevene?
    what is thee befalle?   *what has happened to you*
Lakketh thee either mete or drynk   *do you lack either food or drink*
    in Kyng Herowdes halle?'

'Lakketh me neither mete ne drynk   *I lack neither*
    in Kyng Herowdes halle;
Ther is a child in Bedlem born
    is better than we alle.'

'What aileth thee, Steven, art thou wod,   *are you mad*
    or thou gynnest to brede?   *or are you beginning to rave*
Lakketh thee either gold or fee   *gold or payment*
    or any ryche wede?'   *fine clothing*

'Lakketh me neither gold ne fee,
    ne non ryche wede;
Ther is a child in Bedlem born,
    shal help us at our need.'   *in our necessity*

'That is also soth, Steven,   *that is just as true*
    also soth y-wis,   *just as true, indeed*
As this capoun crowe shal *cock*
    that lyth here in myn dish.'   *lies*

That word was not so sone said,   *was no sooner said*
    that word in that halle,
The capoun crew *Christus natus est*   *Christ is born*
    among the lordes alle. (9–40)

Whatever the doubts concerning the status of these poems as ballads, it cannot be denied that both are written in what, granted irregularities, is basically the ballad stanza form and that both (as the above quotation shows) have other salient characteristics of ballads – dramatic, impersonal narrative marked by sudden transitions, abrupt dialogue in question and answer form, repetitions both formulaic and incremental in nature.

If, then, problems of context (variously understood) have to be recognized and taken into account by readers of Middle English lyrics, the major problem of modality stems from the term 'lyric' itself. In approaching Middle English lyrics, and not least love lyrics, it is essential that expectations generated by the nineteenth-century notion of a lyric, defined by the *OED* in Ruskin's words as 'the expression of the poet of his own feelings', should be set aside. Lyric poets in Middle English do indeed write of love, but not characteristically in poems of an intimate, private, personal nature; rather, their poems are essentially public events operating within and through well recognized conventions, not least those of the lover and the beloved. In lyric after lyric lovers sigh, lie awake, feel condemned to death, plead for mercy, while, true to form, the beauty of the ladies for whom they long is described in almost identical terms from poem to poem. Neither individuality nor sincerity, whether of feeling or expression, is at issue. Middle English poets are happy to use a common currency of word and phrase: the lady is a *byrde in a bour, brightest under bis, geynest under gore*, and *beste among the bolde* – all phrases used as much as anything for their alliteration. However, literary convention does not here make for tedious verse. What is obvious is the relish with which Middle English love poets (many may well have been clerics) made play with a range of literary conventions as they exercised their skill in versification. One prominent convention was the *reverdie*, the description of springtime, the medieval implications of which, however, went beyond mere natural description.

Foules in the frith,	*birdȝ; wood*
The fishes in the flod,	*sea*
And I mon waxe wod;	*must go mad*
Much sorwe I walke with	
For beste of bon and blod.	*finest (creature) of bone and blood*
	(Duncan *MEL*, No. 16)

The mention of the birds in the wood and the fish in the sea in this short poem encapsulates a wider understanding: as with the rest of the natural world these creatures are happily revelling in the joys of springtime love, in love uncomplicated and uncompromised by the conventions governing relationships in human love. Hence the irony of the contrast with the birds and fish here: this poet's lot (like that of many another) is to go mad in anguish for his lady, 'the best of bone and blood'. *Lenten ys come with love to toune* (Duncan *MEL*, No. 20) offers the ultimate *tour de force* in the lyric exploitation of the *reverdie*. Spring's *wynne wele* [wealth of joys] – a profusion of blossoms and flowers, with the singing of nightingales and song thrushes, and with animals of all kinds mating on hillside and riverside – is woven into three flowing twelve-line stanzas leading, once again, to the ironic contrast of man and beast, wittily and provocatively expressed in the alliteratively linked worms and women.

Wormes wowen under cloude,	*worms make love under ground*
Wommen waxen wonder proude,	*become amazingly haughty*
So wel it wol hem seme.	*it becomes them*

What is encountered in this lyric is clearly not any simple evocation of nature; it is more akin to a literary game as this poet sports with a literary convention and its implications. Nor is *Moste I ryde by Rybbesdale* (Duncan *MEL*, No. 25) merely any one lover's account of his beloved. Nowhere is it more self-evident just how literary the traditions and conventions of Harley love lyrics could be. Writers of medieval treatises on poetics like the thirteenth-century Englishman Geoffrey of Vinsauf, author of the *Poetria Nova*, illustrated in detail how the literary topos of the description of a beautiful woman should be handled. Geoffrey's model head-to-foot description details the following features: hair (golden), forehead (lily-white), eyebrows (dark and snow-white between), nose, eyes (shining), face (bright and of rosy complexion), mouth (gleaming), lips (red and warm), teeth (even), breath (fragrance as of scent), chin (polished), neck (a milk-white column), throat (radiant as crystal), shoulders (even), arms (long and slender), fingers (long, straight, white), breasts (jewels side by side), waist (slender), leg (long and slender), foot (small and dainty). What is ostensibly a love lyric is, in fact, another literary *tour de force*: with consummate skill this Harley poet, in seven stanzas (each, again, of twelve lines), engages in a detailed elaboration of Geoffrey's model description, but (astonishingly) without any sense of artificiality or stiffness. Having reached the waist, Geoffrey remarks: *Taceo de partibus infra: / Aptius hic loquitur animus quam lingua* [I am silent concerning the parts below; more aptly does the imagination speak at this point than the tongue]. Evidently a wit, our poet, at the same point in his description, does not fail to echo Geoffrey's reticence:

> Al that Ich you nempne noght,   *do not mention to you*
> Hit is wonder wel y-wroght
>   And elles wonder were. (79–81)   *otherwise it would be strange*

This poem, however, moves beyond the elaboration of a literary topos. The eulogy accorded to the lady in its final three lines is as sudden as it is startling:

> He myghte seyn that Christ hym seye *say; had looked after him*
> That myghte nightes neigh hyre leye: *who might by night lie beside her*
>   Heven he hadde here. (82–4)   *heaven he would have here*

In this hyperbolic tribute one senses here, as elsewhere in the Harley lyrics, a touch of goliardic wit, not least in its whiff of blasphemy.[7] In some ways similar is the contrast found between the stanzas and burden of *Bitwene March and Averil* (Duncan *MEL*, No. 18). Alongside the love-longing of stanza 1, the poet's despair of stanza 2, his nightly anguish of stanza 3, and his final plea of the concluding stanza, the ecstasy of the burden in this poem runs in striking counterpoint:

> An hendy hap Ichave y-hent,
> Ichot from hevene it is me sent,
> From alle women my love is lent
> And light on Alysoun.

---

[7] One may compare the endings of *With longing I am lad* (Duncan *MEL*, No. 1, 37–40) and *A wayle white as whales bon* (Duncan *MEL*, No. 2, 55–9).

This *hendy hap* [good fortune] – no less than heaven-sent! – dances in these lines. However, with the reference to all the women from whom the poet now turns with the advent of Alison (unusually, the beloved is named here) there is a sense of the world at large and of other relationships which would be alien to the singular devotion and claustrophobic atmosphere of many a troubadour lyric. Again, whatever the admiration for ladies professed in *Weping hath myn wonges wet* (Duncan MEL, No. 27), this wittily ironic and somewhat enigmatic poem, with its covert, possibly clerical anti-feminism, is a far cry from troubadour devotion. All in all, in their play of convention, wit and irony, the characteristic modalities of many of the surviving pre-Chaucerian love lyrics are a far cry from nineteenth-century 'lyric' expectations.

'The expression of the poet's own feelings' in the intense and personal mode Ruskin had in mind is no more typical of the best of Middle English devotional lyrics. Whereas a Donne or a Hopkins spoke with a personal, individual voice, the modality of many medieval religious lyrics is one in which the poet's voice is that of Everyman, a voice with which the reader may readily identify, and, indeed, is tacitly invited so to do. However, it is not surprising if in this regard a modern reader can feel more readily at home with Middle English religious lyrics. This modality has always in some measure been characteristic of religious poetry and not least of hymnody. At his finest, in such a poem as *Love bade me welcome*, the seventeenth-century poet George Herbert implicitly invites his reader to identify with the speaking voice however characteristically his own it may be.

If, then, with regard to Middle English poetry, the term lyric in its nineteenth-century sense is potentially misleading, in another sense, that of a song, it is particularly instructive. In the classical literature of ancient Greece, a lyric was understood as a song rendered to the accompaniment of a lyre. The characteristic stanza form of lyric verse found its origin in song, for stanzaic structure is the verbal counterpart of the melodic structure of song. Thus the structure A-A-B, characteristic of many songs, would consist of two melodic units with the first repeated before ending with the second. The corresponding verbal structure would be a stanza in A-A-B form, such, for example, as found in the Harley lyric *With longing I am lad* (Duncan MEL, No. 1) with its stanzas of two tercets followed by a quatrain and the corresponding rhyme scheme **a,a,b / a,a,b / b,a,a,b.** Some Middle English lyrics survive with music. Since copies of such lyrics sometimes survive without music, other lyrics lacking music may also have been songs. Thus the absence of music in the Harley manuscript does not preclude this possibility for some of its lyrics. On the other hand, stanza form established itself as a literary mode independent of music, a development which gave rise to the distinction between 'song lyric' and 'literary lyric'. Typical of the latter was the ballade, a French form, complex and sophisticated, less suited to singing, introduced into English by Chaucer and, thereafter, popular in the fifteenth century. Nevertheless, what has often been claimed to be lyrical even about 'literary' lyrics has in part been perceived to be a certain melodious quality of their language. Meanwhile lyrics of the 'song lyric' kind held their ground throughout the Middle English period. A significant part of the appeal of some of the simpler later Middle English love lyrics, whether they survive with music or not, continues to stem from the song-like qualities of their language which finds its music in a harmony of rhyme, alliteration, and, indeed, rhythm; as the poet laments and pleads in familiar form, there is nothing tough or intellectually challenging to impede the flow of his verse.

> Now wolde y fayne sum merthes mak,   *would I gladly make merry*
> Al only for my ladys sak   *entirely on account of my lady*
>   When y her se;   *see*
> But nowe y am so far fro hir   *far from*
>   It wil not be.
>
>   (Duncan *LMELC*, No. 22, 1–5)

To judge from the early sixteenth-century Devonshire and Henry VIII manuscripts, lyrics in this manner never lost their appeal.

Middle English lyrics often survive in a random, scattered and marginal manner; even where they are found in any number in any one manuscript they are generally part of a miscellaneous collection of literary materials in verse and prose, sometimes partly in Latin and French, often with literary items keeping company with non-literary material. Nevertheless, as shown in the opening chapter of this *Companion*, recent research on their varied contexts of survival has added significantly to our understanding of these lyrics. And certainly the lyrics found in each of such major sources as the Harley, Vernon and Sloane manuscripts manifest their own characteristics and thus offer valuable points of orientation to readers of Middle English lyrics. Only rarely (as in BL MS Sloane 2593) did manuscript collections consist solely of lyrics, and even then the contents of such collections were usually varied. Present-day thematic lyric anthologies – anthologies of love lyrics, of religious lyrics, of war lyrics, of humorous lyrics, or whatever – were virtually unknown in the Middle English period.[8] This is not surprising. In most cases, in Middle English manuscripts of varied contents, items of whatever kind were doubtlessly inscribed as they came to hand. The heterogeneous contents of Middle English manuscripts bespeak a world in which at any one time the availability of material was limited, a world which knew nothing of the possibilities and advantages available to a present-day anthologiser, not least in terms of modern book production. However, it would seem absurd to view the heterogeneity of medieval manuscripts as evidence to suggest that medieval collectors were unaware of the distinctions of theme, category and genre sometimes employed by modern editors. Doubtless, for instance, a well informed medieval reader – more readily, perhaps, than many a post-medieval reader – would have been perfectly able to distinguish lyrics concerning the Fall, the Annunciation and Nativity, the Passion of Christ, Mary at the Foot of the Cross, and Complaints of Christ – to quote only the first five categories employed in Douglas Gray's excellent anthology, *A Selection of*

---

[8]   The Vernon manuscript might be viewed as an instance of a partial exception. Although it contains a variety of items in prose and verse, the final section containing the 'Vernon lyrics' clearly manifests a striking degree of thematic unity. See Gillespie (below), 85–9. Likewise the twenty-four early fifteenth-century lyrics in Bodl. MS Digby 102 constitute a political anthology within that manuscript. See Turville-Petre (below), 179–80.

Religious Lyrics (Gray 1975). Groupings of such a kind offer modern readers by far the best entry into the largely anonymous world of Middle English lyrics.

For this reason most of the chapters in this *Companion* focus on themes, categories and, in the case of the carol, genre. At no point in the history of English literature do sermon lyrics more obviously call for separate consideration than in Middle English, while political poems as a valid medieval category enjoy the unusual confirmation of the lyrics of Bodl. MS Digby 102 and the poems of Laurence Minot which might appropriately be described as political anthologies. Meanwhile, issues of chronology have not been ignored. Even if discussions of early lyrics based on chronology are, as indicated above, at best speculative, it is clear that, in broad terms, the later fourteenth century marks a major watershed in the development of the Middle English lyric. Accordingly, separate chapters on the love lyric are devoted first to the earlier love lyrics and then to lyrics from Chaucer to Henry VIII. Likewise, the chapters on penitential and devotional lyrics respectively address the changes in manner, tone and style which appear in the later fourteenth-century moral poems of the Vernon manuscript and in Chaucer's lyrics (albeit in different ways), and the stylistic and thematic developments which so markedly differentiate fifteenth-century devotional lyrics from their earlier counterparts. The case of Middle Scots lyrics is especially interesting: as the final chapter of this volume demonstrates, these lyrics are not simply a late northern continuation of the Middle English lyric tradition, but, at their best, sophisticated productions of an entirely new order.

One concern of this volume has been to take account of the fundamental scholarship upon which our knowledge of Middle English lyrics rests, from the early pioneering work of Carleton Brown, Rossell Hope Robbins and Richard Leighton Greene, through the outstanding contributions of Rosemary Woolf and Douglas Gray in the last few decades, to more recent insights such as those of gender criticism. It is also the editor's hope that by creating an awareness of the characteristic contexts and modalities of Middle English lyrics, by associating them chapter by chapter according to their kinds, and by offering generous illustrative quotation in a readily accessible and glossed form, this *Companion* may guide readers to familiarity with and a fuller understanding and enjoyment of this important part of our literary heritage, and may also, in some measure, prove an incentive to further research.

1

Middle English Lyrics and Manuscripts

JULIA BOFFEY

The ways in which Middle English lyrics have survived are multifarious and largely resistant to logical classification: perhaps more than any other kind of medieval text, these poems were recorded unsystematically and often simply accidentally, in contexts which offer to posterity little help in interpreting their contemporary functions or appeal.[1] Short poems in Middle English are recorded on parchment rolls and other documents, in parchment and paper codices of various shape and sizes, in some of the earliest printed books produced in England, as well as in an extraordinary range of further locations. Some of the many different purposes which lyrics served are reflected in these diverse contexts. Short devotional poems might be inscribed in public places, or copied into small books which could conveniently be carried about the person for occasions of private prayer, or incorporated into a sermon, with recommendations for their use. Short secular poems might be scrappily copied for personal record (often in the margins or on the flyleaves of another book), or included in an anthology of texts for private reading, or written out with musical notation in a song repertory, perhaps for use by a professional musician or entertainer. Short poems on a number of subjects were evidently convenient for the purposes of pen-trials or inscriptions. Any attempt to survey the modes of survival of poems which range from the pragmatic *Thirti dayes hath novembir* (Robbins *Sec.*, No. 68) to the intensely evocative *Nou goth sonne under wod* (Brown *XIII*, No. 1) is bound to involve the scrutiny of an extraordinary diversity of manuscripts and other forms of record.[2]

More so than with other genres, perhaps, those lyrics which have survived probably represent only a small proportion of the total number which were in circulation. A number of lyrics may have had a purely oral currency and never even have been recorded in written form, and some are known today only by references to their first lines or refrains; the rascally Hervy Hafter, in Skelton's *Bowge of Court*, refers to at least four songs (Scattergood 1983a, 46–61: *Sythe I am no thynge playne*, 235; *Heve and how, rombelow, row the bote, Norman, rowe*, 252; *Prynces of youghte*, 253; *Shall I sayle with you*, 254), only two of which are

---

[1] Defining 'Middle English lyric' is notoriously difficult (see Greentree 2001, 5–37). For the purposes of discussion here I understand the term to mean 'Middle English short poem'.

[2] Some attempts to survey the manuscripts include (on religious lyrics) Woolf, 373–6, Wenzel 1986, 4–8, and (on love lyrics) Boffey 1985; the introductions to Brown *XIII*, Brown *XIV*, Brown *XV* and Robbins *Sec.*; and the 'Bibliography of Original Sources' in Greene, 297–341. Burrow 1979 discusses the interpretation of 'poems without contexts'.

mentioned in other sources.[3] The linguistic situation in England throughout
most of the Middle Ages also meant that those wishing to read or copy or
compose short poems could do so in French and Latin as well as in English. Any
study of lyrics in England during this period needs to remain alert to the
cultural implications of the bilingual or trilingual milieux in which lyrics were
transmitted and copied into manuscripts. Some individual poems are macaronic
(including lines in more than one language; see Wehrle 1933 and Archibald
1992); some authors – Gower certainly, and Chaucer possibly – are credited with
non-English lyric compositions.[4] Many of the short Middle English poems
which figure in the following discussion occur in manuscripts alongside short
poems in French and Latin, or both, to which they might in some cases be
closely connected.

The most significant distinction to be made among lyric manuscripts is probably that between the planned and the random copying of poems. Random
copying is most likely to be the jotting on handily available writing space of
poems which individuals suddenly wished to record, or which they copied for
autograph purposes or for pen-trials. Some of these copies, especially those with
many signs of correction, might be holographs: the author's own original
version (the poem edited by Boffey and Edwards 2001 is one example). A
planned copy of a lyric, or of a sequence or collection of lyrics, would have been
available to a compiler or scribe in advance, offering the possibility of calcu-
lating the space needed for the poem or poems, and for the making of decisions
about layout and presentation. Advance availability need not necessarily imply
the existence of a written exemplar (poems might be carried in a scribe's or a
compiler's head), but it is quite likely to have done. In cases where written
exemplars were available, they might have taken the form of an existing manuscript, or a single gathering, or have consisted of poems copied separately onto
loose leaves or bifolia. Lyrics were also frequently used as fillers in manuscripts,
copied to occupy what would otherwise have been blank space at the end of a
gathering or a whole work. In these situations scribes presumably calculated in
advance what length of lyric to add, or how best to organize the text they had to
hand, in order to fill the space available to them.

Decisions about presentation would have involved consideration of whether
or not lyrics were to be accompanied by music, and whether or not they were
likely to be illuminated or decorated in any way. The proportion of surviving
Middle English lyrics accompanied by written musical notation is in fact very
small (see Bent 1973): what survives tends to be in early manuscripts of monastic
provenance, in collections made by musically literate clerics for their own use, or
in later song repertories associated with particular households or ecclesiastical
establishments. The melodies for many lyrics were probably carried in people's

3   Scattergood 1983a, 46–61; the character Ryotte mentions another song at 360. For further
    discussion, see Scattergood's notes to these lines, and Fallows 1977.
4   Gower wrote at least two series of French ballades, the *Traitié pur essampler les amantz marietz*
    and *Cinkante ballades*; see MacCracken 1908–09. Chaucer cites French lyrics (*Jay tout perdu mon
    temps et mon labour* is mentioned in *The Parson's Tale*, 248 and in *Fortune*, 7; see Benson), uses
    French lyric forms in his own compositions, and has even been credited with the poems
    signed 'Ch' in Philadelphia, University of Pennsylvania MS French 35; see Wimsatt 1982.

heads (as indicated by occasional directions prefacing individual poems with the advice 'sing this to the tune of . . .'), and would have been superfluous in written copies.

Significant illumination and decoration are also relatively rare in English lyric manuscripts. Sometimes they may accompany longer texts in a manuscript but be absent in the section of the manuscript where lyrics are copied: this is the case with the Vernon manuscript, Bodl. eng. poet. a. 1 (see Doyle 1987), and with the large Scottish anthology of Chaucerian verse which is now Bodl. MS Arch. Selden. B.24 (see Boffey and Edwards 1997). Its provision in conjunction with secular lyrics in manuscripts such as Bodl. MS Fairfax 16 and BL MS Royal 16.F.ii (respectively an anthology of Chaucerian verse, and a collection of largely French texts, with some stray English poems) is unusual, and seemingly connected with the fact that the first of these manuscripts was customized for an owner of some status, and that the second was destined for presentation to Henry VII or to a member of his family (see Norton-Smith 1979 and Backhouse 1995). Images and short verse texts are occasionally united on manuscript rolls which would have been publicly displayed: some diagrammatic pedigrees of the kings of England in this form depict individual kings alongside stanzas on their reigns (usually from a text related to Lydgate's *Verses on the Kings of England*, IMEV 3632 and 444; see Mooney 1989 and Scott 1996, II: 221–3), and rolls designed for devotional purposes with images of and verses on the *Arma Christi* (the instruments of torture and comfort associated with the Crucifixion) seem to have been produced in some numbers (see Robbins 1939). Other instances of illustrations in combination with lyrics are almost all of a devotional kind, in books such as the tiny Bodl. MS Douce 1 (see Hirsh 1968), the larger and more comprehensive Cambridge, Trinity College MS R.3.21 (Scott 1996, II: 337–9), and in some of the images which accompany the long allegorical poem called *The Desert of Religion* (Scott 1996, II: 192–4), where lyrics often appear in speech scrolls.

Single-Author Collections

Large compendia of lyrics associated with single authors are notably few: the majority of surviving Middle English lyrics are anonymous, and English writers in general seem to have felt little urge to compose or to collect together large numbers of lyrics on the models offered in Italian by Dante and Petrarch, or in French by Froissart, Machaut, or Deschamps. Chaucer seems to have made no effort to collect together for circulation the *many a song and many a leccherous lay* which he revokes in the *Retracciouns* at the end of *The Canterbury Tales*, and his lyrics survive singly or in small clusters, generally as appendages to other texts (Boffey 1993). The lyrico-narrative cycle of Middle English poems in BL MS Harley 682, parallel in large part to a series of French poems by Charles of Orleans (surviving in his autograph, Paris, Bibliothèque Nationale MS fr.25458), has some claim to be the only extensive collection of secular poems in Middle English attributable to a single author (whether this was Charles himself – a prisoner in England for over 25 years after his capture at Agincourt – or an anonymous translator).[5] The large body of secular lyrics attributable to Dunbar survives largely in post-medieval copies (collections such as the Maitland and Reidpeth manuscripts; see Bawcutt 1991), and Skelton's smaller body of independent lyrics mainly in printed editions dating from the early sixteenth century (Kinsman and Yonge 1967).

Other surviving manuscripts which represent single-author compilations contain only religious lyrics. Bodl. MS Douce 302 collects together a number of poems mostly composed by the blind John Audelay, who was early in life chantry priest to Richard le Strange of Knockin Castle near Oswestry in Shropshire and seems by c.1426 to have lived in the Augustinian monastery of Haghmond (Whiting 1931; Greene, 317; Stanley 1997; Fein 2003, with a facsimile). This collection was carefully put together, copied largely by one scribe and corrected by another, and its individual items are numbered and distinguished from each other by ornamentation and rubrication; it was possibly made in Haughmond, and may in part have been written down from dictation, although a final prayer for Audelay's soul might indicate that he was dead by the date of the completion of the copy. Although the manuscript contains no musical notation, its lyrics may have had some function as songs: a later Augustinian owner, one 'Ihon Barkre', canon of the Augustinian priory of St John the Baptist at Launde in Leicestershire, notes that he obtained the collection from a minstrel of Coventry named Vyott or Wyatt. Whereas Audelay's blindness most probably necessitated dictation to an amanuensis, it is possible that the numerous carols and lyrics by James Ryman in CUL MS Ee.1.12 were copied by their author, a Franciscan attached to the friary at Canterbury, or if not by their author then by another scribe associated with this house (Zupitza 1892; Greene, 321). Although there is no formal notation here, a rough scrap of music has been added on fol. 81r, and the scribal colophon refers to the collection as 'liber ymnorum / et cantorum': a book of hymns and songs, compiled as a purposive whole. There is some evidence that Ryman's poems may have been transmitted outside his own immediate locality, and although Audelay's manuscript found a later home among fellow Augustinians, the fact that at least one of his poems survives in another copy suggests that they may have had a wider circulation outside the confines of his order.[6]

Certain manuscripts which gather together short poems by the prolific Benedictine monk John Lydgate are superficially similar to the Audelay and Ryman collections. Unlike Audelay and Ryman, though, Lydgate wrote a number of much more substantial works, and the totality of his *oeuvre* cannot be comprehended in a single anthology (Renoir and Benson 1980, supplemented by Edwards 1985; Edwards 2000a; Boffey 1996). Typically, his lyrics survive alongside selections from the longer works in manuscript anthologies such as BL MS Lansdowne 699 or Leiden, University Library MS Vossius Ger.Gall.Q.9 (manuscripts whose contents are arrestingly similar and may be in some way related).

[5] For a recent review of the issue, see Pearsall 2000, and on single-author manuscripts more generally, Edwards 2000a.
[6] On the Ryman poem, see Scattergood 1987a; Audelay's *Foresake thi pride and thyn envy* (Whiting 1931, 182) is also copied in Aberystwyth, National Library of Wales MS 334A, endleaf.

The major collections which feature short poems alone include BL MS Harley 2255, apparently made for William Curteys, Lydgate's abbot at Bury St Edmunds, and two further non-metropolitan collections, Bodl. Laud Misc.683, and Cambridge, Jesus College MS 56 – all three perhaps related in some way, on the evidence of correspondences in order and contents. Within London, the circulation of Lydgate's short poems seems to have been influenced by the activities of the scribe John Shirley (Connolly 1998), and by a later circle including the so-called 'Hammond scribe' who had access to Shirley's manuscripts; many of Lydgate's lyrics appear in Shirley's Bodl. MS Ashmole 59 (alongside other material), and in two related anthologies compiled by the Hammond scribe, BL MSS Additional 34360 and Harley 2251.

The impulses which prompted John Shirley to produce manuscripts are not recorded, and may have stemmed from the requirements of his patrons or from his own wish to promote an English literary culture of some definable kind (he copied certain of Chaucer's works, and various other texts, as well as Lydgate's writings). The activities of the Hammond scribe, however, certainly played some part in commercial networks of book production: his hand is detectable in a number of different manuscripts, and he collaborated on occasion with other scribes who worked on commission (Mooney 2000, 2001, 2003). The inclusion of lyrics in these fifteenth-century commercially produced manuscripts (some of which may have been produced speculatively) is significant testimony to the increasing availability of examples of this mode of writing in English – an increase in which Lydgate played no small part. His short poems were copied into manuscripts of all kinds throughout the fifteenth and early sixteenth centuries, and figure too in early printed books.

Groups of Lyrics Attributed to Single Authors

Like Lydgate's short poems in the early stages of their transmission, Thomas Hoccleve's lyrics circulated with other of his writings. Hoccleve, however, was a trained scribe who both organized and copied collections of his writings (surviving in San Marino, Huntington Library MSS HM 111 and 744, and Durham, University Library MS Cosin V.iii.9; see Bowers 1989; Burrow and Doyle 2002).[7] MS HM 111 in particular contains a number of lyrics, on fols 26–42, many of which originally served specific social purposes (some in the 'Court de bone compaignie', a circle of civil servants with whom Hoccleve was friendly). The grouping of the poems together here presumably reflects Hoccleve's own authorial filing system, and perhaps also the occasion or recipient for whom this volume was compiled. The circulation of Chaucer's lyrics seems to have had no such authorial supervision (see Boffey 1993). Some survive in the context of an early attempt to collect Chaucer's works in CUL MS Gg 4.27 (see Beadle and Owen 1977); a few were copied with particular Chaucerian texts with which they might have been associated (the love lyric Rosemounde

---

[7] William Herebert was another such author-scribe-compiler; see below 13.

at the end of *Troilus and Criseyde* in Bodl. MS Rawlinson poet.163; the Boethian lyrics *Fortune* and *The Former Age* with a copy of *Boece*, for example; see Pace 1961); others appear in small clusters (sometimes copied continuously, as if the exemplars available to scribes did not clearly mark beginnings and endings) in the context of more varied anthologies.

Other groups of lyrics in larger anthologies are attributable to single authors. BL MS Cotton Galba E.ix, an early fifteenth-century parchment manuscript, includes a short collection of political lyrics referring to events dating from the reign of Edward III by Laurence Minot conjoined with the romances *Ywain and Gawain* and *The Seven Sages*, and some religious verse, including *The Prick of Conscience* (Hall 1914; James and Simons 1989). Minot's poems are grouped together in the manuscript (on fols 52 onwards) and must have reached the copyist as a body, perhaps in an exemplar formed from a single gathering. A group of short love lyrics in Bodl. MS Fairfax 16, fols 318–26, one of which is duplicated in Charles of Orleans's *Book of Love*, may be the work of Charles's English translator or one of his associates (see Norton-Smith 1979; Jansen 1989; Pearsall 2000).

Lyrics as Components of Anthologies and Miscellanies

If there is a typical manuscript context for Middle English lyrics, it is probably that of the manuscript anthology or miscellany: a collection of texts (often including material in Latin and French as well as English), in which a small number of lyrics have somehow been accommodated.[8] Sometimes the lyrics occur together, in small sequences; in other instances they are copied at intervals throughout the collection, presumably as space became available or as exemplars came to hand. Occasionally musical notation, or references to tunes suitable for the words, is also provided. One of the best known early lyrics, *Sumer is icomen in* (Brown *XIII*, No. 6), occurs in a collection of this sort, BL MS Harley 978 (on fol. 11v), where it is surrounded by liturgical pieces, the *Fables* and *Lais* of Marie de France, and some Latin goliardic poems. The manuscript's contents were copied by a number of different hands, and probably over a number of years, in the first few decades of the thirteenth century; references in some of the texts suggest that the scribes were all in some way associated with Reading Abbey, a milieu in which the parallel Latin and English versions of *Sumer is icumen in* (the English words are written above Latin ones which begin *Perspice, Christicola*) would have been entirely appropriate (see Dobson and Harrison 1979, 143–5; Brown *XIII*, 168–9; Frankis 1986, 176–7; Taylor 2002, 76–136, with a facsimile on p. 80). The conviviality which such lyrics serviced is indicated by Latin directions for the performance of *Sumer is icomen in* which state that 'hanc rotam cantare possunt quatuor socij' [this round may be sung by four companions].

Not unsurprisingly, a number of other thirteenth- and fourteenth-century

---

8   For the purposes of this discussion I use the term 'anthology' to define a manuscript which displays some indications of planned compilation, and 'miscellany' for a collection which seems to have come into being in a more random way. The distinction is not always clear or watertight.

groups of lyrics occur in manuscripts originating in religious houses. The songs attributed to St Godric (d.1170) were diffused in such contexts, presumably in part through the agency of his fellow monks at Durham (Dobson and Harrison 1979, 16). BL MS Arundel 292, containing among other things the Middle English *Bestiary*, various Latin religious and secular prose texts, and some Anglo-Norman poems, seems to have been compiled in the thirteenth century at Norwich Cathedral priory. It contains on fols 3–4 a series of short English verse translations of liturgical texts (the *Credo*, IMEV 1326; the *Pater Noster*, IMEV 787; the Angelic Salutation, *IMEV* 2100; *In Manus Tuas*, *IMEV 1952*) and two lyrics on death (*IMEV* 1422 and 3969; Brown *XIII*, Nos 12 and 13), and later in its existence attracted additions which include the well-known poem on blacksmiths *Swarte smekyd smethes smateryd with smoke* (Robbins *Sec.*, No. 118; Salter 1979; Ker 1949–53, 11, 18). Corpus Christi College, Oxford, MS 59, dating again from the thirteenth century, and including three English religious lyrics (Brown *XIII*, Nos 59, 60 and 61), at least one of which translates a Latin hymn also copied in the manuscript, seems to come from Llanthony Priory in Gloucestershire (Brown 1928). And the late thirteenth-century miscellany which is now MS Bodley 57, and includes a version of *Quanne hic se on rode* (Brown *XIII*, No. 36), was compiled by a monk of the Augustinian abbey of St Mary de Pratis at Leicester (Ker 1964, 113).

Lyrics continued to be copied by religious in contexts of this sort throughout the medieval period. Evidence of provenance also suggests that female as well as male religious found uses for lyrics. A prayer to Our Lady and all the Angels and an alphabetical devotion to the cross (Brown *XV*, Nos 43 and 101) occur in the fifteenth-century register of Godstow nunnery, for example (Clark 1911). But it is also clear that friars and secular clergy – individuals leading unenclosed lives, outside the confines of monastery or nunnery – played significant roles in disseminating lyrics and recording them in manuscripts of various types.

Discussion of some of these collections as 'friar miscellanies' has been somewhat over specific in its suggestions about their provenance and functions, but it has nonetheless been influential, and (especially in respect of its emphasis on an increasing taste for affective piety) has highlighted some clearly developing trends (Robbins 1935 and 1940; Greene, cliii–cliv). The inclusion in Jesus College, Oxford, MS 29 of the famous *Love-Ron* attributed there to 'frater Thomas de hales de ordine fratrum Minorum' (fol. 260) has been used as crucial evidence for a Franciscan influence on the compilation of this and collections which seem, on the grounds of shared contents, to be related to it. But more recent research has suggested that the manuscripts might have been copied by or for secular clerics rather than necessarily in a Franciscan milieu, and without a necessarily specific Franciscan agenda (Frankis 1986, 179–81; Hill 1963 and 1975; Horrall 1986; Cartlidge 1997). The audience for a collection such as Jesus 29 would have been wide, comprehending those sufficiently learned to appreciate the witty sophistication of *The Owl and the Nightingale*, but also possibly the young women to whom the *Love-Ron* is addressed.[9] The lyrics of Jesus 29 – almost exclusively religious, made up of prayers, Marian poems, advice on death and mortality –

---

[9] For a list of English contents and a description with partial facsimile, see Ker 1963.

are in part duplicated in BL MS Cotton Caligula A.ix (Ker 1963, intro.; Brown *XIII*, xxiii–xxiv). The similarities between these two anthologies are pressing. Both manuscripts contain many of the same texts, in English (*The Owl and the Nightingale*, for example) and in Anglo-Norman; both seem of similar date and place of origin (c.1260–80, in the south-west Midlands); and despite some differences (such as the inclusion in Cotton Caligula of Layamon's *Brut*), it seems likely that the two may have shared a common exemplar. But the processes of production were not entirely the same: Jesus 29 was copied throughout by one single scribe, whereas several contributed to the copying of Cotton Caligula.

Cambridge, Trinity College MS B.14.29 (323), which has been grouped with them as another 'friar miscellany', and is of approximately the same date and geographical provenance, has a slightly different flavour, containing a larger number of lyrics (including many Marian poems and the famous Judas ballad, Brown *XIII*, No. 25), and incorporating Latin texts with its English and Anglo-Norman material; like Cotton Caligula, it contains the work of several scribes (Reichl 1973). But once again its specific origins are irrecoverable, and its association with friars or with secular clergy or with enclosed religious a matter of speculation. In practice, many of the distinctions which have been conventionally observed between manuscripts produced and owned by religious or by secular clergy or by laypeople are in the end misleading, since there clearly existed many possibilities for interpenetration among all these categories. A lay household might have maintained priests or supported friars who could have copied texts (its own secular personnel might even have borrowed exemplars); individual members of enclosed orders might have owned or copied texts for private use rather than for the purposes of the monastery library; regular and secular canons might have produced manuscripts both within and outside their houses.

Collections for Household Use

Much more sense can be made of important compilations like Bodl. MS Digby 86, or BL MS Harley 2253, with a more fluid understanding of the environments in which manuscripts were produced. The contents and marginalia of Digby 86 correctly enabled Carleton Brown to place its production in Worcestershire, and to date it roughly to the last quarter of the thirteenth century; the nature of the texts included in the manuscript (some secular, but most religious; and in English, French, and Latin) prompted his deduction that this 'most important collection of lyrics' must have been compiled 'in some ecclesiastical house', almost certainly 'a house of friars' (Brown *XIII*, xxviii–xxxv). Later research has confirmed his observations about place and date of origin but has made a more plausible case for the view that it is a layman's commonplace book or miscellany, very probably copied by Richard de Grimhill II in the environs of Hallow and Redmarley, near Worcester (Miller 1963; Tschann and Parkes 1996; Corrie 1997). The Middle English lyrics in this collection include a famous 'Ubi sunt' poem, a dialogue between Jesus and Mary, a prayer to Jesus, *The Thrush and the Nightingale*, a definition of love , and a 'contemptus mundi' poem paraphrased from the first elegy of Maximian (Brown *XIII*, Nos 48, 49, 50, 52, 53 and 51). All of these are interpolated into a miscellaneous collection of prayers and devotions, romances, works of moral and practical instruction, animal lore, and humour (notably *Dame Sirith* and some grossly humorous anti-feminist pieces). The texts are copied straightforwardly, with minimal decoration; the verse, including the lyrics, is copied in verse lines, usually in two columns. This looks like an unfussy repertoire of material for domestic use.

Scholarly understanding of the origins of BL MS Harley 2253, one of the richest repositories of early lyrics, has followed a pattern similar to that concerning MS Digby 86. Following Thomas Wright, Carleton Brown deduced from the manuscript's inclusion of a Latin legend of St Etfrid, priest of Leominster, that it was compiled at the priory of Leominster in northern Herefordshire (Brown *XIII*, xxxv–xxxvi, and Wright 1842, vii; see also Brook). Only relatively recently has more intensive work on the scribal hands and on the contents of the collection suggested that its compilation may have been undertaken to serve the needs of a lay household, and furthermore that the date of copying (c.1340) was probably later than earlier estimates had suggested (see the essays in Fein 2000, especially Revard). The range of lyrics in Harley 2253 is very wide, covering religious, political and secular poems. Many of these (especially among the political and love poems) are unique survivals, but the manuscript shares a number of its texts with other manuscripts, including Digby 86, and the hand of its main scribe appears in BL MS Royal 12.C.xii, copying the romance of Fulk Fitzwarin in French prose, and some other items, and also in BL Harley 273, a book for instructive and devotional purposes (Ker 1965, xx; Revard 2000). This suggests that he worked in a milieu where exemplars were readily available from a number of sources (some perhaps of a highly local sort), and where scribal expertise was honed in a variety of contexts. The trilingualism of the contents, and the easy modulations from one kind of text to another, suggest practised compilers and readers who could respond in sophisticated ways to the textual interplay of this collection (Scahill 2003; Corrie 2003).

Digby 86 and Harley 2253 are capacious and striking examples of the kind of manuscript which includes lyrics among a selection of texts, both religious and secular, likely to fulfil many different needs. According to the most recent account, Digby seems originally to have been conceived in two separate sections, one incorporating 'prose texts with practical application' (including religious instruction), the other 'secular verse texts for edification or entertainment including some devotional texts'; 'the two sections were originally regarded as two discrete but complementary collections' (Tschann and Parkes 1996, xliii). Although no conspicuous attempt to organize the lyrics has been made in what now forms the second section, they mostly occur in the same few contiguous gatherings to form a sequence of shortish items in both Anglo-Norman and Middle English. Such consistency as there is relates to layout (all the texts here are in double columns, copied by the same hand), and to the fact that the headings throughout are in Anglo-Norman: *Stond wel moder ounder rode* is 'Chancoun de noustre dame'; *Somer is comen with love to toune* is headed 'Ci commence le cuntent par entre le Mauuis et la russinole'. The lyrics in Harley 2253 also occur in a rough sequence, starting after some Anglo-Norman and

Latin saints' lives which now begin the collection. The occurrence of groups of Middle English poems together (and some rough continuities of subject matter: political poems from fol. 58v to fol. 61v; love poems, with a brief interruption, from fol. 63 to fol. 67), interspersed only now and then with Anglo-Norman poems, perhaps indicates that exemplars became available to the scribe in small batches, possibly on single leaves or bifolia. No headings are supplied here, and the scribe has used the writing space with some ingenuity, moving from single to double columns and back again, and occasionally copying verse lines as continuous prose. The evidence of these two important manuscripts suggests that lyrics circulated in some numbers, that scribes and compilers saw fit to group and present them in different ways according to different tastes and contingencies, and that they were not routinely separated off or kept apart from other texts when copied in anthologies.

Lyrics in Anthologies for Religious and Spiritual Instruction

The most striking instances of the careful grouping and arrangement of lyrics are offered by Bodl. eng. poet.a.1, the Vernon manuscript, compiled in the last decades of the fourteenth century in the region of north Worcestershire or Warwickshire, and its sister-collection, BL Additional 22283, the Simeon manuscript, from approximately the same area (Doyle 1987 and 1990). These are enormous books: the leaves of the massive Vernon manuscript (of which there survive about 350 of the 426 it probably had when complete) measure 544 x 393mm in comparison with the more modest 293 x 188mm of those of Harley 2253. Vernon weighs about 22kg, and was clearly designed to be supported on a lectern or a desk (Robinson 1990).[10] Both manuscripts seem to have been designed as self-contained libraries of material for spiritual instruction: Vernon begins with a contents table which announces 'Here begynnen the tytles of the bok that is cald in latyn tonge *salus anime* and in englysch tonge sowle hele' (fol. ia).

The lyrics included in the manuscripts are exclusively religious and moral. A series of Middle English verse prayers and devotions follows 'La Estorie del Evangelie en engleis' and Richard Maidstone's translation of Psalm 50/51 in the second major section of the Vernon MS's construction. A small number of further lyrics are interspersed between the longer items in the manuscript (*IMEV* 3826, *Unkuynde mon*, comes between two prose texts in section IV, for example).[11] But the greatest number of lyrics – twenty-seven in all – are grouped together in a sequence which in Vernon forms a separate gathering, now the last section of the manuscript (fols 407ra–412vb), and in Simeon comes at the end of what is now Part III (fols 128vb–134ra; two further poems are added at the end of the sequence here; Brown *XIV*, Nos 95 to 120). The Vernon copy of the lyrics was executed by one of the manuscript's main contributing scribes, and his copy

[10] The Simeon MS, now defective, is slightly taller (Doyle 1990, 4).
[11] More lyrics may have been included among items which have been lost from the manuscript: see the table of contents in Doyle 1987.

is carefully organized in three-column format. Space has been left for the provision of ornamented capitals to mark the start of each new poem, and individual stanzas are signalled by coloured paraph signs. The consistency of layout matches an unusual consistency of form and style in the poems themselves: all but three are refrain poems, often with proverbial echoes; all are written in eight- or twelve-line stanzas, with occasional decorative alliteration.

The compilers of Vernon (and the Simeon scribes who probably used the Vernon copy of the lyrics as their exemplar) evidently saw fit to group the poems coherently together within the programme of vernacular spiritual instruction which the volume as a whole presents (Burrow 1990 and Thompson 1990). For whatever reason, though, neither the refrain lyrics in the last section of Vernon, nor the prayers and devotions at the end of Section II of the manuscript, are indicated in the table of contents which was provided at the start. The positions of both groups of lyrics – one at the end of a section, the other in a separate gathering which would come at the end of the whole manuscript – perhaps suggests that they were still being copied when the table of contents was made, although it is also possible that their contents were considered difficult to index in any meaningful way. But they must nonetheless have constituted part of the 'sowle hele' which the manuscript offered, alongside the longer texts like *Piers Plowman*, *The South English Legendary*, *Ancren Riwle*, a version of *The Northern Homily Cycle*, and a sequence of Miracles of Our Lady. Whether its audience was composed of readers or listeners is impossible to determine. A manuscript of such size, on a lectern or bookrest, could not easily have been consulted by more than one person at a time, and it might most effectively have been used for reading aloud. The suggestion that its vernacular programme of contents must have been designed for a female audience (nuns, perhaps, or laywomen associated with a monastic house) is attractive, if not provable (Ayto and Barratt 1984, xviii; Doyle 1987, 15; Meale 1990). The desire among lay readers for books of spiritual instruction on this model is suggested by the survival of some multiple copies which preserve identical runs of contents: the texts of Bodl. Douce 322 (including verse prayers and other religious lyrics) are duplicated in the first half of BL MS Harley 1706, while parts of Longleat House MS 30 and Huntington Library MS HM 142 appear to be twins (see Doyle 1958 and Schulz 1939–40).

Anthologies and miscellanies including texts in the vernacular were produced in increasing numbers in the fourteenth and fifteenth centuries, partly as a result of growing lay literacy, and the changes in the materials and procedures of manuscript production which went along with it (Parkes 1973). The efforts of writers such as Richard Rolle and his followers to promote short texts for devotional purposes in English contributed to the numbers of Middle English lyrics in circulation, and small clusters of these and imitative short aids to affective piety survive in numerous collections. Some of Rolle's lyrics are incorporated in his prose texts, particularly the *Ego Dormio*, which was written for a nun of Yedingham addressed as Rolle's 'dere syster in Criste'; others occur in the *English Psalter* and *The Form of Living*, both apparently addressed to a nun of Hampole named Margaret Kirkby who became a recluse in 1348; still other independent lyrics attributed to Rolle accompany the collections of his works in

Longleat House MS 29 and in CUL MS Dd.5.64 (Allen 1927, 287–311; Woolf, 159–79, 380–2; Ogilvie-Thompson 1988, xvii–xxxi).

Lyrics associated with or influenced by Rolle's brand of pious *lufe-langyng* (Brown *XIV*, No. 83, 29) occur in many fifteenth-century collections, available to compilers sometimes, perhaps, through relatively local networks of textual transmission. Some are to be found in BL Additional MS 37049, a copiously illustrated anthology of pious texts in prose and verse which may have been made (after c.1460–70) in or for a Yorkshire Carthusian house; Rolle's home of Hampole was also in Yorkshire (see Hogg 1981; Gray 1997). Others, though, made their way into collections compiled for lay readers, whose desire for spiritual edification, and for textual aids to devotion, could increasingly be satisfied by domestic reading. A number were copied into the volume which is now Lincoln Cathedral MS 91 by a gentleman named Robert Thornton of East Newton in North Yorkshire (d. by 1465), who seems to have attempted to construct in this compilation, and in another which is now BL Additional 31042, a two-volume household library of edifying and diverting material (Brewer and Owen 1977; Thompson 1987; Keiser 1979 and 1983 and 1984). Here (preceded by romances and miracles, and followed by prose tracts and a collection of medical recipes), a number of prose pieces in Latin and English explicitly associated with 'Richerde hermete' are matched with verse prayers, hymns and meditations which focus on topics such as the holy name or the sweetness of Jesus.

Secular and Religious Lyrics in All-purpose Manuscript Anthologies

Thornton copied a varied selection of other lyrics into his two books: prayers, a carol, moral lyrics with refrains (*IMEV* 560, 3533 and 583). His choices typify the range of short poems commonly included in fifteenth-century all-purpose anthologies. CUL MS Ff.2.38 has a similar flavour, its romances and saints' lives interspersed with verse salutations to the Virgin (*IMEV* 1401 and 3685) and short verse formulations of essential matters like the works of mercy, the seven deadly sins, and the twelve articles of the faith (McSparran and Robinson 1979). In another 'household library', NLS MS Advocates 19.3.1, it is possible to discern some attempt to subdivide the contents of the volume among constituent, themed booklets: one contains humorous parodies, another is concerned with teaching good behaviour; one more addresses issues of female piety. The lyrics (mainly religious) occur in three remaining booklets preoccupied with pious and penitential texts, and were supplied by the main scribe, who names himself as Recardus (Richard) Heege, and by some collaborators (Hardman 1978 and 2000). The occurrence of six rather similar lyrics in sequence on fols 89v–96 may suggest that the copyists were working from a small exemplar (a bifolium or a small quire) which grouped them together in this way.

Similar mixed collections for lay readers, with lyrics on all subjects making increasingly frequent appearances, were produced in significant numbers in the fifteenth century (Boffey and Thompson 1989). Some look to have been household productions, with contributions from large numbers of scribes, and relatively inconsistent systems of quiring and layout: CUL MS Ff.1.6 and

Aberystwyth, National Library of Wales MS Porkington 10 are striking examples (see Beadle and Owen 1977, and Huws 1996). Other compilations, particularly those of metropolitan provenance, whose production may have been influenced by commercial methods if not in all cases generated by such, sometimes devote whole gatherings to lyrics. A ten-page quire in Lambeth Palace MS 306 (fols 132–41), for example, contains a mixture of love lyrics, carols, short topical poems, and added medical recipes (see Guddat-Figge 1976, 218–26), and several short series of lyrics are included in Cambridge, Trinity College MS R.3.19 (Fletcher 1987).

Lyrics in Collections of Sermons and Related Material

While the notion of 'friar miscellanies' has now been overtaken, it is nonetheless clear that many individual clerics, especially those with preaching responsibilities, copied lyrics into working collections as aides-mémoires, or as valuable summaries of material, or as effective devices for the rhetorical punctuation of sermons. The semi-autograph collection of the Franciscan friar William Herebert (d.1333), now BL Additional MS 46919, exemplifies this kind of collection.[12] Herebert, who studied at Oxford before apparently returning to the Franciscan priory in what was probably his native Hereford, owned and annotated at least seven other surviving manuscripts, and assembled texts from a variety of sources, a number copied in hands not his own, in the trilingual MS Additional 46919. The collection includes recipes, treatises on falconry and venery, the *Contes Moralisés* of Nicolas Bozon (another Franciscan friar), and preaching material of diverse kinds: sermons in prose and verse, in Anglo-Norman and in Latin; annotations to these; notes for further sermons; and some Latin sermons of Herebert's own composition, copied in his hand. The last gathering in the manuscript is filled with nineteen Middle English lyrics (mostly translations of Latin hymns and antiphons; see Brown *XIV*, Nos 12–25), in holograph copies, with signs of Herebert's revisions and adjustments. A note on fol. 205r confirms 'in manu sua scripsit frater Willelmus Herebert' [Brother William Herebert copied [these] in his own hand].[13]

Various organizing principles could govern the arrangement of sermon collections and material for preachers' use. While Herebert's lyrics are grouped at the end of his collection, the lyrics in another Franciscan friar's notebook, now Edinburgh, Advocates Library MS 18.7.21, are organized alphabetically by sermon topic ('De Avaricia', 'De Amore Dei', and so on), accompanying further sermon notes. Its single scribe, whose identity as John Grimestone is evident in an invitation on fol. 9v to pray for his soul, completed his collection in 1372, including in it no less than 246 short items of Middle English verse (some are in Brown *XIV*, Nos 87–94; see further Wilson 1973). Many of these are simply

---

12 See Reimer 1987; the frontispiece reproduces BL Additional 46919, fol. 171, part of Herebert's copy of one of his sermons.

13 Four further Middle English lyrics (in Herebert's hand, and probably his compositions) occur earlier in the manuscript, two within sermons and two as marginal additions.

couplets, sometimes proverbial, but others are more substantial lyrics, often locatable in other manuscripts as well as this one (Wilson 1973, xi–xii). The label of 'preaching book' is a convenient term for these manuscripts and for many others, and it highlights a crucially important connection between lyrics and sermons, but at the same time it can iron out fundamental differences of organization and tone between individual manuscripts. Recent discussions of the implications of the Franciscan affiliations of the so-called 'Kildare Manuscript', BL Harley 913, which contains a number of Middle English lyrics (and other well known poems such as *The Land of Cockaygne*) demonstrate the difficulties of reconstructing a manuscript's origins, and the implications of these, with any exactitude (Lucas and Lucas 1990; Lucas 1995, 14–24; Cartlidge 2003).

Many collections related to the needs of preachers include lyrics actually within sermons, at points where they would have provided an effective rhetorical flourish (see Wenzel 1986, Spencer 1993, 89–90, and, for some particularly striking examples, Fletcher 1981). Sometimes these are signalled by rubrication or are evident because their verse lines set them apart from their prose surroundings, but more often than not they are hard to spot on the page. Several English lyrics, written as prose, occur in a collection of sermons owned by the Benedictine John Sheppey, later Bishop of Rochester (d.1360), which is now Oxford, Merton College MS 248 (Brown *XIV*, Nos 35–41), and numerous other collections (organized in a variety of ways, sometimes copied by one individual and in other instances by several scribes) contain similar material (Wenzel 1986 cites many examples; see also Grisdale 1939, Ross 1940, and Fletcher 1986). Much of this was freely circulating, with the effect that the same couplet or short lyric can appear in several different contexts, occasionally even in different language versions of the same text, like the famous *Nou goth sonne under wod* (Brown *XIII*, No. 1) in St Edmund Rich's *Speculum Ecclesie*, not in itself originally a preaching text. The formulation of certain standard handbooks for preachers, works like the *Fasciculus Morum* and John Mirk's *Festial*, of which multiple copies survive, also increased the transmission of these verses (Wenzel 1989; Erbe 1905). Clearly, much sermon-related material also gained currency beyond the professional needs of preachers. Thomas Wimbledon's sermon or Richard Lavynham's treatise, or *Dives et Pauper* (in all of which a small number of lyrics occur), could all have been suitable for private reading by laypeople (Knight 1967; van Zutphen 1956; Barnum 1976–80).

Other 'Professional' Collections

Individuals in other walks of life also made use of lyrics among the texts they copied into books for professional use. The notebooks kept by canons and secular clergy occupied with ecclesiastical or parochial duties often include a few religious lyrics, and sometimes songs for convivial use. A Premonstratensian canon of Coverham in Yorkshire, John Gysborn, incorporated into a compilation he assembled in the early decades of the sixteenth century a verse prayer and salutation to the Virgin, a litany, a macaronic song of a schoolboy at Christmas, and a love song and a poem in praise of servingmen (*IMEV* 2444,

2446, 914, 320.5, 1018 and 2654), sandwiching these items between extracts from the liturgy, notes on parochial duties, legal formulae, medical recipes, and useful instructions on matters like preparing parchment and engraving (a brief description is in Greene, 306).

Student notebooks also include material of this sort: among the very diverse contents of CUL MS Additional 5943 (originally a collection of Latin tracts and sermons, with some Latin prose works by Richard Rolle) is a sequence of festive songs and carols with music, probably added when the collection was in the hands of Thomas Turk, a fellow of Winchester College intermittently between 1395 and 1401 before he became vicar of Bere Regis in Dorset and eventually a Carthusian monk at Hinton Charterhouse in Somerset. Other lyrics, possibly intended for singing although lacking notation, were added at different stages in the manuscript's history, as it seems to have passed from Turk to an anonymous minstrel (a 'joculator', as he names himself), and from the minstrel to John Morton, a rector and vicar in various parts of Dorset in the 1420s and '30s (the minstrel's role here recalls that of the intermediary who seems to have been involved in the transmission of John Audelay's poems).[14] Almost a century after Turk recorded his material, a monk of St Swithun's Priory in Winchester compiled a book of texts in Latin, French and English for a range of pedagogical and other purposes, and included in his selection (now BL Additional 60577) a number of English lyrics and songs (Wilson 1981).

Songbooks

Among the important collections of late fourteenth- and fifteenth-century carols (songs 'on any subject, composed in uniform stanzas and provided with a burden' in the widely accepted definition formulated by R. L. Greene: Greene, xxxii–xxxiii) is a number of manuscripts, some with musical notation, which appear to have served as song repertories for individuals or communities. Scribes with the musical literacy necessary for the copying of notation were not numerous, and were most likely to have worked in association with cathedrals, larger abbeys and monastic institutions, educational foundations, or large household chapels, and it is no surprise that the fullest carol repertories seem to have been connected with institutions such as these. Bodl. MS Arch. Selden. B.26 has been associated with Worcester Cathedral, BL MS Egerton 3307 variously with Meaux Abbey and the Chapel Royal at Windsor (Greene, 314–15, 299–300, 317–18). BL Additional 5665, with carols and other lyrics, may have been associated with Exeter Cathedral (the texts are in Stevens 1979, 338–50, and texts and music in Stevens 1975). Cambridge, Trinity College MS O.3.58, a vellum roll onto which carols and musical settings have been copied, probably also served some institutional purpose (Greene, 327). Bodl. MS eng. poet. e.1 and BL MS Sloane 2593, the first with some musical notation and the second with none at all, have sometimes been described as 'minstrel collections', serving the needs of

---

[14] The very full account in Dobson and Harrison 1979, 22–27, corrects the briefer description in Greene, 323–24.

itinerant musicians who would not have needed recourse to written notation, but their contents and annotation suggest clerkly environments, where again they may have had a role in communal diversion. Both are small-format, easily portable volumes; like the fourteen leaves making up Cambridge, St John's College MS S.54 (259), which survive in their original vellum wrapper, they are handy, workmanlike productions.[15]

More comprehensive songbooks, containing lyrics in other forms as well as carols, were produced for use in secular court or household milieux. BL MS Additional 5465 is a carefully produced parchment volume of carols and songs, all secular in the first layer of copying but with some religious additions, and all with music for voices which may or may not have been accompanied. Recent research suggests that it may have been compiled in 1501 to mark the forthcoming marriage between Henry VII's son Arthur and Princess Catherine of Aragon (texts in Stevens 1979, 351–85; texts and music in Stevens 1975; see also Bowers 1995). The slightly later BL MS Additional 31922, roughly the same size, also parchment, and also containing musical notation, contains songs from the early part of the reign of Henry VIII (texts in Stevens 1979, 386–425; texts and music in Stevens 1962).

Lyrics in Manuscripts for Personal Use: Commonplace Books

There are many overlaps in the categories of manuscript discussed here: in some instances an anthology might also have been a preaching book; a songbook might also have been a friar's collection. One of the hardest categories to distinguish and make pronouncements about is the commonplace book, 'a collection of miscellaneous material generally assumed to have been assembled simply for the interest and amusement of the compiler', as the most useful definition puts it (Rigg 1968, 24; the 'Winchester Anthology', BL MS Additional 60577, seems a good example of a collection which could qualify either as anthology or commonplace book). Robert Reynes, a church reeve and alderman of Acle, in Norfolk, in the late fifteenth century, used his commonplace book (now Bodl. MS Tanner 407; see Louis 1980) to record recipes, charms, and matters of local and legal interest (obituaries of local worthies, court proceedings, information about taxes), as well as fragments of plays and pageants and lyrics which include precepts, proverbs, the ubiquitous 'signs of death' (IMEV 4047 and variants), and some moral and devotional pieces. The compiler of Cambridge, Trinity College O.9.38 (see Rigg 1968), evidently someone associated with Glastonbury Abbey, c.1450, copied Latin and English items in prose and verse, of practical and other relevance, into his book along with anti-feminist, moral, and Marian lyrics.

Like Reynes's collection, this shows characteristic variations in script indicating that the copying took place over a relatively long time. And like the commonplace book of the London grocer Richard Hill, Oxford, Balliol College

---

15 Robbins Sec., xxvi, perpetuates the 'minstrel' associations; but see the more specific provenances suggested by Greene, 306–7, 317–18, 325–6.

MS 354, this book is the long, thin shape favoured for account books which could be carried in a holster (Rigg, 1968, 1; Dyboski 1908; Collier 1997). A good deal of Hill's collection is taken up with materials representing his civic and commercial interests – topics that also preoccupied his contemporary, John Colyns, a London mercer, who copied his lyrics alongside London annals and notes on such matters as the assize of bread, as well as alongside romances and other poems (BL Harley 2252, not all in his hand; Meale 1983). For both Colyns and Hill, exemplars were available in the form of printed texts as well as other manuscript copies (this in addition to such texts as they might have copied from memory, of course): Colyns in particular had connections with the world of printers, and as a mercer may have sold books (Meale 1982). Evidence of the compilers' wider reading and means of access to it are often visible in various forms in books such as these. The manuscript compiled over a number of decades in the late fifteenth and early sixteenth centuries by the Cheshire gentleman Humfrey Newton, Bodl. MS Lat. misc.c.66, seems to have begun life as a 'bespoke . . . single professionally produced quire' (Hanna 2000, 282), around which were gathered miscellaneous items in Newton's own hand: charms, notes on physiognomy and palmistry, legal notes, a courtesy book, and fragments from more obviously 'literary' works such as the *Brut* chronicle, *The Knight's Tale*, *The Parson's Tale* and Lydgate's *Siege of Thebes*. Newton's lyrics (some of which are unique, and may well be autograph copies) were supplied in part on loose leaves, informally arranged.[16]

Added Lyrics

Perhaps the most 'informal' way to copy a text is to add it in some inviting blank space in an existing book or document, registering it in response to a quick impulse rather than copying it according to some carefully conceived plan. The brevity of lyrics, and the related fact that so many of them circulated orally, either as songs or as easily memorized poems, made them especially attractive as items to add to other volumes, sometimes as pen-trials, sometimes as personal autographs registering a particular reader's perusal of a particular book, sometimes as annotations to extend, or to qualify, or to comment on the material to which they were appended. Additions of this sort were made to manuscripts of all types throughout the Middle English period (see Dobson and Harrison 1979, 20–1; Robbins 1968 and *Sec.*, xxx–xxxii; Boffey, 1985, 27–9; Richmond 1994). Prayers to the Virgin and to Christ were added in a thirteenth-century hand to a Latin text in a manuscript from the Benedictine abbey of St Albans, now BL Royal 2.F.viii,[17] while some lyrics on women and love (including an extract from *Troilus and Criseyde*) have been appended to the auto-

---

16 Robbins 1950; Marsh 1996; Hanna 2000. The four lines from fol. 127v, beginning *Quene phebus passyd was ye ram*, quoted by Hanna on p. 285, are from the start of Lydgate's *Siege of Thebes*.
17 The manuscript contains the name of 'fr. Willelmus Parys', see Ker 1964, 301; *IMEV* 2687 and 3962; Brown *XIII*, Nos 32C and 63. Occasionally such added lyrics are not copied onto the pages of an existing manuscript, but added on single leaves incorporated in an existing book.

graph copy of the *Chronicle* of the fifteenth-century Augustinian canon John Capgrave in CUL MS Gg.4.12 (Boffey 1985, 28).

Added lyrics of this kind occur singly and in groups, sometimes entered into the same manuscript by more than one compiler. Occasionally they fulfil the role of bookplates, warning other readers to return the book to its proper owner (Robbins *Sec.*, Nos 89–94; some of these are personalized, specifying owners' names). In a number of instances they are added not to manuscript books but to printed books or to documents of other kinds: the thirteenth-century bilingual 'A Prisoner's Prayer' (Brown *XIII*, No. 5) is included in a collection of ancient laws now in the Corporation of London Record Office because two leaves which may have been fragments from a service book belonging to one of the manuscript's main scribes were accidentally bound up with it; the moral refrain poem *Bi a forest as y gan walke / With out a paleys in a leye* (IMEV 560), was added to some churchwardens' accounts from Cowfold, now at Chichester in the West Sussex Record Office.[18] Some lyrics, like the widely circulating *Erthe upon erthe* (Brown *XIII*, No. 73 and later versions), may have been considered more suitable than others for purposes as epigraphs or autograph inscriptions (Murray 1911, xi, xxxv).

Lyrics Elsewhere

Much has had to be left out of this survey of lyric manuscripts, or treated more sketchily than is warranted. Numerous lyrics are identifiable in the context of longer works, for instance, and their origins and transmission are likely to repay study.[19] Many more may indeed remain to be identified in such environments by anyone prepared to read lines which have been copied as prose with some alertness. The copying and circulation of political and topical lyrics – items which may have been posted for public scrutiny, or sometimes recorded in official contexts – also invite separate consideration.[20] And finally, it is worth remembering all the non-manuscript contexts in which Middle English lyrics have survived: the texts in scrolls and the *tituli* in paintings, tapestry, manuscript illuminations and stained glass; the inscriptions on tombstones and tiles, and the graffiti on buildings and elsewhere; the verses on plates and jugs and rings (Edwards 1997). What remains in manuscript can only be a fraction of the lyric material that seems to have played a part in almost all forms of cultural production throughout the medieval period.

---

[18] See Bazire 1982, and for some further instances Boffey 2000b.

[19] These would include lyrics interpolated in longer poems, such as the songs in Chaucer's *Troilus and Criseyde*, and lyrics in longer prose works like the *Speculum Christiani* (Holmstedt 1933).

[20] Scattergood 1971, 22–33 discusses some aspects of this topic. Boffey and Edwards 2000 address the subject of lyrics in chronicles.

2

Middle English Lyrics: Metre and Editorial Practice

THOMAS G. DUNCAN

How are Middle English lyrics to be read? In the Middle Ages many would have been sung: some survive with music. But others (whether originally set to music or not) would have been read, probably read aloud, and, by informed readers at least, with a sense of the movement of the verse – a crucial aspect of lyric form. It is likewise essential that present-day readers should have some understanding of lyric metre if they are to enjoy these poems to the full. More often than not, however, metre is a topic passed over in silence in editions and anthologies of Middle English lyrics. The question of how Middle English lyrics should be read goes hand in hand with the question of how they should be edited. As E. T. Donaldson has observed of Chaucer, 'it is impossible to edit at all without having in mind some fairly strong preconception concerning ... metre' (Donaldson 1974, 99).

Metre

A commonly accepted view has been that lyric scansion is appropriately to be analysed in terms of the number of stresses per line. Representative of this view is G. L. Brook, the editor of the standard edition of the Harley lyrics. According to Brook, stressed and unstressed syllables 'alternate fairly evenly as in Modern English versification'. Nevertheless, some lines have 'fewer stresses than we should expect'; and although Brook accepts that 'some of these lines may be corrupt', he takes the view that it is 'better to regard the occasional substitution of a three-stress for a four-stress line as a form of licence to avoid monotony' (Brook, 18). However, such an account of metre involves several assumptions. One is that the medieval reader entertained the same aesthetic responses as a modern reader. Yet, would a Middle English reader or poet necessarily have felt or shared Brook's (or any modern reader's) notion of 'monotony'? If anything, the evidence tells against any such view. Thus, it seems gratuitous to assume that in a poem so carefully crafted as the Harley lyric *Weping hath myn wonges wet* (Duncan *MEL*, No. 27), where each stanza concludes with a quatrain of 'three-stress' lines, that one line (59) out of 24 such lines should, 'to avoid monotony', happen to be a 'four-stress' line. A second assumption is that it is satisfactory to describe this verse simply in terms of the number of stressed syllables per line. An obvious disadvantage of this approach is that it is often unclear what is to count as a 'stressed syllable'; is it a syllable carrying 'natural' stress, or perhaps 'metrical' or 'rhetorical' stress? A more serious disadvantage is that unstressed syllables are left out of account. It has commonly been thought that English poets, accustomed to a measure of flexibility with regard to the number of unstressed syllables in traditional native alliterative verse, were happy with some variation in the syllable-count of their lines even when writing non-alliterative verse.[1] This may be true of some verse, but as a generalisation it is much too sweeping and may owe less to systematic analysis than to what seems more akin to a form of quaint nationalistic pride as found in George Saintsbury's claim that Middle English verse by 'the admission of extra unstressed syllables . . . refused to surrender . . . [to] mere slavish following of French and Latin forms' (Saintsbury 1907, 376–7). Yet, whatever the truth may be, one crucial question which confronts us in assessing the metre of Middle English lyrics is this: precisely which unstressed syllables in a line *as written* are metrically to be counted?

It is difficult to answer this question for two reasons. First, no contemporary account of the metrical principles and practices of Middle English poets survives, if, indeed, any such treatise was ever written. The second is simply this: whereas it is clear to a present-day reader how many syllables are represented in a modern English text, in a Middle English text this is far from self-evident. For guidance in this matter it is therefore necessary to look, at least in the first instance, to sources of evidence independent of the actual texts. Two such sources immediately suggest themselves: one is the verse tradition from which Middle English stanzaic lyrics derived, French and Latin songs; the other is the music which survives with some of the Middle English lyrics. A fundamental requirement of a song is that its words should fit the tune, and do so for all stanzas – a requirement which calls for a considerable degree of regularity. Indeed, from a study of troubadour and trouvère songs, John Stevens concluded that in the matching of words and music the 'most important single controlling factor is the number of syllables in any given line or stanza'.[2] It may well be, therefore, that in English stanzaic lyrics within this tradition (whether surviving with music or not) the principal poetic constraint continued to be a matter of a syllabic match, line for line and stanza by stanza. Indeed, E. J. Dobson took the view that 'the music . . . may require perfect or near-perfect metrical regularity, in syllable-count and in rhythm'.[3]

On the hypothesis, then, that the number of syllables per line may be a crucial poetic constraint in some Middle English verse (and not least in song lyrics), how, then, is the analysis of syllable-count to be made? The norm for the syllable-count of a line may conveniently be taken as the number of its metrical

---

[1]   The long-held view that the variations allowable with regard to unstressed syllables in Old English verse gave way, in Middle English alliterative verse, to a much looser usage in this regard is to be entertained only as sweeping generalisation. Careful alliterative verse, as, for instance, that of the *Gawain*-poet, evidences tightly controlled patterns in the distribution of stressed and unstressed syllables. See Duggan 1997; Putter and Stokes 2000.

[2]   Stevens 1982, 2. See also Stevens 1986.

[3]   Dobson and Harrison 1979, 32. However, the evidence of surviving musical notation supports rather more flexibility than Dobson allowed, especially concerning the extent to which musical rhythm and word accent should coincide. See Duncan *MEL*, 152–3.

(i.e. pronounced) syllables, counting from the first stressed syllable to the rhyme syllable (but not counting the second syllable of feminine rhymes). Occasionally, as in some lines beginning with the word 'and', metrical or rhetorical stress will determine the first stressed syllable. If, for the purposes of description, an unstressed syllable at the beginning of a line may be regarded as an optional extra syllable, the norm may be varied by such an additional syllable. Two very common lines are those of 5 syllables (optionally 6) and of 7 syllables (optionally 8), i.e. 5(6) and 7(8). As a common variant in lines with the optional extra initial syllable, the stress pattern of the first two syllables may be inverted to give an eight-syllable line in the form / x x / x / x / beside the pattern x / x / x / x /. However, it is to be noted that the regular alternation of stressed and unstressed syllables often depends on imposing a rhythm of 'metrical' stresses, and, as suggested above, the practice of analysing lines of non-alliterative verse in terms of numbers of stresses has its dangers, dangers strikingly apparent in controversy over the analysis of Chaucer's decasyllabic lines in terms of stresses, four stresses or five. The French decasyllabic line was virtually introduced into English poetry by Chaucer. C. S. Lewis believed that English ears used to the four-stress line of traditional English alliterative verse would not have understood Chaucer's long lines in any other way.[4] However, this hypothesis ignores the obvious fact that Chaucer did not write alliterative verse and that he seemed to view alliterative 'rum, ram, ruf' as a provincial and possibly outdated literary mode, alien to a 'Southern man', an attitude doubtless shared by his London literary circles.[5] It is equally obvious that in the trilingual (English, French and Latin) society of Chaucer's England, and not least among the literati of the court of Richard II, there would have been many who were far from unfamiliar with French verse. Now, while it is true that many of Chaucer's lines may be read naturally enough with four stresses (and only with five stresses by resorting to artificial 'metrical' stressing), it is equally true that other lines read more naturally with five stresses. But whatever the number or pattern of perceived stresses may be, the fundamental fact remains that Chaucer's 'decasyllabic' lines are consistent in one significant regard: counting an initial unstressed syllable, each indeed has ten syllables.[6] Likewise, though the lines of the Harley lyric

---

4 Lewis's views on Chaucer's decasyllabic line are found in Lewis 1938. Subsequently, the most outright advocate of the four-stress analysis was Southworth 1962.

5 Cf. Chaucer's Parson's observation:
    But trusteth wel, I am a Southren man;
    I kan nat geeste 'rum, ram, ruf,' by letter. (CT, X. 42–3)

6 See Samuels 1972. Chaucer's understanding of prosody in terms of counting syllables rather than stresses was more widely understood and practised than C. S. Lewis was prepared to allow. Into the fifteenth century one finds Hoccleve writing in the same manner. See Burrow 1999, xxviii: 'There can be little doubt that the prime general metrical rule for Hoccleve, as for his French contemporaries, concerned the number of syllables, not the distribution of stresses'. Of course, the decasyllabic norm in Chaucer allows for variation – from a possible eleven syllables in lines with feminine rhymes to nine syllables in headless lines. It may also be that Chaucer tolerated trisyllabic feet; see Barney 1993, 98. It should be added that to insist on the importance of syllabic count as a poetic constraint is in no way to discount the importance of stress patterns in Middle English verse, not least in view of the fact that, unlike French, English is a stress language. Clearly stress patterns were important in Chaucer's verse which, for instance, does not permit a clash of stresses other than after grammatical caesura.

With longing I am lad (Duncan *MEL*, No. 1) may be described as three-stress lines, such a description only makes sense in terms of 'metrical' stressing, for in natural speech rhythm many of the lines read more convincingly with two stresses: e.g., *With lónging I am lád*, or *For sélden I am sád*, or *That sémly for to sée*. It makes more sense, then, to view lines of non-alliterative verse not as fixed in number of stresses (some merely 'metrical'), but rather (at least, in careful verse) as basically constant in number of syllables, with flexibility in the number and pattern of natural stresses. Such a view accords well with Stevens's claim that the rhythm of Middle English verse is that of 'very speech itself' (Stevens 1982, 7). Hence, where the poetic constraint is a count of syllables rather than of stresses, any reading of such verse may appropriately follow the natural rhythms of speech.

How well, then, does an analysis in terms of syllable counting work with the surviving lyric texts? Unfortunately, as already stated, it is not immediately self-evident from a Middle English text which unstressed syllables are to be pronounced. In reading a Middle English poem aloud some syllables in the text *as written* may not be sounded depending on the operation of phonetic principles such as elision, syncope, synizesis and apocope. There is, moreover, the considerable problem of the interpretation of the word endings '-e', '-est', '-eth', '-ed' and '-es'. A brief review of these linguistic matters is essential at this point as they are fundamental to any appraisal of metre.[7]

Elision, syncope, synizesis and apocope are processes of phonetic reduction operative within the spoken chain of speech, processes often masked by spelling in Middle English texts. Elision arose where a vowel at the end of a word was absorbed by an initial vowel (or 'h' plus vowel) of the following word. Thus, the final '-e's of *grede* and *grone* were elided so that the line *Y grede, Y grone unglad* (Duncan *MEL*, No. 1, 4) would have been spoken with six syllables as 'Y-gred-Y-gron-un-glad'. The common words *ne* and *the* were frequently subject to elision. By syncope an unstressed syllable was removed within a word or word sequence. Middle English *comely*, *every* and *lovely* could be pronounced as three syllables, or two, as in present-day English with the loss by syncopation of the medial syllable, and are, indeed, sometimes spelt as two syllables. Syncope frequently occurred where words ending in '-el', '-en' or '-er' were followed by a word beginning with a vowel (or 'h' plus vowel). In the line *Mirie it is while summer ilast* (Duncan *MEL*, No. 36, 1, manuscript spelling) the last two words are to be read as three syllables (i.e. 'sum-ri-last') with the reduction by syncope of the second syllable of *summer*. Synizesis is a form of elision in which the vowel /i/ (in Middle English spelt 'i' or 'y') immediately followed by another vowel becomes the corresponding semi-vowel /j/ (the sound of 'y' in 'yet') and so the first element of a diphthong with the following vowel and thereby a single syllable. By this process, *Mirie it is* in the line just quoted would be pronounced 'Mir-yi-tis' in the speech chain. Apocope involves the suppression of a final unaccented vowel before a following consonant. In Middle English lyrics a weak syllable was sometimes eliminated in this way to preserve the

---

7   For a more detailed account, see Duncan *MEL*, 254–7. See also Smithers 1983 for an excellent discussion of such matters with reference to the metre of *Havelok*.

rhythmic pattern of a single weak syllable between two accented syllables. Thus, in the line *That whilom bar that swéte savóur* (Duncan *MEL*, No. 53, 2) the final '-e' of *swete* is silent by apocope whereas in *that swetë lide* of the following line, the final '-e' in *swete* is pronounced. All four phonetic processes are operative in speaking the line *Mirie it is while summer ilast*. At first sight one may wonder how many of the syllables here *as written* are to be pronounced? A puzzled present-day reader might be comforted to know that the spelling misled a medieval music scribe to count eleven syllables. However by the phonetic processes just discussed, in speech or song this line reduced to seven syllables (i.e. 'Mir-yi-tis-whil-sum-ri-last') in keeping with a seven-line stanza form of 7a, 5b, 7a, 4b, 7b, 7b, 7a. An initial line of eleven syllables would clearly have been highly incongruous.[8]

By the early fifteenth century, '-e' at the end of words had ceased to be pronounced in ordinary speech. It has commonly been held that this was the end result of a gradual and steady loss of final '-e', which began in more northerly dialects in the thirteenth century and advanced through midland and then southern dialects in the course of the fourteenth century. However, the linguistic processes which led to the loss of final '-e' were complex. Probably from early Middle English the possibility of elision and apocope within the spoken chain of language would have given rise to the existence of forms of the same word with and without sounded final '-e' in any dialect. Furthermore, the process of the loss or reduction of unstressed syllables in Middle English doubtless first took place at a colloquial level of speech, from which endingless or reduced forms would begin to appear, however gradually, in more formal registers. In effect, in midland and southern dialects until the end of the fourteenth century, the presence or absence of pronounced historical final '-e' (that is, the grammatically or etymologically authentic inflexion as distinct from mere random spellings) depended on formality of register, and poets would have had at their disposal optional forms of words with and without final '-e'.[9]

Reduced forms of the second and third person singular present indicative had been current in southern dialects since the Old English period. They may have been available to poets in other dialects either from their awareness of the southern forms, or from the operation of syncope, or by analogy with such contracted forms as *saist* and *saith* beside *sayest* and *sayeth*. As the evidence of Chaucer's metre conclusively demonstrates, even when the endings '-est' and '-eth' were spelt as full forms they were sometimes pronounced as reduced forms. The evidence of metre would suggest that this was also true for many Middle English lyrics. Where lyrics survive in more than one manuscript, variation from copy to copy between full and reduced spellings of the same words is not uncommon.

Again, it has usually been supposed that after monosyllabic stems the endings '-ed' and '-es' retained their full forms until the fifteenth century. However, as with the loss of final '-e', it is likely that reduced forms first arose in colloquial usage before establishing themselves in more formal speech. The

8   See Duncan 1994 for a full discussion of the metre of this lyric.
9   For a detailed discussion of this issue in the light of the evidence of *Havelok*, see Smithers 1983.

reduction of these endings has been attributed to the effect of syncope,[10] a process which was not new in Middle English and which was operative long before the fifteenth century. Even in lyrics from the mid-thirteenth and early fourteenth centuries, it seems metrically plausible to view '-ed' and '-es' in sequences like *Y-lóved Ich háve*[11] and *táles untóun*[12] as early instances of reduction by syncope. Occasional thirteenth-century reduced spellings also occur as, for instance, *frents* [friends][13] and *þar wils* [there whiles].[14] It is true that such spelling evidence is scarce, but if the loss of final '-e' is more often signalled by a tendency on the part of scribes to add '-e' to words at random rather than to omit silent '-e' from spelling, there is no reason why the conventional spellings '-es' and '-ed' should not sometimes mask reduced forms. Indeed, even in the late fourteenth century, when spellings like *tornd* [turned] and *tempt* [tempted] are found in the Vernon manuscript,[15] such evidence of reduction disappears under the cloak of spelling convention in the spellings *turned* and *tempted* of the companion manuscript, BL Additional 22283.

Even if Middle English lyrics had survived in authorial copies, an understanding of their metrical form would be possible only in the light of such considerations. However, many of the surviving lyric texts are manifestly the end product of successive scribal transcriptions, and possibly, in some cases, versions made from dictation or from memory. Such copies are notoriously unreliable.[16] Since Middle English scribes wrote in accordance with the pronunciation and usage of their own dialects and the spelling habits which prevailed in the schools or scriptoria where they had learned to write, they tended to alter the language of the texts they copied to conform with the spellings and forms familiar to them. Clearly metre and rhyme were vulnerable to the changes resulting from such scribal linguistic revision. Chaucer himself was all too aware of this danger as his famous plea at the close of *Troilus and Criseyde* makes clear:

> And for ther is so gret diversité   *because; diversity*
> In Englissh and in writyng of oure tonge,
> So prey I God that non myswrite the,   *thee*
> Ne the mysmetre for defaute of tonge.   *lack of skill in language*
>   (*Troilus* V, 1793–96)

[10] See Luick 1914–, § 456.2.

[11] Duncan *MEL*, No. 40, 23. See Brown *XIII*, Nos 32A, 23; 32B, 33; and 32C, 33 for variant spellings in surviving copies of this lyric.

[12] Duncan *MEL*, No. 27, 37.

[13] See Brown *XIII*, No. 28A, 34 for this form in Cambridge, Trinity College MS B.14.39.

[14] See Brown *XIII*, No. 46A, 49 for this form in BL MS Arundel 248. The reduction of '-es' is, of course, well attested from the beginning of the fourteenth century for the East Midland dialect from scansion in Robert Mannyng's *Handlyng Synne* (1303), as in line 9153: *Goddys mércy déd hyt fró hem wére.*

[15] In *Whan men ben meriest at her mele*, Duncan *MEL*, No. 60, 24 and 134.

[16] Readers unfamiliar with the extent of textual corruption in ME lyrics – words added or omitted, word order, line order and even stanza order altered, stanzas added or omitted – not to mention the effects of scribal linguistic revision (see below), need only compare the different versions of Brown *XIII*, Nos 10, 17, 28, 32, 46 and 49, or the texts of Brown *XIII*, No. 63 from BL MS Royal 2.F.viii and Brown *XIII*, No. 64 from Bodl. MS Digby 2 with the versions of the same lyrics in BL MS Harley 2253, Brook, Nos 18 and 22.

Evidently Chaucer did suffer from a great deal of 'miswriting' and consequent 'mismetering'. E. T. Donaldson offers a telling illustration of the problem by detailing the eleven different versions of line 19 of the 'General Prologue' found in twenty-seven authorities (Donaldson 1974, 99). These are:

Bifel that in that sesoun on a day
Bifel that <u>on</u> that sesoun on a day
Bifel that in that sesoun <u>upon</u> a day
Bifel it in that sesoun on a day
Bifel ___ in that sesoun on a day
Bifel ___ in that sesoun <u>upon</u> a day
<u>And</u> fel ___ in that sesoun on a day
<u>It</u> bifel that in that sesoun on a day
<u>It</u> bifel <u>than</u> in that sesoun <u>upon</u> a day
<u>So</u> bifel <u>it</u> ____ that sesoun on a day
<u>So</u> <u>it</u> bifel ___ that sesoun on a day

Numerous words in Middle English, including prepositions, adverbs, nouns and especially verbs, had the endings '-en' or '-e' as variant forms. Scribes readily copied '-en' instead of '-e' or *vice versa*. Since '-e' frequently disappeared with elision which was prevented by '-en', it is evident how easily metre could be distorted by such alterations alone. Among other common variants affecting metre were: *hauest / hast; haueth / hath, haueth / hauen / haue / han, haued / had, for to / to; upon / on; unto / to; other / or; also / so, as; muchel / much; loverd / lord; lavedy / lady; heved / hed; ne wot / not;* and single *ne, nought* and double *ne . . . nought* negatives.[17]

Nevertheless, such problems notwithstanding, when analysed in the light of the linguistic principles mentioned briefly above – elision, syncope, synizesis and apocope – and also the possibility of hiatus, many of the non-alliterative lyrics do reveal a marked consistency in syllable count.[18] When a lyric is characteristically regular in its metre, it is reasonable to assume that an occasional irregularity in the text may well have resulted from the hazards of 'linguistic revision'. Where an alternative form – e.g. *to* instead of *unto* – readily rectifies the metre, there is a strong case for adopting that alternative form in an edited text. However, where no obvious alternative form suggests itself, an exceptional irregularity in a context of apparent overall metrical regularity may call for emendation, especially where suspect sense or syntax is involved; and even if emendation can never guarantee to restore the original text – for all emendation must remain to a degree speculative – the restoration of metre is a positive editorial gain.

---

17 Numerous examples of 'mismetering' and spoilt rhymes caused by variants adopted by scribes other than the forms of the original authors are readily to be seen by comparing the texts of lyrics printed from more than one manuscript in Brown *XIII*. See also Duncan *MEL*, No. 75, Commentary, 14 n.

18 Hiatus: where, for the sake of the metre, a vowel at the end of a word is retained and not elided with the initial vowel, or 'h' plus vowel, of a following word.

Editorial practice

With the noteworthy exception of E. J. Dobson, editors of editions and anthologies of Middle English lyrics have all too often ignored or been reluctant to
recognise the need for emendation to restore metre in corrupt texts. Two blatant
instances well illustrate this point, the first in the lyric *Now I se blosme sprynge*
(Duncan *MEL*, No. 69). This poem survives in two manuscripts, BL MS Royal
2.F.viii, and BL MS Harley 2253. Its scansion is very simple. It is written in
ten-line stanzas. Almost all the lines are of the same length, 5(6) syllables, mostly
6. This lyric has been printed from the Royal MS by Carleton Brown, by Bennett
and Smithers, by Silverstein, and by Celia and Kenneth Sisam.[19] All these
editors, following the Royal MS, give the third line of the poem as *A swete
longinge*. But even if the final '-e' of *swete* is pronounced (as indicated by the
Sisams), the line is still obviously metrically short (unless one were to resort to
taking the first word *A* and the final '-e' of *swete* as stressed – a bizarrely unnat-
ural analysis!). The Harley reading of this line is *A suete loue-longynge*. It is, of
course, true that where another manuscript gives a metrically satisfactory
reading of a line, there is no guarantee that the version of that manuscript is
necessarily that of the original poem; it could represent an independent scribal
improvement. In this case, however, there is little room for doubt. It is over-
whelmingly likely that the Royal reading *longinge* has arisen by the common
process of haplography:[20] an original *louelongynge*, or perhaps *loulongynge*, (with
the minim letters 'u' and 'n' of identical or virtually identical appearance) has
been miscopied as *longynge*. And even for anyone so sceptical as to cling to the
view that, in the nature of things, there can be no final proof that the original
reading could have been none other than *louelongynge*, there is, nevertheless, no
denying that by this emendation faulty metre is rectified. It is true that reserva-
tions have sometimes been expressed concerning what has been suspiciously
spoken of as the smoothing out of metrical irregularities, almost as if irregularities themselves were somehow self-evidently and automatically self-justifying.
Certainly, each poem must be assessed in terms of its overall metrical form. In
the case of this lyric, metrical regularity is beyond question. It is evident to the
ear from reading even the first four lines of the poem with the Harley reading of
line 3 –

> Now I se blosmë sprynge,   *blossom flourish*
> Ich herde a foulës song,   *I heard a bird's song*
> A swetë love-longynge
> Myn hertë thurghout sprong   *throughout; has sprung up*

– that the short third line of the Royal version is unacceptable, the product of
readily explicable corruption.

---

[19] Brown *XIII*, No. 63; Bennett and Smithers 1968, VIII W; Silverstein 1971, No. 15; Sisam and
     Sisam 1970, No. 23.
[20] Haplography: the unintentional writing of a letter (or series of letters) once when it (they)
     should have been written twice.

The well-known lyric *Adam lay y-bownden* (Duncan *MEL*, No. 108) may serve as a second illustration. This poem is sometimes printed in eight long lines (as in the manuscript), and sometimes as sixteen short lines. In the short-line version, lines 7 and 8 are variously printed as:

> As clerkes fynden writen
> in here book

or as:

> As clerkes fynden
> writen in here book.

Edmund Reiss opens his discussion of the long line version of this poem with the observation that:

> On the surface a naive, unsophisticated ballad like piece, even revealing faulty meter – as in line 4 – this lyric still has a compelling quality that stems from its simple language and the combination of its rhythms and sounds.
>
> (Reiss 1972, 139)

However, Reiss does not clarify his point about 'faulty meter'. Yet, if, as he claims, 'the combination of its rhythms and sounds' so significantly determines this poem's 'compelling quality', a metrical anomaly surely invites further comment. Stephen Mannyng speaks of lyrics which 'so relate sound and sense that the sound structure buttresses the sense' (Mannyng 1962, 3). Since he offers the poet of *Adam* as his example of one who 'exacts this very quality from his meter precisely because he has penetrated the significance of his topic' (Mannyng 1962, 6), it would be reasonable to expect him to address himself to the metrical peculiarities of lines 7 and 8, and line 12 in this poem. This, however, he does only briefly:

> In fact, lines 7–8 and line 12 have to be squeezed into the meter, to be syncopated as it were, yet this is precisely what the poem demands. (Mannyng 1961, 6)

How this process of metrical squeezing works and why it is 'precisely what the poem demands' are matters which, alas, Mannyng leaves unexplained. It is clear that for Mannyng the integrity of the text as it stands in the manuscript is accepted without question. In the case of Middle English lyrics, however, such an assumption is wholly unwarranted.

In attempting textual emendation, vital clues may sometimes be found by re-examining the source manuscript. It was the practice of the scribe of BL MS Sloane 2593 to write his poems in long lines and sometimes to divide these lines into two parts by marking the end of the first unit with a point. Thus he copies this lyric in eight long lines, six of which he divides in this manner with points after *y-bownden* (line 1), *wynter* (line 2), *appil* (first occurrence, line 3), *writen* (line 4), *lady* (line 6), and *singen* (line 8). It is clear that the scribe was at pains to save space. The manuscript pages are small and in many poems he fills up his page by copying the last line of each stanza in the space between the end of the previous lines and the right-hand edge of the paper. Furthermore, each poem is divided off from the next not by a space but simply by a line drawn right across the page. It may therefore be that the scribe did not regard his written lines as units of structure as the word 'line' is now used with reference to poetic form. Rather it seems that his long lines may merely have been an economic way of combining two units to save space. In this case this poem is more appropriately to be viewed as one of sixteen units or (expressed in modern terms) sixteen lines and, when economy of space is not at issue, more appropriately so to be printed.[21]

Granted a 16-line arrangement, lines 7 and 8 are the first and second parts of the long line 4 of the manuscript copy. Evidently, as with the other five cases of lines he divided by a point, the scribe took the first part of this line (up to *writen*) as a complete unit. Line 7 should, therefore, read:

> As clerkes fynden writen.

It is line 8, *in here book*, which is evidently imperfect and which calls for emendation. The required emendation readily suggests itself: lines 7 and 8 should read:

> As clerkes fynden writen,
>   writen in here book.

The addition of 'writen' in line 8 restores the otherwise faulty metre. It also complies with a strikingly characteristic feature of this poem, repetition, as in the repetition of *y-bownden* of line 1 as *bownden* in line 2, the repetition of *an appil* of line 5 in line 6, and of *the appil take ben* in line 9 as *the appil take ben* in line 10. Moreover, the presumed omission of *writen* by the Sloane scribe (or in an earlier copy) would again have arisen from that previously mentioned common scribal error, haplography.

What Mannyng and Reiss fail to notice is the problem in the Sloane reading of

---

[21] With rhyme schemes as a guide, the stanza forms of Middle English lyrics are in most cases self-evident. However, the convention of representing units of verse as separate lines is largely a post-medieval practice. The representation of poetic form was often at best a matter of secondary importance to a medieval scribe; his over-riding concern was usually with economy – with saving space. Hence, in the manuscripts, these poems were frequently written out as prose or in long lines (i.e. with two or more lines written as one line) in order to make the maximum use of every page. The way a poem was copied sometimes depended on how the page on which it was begun had been divided for the previous item. Thus, in BL MS Harley 2253, the beginning of the lyric *Of rybaudz I ryme* (Ker 1965, No. 88) is written out in short lines because the page on which it starts had already been divided into two columns; but when the scribe began a fresh page he changed to copying the rest of the poem (from line 24 on) in long lines. Similarly, John of Grimestone in his Commonplace Book (NLS MS Advocates 18.7.21) copied the first stanza of the lyric *Why have ye no routhe on my child?* (Duncan *MEL*, No. 92) as four short lines, and then, to fill space at the bottom of the page, he copied the second stanza as two long lines. Like many others, the scribe of BL MS Sloane 2593 sometimes marked the division of his long lines into separate units by punctuation marks; he also had the not uncommon habit of saving space by copying the last line of a stanza in the right-hand margin. The copying of lyrics in abbreviated form represents the extreme of scribal economy as in the case of *Maiden in the more lay* (see below). The line division and stanza form of Middle English lyrics as printed in modern editions are, therefore, for the most part editorial. But if editors have never felt tempted to print lyrics as prose where (as often) they are so found in the manuscripts, it is a pity that in some editions more care has not been taken in following the modern convention of representing units of verse by separate lines.

line 9: *Ne hadde the appil take ben.* Ending with the word *ben*, this line has one syllable too many, indeed, one stress too many, and introduces a rhyme with the following line (a self-rhyme, in fact) which is at variance with the rhyme scheme of this poem. Again, a simple emendation readily suggests itself – the omission of *ben* in line 9. Lines 9 and 10 should read:

> Ne hadde the appil take,
> the appil take ben.

So emended the metre is restored. The extra *ben* after *take* in line 9 is readily to be accounted for as a mistake in copying deriving from a scribe's eye having caught *take ben* of the next phrase, i.e. an instance of eye-skip, another common kind of scribal error. Moreover, this emendation restores here the incremental repetition so characteristic of this poem.[22] It is surely preferable to recognise textual corruption for what it is rather than to base on faulty metre aesthetic assertions as dogmatic as they are dubious; and in this instance it is to be noted that the metrically regular restored version of this poem in effect strengthens Mannyng's contention that here 'the strong beat supports the sense of joy' (Mannyng 1962, 7) – and that without recourse to ungainly squeezing and syncopating.

If metrical corruption in Middle English lyrics has frequently been left unattended to, corrupt rhymes have fared rather better. Even highly conservative editors like Carleton Brown have been more readily disposed to resort to emendation to restore spoilt rhymes. Such efforts, however, have at best been haphazard and random; spoilt rhymes have often been left standing even where plausible emendation readily suggests itself. For instance, the Grimestone lyric *My folk, now answere me* (Duncan *MEL*, No. 100) is written in four-line stanzas rhyming a, b, a, b. The eighth stanza of this poem is printed by Brown as:

A kingges yerde i the be-tok	*king's scepter I granted you*
til thu were al be-forn;	*until; above all (others)*
& thu heng me on rode tre,	
& corounnedist me with a thorn.	*crowned*
	(Brown *XIV*, No. 72, 29–32)

Brown ignores the obvious fault in the rhyme scheme here. This, however, may easily be corrected by the reversal of the order of the last two words of the first line, i.e. *the be-tok* to *be-tok the*. Initially, this seemed to me a likely emendation; scribes not infrequently inverted word order as they copied. In the event, an examination of the manuscript proved gratifyingly rewarding. Close inspection revealed that the word *the* had been marked by double ticks for transposition. The line was indeed correctly to be read as: *A kingges yerde i be-tok the*.

Dislocation of stanza order is not uncommon in Middle English lyrics. This is immediately apparent from many lyrics surviving in more than one manuscript. But even in the face of the clearest evidence of corrupt stanza order, editors have tended to resist appropriate emendation. A striking example is the case of the

---

[22] See Duncan *MEL*, No. 108 for the complete text of this lyric as restored with these emendations. See also Duncan 1987 for a fuller account of the textual problems in this lyric.

Harley lyric *A wayle whyt ase whalles bon,* written out as prose on f. 67 of BL MS Harley 2253. A stylistic feature of this poem is stanza linking by the repetition of a word or words from the last line of each stanza in the first line of the following stanza. Partly on the evidence of this stanza linking, J. A. Gibson, as long ago as 1914, pointed out that what appears in the manuscript copy as the first stanza must in fact originally have followed the eighth stanza: stanza 8 ends with the line *that wayle whyte;* the first stanza (in the Harley copy) begins with the line *A wayle whyt ase whalles bon.* On the basis of this and other evidence, Gibson proposed a reconstruction of this lyric which I follow in my text of the poem (Duncan *MEL,* No. 2).[23] However, in other editions and anthologies this lyric has continued to be printed as found in the manuscript despite Gibson's clear demonstration of the corrupt stanza order of the Harley text.

Another example of corrupt stanza order is to be found in a lyric entitled by Carleton Brown 'Penitence for Wasted Life' (Brown *XIII,* No. 2). Brown prints this poem as found in the manuscript, BL MS Additional 27909, with the last two stanzas of the poem as:

Leuedi sainte marie, understond nu seonne mine;	*my sins*
ber min erende wel to deore sune thine,	*petition*
hwas flech & blod ihalwed is of bred, of water, of wine,	*consecrated*
that us ischulde he eure fram alle helle-pine.	*protect us; pains of hell*
Inne mete & inne drinke ic habbe ibeo ouerdede,	*excessive*
& inne wel sittende schon in pruttere iwede;	*shoes; sumptuous clothes*
hwanne ich ihurde of gode speke ne hedd ich hwat me sede –	*heeded*
hwan ich hier-of rekeni shal, wel sore me mei drede.	*shall take account*

This lyric has eleven four-line stanzas. In stanza 1 the poet appeals to the Virgin for help as, in perplexity, he reflects on his sinful life. Stanzas 2–8 give an account of his sins: they are many and varied. Now he wishes to escape from the sleep of sin before his eternal sleep and to be a warning to others. The sleep of sin has stolen his life as his hair has turned white and his flesh has withered. He repents sins of word and deed, in bed and at board, drunkenness, extravagance, indifference to charity and to the needs of the hungry, the naked and the igno-rant, and his sins 'with all my limbs'. In stanza 9 he again addresses the Virgin, praying for help to reform, to curb his fleshly desires, to defeat the Devil, and to love charity, God and man. He asks Mary, in stanza 10, to bear his petition to Christ, in order that Christ, through the sacrament of his sacrifice, should protect us from hell.

It is at this point, where the poem might have been expected to end, that another stanza follows, a stanza which does not fit any thought sequence and which makes for a rather odd and inappropriate ending to this penitential poem. Carleton Brown, in comparing this poem with the prose *Lofsong of Ure Lefdi* states that 'both . . . conclude with an appeal for her [the Virgin's] interces-sion' (Brown *XIII,* xvii), yet this is clearly not true of this lyric as it appears in the manuscript and as printed by Carleton Brown.

---

[23] For a fuller discussion of editorial problems in this lyric, see Duncan 1992.

However, the problem of the final stanza in the manuscript can readily be solved if it is reconsidered in the context of the overall sense-development of the poem. At stanza 7, the poet turns to charitable deeds which he defines as feeding the hungry, clothing the naked and guiding the ignorant. He ends this stanza with an injunction to love God and *of him habbe drede*. The anomalous final stanza in the manuscript would follow naturally at this point for in it the poet confesses that, by contrast, he has overfed himself, overclad himself, and has thereby ignored God's word (i.e. to 'feed the hungry' and 'clothe the naked' mentioned in stanza 7); therefore, he concludes, *wel sore me mei drede*.

How then did this anomalous final stanza come to be misplaced at the end of the poem? In the manuscript this poem is written out as prose. Coloured initials, alternately green and red, mark the beginnings of the stanzas. These initials as effectively draw attention to the final as to the first word of each stanza. In the original stanza order, with the anomalous final stanza following stanza 7, there would have been two successive stanzas ending with the same rhyme word *drede*. Obviously, a scribe, having copied the word *drede* at the end of stanza 7, has looked back to his exemplar to have his eye caught by *drede* at the end of the following stanza (the original stanza 8) and has therefore moved on to copy the next stanza (the original stanza 9). On looking over his finished copy, the scribe noticed that he had missed out a stanza; this he then added at the end of the poem. With the final stanza of the manuscript thus restored to its rightful place, the penultimate stanza of the manuscript copy, with its petition to the Virgin, emerges in its true role as the proper conclusion of this poem.

Dislocation in lyric transmission affects not only stanzas but also individual lines; sometimes lives are inverted, sometimes omitted. Such corruptions may in some cases be corrected from other manuscripts where more than one copy of a lyric exists. Otherwise, the rhyme scheme may help in restoring correct order. What, however, if a line is missing in a sole copy? At the very least, an editor ought to indicate this in his printed text. But occasionally there may even be a case for supplying a missing line, however speculative this course of action must inevitably be. The fifteenth-century lyric *Freers, freers, wo ye be!* (Duncan LMELC, No. 141) offers an interesting case in point. As printed by Robbins (Robbins *Hist.*, No. 67), the last line of this poem reads *ffilius atque fflamen*, and the words *Omnes dicant Amen* are printed in smaller pointage below the poem as if they were some kind of appendage or rubric. However, inspection of the manuscript (Cambridge, Trinity College MS O.2.40) reveals that this poem, written out as prose, ends with the words *Omnes dicant Amen* as part of the poem – words in no way distinguished from the rest of the text, whether by colour of ink, by underlining, or by any other means. Furthermore, the alternating English and Latin lines and the rhyme scheme show that this lyric is made up of a sequence of quatrains. In the light of these facts it is clear that one line (the second English line) is missing from the final quatrain. This missing line must have rhymed with *trinité* of the first line of the final quatrain, and, as part of a Trinitarian conclusion, the rhyme-word corresponding to *trinité* must almost certainly have been *thre*, ending a line something like 'Three in one and one in three'. Trinitarian endings are not uncommon in Middle English lyrics and the required rhyme, metre and sense of the missing line here can be supplied by the line *All one God and persones thre* from another lyric, *Almyghty God, fadir of hevene* (Duncan *LMELC*, No. 84, 18), a prayer to the Trinity found in several Middle English manuscripts.

Some, of course, may shrink from such creative emendation. However, the editorial task requires that in editing a poem full account should be taken of verse form as well as manuscript evidence. In this case, a missing line is clearly indicated by the verse form of this poem. At the very least, this fact should be recorded and indicated in the edited text. Some may consider that the editor's duty should end here. Where, however, it is possible convincingly to suggest the probable sense of the missing line, it may be felt that a line which fulfils the requirements of metre, rhyme and that sense may appropriately be supplied, provided, of course, such an emendation is properly noted in the textual apparatus and defended in the textual commentary. In the case of this lyric, it is surely better to supply a plausible version of the line missing from the final quatrain, an emendation which completes the sense and verse structure of this lyric, than to leave the defective text misleadingly enshrined in print without comment.[24]

Although Middle English lyrics often survive written out as prose or in long lines, stanza form can usually be reconstructed without difficulty not least with the guidance of rhyme schemes. However, this is not always so. Scribes sometimes jotted lyrics down in abbreviated form. The reconstruction of such lyrics can be problematical. A striking instance is that of the famous lyric *Maiden in the more lay* (Duncan *MEL*, No. 118). This lyric survives on a leaf of parchment bound into Bodl. MS Rawlinson D.913. It is copied out as prose in a seemingly casual manner, as follows:

> Maiden in the mor lay in the mor lay. seuenyst fulle
> seuenist fulle maiden in the mor lay in the mor
> lay seuenistes fulle ant a day Welle wat hire mete
> wat was hire mete þe primerole ant the þe pri
> merole ant the welle was hire mete wat was
> hire mete the *pri* merole ant the violet Welle
> wat was hir*e* dryng þe chelde water of [ ]
> Welle spring Welle was hir*e* bour wat was hire
> bour þe rede rose ante lilie flour [Next item begins]

This poem appeared in print for the first time in 1907 (Heuser 1907, 175, No. 8). The editor, W. Heuser, simply arranged the manuscript prose text in verse lines as guided by rhyming words, and, in the absence of any indications in the manuscript, made no attempt to divide the lines into stanzas. Since then, the

---

24 Similar editorial courage is shown by Celia and Kenneth Sisam in supplying a plausible version of the missing seventh line of the first stanza of the lyric *Bon jour, bon jour a vous!* (Sisam and Sisam 1970, No. 259). In Robbins *Sec.*, No. 1 and Greene, No. 420, this missing line is indicated by a series of dots. To complete the required nine lines of this stanza, an earlier editor, Roman Dyboski, divided the third line into two lines (Dyboski 1907, No. 100). This procedure, however, was clearly mistaken: it ignored the stanza structure of this lyric. In Dyboski's version the third and fourth lines of the first stanza have two rather than four stresses and the rhyme scheme becomes aaaabccbd rather than aaabcccbd as in the other stanzas.

structure of this poem has remained a matter of doubt. Recognising that the Rawlinson text was an abbreviated version of the poem, Kenneth Sisam, in 1921, printed the poem as four stanzas, the third and fourth of three lines each (Sisam 1921, XV E). In 1952, in a bolder attempt to reconstitute the poem, Robbins expanded the third and fourth stanzas to 7 lines each on the model of his seven-line second stanza (Robbins *Sec.*, No. 18). In the same year, R. L. Greene drew attention to the fact that the incipit '[M]ayde y[n] the moore [l]ay' was to be found prefixed to one of the Latin lyrics in the *Red Book of Ossory*.[25] These lyrics were written by Richard de Ledrede, Bishop of Ossory from 1317 to 1360. In order to prevent his vicars, priests and clerks from being 'polluted by songs which are lewd, secular, and associated with revelry',[26] he composed devout poems in Latin which could be sung to the tunes of the proscribed secular songs. This evidence confirmed that *Mayden in the more lay* was indeed a song. Furthermore, it seemed likely that the lyric *Peperit virgo*, Ledrede's *contrafactum*[27] of the English song, would offer definitive evidence concerning the latter's form and structure since in order to make his Latin poem fit the tune of *Mayden in the more lay*, Ledrede would have had to match the verbal structure of the English lyric in line length and stanza form. The first stanza of the Latin poem is as follows:

> Peperit virgo,
>   Virgo regia,
> Mater orphanorum,
> Mater orphanorum;
> Peperit virgo,
>   Virgo regia,
> Mater orphanorum,
> Mater orphanorum,
> Plena gracia. (Greene 1974, x)

There is one obvious danger in seeking to establish the form of the English lyric by comparison of the Rawlinson text and Ledrede's Latin *contrafactum*. However likely it may be that the Rawlinson scribe (or a predecessor) and the Irish bishop knew the same tune and therefore the English poem in exactly the same form, this cannot be assumed. It is, therefore, not sufficient simply to show how an English version to match the Latin could somehow be manufactured out of the Rawlinson text; it is necessary, rather, to explain how the method of abbreviation behind the Rawlinson text worked, and how, in the light of that, the abbreviated copy can readily and credibly be expanded into a complete poem – and if this in fact turns out to match the Latin, well and good.

Fortunately, the system followed by the scribe who first copied the poem in this abbreviated form is, when recognised, clear as well as economical. How-

---

25 See Greene 1952, 504–06. A variant of another of the English snatches accompanying Latin lyrics in the *Red Book* occurs in Lambeth Palace Library MS 352. See Wenzel 1983, 105–8.

26 Greene 1974, iv, translating 'ne . . . polluantur cantilenis teatralibus, turpibus et secularibus', part of a memorandum marked 'Nota' found in the manuscript at the bottom of the first page of the Latin lyrics.

27 Contrafactum: words in versified form in another language made to fit the music of a poem in its original language.

ever, in all probability, the working of this system depended to no small extent on the way the music of the song was able to prompt him when he came to recreate the full text of the poem out of his *aide-mémoire* of a copy. This was not too difficult an undertaking in this case since this poem had a very clearly defined form. Its basic structure was immediately made apparent in the first four lines of the first stanza, in which fundamental patterns of repetition and partial repetition were established as follows: (1) the first line; (2) the partial repeat of the first line; (3) the third line; (4) the third line repeated in full. The scribe then recorded line 5 (a repetition of line 1) from which, with partial repetition as in line 2, *In the more lay* would follow as line 6, and thereafter he abbreviated the rest of the stanza to *seuenistes fulle ant a day*, words which some editors have taken to be one line, but which in fact represent (in abbreviated form) three lines; for, on the model of the repetition of lines 3 and 4 and, crucially, guided by the music, he would know that *seuenistes fulle* had to be repeated as lines 7 and 8. Confirmation of this is readily to be found in the form of abbreviation used for stanza 4: *Welle was hire bour wat was hire / bour þe rede rose ante lilie flour*. Obviously, this form of wording, as far as the words *an te* must allow for expansion into four lines (as required on the model of stanza 1) for the first four lines of this fourth stanza, and must, therefore, imply the repetition of *þe rede rose an te* as follows:

> Wele was hire bour,
> Wat was hire bour,
> Þe rede rose an te –
> Þe rede rose an te –

and there is no reason why the same words should be expanded in any other way for the subsequent lines of the stanza, to give, that is, anything other than a second full quatrain. Likewise, since the form of words used for the second part of the first stanza – *maiden in the mor lay in the mor / lay seuenistes fulle ant a day* – is identical, it is evident that these words as far as the word *fulle* should again, with the repetition of *seuenistes fulle*, represent a full quatrain, i.e.

> Maiden in the mor lay,
> In the mor lay,
> Seuenistes fulle –
> Seuenistes fulle –.

With the second stanza the scribe adopted the same procedure: he copied the initial quatrain in full and abbreviated the rest of the stanza, again in the same form of words.[28]

There remains the question of the form of the final line. Once more, this presents no difficulty. It is obvious that all the words required for the full text must be present in the abbreviated text which, of course, only omitted some of the

---

[28]   A slight variation in the form of the second stanza is to be noted. Like the first stanza, its second line was still a partial repeat of the first line, but now with the addition of the word *wat* – a pattern repeated in stanzas 3 and 4.

repeats so characteristic of this poem. In determining what the final line should be it is essential to bear in mind that the Rawlinson text was *written out as prose* with no indication as to where line divisions were to be made. One possibility for the first stanza would be to take the remaining words of the text, namely the last three words *ant a day*, as the final line. Granted, however, that this is an abbreviated text, there is no guarantee that these words form the complete line. Alternatively, it would be just as easy to take the last four words of the Rawlinson text, *fulle ant a day*, as the required line. It would be wholly in keeping with the patterns of full and partial repetition of this poem and with the scribe's method of abbreviation that this line should include some element of repetition as well as the remaining words of the text of the first stanza. Since, then, the Rawlinson copy itself readily allows for either interpretation, this is a situation in which an appeal for confirmation may legitimately be made to Richard de Ledrede's Latin counterpart. The stanzas of *Peperit virgo* end with lines of 5 or 6 syllables – 5 syllables in the case of the last line of the first stanza, *Plena gracia*. In the light of this evidence it is clear that of the two possible interpretations of the Rawlinson text offered above, the former, *ant a day* (with three syllables), is suspect, and the latter, *fullë ant a day* (with five syllables) is to be preferred as the final line of the English poem. For the stanza structure of *Maiden in the more lay* in its complete rather than abbreviated form, therefore, the first two syllables of the final line were repeated from the last word (or words) of the previous line, the very word (or words) which had already chimed throughout the stanza at the end of the third, fourth, seventh and eighth lines.[29] Thus, the last three lines of the first stanza should be:

> Seueniates fullë
> Seuenistes fullë –
> Fullë ant a day.

Indeed, had the same scribe abbreviated *Adam lay y-bownden* in the same manner, he would have copied *and al was for an appil, an appil þat he tok* simply as *and al was for an appil þat he tok*, knowing that in performance the repetition of *an appil* in the second half of the line would be required both by the style of the lyric and by the its music. It thus emerges that the stanzaic structure of *Maiden in the more lay* in the light of the *modus operandi* of the method of abbreviation used in Rawlinson text does in fact match that of the Latin *contrafactum*.[30]

So far, emendation has been considered on the basis of such formal criteria as syllable-count, rhyme scheme, stanza form, stanza order, line order and line omission. Emendation may also be considered on account of failure of sense, though only with the greatest caution, and especially so in the case of poetry. An instance where sense, indeed poetic sense, would seem to call for emendation

---

[29] It is to be noted that the final '-e' of *fullë* has to be pronounced to give the necessary five syllables for the final line of this stanza. However, if so pronounced at the end of lines 3, 4, 7 and 8 there would be no difficulty in continuing with sounded final '-e' (by hiatus) before the following *ant* in line 9.

[30] For a more detailed analysis, see Duncan 1996, where the reconstituted text of this lyric is printed. See also Duncan *MEL*, No. 118.

arises in the fifteenth-century lyric, *Whan netilles in wynter bere roses rede* (Duncan *LMELC*, No. 136). This lyric is based on the rhetorical figure 'adynaton'. This is a device originating from ancient and classical literature which involves the stringing together of a series of impossibilities. It is a characteristic means of expressing the topos of the 'world upside-down', a notion common in medieval literature – the depiction of a crazy world in which absurdities prevail and, typically, roles are reversed: the ass plays the lute, the ox dances, the hare is bold, the lion timorous, and so on.[31] In the second stanza of this poem, this thematic absurdity involves the notion of fish hunting animals, a bizarre notion which, however, breaks down in lines 11–12:

> And gornardes shote rolyons
>   owt of a crosse bowe,
> And grengese ride huntyng
>   the wolf to overthrowe.[32]

Here, inconsistently, fish hunt fish (i.e. *gornardes*, a type of sea fish, hunt *rolyons*, another type of fish). This defect is easily made good if it is assumed that a scribe has mistakenly transposed *grengese* and *rolyons* in lines 11 and 12. The sense of the emended text thus becomes: 'And gurnards shoot goslings from a cross-bow, / And roullions ride hunting the wolf to overthrow'. The resultant alliteration, of *gornardes* and *grengese* in line 11, and *rolyons* and *ride* in line 12, supports this emendation. It would also appear from the reading *rokes* for *rolyons* in line 11 of one of the other two manuscripts that at least one medieval scribe spotted the inconsistency of fish hunting fish in this stanza.

  E. J. Dobson described the surviving copies of Middle English poetry as often 'lame and deformed' (Dobson and Harrison 1979, 30). 'No one,' he stated, 'who has closely studied the texts of Middle English poems, and especially perhaps of the lyrics, which were so often hastily jotted down on whatever was available, is prepared to allow much credence to the scribes and their work; a few were good, many were downright bad, and none is to be blindly trusted' (Dobson and Harrison 1979, 28). Dobson further observed that hitherto editors of collections of Middle English lyrics had printed texts 'without the most obviously necessary changes: abnormal spellings, false forms, bad rhyme and worse metre, irregular or impossible accidence and syntax, and even sheer nonsense are left uncorrected', and gave the following bold statement of his own editorial aim: 'It has not been my object to reproduce the texts given by the scribes, but to recover as far as might be the text written by the original author; and I would rather go wrong in the attempt than fail to make it' (Dobson and Harrison 1979, 27). Though more conservative in practice, I salute Dobson's principles and his zeal in undertaking to the full the duties of an editor. It is evident to me that the task of an editor of Middle English poetic texts, and especially of Middle English lyrics, manifestly corrupt as they frequently are, must begin with a well-

---

[31] See Curtius 1953, 94–8.
[32] The version of this lyric as found in Oxford, Balliol College MS 354. For the variant readings of the two other manuscripts, see Duncan *LMELC*, 257.

founded conception of metre, must include a commitment to rigorous examination of rhyme schemes, stanza forms, stanza order, and the order of lines within
stanzas, must, however cautiously, be alert to nonsense as a product of corruption, and, above all and not surprisingly, must at all times scrutinise the
evidence of manuscript sources as an essential prelude to emendation.

Should an editor attempt to offer guidance, however limited, to the reader in
the matter of metre? This is, admittedly, a hazardous task. As previously
suggested, it may well be that as in the verse tradition from which Middle
English stanzaic lyrics derive – that of French and Latin songs – so also in
English stanzaic lyrics the principal poetic constraint may have continued to be
a matter of a syllabic match, line by line and stanza by stanza. And indeed, in the
light of linguistic analysis, not least of phonetic processes operative within the
speech chain, and of plausible editorial restoration, it may be claimed that a fair
proportion of surviving stanzaic lyrics were composed with such a kind of
metrical regularity in view. In the case of such lyrics, it is clearly helpful, not
least for readers with a limited linguistic command of Middle English, if an
editor should indicate which of the syllables in the text *as written* were probably
to be counted metrically. Yet, if some lyrics are arguably metrically regular,
many others evidently are not. Lyrics of a more popular kind, as one might
expect, often appear to be freer in their scansion. Sometimes metre seems to defy
consistent analysis. *Levedy seynte Marie* (Duncan *MEL*, No. 37), for instance,
seems to fluctuate between alliterative and syllabic verse. In some of the later
lyrics (in striking contrast with Chaucer) lines with extra weak syllables are
common. This is true, for instance, of the Vernon lyrics. The considerable textual
discrepancies between the two manuscript versions of the lyric *In the vaile of
restles mynd* (Duncan *MEL*, No. 73) make it impossible to tell how authentic the
apparently loose metre of this lyric, written c.1400, really was. However, even in
the case of such poems or, indeed, despite the flexibility in the count of
unstressed syllables to be expected in lyrics in alliterative verse form, it is
possible to suggest plausible modes of reading based on linguistic judgments
taking into account what pronunciations may have been likely in terms of the
date and dialect of the language of the lyrics. For instance, in the broadest of
terms it may reasonably be claimed that the later the date of a lyric within the
Middle English period the less likely it will be that final '-e' will be pronounced
even if, even into the fifteenth century, such a syllable may sometimes count
metris causa.[33] Likewise, reduced pronunciations of the endings '-es' and '-ed'
become ever more likely the later the language of the lyrics. Inevitably, attempts
at suggesting plausible ways of reading Middle English verse remain a matter of
judgment and taste on the part of an editor. And, indeed, one can hardly doubt
that there were variations in the performance of these lyrics among Middle
English readers themselves. However, guidance in the matter of which syllables

---

[33] E.g. Hoccleve's use of final '-e'. See Burrow 1999, xxix: 'There can be no doubt that wherever
Hoccleve writes 'e' in unstressed position . . . it is to be pronounced', and, moreover, 'he
evidently felt able to assume that [readers of suitable competence] would be familiar with the
rules governing unstressed *e* in verse of his kind'.

in Middle English verse are plausibly to be sounded, such as given, for example, in the Sisams' *Oxford Book of Medieval English Verse* and in my *Medieval English Lyrics: 1200–1400* and *Late Medieval English Lyrics and Carols: 1400–1530,* may help less expert readers; it can easily be ignored by others.

3

The Love Lyric before Chaucer

JOHN SCATTERGOOD

I

In the late thirteenth century an anonymous English poet closes his poem on the problematic nature of love with the following lines:

Love is wele, love is wo,	*happiness; woe*
love is gladhede,	*gladness*
Love is lif, love is deth,	*life; death*
love mai us fede.	*feed*
Were love also longdrei	*as long-lasting*
as he is first kene,	*eager*
Hit were the wordlokste thing	*it would be the most precious thing*
in world were, Ich wene.	*in the world that might be, I suppose*
Hit is y-said in an song,	
soth is y-sene,	*the truth is evident*
Love comseth with care	*begins*
and endeth with tene,	*suffering*
Mid lady, mid wive,	*with lady, with woman*
mid maide, mid quene.	*with queen (or harlot)*

(Duncan *MEL*, No. 6, 22–8)

It is not clear to what 'song' the poet refers, but it is obvious that he is conscious that he is writing in what is an already well-established tradition of love poetry. The importance given to the sentiment of what is variously known as *fin amor*, *amour par amour*, or in English *fyn lovynge*, however, is notable, particularly since, in the view of most scholars, it was a fairly recent development in European culture, though Peter Dronke has argued strongly that it was of much more ancient provenance.[1] The conception of an ideal and exalted relationship between men and women may have drawn ideas from sources as diverse as Plato's *Phaedrus*, Ovid's *Amores*, and the cult of the Virgin Mary, but its earliest, most complete and most significant articulation was in eleventh- and twelfth-century texts such as the troubadour poetry of Provence, the romances of Chrétien de Troyes, and Andreas Capellanus's *De Amore*.[2] Here appears, time

---

1 See Dronke 1968a, particularly I, 1–97.
2 The literature on this subject is extensive. For C. S. Lewis's highly influential treatment see Lewis 1936, 1–43. For an interesting set of documents and texts relating to the concept see O'Donoghue 1982. For Peter Dronke's ideas see Dronke 1968a, I, 57–97. I have also found

after time, in text after text, the idea that love is the most important aspect of life, the conception of the idealised lady, worshipped or deferred to in an almost feudal manner by her devoted and obedient lover who believes that in her lies all the happiness that life can give if he can win her love, and all the despair and suffering if he fails to attain it: as this English poem affirms, *love is lif, love is deth*. In such eleventh- and twelfth-century texts too appear the ideas that love is independent of marriage and may be adulterous, that secrecy and discretion are a necessary part of it, and that the jealous and rumour-mongers are its enemies. In this ethos, love was all-powerful and irresistible so that its effects could be seen in all ranks of society: as the English poem puts it, *Mid lady, mid wive, mid maide, mid quene*. All should be equal in love's court without social distinction, asserts Andreas Capellanus, and the belief grew up that love could ennoble the activities of anyone, so that a suitor of humble origins might aspire to the most socially distinguished and sophisticated of ladies – in theory at least.[3]

But in relation to this set of ideas it was the lyric which had the seminal role. Andreas's elaborate codification of this particular ethos of *amor* was not created *ex nihilo*, but is likely to have been conceived and formulated as a response to the aristocratic code of love set out in the Provençal lyrics. Moreover, Chrétien's romances, whether they deal with married or adulterous love, ought to be read in one sense as a 'translation' of these same ideals of the lyric into a different narrative mode. And, finally, in the thirteenth-century *Roman de la Rose*, the ideals which had originated in the lyric were again 'translated' – this time into what was considered to be the most venerable of literary modes, allegory. In this way, the essence of the ethos of *fin amor*, including such central tenets as the virtue (*proezza*) and nobility of the lover, the concept of love as privation or absence (*amor de lonh*), and the multiplicity of obstacles (marriage, spiteful guardians, geographical distance, social distance) barring the way to fulfilment, were set out in a text which would have a profound influence on medieval English writers – especially Chaucer. But these sentiments, and refinements and variations of them, by whatever means they reached England, also form the ideological nexus of the Middle English love lyric.

'No lyric poetry is extant from the Old English period' – so R. M. Wilson in 1939, though he does allow that what he calls 'a small group of poems which are better classed as elegies' may contain lyrics (Wilson 1968, 250). This is an unfortunate statement, if taken as authoritative, because it effectively precludes any consideration of what may be significant continuities in the English tradition. *Deor* (Krapp and Dobbie 1936, 178–9), a poet's lament for his loss of status and lands, his displacement by Heorenda 'a man skilled in songs', is certainly structured like a lyric, with its six parallel sections illustrating changes in fortune and its refrain: *Þæs ofereode, þisses swa mæg* [That passed away, so may this]. And the tantalising, perhaps fragmentary lines usually called *Wulf and Eadwacer* (Krapp and Dobbie 1936, 179–80) which follow *Deor* in the Exeter Book, look as if they may form a love lyric with what is perhaps a refrain: *ungelice is us* [? our fates are

---

much of use in Burnley 1998a, 148–75. For a sceptical view of the matter see Donaldson 1970, 155–64. For a collection of essays on various aspects of this subject see Newman 1968.
3   See Walsh 1982, I, 6, 71–2.

different], which appears twice. Laconic and allusive, the poem does not deliver a narrative situation in any completeness, but it is clearly meant to be spoken by a woman. It has been argued that, like *The Wife's Lament*, it is a *frauenlied*, a lament by a woman for her lover Wulf, detailing her sorrow and sickness, because she is separated from him:

> Wulf is on iege, ic on oþere.
> Fæst is þæt eglond fenne biworpen.
> Sindon wælreowe weras þær on iege . . . (4–6)

> [Wulf is on one island; I am on another. That island is secure, surrounded by fens. There are deadly cruel men on the island . . .]

A Middle English fragment testifies to a similar situation, especially if the last line refers to lovesickness, of lovers separated by water:

> I ne may cume to mi lef bute by the watere   *my sweetheart only*
> Wanne me lust slepen thanne mot I wakie –   *when I want to sleep I must*
> Wonder is that I livie.   *live*   [*lie awake*
> (Bennett and Smithers 1968, 128)

And generally, of course, there is a continuity from Old English into Middle English in the survival of numerous alliterative formulae, which are part of the standard poetic diction – though these are not confined to lyrics.

Nevertheless, it is clear that the main influences on the forms and genres of the Middle English love lyric do not derive from the native tradition.[4] The staple genres of the love lyric – the spring song, the love song, the *chanson d'aventure* and its more particular manifestation the pastourelle, the debate, the dawn song – are all found in the Latin literature of the Middle Ages, in the works of the troubadours of Provence, and in Northern French trouvère poetry. Peter Dronke has argued powerfully and at length that the European love lyric has its origins in late antique Latin poetry – though precise influences on Middle English are not immediately apparent.[5] And H. J. Chaytor, long ago, suggested the possibility of direct influence from the troubadour poetry of Provence on the early Middle English lyric, which is plausible enough in historical terms since the early Angevin and Poitevin kings of England married southern French princesses, spent a lot of time in France, and were intimately involved in the politics of France. Marcabru may have visited England, and Bernart de Ventadorn was certainly there in the train of Henry II. What is more, troubadours sometimes wrote about English politics. There are also correspondences of expression and of ideas of some singularity between troubadour poetry and English love lyrics. Chaytor draws attention, amongst other things, to Bernart de Ventadorn's desperate shape-shifting fantasy for overcoming the difficulty of access to his lover:

---

4   I have found the following studies of the Middle English secular lyric generally useful in the preparation of this essay: Boffey 1985; Gray 1983 and 1986; Moore 1951; Oliver 1970; Reiss 1972.

5   See Dronke 1968a, especially I, 112–25.

Ai Deus! Car no sui ironda
Que voles per l'aire
E vengues de noih prionda
Lai dins so repaire?

[Ah, God! Why am I not a swallow, which might fly through the air,
and come at dead of night there in her dwelling place?] [6]

He compares the similar, but more extremely erotic avian fantasy which closes *A wayle whyt ase whalles bon* (Brook, No. 9) from BL MS Harley 2253:

Ich wolde ich were a threstelcok,	*song-thrush*
A bountyng other a lavercok,	*bunting; skylark*
Swete bryd!	*sweet bird*
Bitwene hire curtel and hire smok	*gown; undergarment*
Y wolde ben hyd. (51–5)	

Here, though, the song thrush, the bunting and the lark are birds often kept caged (for their song) and so, like Jane Scrope's sparrow, intimates, as it were, of the household.[7] He is on stronger grounds, however, when he argues that the structure of the stanza forms of a number of Middle English lyrics parallels that of Provençal poems. But whether these were imitated directly from Provençal, or whether they were mediated through northern French is an open question, though the second of these alternatives has traditionally been regarded as the more likely.

But the question is a difficult one, as can be seen from a brief consideration of *Nou sprinkes* [springs] *the sprai* (Brown *XIII*, No. 62). This poem is preserved on one of the end flyleaves of London, Lincoln's Inn Hale MS 135, a copy of Bracton's *De Legibus Angliae*, which belonged to Adam de Thornton, who was in the employ of the Abbot of Ramsey. The poem is written in a hand, different from the main hand of the book, which was responsible for a number of entries concerning swans dated between 1302 and 1305.[8] It is in the pastourelle genre and bears similarities both to a Provençal and a northern French poem. In *L'autrier cavalcava*, by the Limousin troubadour Gui d'Ussel, the poet overhears a *pastorella* [shepherdess] lamenting in sadness: *Las, mal viu qui pert son jauzimen* [Alas, one leads a sad life whose joy is lost]. He immediately approaches her:

Lai ou il chantava
Virei tost mon fre . . .

[I made my way quickly to where she was singing . . .][9]

He gets down from his horse, greets her, and asks her about her sorrowful song. She tells him that she has been abandoned and forgotten by her lover. The

6   See Chaytor 1923, especially 34–97 for the troubadours and English politics, and 108–9 for
    Bernart de Ventadorn.
7   See Scattergood 1983b, No. 7, 120–7, 159–74.
8   For a description of the manuscript see Greene, 313.
9   For the poem see Audiau and Lavaud 1928, 287–90. For Gui d'Ussel see Gaunt and Kay 1999,
    284.

narrator too, it transpires, has been deserted for another. The shepherdess proposes that they console each other and turn their suffering *en joi et en deport* [into joy and gaiety] – to which the narrator readily consents. The general movement of this poem, and some of its phrasing, has found its way into an anonymous northern French pastourelle beginning *L'autrier defors Picarni*. Here again the poet overhears a lamenting *pastoure*: *Lasse, ke ferai? / jeu ai perdu mon ami . . .* [Alas, what shall I do? I have lost my love . . .].[10] The poet, as in the troubadour lyric, follows the sound of her song and finds the shepherdess *deles un arbre foilli* [under a tree in bloom]. In response to the narrator's questions the shepherdess reveals that Robins, her lover, has made her unhappy, and, as in the Provençal lyric, the narrator successfully woos her.

The English poem follows much the same development as its predecessors, with what may be echoes of their wording. The lament of the *litel mai* [little maiden] begins with *Wai is him i louve-longinge / Shal libben ai* [Woeful is anyone who must live for ever in love-longing] (9–10) and the poet's approach suggests the immediacy of his reaction:

> Son Ich herde that mirie note,   *as soon as*
> Thider I drogh . . . (11–12)   *thither I drew*

But though the poem looks to be dependent on its predecessors, which seem to leave intertextual traces, it finds its own way after a certain point, and this makes the question of the sources of its inspiration very difficult to determine. In the English poem the forsaken girl has her own demotic language and her own violent sentiments, which she articulates in a vengeful manner. At one point she wishes for her lover's death: *the clot him clingge!* [may the earth stick to him!] (8). At another she merely wishes to make him sorry:

> 'Mi lemman me haves bi-hote   *my lover has made me a pledge*
>   Of luve trewe;
>   He chaunges anewe.   *again*
> Yiif I mai, it shal him rewe   *he will regret it*
>   Bi this day'. (20–4)

She is not interested in what Audiau calls 'consolations réciproques' (Audiau and Lavaud 1928, 287) – unless there is a lost conclusion to this poem – but in revenge, and another kind of reciprocity, the exaction of suffering for suffering.[11] Though the English poem may be dependent on one or other of its Provençal or northern French predecessors – or perhaps both – it asserts its own individuality of manner and attitude, which here releases the violent and destructive emotions which can result from betrayal and disappointed love. As it stands, this is a tougher and more uncompromising poem that either of its rather sentimental predecessors.

---

10 For the text of this poem see Bartsch 1870, § II, 7. For a detailed comparison of the two poems see Sandison 1913, 47–8.
11 For a study of this poem in relation to its Provençal and French predecessors see Scattergood 1996, 66–8.

II

Before Sir Thomas Wyatt no English poet acquired a substantial reputation for writing secular lyric poetry. There was no substantial tradition of high-style art lyric in early medieval England as there had been in twelfth- and thirteenth-century Provence: there was no English equivalent to love poets like Bernart de Ventadorn or Jaufre Rudel. When Chaucer mentions his lyric poems, moreover, it is always at the end of lists of his works: in one place he claims to have written many songs in praise of Love's *halydays / That highten balades, roundels, virelayes*; and in another he refers rather offhandedly to *many a song and many a leccherous lay*, though many of his lyrics are on religious or profoundly moral matters.[12] No manuscripts devoted principally to lyrics appear before the fifteenth century: then Charles of Orleans's carefully produced book of his English love poems, mainly ballades and roundels, BL MS Harley 682, was written around 1439–40;[13] and a number of less expensively produced manuscripts containing carols appeared later, such as BL MS Sloane 2593, Bodl. MS eng. poet. e.1, and Cambridge, St John's College MS S.54. And secular lyrics begin to appear in commonplace books or miscellanies: the London grocer Richard Hill was apparently fond of lyrics, many of which were copied into his book, Oxford, Balliol College MS 354.[14] Though it acquired status later, the lyric – particularly the secular lyric – was apparently little regarded in the early Middle Ages in England.

Indeed, the manner in which a number of lyrics have survived gives support to this notion. Few scholars would disagree with the view that 'the extant lyrical poetry represents a mere fraction of that which was actually composed. Much of our knowledge of it depends on the chance preservation of a few manuscripts' (Wilson 1952, 175). What is more, lyrics tend to be jotted down in odd places, blank pages in manuscripts or in invitingly wide margins. Some snatches of secular lyrical poetry have survived only because they were included in other texts. Giraldus Cambrensis in his *Gemma Ecclesiastica* tells a famous story in which a parish priest of Worcestershire was kept awake all night by revellers dancing in his churchyard, so much so that when he began his early morning service the next day, instead of the correct *Dominus Vobiscum* [the Lord be with you] he intoned the refrain of the secular song he had heard the night before: *Swete lemman thin are* [Sweet beloved, thy mercy].[15] The song was proscribed within the limits of his diocese by the Bishop of Worcester, who was appalled at the scandal. In a twelfth-century sermon a snatch of secular song appears tantalisingly as a 'text':

---

[12] For Chaucer's references to his lyrics see *The Legend of Good Women* F Prologue, 422–3; cf. G Prologue, 410–11; and *CT* X, 1086. See further Scattergood 1995, especially 455–8.

[13] See Steele and Day, 1941–6 for Charles of Orleans's English poems. For a study of BL MS 682 and of a manuscript of Charles's French poems produced in England, Paris, BN fr.25458 see Arn 2000, 61–78.

[14] For these manuscripts see Greene, 306–7, 317–18, 325–6, 320–1. For a recent study of the lyrics in MS Sloane 2593 see Boklund-Lagopoulou 2002, 63–86.

[15] For a discussion of this story see Wilson 1952, 173–4.

'Atte wrastlinge mi lemman I ches   *my sweetheart I chose*
and atte ston-kasting I him for-les.'   *I abandoned him*

. . . Mi leve frend, wilde wimmen and golme i mi contreie, wan he [when they]
gon o the ring, among manie othere songis, that litil ben wort [worth] that tei
singin, so sein thei thus: 'Atte wrastlinge mi lemman . . .'[16]

The context of the preservation of this couplet is interesting for a number of
reasons: the song may well be local (*i mi contreie*) or even rural; it is evidently
conceived in the context of rural sports (wrestling, putting the stone); it is a situation predicated on love (*lemman*). But what emerges most clearly is the clerical
disapproval of this poetry: the women who sing the song are adjudged to be
wilde and *golme*, that is, wanton or lecherous, and the song evidently associates
with immoral activity. Rural sports, perhaps associated with holiday, are the
occasion for unsanctioned sexual activity. And so, by implication, is dancing, for
the phrase *wan he gon o the ring* suggests that the song was part of a *carole*, a
ring-dance accompanied by a song: one performer would sing the verse or
stanza; all would contribute to the refrain which was characteristic of *caroles*.[17]
And the phrase *among manie othere songis* suggests that there was a rich secular
culture of this sort which worried the more staid churchmen of the age, for
whom attractive popular literature about love was problematic in that it might
induce immorality. And this point emerges from another such song, perhaps
from a little later, when the clerical author of the *Ancrene Wisse* warns the
anchoresses he is advising against listening to protestations of love from those
who visit them, lest the words lodge in their hearts. In support of this he quotes
a snatch of what appears to be a popular lyric which makes a similar point:

Ever is the eie   *eye*
To the wude leie   *turned to the wood*
Therinne is thet ich luvie.   *wherein is the one I love*
                                    (Morton 1853, 96–7)

This is evidently part of a love song which makes the point that love songs are
dangerously seductive and may itself be so.

    These snatches of love poetry are preserved, as it were, by accident, as the
authors of the documents in which they appear seek to make different points,
sometimes disapproving of the poetry quoted. And early secular lyrics are often
preserved in similar unofficial circumstances. The most fragile is perhaps
Though I can wittes ful-iwis (Duncan *MEL*, No. 7) which is jotted down (very
faintly) in the top margin of BL MS Royal 8.D.xiii fol. 25r. The poem opens with
the poet asserting that, though he is intelligent, it is of no help in procuring
worldes blisse, and all because of love, because the object of his affection is
unattainable:

Sithen first that she was his   *since*
Y-loken in castel wal of ston,   *locked; wall of stone*

---

16 For this text see Wilson 1952, 174–5. For comments on its implications see Greene, cxlvii, and
    Boklund-Lagopoulou 2002, 23.
17 See Greene, xxi–xxxiii and xliii–lxiv; also Reichl (below), 161–4.

Nas Ich hol ne blithe iwis,   *I was not well nor happy indeed*
Ne thrivinge mon. (5–8)   *nor a prospering man*

'Locked inside the stone wall of a castle' suggests that the lady is unattainable because she has become the wife of a powerful lord. Grief *hongeth* [weighs] (13) on him, he says, and he looks for death: *Ned* [of necessity] *after my deth me longeth* (11). The implication of this lyric may be that at some time the lover was more successful with the *lady that is pris* [the most excellent] (3), before her circumstances changed.

But long-lasting devotion, so much prized as part of *fin amor*, does not always guarantee success, as a snatch of lyric written in Worcester Cathedral Library MS Q.50 by 'Robertus Seynte Mary Clericus' makes plain:

Ich have ydon al myn youth   *I have loved* (lit. *done*)
Ofte, ofte, and ofte;
Longe y-loved and yerne y-beden –   *eagerly desired*
Ful dere it is y-bought!   *very dearly has it cost me*
                                     (Duncan, *MEL*, 13. 1–4)

– though whether this is a farewell to love or simply a rueful lament at failure is not easy to determine. Even more difficult are four lines which precede this poem in the same manuscript, though here the lover hopes for greater success, or, in a different reading, may have accomplished it:

Dore, go thou stille,   *door; quietly*
Go thou stille, stille,
That Ich have in the boure   *until; bower*
Ydon al my wille, wille.   *accomplished; desire*
                                     (Duncan, *MEL*, 12. 1–4)

The first word of line three may be *That* (the reading adopted here) or *Yat* [gate]: whether the initial letter is 'þ' ('thorn', a Middle English letter equivalent to 'th') or 'y' is difficult to determine. Duncan, who prefers the second reading, puts the alternatives plainly: 'Either the poet addresses first the chamber door and then the outside gate as he leaves after a fulfilling tryst, or, with the reading *that* 'until', the poet, on entering the chamber, bids the door be silent until his love-encounter is completed' (Duncan *MEL*, 186). And another quatrain, preserved in a Tübingen Latin manuscript, which looks like a wry and witty statement about long service and the difficulty of access, is rendered problematic by its context:

So longe Ich have, lady,
Y-hoved at thi gate,   *lingered*
That mi fot is frore, faire lady,   *frozen*
For thy love faste to the stake.   *(gate-)post*
                                     (Duncan, *MEL*, 14. 1–4)

The hermeneutic difficulty here stems from the fact that this text is preserved in a religious manuscript, and is preceded by *Deum ad cor intrare volentem excludunt* [God wishing to enter the heart they exclude]. Though it may have originally been a snatch of secular song, it may have been read in this context in terms of the allegory of Christ the lover-knight seeking entry to man's soul.

III

Problems arise in interpreting and understanding these texts partly because they are brief and laconic, and one is never sure whether what one is dealing with is the whole text or simply part of it – a stanza, perhaps, or a refrain. But they are also, in John Burrow's memorable phrase, 'poems without contexts' in the sense that the circumstances of their preservation are often unhelpful to understanding them and occasionally hostile to what they apparently are and mean.[18]

The immediate subjects of his comments are the twelve poems preserved on a strip of parchment, measuring 11 inches by 4, which is now part of Bodl. MS Rawlinson D.913, a collection of fragments bound together. Palaeographically, the handwriting indicates a date of about 1325, but there is little else that it can tell the scholar. Three of the poems are simply indicated by their first lines. Of the others, one is a 'song of good company' in French, another is a hilarious drinking song, and another a *chanson de mal mariée* with a chillingly 'consolatory' refrain:

> Ami tenez vous joyous,
> Si murra lui gelous.

> [Lover, stay happy; the jealous one will die.][19]

The other six poems are all apparently secular, and all deal, in one way or another, with love. Understanding them in the absence of external contexts such as the name of the author, the occasion, the audience, depends largely on the genre of the text. As Burrow puts it: 'The text must clearly declare itself as belonging to a known genre or type, and that genre must be such as to determine specific types of meaning' (Burrow 1984, 23). This is a somewhat reductive methodology – poets are capable of using genre in a deliberately misleading way – but it is as good a starting point as one can find.

Easiest to understand is the love song because the medieval stereotypes of the beautiful lady and the suffering lover, whose salvation depends on her favour, are implicit:

Al gold, Janet, is thin her,	*hair*
Al gold, Janet, is thin her;	
Save thin Jankin, lemman dere,	*sweetheart dear*
Save Jankin, lemman dere,	
Save thin onlye dere.	*only beloved*
	(Duncan, *MEL*, 11, 1–5)

Here the names – which are both diminutives – are popular and this may be a snatch of popular song. And similarly transparent is *Of everykinne tre* (Duncan *MEL*, No. 9) where the superlative sweetness of the hawthorn is compared to the *lemman* who is *fairest of every kinne* – a feature of the spring song is associated, as

---

18 See Burrow 1984, 1–26, where the lyrics are also printed.
19 Printed by Burrow 1984, 24.

often, with a feature of the love song. The understanding of this poem depends on the associative literary imagination of the audience, as does the seemingly enigmatic stanza:

> Al night by the rose, rose,
> Al night bi the rose I lay.
> Dorst Ich nought the rose stele,   *dared; steal*
> And yet I bar the flour away.   *bore the flower*
>
>   (Duncan *MEL*, No. 10)

Superficially this is deliberately riddling: how can one not steal a rose but at the same time carry off the flower? But nobody who knew the *Roman de la Rose*, the erotic allegory of Guillaume de Lorris and Jean de Meun, would have had any doubt that the *rose* is the beloved, and the *flour* is her virginity: the lady here is unattainable, but is sexually accessible. And *Ich am of Irlande* (Duncan *MEL*, No. 117) is positively inviting. Even without the cue *Come and daunce with me* (6) this poem would be recognisable as a dance song, with a burden which precedes what is presumably the first stanza:

> *Ich am of Irlande,*   *from Ireland*
> *And of the holy lande*
>   *Of Irlande.*
>
> Gode sire, pray Ich thee,
> For of saynte charité,   *for holy charity*
> Come and daunce with me
>   In Irlaunde.

But the form of the poem does not help much in interpreting it. W. B. Yeats adapted it and added to it, making it applicable to the world of contemporary politics where the invitation is towards a commitment to an idealism to which few are prepared to listen and to which none is prepared to respond.[20] But the invitation here is not to a political Ireland so much as to a religious one. The *holy lande* of Ireland alludes perhaps to its ancient reputation as being 'the island of saints and scholars' and the invitation to *Come and daunce with me* may be read allegorically in a religious sense: after all it is said to be *For saynte charité*, where the religious insistence is doubly plain in the vocabulary. This is a somewhat problematic love lyric, if it is one. Perhaps it is a love lyric which has been subverted to a religious purpose.

Problematic too is *Wer ther outher in this toun* (Robbins *Sec.*, No. 9) with its irregular form and its disconcerting shifts of focus and tone. It fits into no literary genre, and has to be quoted in full:

> Wer ther outher in this toun   *were there either*
> Ale or wyn,   *wine*
> Ich hit wolde bugge   *I would buy it*
> To lemmon myn.   *for my beloved*
> Welle, wo was so hardy   *alas, who; so rash*

---

20 See Yeats 1973, 303–4.

For to make my lef al blody?	*dear one; bloody*
Thaugh he were the kynges son	
Of Normaundy,	
Yet Icholde a-wreke boe	*I would be avenged*
For lemman myn.	
Welle wo was me tho!	*alas, woeful was I then*
Wo was me tho!	*woeful was I then*
The man that leseth that he loveth	*the man who loses the one whom*
Hym is also.	*(woe) is his also*
Ne erle ne lerde,	*neither earl not lord*
Ne – no more I n'can!	*nor – I can do no more!*
But Crist Ich hire biteche	*to Christ I commit her*
That was my lemman.	*who*

This poem appears to be about bereavement, or at least loss, and memory. The male narrator suffers *wo* because he is in the state of a *man that leseth that he loveth*. His *lemman* appears to have been taken away by violent assault which left her *al blody*: indeed, she is perhaps meant to be dead since the final two lines commend her to Christ and use the past tense (*was*). He vows vengeance (*a-wreke*) for the injury to or death of his beloved, but appears frustrated in that course of action because he does not know who is responsible: hence the question in lines 5–6 and the extravagant claim in lines 6–7. It may be tempting to see the narrator as somebody who consoles himself with drink because nobler courses of action are unavailable, and to see this as a poem which examines male pretensions to heroism. But it is more likely that what is being referred to in lines 1–4 is a *myndale*, a memorial drink to a dead person.[21] Either way, this is by no means a conventional love lyric.

Nor is the enigmatic *Maiden in the more lay* (Duncan MEL, No. 118). This consists of four nine-line stanzas, full of hesitations and repetitions, which develop from the situation described, or better, hinted at in the opening:

Maiden in the more lay,	*dwelt in the moor*
In the more lay –	
Sevenighte fulle –	*for full seven nights*
Sevenighte fulle –	
Maiden in the more lay,	
In the more lay,	
Sevenighte fulle –	
Sevenighte fulle –	
Fulle and a day. (1–9)[22]	

In the following stanzas we are told that the maiden's *mete* [food] was the *primerole* [primrose] and the *violet* [violet], that her drink was the *colde water* of

---

21 In the Middle Ages particular brewings of ale were made for all sorts of reasons: 'church ales' to provide for parochial expenses, 'bride ales' to endow marrying couples, 'help ales' to assist people fallen on hard times. See Bennett 1992. This appears to be a memorial drink to commemorate a dead person, perhaps on the anniversary of that person's death. See *Wynnere and Wastoure* (Trigg 1990, line 304). For fuller discussion of this lyric and references to other proposed interpretations, see Burrow 1984, 9–11, and also the Introduction (above), xvii–xviii.
22 See Duncan (above), 32–5.

the *welle-spring* [spring], and that her *bour* [shelter] was the *rede rose* and the *lilie flour*. The hermeneutical problem here is extreme and extreme solutions have been proposed. D. W. Robertson interpreted the poem allegorically: the moor is the 'wilderness of the world under the old law', and the maiden is the Virgin Mary, awaiting the coming of Christ. In this view the roses are martyrdom or charity, the lilies are purity, and the *welle-spring* is the grace of God.[23] Peter Dronke goes to folk belief and anthropology for an alternative explanation: the maiden is a water-sprite who lives by a spring on the moors.[24] Talbot Donaldson's reading is more humanistic and ahistorical. He compares the maiden to Wordsworth's Lucy who, like the maiden, is exposed to the vast forces of nature: 'the Middle English lyric suggests the mystery by which these forces are, at times, transmuted into something more humane, more benevolent, by their guardianship of the innocent maiden'.[25] This may feel right, but the poem is not a romantic one but one which is steeped in the culture of the Middle Ages, and it is articulated and framed, it seems to me, within that culture – though it does present an alternative to the conventional wisdom.

It is clearly about privation and survival in unconventional circumstances. But the division of the subject into *mete* [food], *dring* [drink] and *bour* [shelter] might have been familiar to a medieval audience from Ecclesiasticus 29, 28:

Initium vitae hominis aqua et panis, et vestimenta, et domus protegens turpitudinem.

[The essentials of the life of man are water and bread, and clothes and a house to cover one's shame.]

These are the necessities of common use (*communis usus*) as defined by Gratian, and repeated down the ages.[26] So if this is the right context in which to see it, the poem may have a religious frame of reference: it may be about the deliberate rejection of these necessities for reasons of abstinence and penance. But this is not how Bishop Richard Ledrede saw it at some time before 1360: *Maiden in the more lay* (of which the first line is quoted as *mayde yn the moore lay*) is among a number of secular songs (*cantilenae*) which he refers to in the Red Book of Ossory.[27] It is referred to again in a sermon collection dated about 1360 where it is used in the context of a description of the 'golden age', when, according to Ovid and Boethius, mankind lived only on the foods which nature provided without cultivation of any sort. 'And what did they drink?' asks the sermonist, and quotes a *karole* called *the mayde be wode lay*, noting in the margin *the cold water of the well spryng*.[28] When the myth of the 'golden age' was invoked in the late Middle Ages it was usually, as in this sermon, as a way of criticising the present, lamenting the moral deterioration of an increasingly materialistic society. Clearly, the *maiden* in this poem is no sort of conventional heroine, and

---

[23] See Robertson 1951, especially 26–7.
[24] See Dronke 1968b, 195–6.
[25] See Donaldson 1970, especially 151–2.
[26] See Langland's treatment, for example, in *Piers Plowman* B, Passus I, 17–42.
[27] For the implications of this mention of the poem see Greene 1952.
[28] For this sermon and its implications see Wenzel 1974.

is perhaps meant to be exactly the opposite. When Chaucer speaks of the 'former age' he makes the point that, unlike in modern society, people ate *that the feldes yave hem by usage*, that they *dronken water of the colde welle*, and that *slepten this blissed folk withoute walles*. Perhaps the author of this enigmatic lyric wishes to present a heroine who is not, to use another phrase from Chaucer, *forpampred with outrage* [overindulged with excess], and who uses the resources of medieval Christian asceticism and 'golden age' associations to construct an alternative.[29] Perhaps she is where she is as a result of an unhappy love affair. The lover in *I must go walke the wood so wyld* (Robbins *Sec.*, No. 20) proposes to retreat to a wild wood because he has been *banysshed ffrom [his] blys . . . fautles without offens* and despairs of returning:

> My bed schall be under the grenwod tre,
> A tufft of brakes under my hed . . .   *ferns*
>
> The ronnyng stremes shall be my drynke,
> Acorns schal be my ffode . . . (11–12, 16–17)   *food*

The enigmatic 'maiden' inhabits this same world of privation which, neverthe-less, enables a different, in some ways more romantic, life to be sustained: the replacements for food, drink and shelter, the necessities of civilisation, which nature provides, are all described approvingly in stanzas 2, 3 and 4 as *well* [excellent].

IV

These astonishing and strange texts, casual in their preservation, without order seemingly in their transcription, afford a glimpse into a rich world of secular poetry which has all but disappeared. The view that it was an extensive tradi-tion, probably popular, probably largely oral, receives some support from another set of not dissimilar fragments preserved in Ireland in the Red Book of Ossory. The manuscript consists of eighty parchment leaves bound in red oaken boards (which give it its name) preserved in the episcopal palace in Kilkenny. It is a miscellany consisting of diocesan documents relating to Kilkenny, a number of political documents, some proverbial verses in French, and sixty Latin hymns evidently composed by Ledrede. A note advises the reader that he has made 'these songs for the vicars of the cathedral church, for the priests and for the clerks, to be sung on important holidays and celebrations, so that their throats and mouths, dedicated to God, may not be polluted by songs associated with revelry (*teatralibus*), lewd and secular'. Since they are trained singers, he continues, they should provide for themselves suitable tunes. Snatches of verse, in French and English, are attached to some of the Latin hymns, presumably to indicate the 'suitable tunes' to which they could be sung, and most of the snatches appear to be from love songs.[30]

---

[29] See *The Former Age*, 3–8.
[30] For studies of this manuscript and for editions of the texts it contains see Greene 1974; Colledge, 1974; and Stemmler 1975. The texts of the snatches of French and English verse are

Mayde yn the moore lay, the opening line of the lyric discussed above, appears in the margin of a nativity hymn to Mary on fol. 71r col. a. The line on fol. 72v col. a *Have god day, my lemman*, etc. looks as though it may be the opening of a love song. Two snatches of French and, perhaps, English on fols 71v col. b and 74v col. b record betrayal and unhappiness in love:

> Harrow, ieo su trahy,
> Par fol amour de mal amy . . .
>
> [Alas, I am betrayed by foolish love for an evil lover . . .]
>
> Heu, alas, par amour,
> Qy moy myst en taunt dolour!
>
> [Alas, alas, for love, who has put me to so much suffering!]

Another couplet is perhaps from a betrayed maiden's lament, since it exploits the traditional association of willow with forsaken love, and perhaps is meant to contrast 'wearing the willow' with the wearing of green garlands by lovers in Maytime:

> Gayneth me no garlond of greene   *no green garland is suitable for me*
> But hit ben of wythoues ywroght.[31]   *unless it is made of willows*

On fol. 71v col. a appears what is certainly a stanza from a *chanson de mal mariée*, a type of love lyric not otherwise found until the fifteenth century:

> Alas, hou sholde I singe?   *how should*
> Y-loren is my playinge.   *lost; happiness*
> Hou sholde I with that olde man
> To live and let my lemman,   *abandon my lover*
> Swetest of al thinge?   (Duncan *MEL*, No. 26)

Whether this is regarded as a conventional generic gesture, or whether it reflects a serious protest at the coercive realities of medieval marriage, it articulates the voice of a young woman unhappy in her powerlessness – because she is young and because she is a woman – in relation to normative social protocols. She associates singing with *playinge* which may mean 'amusement' or 'joy', or, more precisely, 'love play', of which she would be deprived in marriage to an old man. And yet she does *singe* about her paradoxical situation, about the emotional and social impossibility into which she has been forced. There is also, on fol. 72r col. b (repeated with a minor variation on fol. 74r col. a), what may be a farewell to love, making use of the idea of the nightingale:

> Do, do, nihtyngale,
> Syng ful myrie,   *merrily*

---

taken from Stemmler 1975, 110–13. For a later analogous situation compare Lorenzo de' Medici's *Laude* of 1491 where he specifies that the religious songs are to be sung to the tunes ('cantasi come . . .') of ribald dance songs and carnival songs: see Toscani 1990. See also Duncan (above), 33 and 35.

31   For the proverbial association of a willow garland with forsaken love see Tilley 1950, W 403.

| Shul y nevre for thyn love | *I* |
| Lengre karie. | *be sad* |

The bird, which sings throughout the Middle Ages as a provocation to love, has, at least, for this poet, lost its efficacy.

V

When love lyrics in English appear in any significant number it is in the Harley manuscript, BL MS Harley 2253. This is a miscellany, copied in about 1340 in the Ludlow area of Shropshire by a scribe who is known to have copied other documents (mainly administrative and legal) as well as literary items in BL MS Harley 273 and BL MS Royal 12.C.xii. There are items in Latin, French and Middle English which address a variety of subjects – devotional, political, secular. Both prose and verse items appear. Some of these are to be found elsewhere, but others, including all the secular love lyrics, are unique to this manuscript, and it is no exaggeration to say that this is the single most important surviving source for the love lyric before Chaucer. It is also notable that in this manuscript the secular poetry is given equal status with other items.[32] The English lyrics are often written in elaborate stanza forms, and a number use alliteration as well as end-rhyme. The diction is highly formulaic in places. Derek Pearsall characterises them as follows: 'Generally speaking, they lack the theorising, abstraction, analysis and paradox of courtly Provençal and French lyric, the cult of pseudo-logic, of extremes of argument and sensibility. Instead, they are fundamentally simple and direct, much more like the anonymous semi-courtly love-poetry of thirteenth-century France, often given to homely and rustic imagery' (Pearsall 1977, 128). And there is much truth in this.

Studies in the dialects of the Middle English items reveal that not all were composed in the West Midlands, so MS Harley 2253 does not represent a simply local tradition, but the literature of provincial England more generally.[33] And what is English sits easily with what is written in Latin and French. In fact, some poems are macaronic, like *Dum ludis floribus velud lacinia* (Brook, No. 19) – a love lyric in Latin, French and English, written in five monorhyming quatrains, with Latin rhymes in the first four and rhymes in all three languages in the final stanza. It is highly conventional in its sentiments. While his lady disports herself among flowers, the poet is the epitome of suffering and misery (*de duel et de miseria*, 3) because he cannot win her love. He is fevered and may die (*hoc saeculum relinquere*, 7). Why she is so unattainable does not emerge, but there may be a problem of social class. In the following stanza he speaks of her as beautiful and noble as if she were the daughter of an emperor (*imperatoris filia*, 10) and she would be pre-eminent for her fine appearance and handsome countenance in the court of every king (*in omni regis curia*, 12). He is not prepared to

---

[32] The best studies of this important manuscript are Ker 1965, and the collection of essays in Fein 2000. For the scribe see Revard 2000.
[33] See Brook 1933; also McSparran 2000.

worship her from afar, however, and his unmistakable sexual intention is clear
when he asks God to help so that he might kiss her and do all those things which
follow (*beyser e fere que secuntur alia*, 16). But this generalised conventional
lament becomes particular in the final stanza:

> Scripsi hoc carmina in tabulis;
> Mon ostel est en mi la vile de Paris;
> May y sugge namore, so wel me is;   *I say*
> Yef I deye for love of hire, duel hit ys. (17–20)   *a grievous thing it is*

> [I wrote these verses on tablets; my dwelling place is in the middle of the
> town of Paris . . .]

This is a self-consciously virtuoso performance in the way it deploys the conventions of *fin amor* in three languages. Since he uses English only in the final two
lines, when he is signing off from the poem, it is likely that the poet was English
– perhaps a postgraduate student at the university of Paris.[34] One only has to
look at a brief poem such as this to see that it has a reach and scope which takes
it well beyond the local, and that it reminds us that these lyrics reflect a highly
developed European tradition of writing.

The love lyrics preserved in the Harley manuscript are not different in kind
from those which occur elsewhere, but formally they are more elaborate and
developed. Poems written in the familiar genres appear and reappear. A case in
point concerns *reverdies* or spring songs. The famous 'Cuckoo Song' *Sumer is
icumen in* (Brown *XIII*, No. 6), preserved in BL MS Harley 978 with music which
demonstrates it was sung in canon as a part-song, is perhaps the simplest spring
song in English:

> Sumer is icumen in,
> Loude sing cuccu!   *sing loudly, cuckoo*
> Groweth sed and bloweth med   *seed grows; the meadow blossoms*
> And springth the wode nu.   *the wood comes into leaf now*
> Sing cuccu! (1–5)

This stanza concentrates on vegetation. After a refrain, a second stanza refers to
animals (ewes and lambs, cows and calves, bullocks, bucks) and their joy at the
renewal of the year – which formally, for most purposes, began on 25 March, the
feast of the Annunciation. Often, though, the rejoicing at the coming of spring,
so evident in the animal kingdom, is contrasted with the unhappiness of men,
particularly lovers:

> Foules in the frith,   *birds; wood*
> The fishes in the flod,   *sea*
> And I mon waxe wod;   *I must go mad*
> Much sorwe I walke with
> For beste of bon and blod.   *finest (creature) of bone and blood*
>   (Duncan *MEL*, No. 16)

---

[34] See Dove 2000, 332–4.

This is also preserved with music, in Bodl. MS Douce 139. It is complete and self-contained. The gestures of the genre are all here in little: the natural world is seen as a contrast to the demented lover, suffering because of an idealised lady. In *Lenten ys come with love to toune* (Brown *XIII*, No. 81) the same gestures appear, but here with an amplified copiousness and, for the most part, a studied orderliness which might make one suspect that the author had read up on how to write a *descriptio naturae* from a rhetorical manual. The poem is essentially a list which catalogues the growth of plants and the re-energised activities of birds and animals. It is a mixture of elements which one might expect to find and features which are unusual: *nyghtegales* sing with *notes swete* (5) but *wilde drakes* (19) also appear; there are roses and lilies (13, 17) but also the woodruff (9), fennel and chervil (18). The landscape is particularly English, and the poem looks as though it was at least in part based on the poet's own observation. But the final stanza is extraordinary in its apparent *non-sequiturs*, its strange imagining, its absurdist logic:

The mone mandeth hire lyght,	*sends forth*
So doth the semly sonne bright	*fair sun*
When briddes singeth breme;	*gloriously*
Dewes donketh the dounes,	*dews moisten the downs*
Deores with here derne rounes	*animals with their secret cries*
Domes forte deme;	*expressing their wishes*
Wormes woweth under cloude,	*worms make love under ground*
Wymmen waxeth wounder proude,	
So wel hit wol hem seme.	*so well it becomes them*
Yef me shal wonte wille of on,	*do without the favour of one*
This wunne weole y wole forgon,	*wealth of joys; I shall forgo*
And wyght in wode be fleme. (25–36)	*and straightway; fugitive*

The poet appears to be disoriented and perplexed by multifarious activities generated by the coming of spring: he runs together day and night; his mind jumps from worms to women, perhaps for no other reason than that they alliterate. He is also marginalised grammatically. Everything about the spring is rendered in the present indicative, figuring the direct instincts of the natural world. In the last three lines of the poem, though, conditionality and futurity reflect the problematic nature of human relationships, and evasion and flight seem to be his response to these complications.

Characteristically, the love songs begin with a springtime setting.

When the nyghtegale singes the wodes waxen grene,	*grow green*
Lef and gras and blosme springes in Averyl, y wene,	*leaf; I know*
And love is to myn herte gon with one spere so kene,	*spear; sharp*
Nyght and day my blod hit drynkes, myn herte deth me tene. *pain*	

(Brown, *XIII*, 86, 1–4)

So opens another Harley lyric, and as the 'song' develops the narrator expatiates on the beauty of his mistress – who has no equal in the East Midlands *bitwene Lyncolne and Lyndeseye, Norhamptoun and Lounde* (17) – and his own lovesickness, from which only the lady can cure him: *a suete cos* [kiss] *of thyn mouth mighte be my leche* [physician] (12).[35] Another poem from the same manuscript, usually entitled 'Alysoun', begins with spring and quickly introduces the most beautiful woman in the world and the stereotypical suffering lover:

> Bytwene Mersh and Averil   *March and April*
> When spray biginneth to springe,
> The lutel foul hath hire wyl
> On hyre lud to synge.   *in her language*
> Ich libbe in lovelonginge   *live*
> For semlokest of alle thynge;   *the fairest*
> He may me blisse bringe,   *she may*
> Ich am in hire baundoun.   *power*
>
>   (Brown, *XIII*, No. 77, 1–8)

The beautiful lady is elaborated in a rhetorically conventional itemising head-to-foot description, and an inexpressibility topos:

> In world nis non so wyter mon   *there is no man so wise*
> That al hire bounté telle con. (25–6)   *who can recount her excellence*

The lovesickness of the poet consists of lying awake all night (22), with *wonges . . . won* [pale cheeks] (23), and a despair of living unless she will take him to be her *make* [companion] (18–19). This is all fairly traditional. But the routine nature of the sentiments of this poem are contradicted by the refrain, in which the narrator expresses joy and gratitude, despite his sufferings, at falling in love:

> An hendy hap ichabbe yhent,   *good fortune I have received*
> Ichot from hevene it is me sent –   *I know; sent to me*
> From alle wymmen mi love is lent,   *has gone*
> And lyght on Alysoun. (9–12)   *alighted*

The poem becomes dialogic, therefore, in a way always open to the writer of carols, and begins to explore the paradoxical nature of love. And another poem from the same manuscript, written in tight tail-rhyme stanzas and heavily alliterated, has a surprise in store, though it opens conventionally with spring, the beautiful lady and the lover:

> In May hit murgeth when hit dawes   *it is pleasant; dawns*
> In dounes with this dueres plawes,   *on hillsides; frolicking animals*
> And lef is lyght on lynde;   *leaf; (lime) tree*
> Blosmes bredeth on the bowes,   *flourish; boughs*
> Al this wylde wyghtes wowes,   *wild creatures make love*
> So wel ych under-fynde.   *as I well perceive*
> Y not non so freoli flour   *I do not know; excellent*
> Ase ledies that beth bryght in bour,
> With love who mighte hem bynde;
> So worly wymmen are by west –   *splendid*

---

[35] 'Love-sickness' was recognised as a disease by some medieval medical authorities: see Wack 1990.

| One of hem ich herie best | *I praise above all* |
| From Irlond in to Ynde. | *India* |

(Brown *XIII*, No. 82, 1–12)

Instead of developing the subjects of the beauty of the lady or the predicament of the lover, this poem dilates, unusually, on what is implicit in the line *With love who mighte hem binde*. In love poems of this sort it is usually the male wooer who is 'bound' or 'enslaved' or 'fettered' by his love for the lady, but here it is ladies who are constrained by love. And it is their susceptibility to love and their commitment to it which makes women, according to this poet, exploitable by men who are deceivers, and he warns them against men *when love you hath ybounde* (36):

Wymmon, war the with the swyke	*guard yourself; dissembler*
That feir and freoly ys to fyke –	*pleasant and comely; flatter*
Ys fare is o to founde.	*his conduct is always to be tested*
So wyde in world ys huere won,	*ubiquitous; their dwelling*
In uch a toune untrewe is on	*every town; false; one*
From Leycestre to Lounde. (25–30)	

The place names mentioned earlier as part of the praise of the pre-eminence of the lady appear to define the geographical limits of the known world, west to east, or, as it may have appeared on a contemporary *mappamundi* from the bottom left of the known world to the top right.[36] The place names defining the spatial activities of deceivers, however, appear to confine them to the English East Midlands, and one may suspect that there is some personal animus in the close of the poem where the narrator addresses the lady directly:

Ah, wolde lylie-leor in lyn	*would the lily-white; linen*
Yhere levely lores myn,	*listen willingly to my advice*
With selthe we weren sahte. (46–48)	*with joy; reconciled*

It may be that the object of the poem is to warn the lady against the intentions of somebody who may be a rival.[37] These three poems all make use of essentially the same materials, but for different ends. It is a testimony to the highly developed nature of the tradition and to the confidence and versatility of those writing within it that this should be possible.

Some of the love songs from MS Harley 2253 are highly elaborate and of great technical virtuosity – especially those which deal mainly with praise of the lady: it is as if the display of poetic virtuosity itself contributed to the honour of the subject. The lady in *Mosti ryden by Rybbesdale* (Brook, No. 7) is described from head to foot in some eighty-four lines, in orthodox rhetorical manner and with conventional comparisons: her hair is like the *sonnebeem* (14); she is as graceful and tall as a *lylie* (10); her complexion of white and red is like roses (34–6); her

---

36 *Mappamundi* had east at the top, so the British Isles appeared on the edge of the world in the bottom left hand corner. See Harvey 1996, where most of the known maps of this sort are reproduced.

37 For the idea that this poem is meant to be paired with *Lenten ys come with love to toune* see Howell 1980.

neck is like a swan's (43–4).[38] Reverence for the lady, however, produces irreverence in the playful licence of this lyric: the poet would rather wait for her to appear *Then beon pope and ryde in Rome* (47); her breasts are like *apples tuo of parays* [paradise] (59);[39] a stone in the buckle of her belt performs one of Christ's miracles in that it changes water *al to wyne* (70–2). The poem ends with an astonishing statement, which is, nevertheless, logical within its own terms:

> He myghte sayen that Crist hym seye   *say; had looked after him*
> That myghte nyghtes negh hyre leye,   *who; by night; near; lie*
> Hevene he hevede here. (82–4)   *he would have heaven here*

Whether he means that, for the opportunity of sleeping with her, he is willing to risk damnation is not clear, but that is frequently the implication of the phrase 'to have one's heaven on earth'.[40] Another poem, celebrating a lady from the 'west' similarly described in terms of roses and lilies, ends with much the same sentiment:

> This wommon woneth by west,
> Brightest under bys;   *fairest in fine linen*
> Hevene y tolde al his,   *I would consider*
> That o nyght were hire gest.   (Brown *XIII*, No. 78, 37–40)

The author of *A wayle whyt ase whalles bon* (Brook, No. 9) protests that sorrowful love disables him from writing: *Hou shal that lefly syng / That thus is marred in mournyng?* [How shall the man sing well who is thus afflicted with sorrow?] (19–20). No fire in hell, he continues, is so hot as the torment he boils in because he is committed to secrecy: he is someone *that loveth derne* [in secret] *and dar nought telle* (43). But he does write a highly proficient poem, elaborately stanza-linked, to the lady.[41] Apart from the fantasy about becoming a bird and flying at dead of night into her chamber, already referred to, the poem is unusual in a number of ways, not least in the offer the poet makes to the lady's *fere* – perhaps 'husband', or 'lover', or maybe 'companion':

> Wolde hyre fere beo so freo
> And wurthes were that so myghte beo,   *equivalents*
> Al for on y wolde yeve threo   *one*
>   Withoute chep. (31–4)   *haggling*

We usen here no wommen for to selle says the high-minded Ector in Chaucer's

---

[38] See Brewer 1955 for a study of the rhetorical basis of these descriptions.

[39] In his description of Egypt, Mandeville speaks of bananas as *apples of Paradys*: see Seymour 1967, 35. But it would be strange if this poet has bananas in mind. These *apples* are probably meant to represent temptation, or perhaps ideal beauty.

[40] Compare *Here* [their] *paradis they nomen* [took] *here, / And now they lye in helle y-fere* [together] (Duncan *MEL*, No. 47, 19–20).

[41] I accept the ordering of the stanzas as they appear in the manuscript. Others, on the basis of internal evidence – most notably stanza linking, a prominent feature of this poem – have argued for an emended version: see Gibson 1914; Stemmler 1962, 121–7; Duncan 1992. The text in emended form is found in Duncan *MEL*, No. 2. Degginger 1994 adopted the same re-ordering of the stanzas. See also Duncan (above), 29–30.

Trojan debate over the proposed exchange of Criseyde for Antenor (*Troilus and Criseyde*, Bk. 4, 182), but this poet has no such scruples: if the lady's *fere* is willing and if suitable equivalents are available, he says, he would give three for one in exchange without haggling. And though this poet cannot name his pre-eminent lady another poet feels that he can, though in a coded way. He does not describe her but rather evokes her virtues, stanza by stanza, in a series of virtuoso comparisons: by turns she is compared to jewels, flowers and plants, birds, spices, and finally heroes of romance. Where she lives and her identity emerge in the centre of the poem, though the reader is asked to be discreet about it and to whisper it to *Johon*:

From Weye he is wisist to Wyrhale;	*river Wye; she is wisest*
Hire nome is in a note of the nyghtegale.	*name*
In Annote is hire nome – nempneth hit non!	*let no one mention it*
Whose ryght redeth roune to Johon.	*if anyone guesses right whisper to John*
	(Brown XIII, No. 76, 27–30)

But this is a puzzle which is meant to be solved. She is clued very easily in the consecutive letters of line 28, and the answer is given (a little redundantly to a reader, perhaps, but not to a listener) in the following line. Line 30, with its mention of *Johon* presumably allows the poet to sign his technically impressive poem, as does the last line with its mention again of *Jon*.

But perhaps the most interesting of these elaborate love songs is *Blow, northerne wynd* (Brown XIII, No. 83) which is written in tail-rhyme stanzas with a simpler four-line burden. Of this burden R. T. Davies writes that it 'may well be that of a popular song: its character – in rhythm, imagery and directness – is quite different from that of the rest of the poem'. He finds much of the poem 'very bad, because merely and uncreatively and repetitiously conventional' (Davies 1963, 317). The noble and attractive lady (*menskful maiden of might*, 7) is certainly described in the routine head-to-foot fashion (13–36), and her moral virtues are listed through comparisons with the qualities of jewels and flowers (45–52) – which is hardly original, but which is worked through with a rich complexity.[42] And the narrator suffers the usual pains of frustrated love: grief, paleness, sleeplessness (77–84). But embedded in the poem is a vignette which defines the relationship in terms of contemporary social and political problems associated with bastard feudalism and the bullying behaviour of the retinues of aristocrats:

To Love, that loflich is in londe,	*who is dear everywhere*
Y tolde hym as ych understonde	*I*
Hou this hende hath hent in honde	*how this gracious one has seized*
On huerte that myn wes;	*a heart that was mine*
And hire knyghtes me han so soght,	*have sought*
Sykyng, Sorewyng, & Thoht,	*Sighing; Sorrowing; Perplexity*
Tho thre me han in bale broght	*these three; grief*
Ayeyn the poer of Pees. (53–60)	*against the power of Peace*

---

[42] For a fine analysis of this poem see Spitzer 1951, 1–22. See also the brief but interesting comments of Dronke 1968a, I, 124–5.

This is constructed in the terms of a formal complaint to an overlord, Love, about the way in which the lady and her knightly servants have injured the speaker. His grievance is framed in quasi-legal language: she has taken into her possession something which rightfully belonged to him – his heart – and her three knights have brought him to grief against the peace. He puts further *pleyntes* [complaints] (61) that the three knights have threatened to imprison and kill him *unlaghfulliche* [unlawfully] (68). It is not unusual in the poetry of *fin amor* for the lover to see himself in the role of a social inferior, but here the quasi-legal language suggests a more precisely imagined and articulated situation. And Love's judgment, which is perhaps meant to be given from the bench (*bord*, 70) is a standard quasi-legal one: the lover must recover what has been wrongfully taken away from him, his *huerte hele* [heart's salvation] (72), and ask for compensation (*bote*, 75) for his injuries. The allegory of love is here sustained by a running comparison with a social complaint.[43]

Social issues, however, more usually appear in *chansons d'aventure* or pastourelles. In its typical manifestation, the pastourelle involves a confrontation in the formal poetic terms of a debate or dispute: after a brief first-person contextualising introduction, the main body of a pastourelle is usually taken up by the alternating speeches of two characters. But this formal confrontation is merely the reflex of larger social confrontations in terms of gender and class. In pastourelles a man, usually a knight in the French poems, or sometimes a cleric, seeks to seduce a woman who may be a shepherdess (hence 'pastourelle') or some other countrywoman, usually in a country setting. Sometimes he is successful; sometimes he fails abjectly and comically. There are ethical and moral confrontations too. But primarily what is striking is the linguistic clash: the courtly language of the man, with all its associations and implications, meets a coarser, more demotic form of speech which incorporates a different ideology, which is more sensible, down to earth, practical.[44]

In a fryht as y con fare fremede (Brook, No. 8) is the most fully articulated pre-Chaucerian example of this genre. In many ways it is a virtuoso performance – intricately rhymed, heavily alliterated and with elaborate stanza-linking – but the story it tells is the familiar one of the successful seduction of a country girl, and many of the traditional arguments and narrative shifts appear. The man's instincts are acquisitive and predatory: the girl he meets is *a wel feyr fenge* (2), *fenge* meaning 'booty' or 'prize'. When he asks her who she is he is rebuffed: *heo me bed go my gates lest hire gremede* [she bade me go away lest she became angry] (7). He offers her fine clothes, but she rejects them saying it is better to wear what she has *then* [than] *syde* [ample] *robes and synke into synne* (16). Initially the girl rejects all of her suitor's not very plausible advances but abruptly changes her mind. What breaks her resolve, however, is not an argument or a promise, but the prospect of being married (or betrothed) to a man she does not love and who appears to be violent:[45]

---

43   See further Scattergood 2000, especially 191–2.
44   For a brilliant overview of this genre see Zink 1972. For a study of English pastourelles see Scattergood 1996, 61–80.
45   The ending of this lyric is problematical: it is sometimes hard to know who is speaking, and there may be textual losses. See Anderson 1980; also Reichl 2000, 233–5.

Betere is taken a comeliche y clothe   *a well-attired person*
In armes to cusse and to cluppe   *kiss; embrace*
Then a wrecche ywedded so wrothe: *than be married to such an ill-tempered wretch*
Thagh he me slowe ne myhti him asluppe. (36–40)   *though he beat me I could*
                                                  [*not escape him*

As Rosemary Woolf has shown, the poem owes something to the *chanson des transformations*, in which the woman thinks of shape-shifting as a means of escaping her would-be seducer (Woolf 1969, 55–9). But here this is rejected as a possibility:

Mid shupping ne mey hit me ashunche;   *it cannot be evaded by shape-shifting*
Nes y never wycche ne wyle. (45–46)   *I was never; witch; sorceress*

She capitulates, but the poem ends on an unexpectedly ambiguous note: *Luef me were gome bute gyle* [Dear to me would be a man without guile] (48). The predicament of the lower class mistress of the upper-class lover is here explored in a disabused and chilling way. She knows that if she listens to his offers he will probably quickly abandon her, which will not only cause her personal unhappiness but will also bring with it disapproval by her family and social ostracism:

Such reed me myghte spaclyche reowe   *advice; soon regret*
When al my ro were me atraght,   *my peace; taken from me*
Sone thou woldest vachen an newe,   *seek afresh*
And take another withinne nyye naght.   *nine nights*
Thenne mihti hongren on heowe,   *I'd starve in (my) family*
In uch an hyrd ben hated and forhaght,   *in every household; despised*
And ben ycaryed from alle that y kneowe,   *separated; had known*
And bede clevyen ther y hade claght. (29–36)   *and bidden to cling where I had*
                                                  [*clung*

The poem exposes a joyless and uncomfortable social reality – one which is adverted to in several pastourelles and in other texts where the sexual relations between persons of unequal social rank are involved. It is addressed most forthrightly in the sixth dialogue of the *De Amore*, where Andreas Capellanus has the lower-class woman reject the advances of her noble suitor on two grounds: firstly that 'if the affair came to the ears of the common people they would ruin my good name by blaming me openly that I had gone far outside my natural limits'; and, secondly, because 'it is not usual for a man of higher rank to love faithfully a woman of a lower one, and if he does he soon comes to loathe her love, and he despises her on slight provocation' (Walsh 1982, I, 6. 292–3). The problem of relationships between upper-class men and lower-class women was clearly one which was of some interest to a broad range of courtly writers and readers, and it looks as though the author of this English lyric was familiar with its main issues.

None of these questions, however, are raised by *As I stod on a day* (Duncan *MEL*, No. 23), a sophisticated and enigmatic pastourelle from London, College of Arms MS 27, for the simple reason that the narrator makes no progress in his suit. It is not that he does not know or use the conventional gestures: he praises the woman as *the fairest may that I ever met* (13); he offers to be her servant (*man*,

16); he commits himself to secrecy, *for nothing in hird* [in public] *fonden* [attempted] *wolde I let* (17); he asks for her *love* (23). He is, according to the canons of *fin amor*, properly appreciative of her, deferential and respectful. However, her response is proud and haughty, because she is no humble shepherdess but a well-to-do, educated woman. She is expensively dressed:

Of a blak burnet	*dark fine brown cloth*
al was hir wede,	*attire*
Purfiled with pellur	*trimmed with fur*
doun to the ton;	*toes*
A red hod on hir heved,	*hood; head*
shraged al of shredes,	*edged; with strips (of cloth)*
With a riche ribban,	*precious ribbon*
gold-begon. (4–7)	*embroidered with gold*

Unless she is breaking the sumptuary laws with regard to her dress (which was not unknown) this lady is of high social rank. She wears fur, and a statute of 1337 expressly forbade it 'only except' for the royal family, prelates, earls, barons, knights and ladies, and 'people of holy church, which may expend by year £100 of her [holy church's] benefices'. And subsequent legislation reinforces these stipulations.[46] And the gold-embroidered headband adds to the impression of her wealth. But, more importantly, she is educated: *That bird rad on hire boke evere as she yede* (8). At this date, literacy among seculars was rare, especially among women.[47] And, as the poem develops, it emerges that the woman is more intelligent, better educated than her would-be seducer, and more verbally acute. She begins by appearing to lead him on:

'Sir, God yeve thee grace	*give*
god happes to have,	*good fortune*
And the lyinges of love,'	*joys*
thus she me gret. (14–15)	*greeted*

To wish that he might have good fortune is clear enough, but *the lyinges of love* might mean 'the joys of love' because *lyinges* can mean 'sexual intercourse',[48] or it might mean ironically 'the untruths of love', a premonition of what he is going to propose to her. At any event, she is not prepared to be amenable to his advances. She tells him he is insane to try to seduce her:

She bar me fast on hond	*she speedily accused me*
that I began to rave,	
And bad me fond ferther	*try elsewhere*
a fol for to fet;	*fool; find*
'Wher gospelleth	*what is the message of*
al thy speche?	*(pious) talk*

---

46 See *Statutes of the Realm*, I, 280–1, 380–2; II, 399–402, 468–70 for medieval sumptuary legislation. See further Scattergood 1996, 240–57.

47 On this difficult subject see Cressy 1980, 176; Moran 1985, 178 and 181.

48 See *MED*, liinge ger. (I). 1(d) 'act of sexual intercourse' for this sense. This is the way Duncan reads the line: see *MEL*, 192.

| Thou findest hir noght here | *her not here* |
| the sot that thou seche.' (18–21) | *fool; seek* |

The insane (i.e. those who rave) can only be successful with fools, is what she seems to be saying, and she is no fool. And, because he persists, she advises him he is wasting his words (26), and then insults him, seemingly because of the deference of his approach, and implies that it suggests that he is sexually inexperienced:

Ther most a bolder byrd	
billen on the bow;	*sing; bough*
I wende be your semblant	*would imagine; demeanour*
she chese you for chaste. (27–8)	*might chose*

Perhaps she would prefer a knight and the narrator here appears to be a cleric, as implied by the use of the words *gospelleth* and *chaste*.[49] Inevitably she dismisses him without ceremony or any face-saving formula: *Wend fort* [move on] *there ye wenen* [expect] *better to spede* [succeed] (31). Here in the manner of many pastourelles the narrator is rebuffed and his shortcomings are ruthlessly exposed.

The debate poem *My deth y love my lyf ich hate, for a leuedy shene* (Brown XIII, No. 85) shares many of the characteristics of the pastourelle: it is a seduction poem, but there is no narrative introduction relating to the circumstances of the encounter, and no rural setting. Indeed the girl seems to be distinctly well-to-do: she refers at one point to her *boure* (19), which may mean 'dwelling' but which here probably means 'inner apartment' or 'bedroom', and if she had her own room she was almost certainly not lower class. At one point in the conversation she uses a socially loaded proverb warning against presumption: *The is betere* [it is better for you] *on fote gon, then wycked hors to ryde* (12), virtually telling the clerical wooer that he may not be good enough for her, since only the better off rode horses.[50] But the cleric does not despair and sets about persuading her to accept him by deploying the tropes and language of *fin amor*.

My deth y love, my lyf ich hate, for a levedy shene,	*radiant*
Heo is bright so daies-light, that is on me wel sene;	*she*
Al y falewe so doth the lef in somer when hit is grene.	*I fade; leaf*
Yef mi thoght helpeth me noght, to wham shal y me mene?	*complain*
Sorewe & syke & drery mod byndeth me so faste	*sighing*
That y wene to walke wod yef hit me lengore laste. (1–6)	*I expect; mad*

The paradox, the imagery, the personification allegory of line 5, and in partic-

---

49 For the 'question' of who makes the better lover, a clerk or a knight, see Oulmont 1911 where a number of apposite texts are printed.

50 See Whiting and Whiting 1968, F 464, but the only instance given. However, compare Boccaccio's *Decameron*, VI, 1, where Madonna Oretta, bored by a story incompetently told by a gentleman with whom she is riding and not wishing to give him offence, asks to be allowed to walk and blames the gait of the animal: *questo vostro cavallo ha troppo duro trotto, per che vi priego che vi piaccia di pormi a piè* [that horse of yours has too hard a trot, so I ask you to please set me down on my feet].

ular the tropes of 'dying for love' and 'love's madness', all mark this off as the standard discourse of *fin amor*, which initially does not impress the girl at all. She literalises his metaphorical gestures. His threat to go mad gets the response of *thou art a fol* (9, 17). His wish for death, she says, may come to him if her father and her family catch him in her *boure*, as they will not hesitate because it is a *synne* from locking her up and killing him, *the deth so thou maght wynne* (19–20). But her sensible, disparaging, clear-eyed wisdom is dissipated by the cleric's appeal to past happiness: *In a wyndou ther we stod we custe* [kissed] *us fyfty sythe* [times] (23).[51] She capitulates to his advances, asserts that she is willing to go against the wishes of her family, and is unwilling to submit the cleric to the 'wounds of love':

Thou semest wel to ben a clerc, for thou spekest so scille;[52]	*so cleverly*
Shalt thou never for mi love woundes thole grylle.	*suffer; terrible*
Fader, moder, & al my kun ne shal me holde so stille	*kin; subdued*
That y nam thyn, & thou art myn, to don al thi wille. (33–6)	*I shall not be*

Arguably, however, the most important part of her final, complicit, speech is her recognition of the cleric's skill with language. He gets her to accept his way of thinking by getting her to speak in the terms of his own discourse. Her adoption of these terms signals her capitulation: in a precisely literalistic way he talks her into loving him. And this is what is so extraordinary about the poem: it is all talk. There is nothing in it except conversation, and that has to carry both the narrative and the meaning. There are earlier and later texts in Middle English which deal with the issue of the clerical wooer, but none, like this, takes him seriously. It is tempting to see this poem in relation to those poems, written in France in Latin and the vernacular, which debated the problem of who makes the better lover, a knight or a cleric. As one female speaker in *Le Concile de Remiremont* says:

> Clericorum probitas, et eorum bonitas,
> Semper querit studium ad amoris gaudium,
> Sed eorum gaudia tota ridet patria.
> Laudant nos in omnibus rithmis atque versibus.

> [The honesty of clerics and their goodness always prompt in them a study of the joy of love; the whole country rejoices in their pleasures. They praise us in all sorts of rhyme and in all sorts of verses.][53]

---

[51] I accept the view that the fifty kisses were exchanged with the same clerk; some have argued that it was a different clerk and that the girl changes her mind because she simply likes clerks: see Reichl 2000, 235–6 for a summary of the arguments.

[52] The reading *scille* is problematic; some editors prefer *stille*. Though self-rhymes are not unknown in Middle English verse, *scille* may seem preferable as giving a full rhyme with *stille* (35) and here it would mean 'eloquently'. However, the form *scille*, with the spelling 'sc' rather than 'sh' for Old English 'sc' is anomalous in the Harley manuscript. According to Reichl, the manuscript reading is definitely *stille* which here would make good sense in a range of meanings 'from "quietly" ("soft-spoken") to "secretly," a sense according well with the demands of *derne love*' (Reichl 2000, 236).

[53] Oulmont 1911 for a text of this poem. The translation is mine.

Certainly the literary accomplishment of this English poem would qualify its author for such praise.

VI

It is strange that the pre-Chaucerian love lyric provides no example of the dawn song, particularly since Chaucer was so familiar with its conventions and wrote several of both a serious and a parodic kind, usually inset into longer narratives.[54] It seems likely that its non-appearance before Chaucer is a result of a loss of texts.

But poems in the other major lyric genres appear in some numbers, and it is a particular testimony to the strength of the tradition that the conventions of the love lyric should be adopted and used in other types of poem. In the light of the way Bishop Richard Ledrede regarded love poems it is hardly surprising that writers of religious lyrics were evidently very aware of the conventions of the secular tradition and adapted them for their own purposes. On fols 128r and 128v in MS Harley 2253 appear two poems, one secular and one religious, which begin identically, *Lutel wot hit any mon*, and have an identical stanza-pattern, and a similar refrain. It looks as though the secular version came first, but, as Michael Kuczynski puts it: 'The two are meant to be read together. They juxtapose the sure love of Christ, demonstrated by his death on the Cross, and the fickle love of woman' (Kuczynski 2000, 154). Two parallel couplets in these poems (Brown *XIII*, Nos 90 and 91) make the point in a particularly clear way:

> The love of him us haveth ymaked sounde,
> And cast the grimly gost to grounde . . . (No. 90, 5–6)

> The love of hire ne lesteth no wyght longe,   *her love lasts not long at all*
> Heo haveth me plyght & wyteth me wyth wronge . . . (No. 91, 5–6)
>   *she; promised; blames me wrongly*

Again, the opening six lines of *Lenten ys come with love to toune* (Brook, No. 11), a secular *reverdie*, are replicated fairly exactly in the bird-debate, usually called *The Thrush and the Nightingale* (Brown *XIII*, No. 52), which begins *Somer is comen with love to toune* and ends with an assertion of religious values over those of secular love. Yet again, the Harley lyric *Nou skrinketh* [withers] *rose and lylie-flour* (Brook, No. 23) exploits the love lyric by seeming to offer a pastourelle, but the narrator's initial thoughts of finding an earthly mistress are quickly replaced by a transfer of his affection to Mary as he realises the *folie* (13) of secular love, and a transposition of the language of *fin amor* (*mournyng*, *merci*) into a religious prayer:

> From Petresbourh in o morewenyng,
> As y me wende of my pleyyyng,   *took my way for pleasure*
> On mi folie y thoghte;   *I*
> Menen y gon my mourning   *I addressed my complaint*

---

[54] See Scattergood 1987b, 110–20.

To hire that ber the hevene kyng,   *who bore*
Of merci hire bysohte. (11–16)   *begged her for mercy*

And lyric moments also occur in longer poems, such as the thirteenth-century
romance *Of Arthour and Merlin*, which is notable for the seasonal headpieces the
author uses to establish the temporal settings for his story. Some of these may
derive from the epic tradition, but others draw on the conventions of the love
lyric. The contrast between the lover's constancy and the transitoriness of
seasonal beauty declares the origin of this example:

In tyme of winter alange it is: *dreary*
The foules lesen her blis,
The leves fallen of the tre,
Rein alangeth the cuntre.   *makes dreary*
Maidens leseth here hewe;
Ac ever hye lovieth that be trewe.   *they*
                              (Macrae-Gibson 1973, I, lines 4199–204)

As G. V. Smithers puts it: 'This could never have been composed without the
medieval love-lyric as a model' (Smithers 1957, II, 36).

And finally there is the compliment of parody, which comes so memorably in
Chaucer. In a celebrated essay, Talbot Donaldson argued that there were
intertextual traces of earlier texts from the lyric tradition in *The Miller's Tale*,
particularly in relation to the language used of and by Alison, Nicholas and
Absolon: 'One of the devices he used most skilfully was that of sprinkling these
characterisations and conversations with clichés borrowed from the vernacular
versions of the code of courtly love – phrases of the sort we are accustomed to
meet, on the one hand in Middle English minstrel romances and, on the other, in
secular lyrics such as those preserved in Harley MS 2253' (Donaldson 1970,
16–17). *Hende* [courteous] Nicholas's wooing of Alison is set out in unmistakably
allusive and parodic terms. He first seizes her and then speaks,

And seyde, 'Ywis, but if ich have my wille   *truly, unless I have*
For deerne love of thee, lemman, I spille.' *secret; sweetheart; die*
And heeld hire harde by the haunchebones,   *thighs*
And seyde, 'Lemman, love me al atones,   *at once*
Or I wol dyen, also God me save!'   (CT, I, 3277–81)

Here the adjectives *hende* and *deerne* suggest that Chaucer was aware of the
earlier traditions of love poetry, which, incidentally, often used alliteration: line
3279, which is a perfect alliterative line, appears to be a recognition of this.
Nicholas calls Alison *lemman* and says that he wants his *wille* with her – both
words common in the earlier tradition – and he uses the familiar 'dying for love'
trope in order to help make his case. This is a story of sexual intrigue and oppor-
tunism set amongst the provincial urban proletariat, and Chaucer may be
suggesting that there is something déclassé about this sort of poetry.

At any event it was not the sort of lyric poetry he wrote.[55] And it was

---

[55] For a study of his lyrics see Scattergood 1995, 455–512; and for a book-length study see Ruud
   1992.

Chaucer's essentially metropolitan manner – using the *formes fixes* of the ballade and roundel, genres such as the complaint, and a highly aureate vocabulary – which sustained the love poetry of the fifteenth and earlier sixteenth centuries, displacing the early medieval mode from its centrality in the English tradition, but not erasing it.[56]

---

[56] I wish to thank Karen Hodder of the University of York and my colleagues Helen Cooney and Corinna Salvadori Lonergan for help in the preparation of this chapter.

4

Moral and Penitential Lyrics

VINCENT GILLESPIE

I

It is in the nature of preliterate and partially literate societies that their moral values and ethical principles will be encoded in and transmitted by memorial verse. Anglo-Saxon poetry bristles with proverbs and maxims, some perhaps of pre-Christian origin, others refracted from the so-called 'wisdom' books of the Old Testament such as Ecclesiastes, Ecclesiasticus and Proverbs, representing the collected aphorisms of another tribal society that had suffered displacement from its homeland. The hortatory tone of poems like *Maxims I* and *II*, *Precepts*, *Vainglory* and *Fates of Men* repeatedly stresses the importance of such proverbs and maxims in providing navigational tools for man's passage through the stormy seas of life (Shippey 1976; Larrington 1993).

The dramatic monologues of the Exeter Book are suffused with this proverbial lore, exploring its application to the challenging and changeful circumstances of each protagonist's life on earth, and revealing how such knowledge can be used in a prudent and wise manner. It is not accidental that one of the Wanderer's greatest hardships is the absence of his beloved lord's *larcwidum* [teaching words] and *cuðra cwiddegiedda* [known stories or utterances] (Mitchell and Robinson 2001, No. 16, 38 and 55). His exile has removed him from the familiar but reassuring guidance of tribal maxim and exemplary story. More ambitiously, *The Seafarer* dramatises its protagonist's search for a remedy for the *sorge* [sorrow] and *longunge* [longing] suffered by the earth-bound soul, allowing him to address the primal anxieties of death, judgement, heaven and hell (the fearful Four Last Things of Christian tradition). That poem's conclusion, *Dol biþ se þe his Dryhten ne ondraedeþ; cymeð him seo dead unþinged* [Foolish is he who does not fear his Lord; death comes to him unreflected on] (Mitchell and Robinson 2001, No. 17, 106), aligns itself ideologically and verbally with the proverbial lore found elsewhere in the Exeter Book:

> Dol biþ se þe his dryhten nat, to þaes oft cymeð dead unþinged;
> snotre men sawlum beorgað, healdað hyra soð mid ryhte.

> [A man who does not know his lord is a fool: death often comes unexpectedly to him. Wise men look after their souls, they uphold their integrity with justice]
> (*Maxims I*, 35–6, Shippey 1976, 64)

Wisdom only comes when the abstract knowledge of moral codes and appropriate behaviours is catalysed by experience into something more personal and immediate, capable of powerfully engaging man's emotions of fear and awe and of channelling his spiritual energies. As *Soul and Body I* puts it:

> Certainly it is necessary for every man to consider for himself the journey his soul will have to make, how terrible it will be when death comes and separates the kinsmen who were once joined: the soul and body. (Shippey 1976, 105)

The route followed by later medieval travellers on this journey to wisdom is not markedly different than that trodden by their Anglo-Saxon forebears.[1] The moral and penitential lyrics surviving from the Middle English period must be interpreted as part of a wide spectrum of didactic writing in which portable piety and aphoristic wisdom played a central role. For medieval Christians, the fear of the Lord was always the beginning of Wisdom (Ecclesiasticus 1.16).

II

Existential anxiety is fuelled by the uncertainties of life and the certainty of death. Three Sorrowful Things haunted human consciousness: the inevitability of death, the uncertainty of its time, and the unknowability of the soul's fate after death – themes tellingly evoked in the Middle English period even in the briefest lyrics:

> Whan I thenke thinges thre,   *ponder*
> Ne may I never blithe be: *happy*
> That on is that I shal away,   *one is; must depart*
> That other is I not which day,   *I do not know*
> The thridde is my moste care,   *my greatest anxiety*
> I not whider I shal fare.   (Duncan *MEL*, No. 42)[2]

Timor mortis conturbat me [the fear of death confounds me] recurs as one of the most common refrains found in moral lyrics from the thirteenth to the early sixteenth centuries, a literary tradition elegantly and knowingly deployed in William Dunbar's famous *Lament for the Makaris* (Bawcutt 1998a, I, No. 21).[3] Earlier, in a lyric in carol form, *Dred of deth, sorrow of syn* (Duncan *LMELC*, No. 89), John Audelay, who was both blind and deaf, used this refrain as, with exceptional poignancy and humility, he self-referentially dramatised the physical plight and mental attitude invoked by the penitential scenario of such *Timor mortis* poems:

> As I lay seke in my langure,   *sick in my infirmity*
> With sorow of hert and teere of ye,   *eye*
> This caral I made with gret doloure –   *carol; great sorrow*

---

1 Several ME lyrics, e.g. *Ihereth of one thinge that ye owen of thenche* (Brown *XIII*, No. 29b), show clear signs of the influence of this older tradition of soul and body debates.
2 See also Brown *XIII*, Nos 11–13; *Bi a wode as I gon ryde* (Brown *XIV*, No. 117, one of the Vernon refrain poems); Heffernan 1981; Heffernan 1982; Breeze 1989.
3 The phrase comes from the liturgical Office for the Dead. On *Timor mortis* poems see Woolf, 333–6 and Greene 1933.

Passio Christi conforta me.   *Passion of Christ strengthen me*
Lady helpe! Jhesu merci!
Timor mortis conturbat me. (45–50)

Latin prose meditations deploring the vileness of human conception and birth, the brevity of human life and the inescapable brutality of death were repeatedly quarried for sermons, reworked into Latin poems and translated into vernacular exhortations of the bleakest and most minatory kind.[4] *Whi is the world beloved, that fals is and vein?* (Brown *XIV*, No. 134), the most common English vernacular version of the hugely popular Latin transience poem *Cur mundus militat*, usually occurs in manuscripts as part of a short sequence of texts on eschatology, all translated from Latin works attributed to fathers of the church like Augustine and Bernard or from the *Counsels of Isidore*, a popular collection of precepts *whiche ben good and holsume, yf there be hade in the reders and lovers of hem wylfulle execucyon* (Horstmann 1896, II, 374).[5] This lyric, with its powerfully imagistic and dramatic couplets, might be considered to be functioning in this largely prose context as the affective catalyst encouraging the reader to bring the teachings of the other texts to *wylfulle execucyon*:

Whi is the world biloved that fals is and vein?
Sithen that hise welthis ben uncertein.   *since its blessings are*
Al so soone slidith his power away   *its power*
As doith a brokil pot that freisch is and gay.   *brittle*
Truste ye rathir to lettirs writen in th'is   *the ice (i.e. they melt away)*
Than to this wrecchid world that ful of synne is. (1–6)[6]

In the late twelfth century, as a new drive for penitential self-awareness was launched by the institutional Church, Pope Innocent III asserted that human life was a miserable, fallen condition in need of God's redemptive grace as its only hope of escape from eternal damnation. His message that man was dust and food for worms rang out through the later Middle Ages, not least in such chilling lyrics as:

Whan the turuf is thy tour,
And thy pit is thy bour,   *grave; bower*
Thy fel and thy white throte   *skin*
Shullen wormes to note.   *shall be the business of worms*
What helpeth the thenne   *thee*
Al the worilde wenne?   *world's delights*
(Duncan *MEL*, No. 45)

– a message to be translated by Chaucer and repeated as a pious cliché on the lips of Shakespeare's dying Harry Hotspur. Texts like the *Meditationes piissimae*

---

4   The two most famous meditations are the *Meditationes piissimae de cognitione humanae conditionis*, often attributed to St Bernard (*PL* 184, cols 485–508), and Lotario dei Segni (Pope Innocent III), *De miseria condicionis humane* (Lewis 1978).
5   The *Concilia Isidori* contain such exhortations as *O man, knowe thi-sylfe* and sections devoted to *Dyspyte of the worlde*. The sequence as it appears in BL MS Harley 1706 is printed by Horstmann 1896, II, 367–80.
6   *IMEV* 4160. There are at least 11 copies of this version in Middle English. Cf. also *IMEV* 3475.

de cognitione humane conditionis (often attributed to St Bernard) provided the Middle Ages with a powerful vocabulary of anxiety, self-loathing and aphoristic stoicism. In its English vernacular version, usually known as *The Sayings of St Bernard* (Furnivall 1901, 511–22), it taught men how to fear the world, the flesh and the devil, how to look askance at human success and prosperity, and, most hauntingly, how to ask in English the core question of Latin complaints against transience:

Where ben heo that biforen us weren	*where are they who*
That houndes ladden and haukes beeren	*who led hounds; carried hawks*
And hedden feld and wode;	*possessed*
This riche ladys in heore bour,	*their bower*
That wereden gold in heore tressour,	*wore; head-dress*
With heore brighte rode?	*complexion*

(Furnivall 1901, 521)

So popular was this theme that a number of stanzas from *The Sayings of St Bernard*, beginning with the one just quoted, enjoyed separate circulation as a powerful independent lyric (Duncan *MEL*, No. 47), entitled in one manuscript (Bodl. MS Digby 86) *Ubi sount qui ante nos fuerount?* [Where are those who were before us?].[7] Such meditations provided the lexical groundswell that carried many moral and penitential commonplaces out into the devotional and didactic mainstream:

Unstable is thi lyt i-dight,	*destined*
Nou art thou hevy, nou artou light,	
Sturtynde as a ro;	*restless as a roe*
Nou thou richest, and nou thou porest,	*now art thou*
Nou art thou sek, now thou rekeverest,	*sick*
In wandreth and in wo.	*misery; woe*

(Furnivall 1901, 513)[8]

Such texts generated a spiritual agenda of formulaic fear and pro-forma penitence, drawing on a tradition of writing on the theme of *nosce teipsum* [know thyself] that can be traced back to the stoics through the early fathers of the Church.[9] They sought to teach men how to know their own weakness and frailty, and, in recognising their own impotence, how to seek mercy and forgiveness from the Almighty. *Kyndeli is now mi coming* (Brown *XIV*, No. 53) typifies this kind of moral verse which codifies the miseries of the human condition, but in so doing it also consoles by the universality of the experience it describes:

Kyndeli is now mi coming	*according to nature*
Into this werld with teres and cry;	*world*

---

7 Woolf, 93–7, 108–10; Gray 1972, 186–90.

8 Cf. an uncontrolled version of these paradoxes in *The siker sothe whoso seys* (Brown *XIV*, No. 27), and the very effectively controlled (and therefore stronger) version in the Vernon poem *I wolde witen of sum wys wight* (Brown *XIV*, No. 106).

9 On this strand of Christian asceticism, see Courcelle 1974–5; Morris 1972. For typical handlings of the theme, see *In a pistel that Paul wrought* (Brown *XIV*, No. 100) and several of the poems in Bodl. MS Digby 102 (e.g. Kail 1904, Nos 1, 7 and 22).

Litel and pouere is myn having,   *what I possess*
Britel and sone i-falle from hi;   *precarious; high*
Scharp and strong is mi deying,
I ne wot whider schal I;   *I do not know; I shall go*
Fowl and stinkande is mi roting –
On me, Jesu, yow have mercy!

One grim lyric, *Lullay, lullay, litel child, why wepestou so sore?* (Duncan *MEL*, No. 50), the first English lullaby and the only surviving poem of this kind in Middle English in which the baby addressed is a human child rather than the infant Jesus, reminds us that we are all born astride a grave:[10]

Child, thou art a pilgrim
    in wikkednes y-born,
Thou wandrest in this false world,
    thou loke the beforn!   *look ahead*
Deth shal comen with a blast
    out of a well dim horn,   *very dim horn*
Adames kin adoun to cast –
    himself hath don beforn.   *as he (Death) previously cast down (Adam)*
Lullay, lullay, litel child,
    so wo thee worth Adam,   *thus Adam became your misfortune*
In the lond of paradis,
    through wikkednes of Satan. (49–60)

The chilling prognosis offered by the mother here, contrasting with the innocence and vulnerability of the infant, too young to understand what is said to him and yet already marked out by Adam's Fall for a life of suffering and uncertainty, creates a powerful emotional frisson. From cradle to grave, the days of our failing life pass like a shadow. The pity, sorrow and fear generated by such a poem provided the affective focal point for the didactic message that it is never too soon to start preparing for and thinking about the Last Things. Purveying for the Last Things became a growth industry in the medieval period. Moral writing in the vernacular (whether in English, or, more commonly in the earlier part of the period, in Anglo-Norman or French) fed off the Christian Church's rich intellectual resources. Moral verse in medieval England was always in productive dialogue with the various Latinities (scriptural, liturgical, theological, academic and even pagan classical) available to medieval readers and writers.[11] As a result it was both responsive to human anxieties and uncertainties in matters of moral choice, penitential reformation and spiritual salvation, and also served to form, shape and give voice to a popular expression of those anxieties and uncertainties that was both timely and timeless.

Although still drawing heavily on the maxims and axioms of earlier ages, the moralists of the Middle English period were able to benefit from a framework of moral philosophy and theology more systematic and centralised than that

---

[10] Woolf, 155–6.
[11] Baswell 1999; Woods and Copeland 1999.

enjoyed by their pre-conquest predecessors.[12] They also benefited from a striking technologising of preaching as a primary instrument of instruction and exhortation; the form of sermons changed to a more systematic structure that encouraged lists and subdivisions (or *distinctiones*) to flourish. Manuals for the clergy appeared that provided lists and tables of such *distinctiones*, often rhyming to assist remembrance.[13] The sermon notebooks of friar John Grimestone (c.1375) preserve many such sets of *distinctiones*, which are easily mistaken for crude vernacular lyrics when considered outside of their proper context:

> Mors:
> It is bitter to mannis mende;   *mind*
> It is siker to mannis kende;   *certain; state*
> It is delere of al oure ende.   *the dealer*   (Wilson 1973, 23)[14]

Such listings, and similar *formulae* outlining the Twelve Abuses of the Age, or the Fifteen Signs before Doomsday (both derived from Latin antecedents, but widely circulated in vernacular contexts), or the Twelve Uses of Tribulation, or the errors of the world and the follies of human behaviour, became part of the preacher's stock in trade:

> *De Gloria Mundi*
> Werdis joye is menkt with wo;   *world's; mingled*
> He is more than wod that trosteth therto. *mad*
> Werdis gile is wol michil;   *very great*
> Therfore it is bothe fals an fikil.   *and*
> The werd passeth evere mo,   *world*
> And werdly love doth also.   *does*   (Wilson 1973, 18)

The narrative baldness and syntactic simplicity of such texts when presented as 'lyrics' reflect the fact that in their sermon or manual contexts they were never intended to stand alone, but operated as keynotes and catalysts within much longer explorations and expositions of moral doctrine.[15] But the occurrence of similar simply rhymed mnemonic tags and listings in books compiled or owned by the laity from the mid-thirteenth century onwards suggests that their mnemonic force soon carried them over from clerical contexts into wider circulation, along with more ruminative lyrics,[16] as one of the subtler poems in the

---

12 See Newhauser 1993. For a powerful exploration of the penetration of the psychology of confession and the new rhetoric of penance into vernacular literature, see Patterson 1991.

13 See Wenzel's various publications for a full account of this development and the role played in it by vernacular verse; see also Fletcher, 195–7 (below).

14 See the similar mnemonic and homiletic verses in the early fourteenth-century Franciscan preaching manual *Fasciculus Morum*: Wenzel 1978, 152; Wenzel 1989, 102.

15 The *Speculum Christiani*, a popular pastoral handbook designed to help priests exercise their care for souls, is peppered with mnemonic verses covering the catechetic syllabus, and longer verses (headed *Mores mundiales* in some copies) that rehearse the commonplaces of the *Cur mundus militat* and *contemptus mundi* traditions (e.g. Holmstedt 1933, 132–59).

16 For a discussion of this process in the Heege manuscript (NLS MS Advocates 19.3.1), see Hardman 2000, who comments: 'Booklet anthologies of moral and religious verse . . . must have been available to professional and private copyists both as copy texts and as a source from which selections and adaptations of material could be made' (15).

collection of tags and verses by the East Anglian churchwarden Robert Reynes shows:

> O Jesu mercy! What world is thys?
> Frendys be feer and feynte at nede.   *are distant and unreliable*
> Wo is hym hath don amys,
> And lyeth in peyne and may not spede.   *prosper*
> What Fortune will have it schal be had,
> Whosever will say nay.
> Therfor, lete it passe, and be not sad,
> And thynke upon Hym that alle amende may.   (Louis 1980, 254)

Although still essentially end-stopped, the syntax is more complex, the rhyme scheme (*ababcdcd*) slightly more ambitious, and the devotional psychology relies on manipulating the reader into faith and hope in Christ by the earnest reasonableness of the poem's voice. This tone is often found in longer, more accomplished lyrics reflecting on the fickleness of the world's glory. One such (which survives with music) is *Worldes blis ne last no throwe* (Duncan *MEL*, No. 38). Placing trust in this world's joys is tantamount to licking honey from a thorn:

> Man, why setstou thought and herte   *why do you set*
> On worldes blis that noughte ne last?   *does not last*
> Why tholstou that thee s'ofte y-smerte   *do you allow yourself so often to suffer*
> For thing that is unstedefast?   *transitory*   *[anguish*
> Thou lickest hony of thorn, iwis,   *honey; indeed*
> That setst thy love o worldes blis   *set your love*
> For ful of bitternes it is. (31–7)

It is, of course, not accidental that the growth of popular affective piety centering on the Passion of Christ happened at the same time as the upsurge in the circulation of moral and penitential lyrics. Devotion to the suffering Christ went hand in hand with a growing personal awareness of sin and guilt:

> O Jesu, lett me never forgett thy byttur passion,
> That thou suffred for my transgression,
> For in thy blessyd wondes is the verey scole,   *school*
> That must teche me with the worlde to be called a fole.
>
>   (Brown *XV*, No. 98, 1–4)

III

Whatever its stylistic and formal sophistication, vernacular moral and penitential verse still displays its appetite for proverbs and maxims. The avian protagonists of the early thirteenth-century *The Owl and the Nightingale* pepper their discourse with appeals to and citations from vernacular proverbial collections such as *The Proverbs of Alfred*. And the growth of Latin literacy through the teaching provided in medieval grammar schools served only to fuel and extend the taste for aphorisms. The Latin verse texts which students read and construed in these schools were always expounded in a carefully moralised light, and commentaries on those texts often used further proverbs and maxims to explain them.[17] The collection of set texts was always headed by the *Disticha* attributed to Cato, whose sententiousness appealed to contemporary taste. The *Disticha* were translated into English on several occasions, and collections of other proverbs and rhyming precepts in Latin and in English survive scattered in the margins and on the flyleaves of many English books.[18] One late medieval collection of proverbial couplets dramatises the interface between the sententious commonplaces of the Latin tradition and their equally formulaic vernacular equivalents:

> *Si quis sentiret, quo tendit, et unde veniret,*
> *Numquam gauderet, sed in omni tempore fleret.*
> Who would thynke of thynges two
> Wheyns he came and whyther to go
> Never more joye should se,
> Bot ever in gretynge be.   *weeping*   (Horrall 1983, 359)

Collections of this kind are part of the aphoristic bedrock of the lyric tradition.

It is entirely unsurprising, therefore, that a major collection of conventional and orthodox religious writing like the late-fourteenth-century Vernon manuscript not only contains one of the most substantial and important collections of moral lyrics but also prefaces that collection with bi- and trilingual sequences of proverbs derived from Scriptural, pagan and secular sources and retooled for the didactic purposes of Christian catechesis. Vernon's Anglo-French version of *Little Cato*, for example, renders the Latin maxim *Literas disce, consultus esto* [Study literature, be wise] with this much more explicitly targeted quatrain:

> Let holy writ beo thi mirour
> In word and eke in dede.   *also*
> Of wyse men tak thi counseyl
> That con the wisse and rede.   *can direct and advise thee*
>   (Furnivall 1901, 559)

The *Great Cato* (a translation of the expanded *Disticha*), meanwhile, has exhortations not to enquire into God's *privetees* [secret purposes] but also encouragements to pursue learning, as in the following, translating the evocative line *Nam sine doctrina vita est quasi mortis ymago*:

> Forthure thi wille with wisdam   *support*
> And sese not for to lere;   *cease; learn*
> Monnes lyf is lyk a ded ymage,
> Witles yif it were.   *without learning*
>   (Furnivall 1901, 587)

But the impact of those school texts was not always as predictable as it might appear. On the face of it the Latin *Elegies* of Maximian, with their laments for old

---

17 Bonaventure 1961; Hunt 1991; Woods and Copeland 1999; Gillespie 2005.
18 See the survey and bibliography in Louis 1993. The London grocer Richard Hill's collection of poems in Oxford, Balliol College MS 354 contains many proverbs in Latin and English: Dyboski 1907, 128–41.

age and lusts for young flesh, are not the most obvious subjects for study by impressionable schoolboys. But school commentaries on Maximian typically argued that the subject matter of the text was *gloria mundi* (generally understood in the sense of *sic transit gloria mundi* [thus passes away worldly glory]), and therefore to be assimilable to the moral theme of *contemptus mundi* [contempt for the world]. Maximian's poems left their mark on English vernacular poetry. *Herkneth to mi ron* (Brown *XIII*, No. 51) is a lyric version of his first elegy (admittedly the most morally explicit of the collection), preserved with the manuscript title of *Le regret de Maximian*. Maximian is described in the heroic terms of romance as *a modi* [valliant] *mon*

| That muchel of murthe won | *gained great joy* |
| In prude and al in pes. (5–6) | *honour; peace* |

The elegiac complaints of Maximian against the depredations of time and old age are aligned in this poem with the common stock of laments about transience. Maximian is the fairest man *with-houten Apselon* [apart from Absalom] (17), assimilating him at a stroke to the Nine Worthies whose passing is conventionally lamented in such *ubi sunt* poems. Maximian's haunting lament for the man who has lived too long embraces the key paradoxes, oxymorons, and inversions of such poems – *this day me thinketh night* (69); *Ich walke as water in wore* [I am like water in a muddy pool] (151) – and deploys the key trigger images of the fading of earthly beauty and joy:

Wen rose blostme blewe,	*when; flourished*
Me was murthe newe,	*happiness*
And nou ich am aswounde.	*I languish*
Wo is me the sithe,	*time*
Ne worthe I never eft blithe,	*I shall never again be happy*
I-brought ich am to grounde. (172–77)	

His long-suffering search for death, bolstered here by appeals to God for mercy, create a plangent and powerful effect. In effect, Maximian's Latin elegy has been brought into the popular lyric sub-genre of the Old Man's Lament (to which it may in fact have given shape). In this sub-genre, a dramatised *persona* laments his past misdeeds and the pains of his present existence as he awaits death with a paradoxical mixture of dread and longing, fuelled by a desire to be free from the sufferings of human existence and a fear of the judgement that his sinful life will have merited. The gloomy world of Old Testament transience is placed into the dynamic context of the romance hero who has fallen on hard times; his previous exploits in hall or on horseback serve only to highlight the steepness of his decline. *Hye Loverd, thou here my bone* (Duncan *MEL*, No 51), a lyric from the important collection in BL MS Harley 2253, similarly explores the passing of vigour and prowess in its poignant contrasts between past energy and dynamism and present weakness and decrepitude:

When I se stedes stithe in stalle,	*see strong steeds*
And I go halting in the hall,	*limping*
Myn herte ginneth to helde.	*sink*

That er wes wildest inwith walle   *one who formerly was*
Nou is under fote y-falle
And may no finger felde. (35–40)   *clasp*

The young blood of former days, 'wildest within castle walls', has now fallen on
evil times ('under foot'); no longer for him romantic dalliance ('holding hands')
with ladies. The poem manages to reinforce the corrosive effects of the Deadly
Sins in an elegantly concise analysis of the reason's for the Old Man's collapse,
reminding the reader of the applicability of the core catechetic teachings of the
church to the course of our lives as well as to the fate of our souls:

Evel and elde and other wo   *misfortune and old age*
Folewen me so faste
Me thinketh myn herte breketh a-two!   *heart will break in two*
Swete God, whi shal it so,
How may hit lenger laste? (47–51)   *longer*

The voices of such lyrics can say with Shakespeare's Richard II, 'I wasted time,
and now doth time waste me':

Slep me hath my lif forstole   *sleep (i.e. of sin); stolen away*
   right half other more;   *or more*
Away! too late Ich was y-war   *aware*
   now hit me reweth sore.   *now I regret it bitterly*
In slepe ne wende Ich ende nought   *I did not intend to end*
   though Ich slepe evermore,   *shall sleep*
Whoso liveth that wakerer be   *more vigilant*
   think of my lore.   *advice*
           (Duncan *MEL*, No. 37, 10–13)

In the fifteenth century, similar poems dramatise a meeting with an Old Man.
One such, Brown *XV*, No. 147, typically begins in the manner of a *chanson
d'aventure*:

As I went one my playing,   *for my pleasure*
Undure a holt uppone an hylle,   *beside a forest*
I sawe an ould mane houre make mornyng. (1–3)   *hoary old man*

The Old Man laments the speed with which life passes:

Owre levyng ys but one daye,   *life lasts but a day*
Ayeynst the world that evyre schal be; *compared to*
Be this matter I dare well saye,   *concerning this subject*
This world is but a vannyte. (61–4)

The final line (which serves as a refrain for the whole poem) is firmly and
emphatically invoked, as if its very conventionality gives it particular power to
close the issue and decide the debate. There is no interaction between the characters: the Old Man serves as a *memento mori*, a voice crying in an empty wilderness perpetually lamenting the end of his life's day as the shadows gather round
him.

This strand of the lyric tradition lies behind Thomas Hoccleve's presentation of his *hevy man* in the *Series*, where material derived from the *Synonyma* of Isidore of Seville (a text revealingly better known in the Middle Ages as his *Soliloquies*) is presented using the form of the Old Man lament:

> My liif is unto me ful encomborus   *burdensome*
> For whidre or unto what place I flee
> My wickidnessis evere folowen me,
> As men may see the shadwe a body sue, *follow*
> And in no maner I may hem eschewe.   *escape them*
>
>   (*My Compleinte*, Ellis 2001, 318–22)

Such poems serve to remind us that we have 'nor youth nor age, but as it were an after dinner sleep dreaming on both':

> Al that we have lyved here
> It ys but a dreme y-mete,   *is only a dream dreamt*
> For nowe yt ys as yt never were.   *as if it had never been*
> And so ys yt that ys to comynge yit. *yet to come*
>
>   (Brown *XV*, No. 148, 73–6)

IV

The unashamedly pragmatic moral strategy at the core of such poems ('don't leave it too late, as I did') remains relatively unchanged throughout the medieval period. In the fifteenth-century lyric, *In a noon-tiid of a somers day* (Duncan *LMELC*, No. 95),[19] a prosperous gentleman, equipped with the hawk and hound of lyric convention, describes how, while out hunting for sport, his leg becomes entangled on a briar whose every leaf has the word *revertere* written on it. Struggling to pull the briar away from his leg, he realises that he has himself become too entangled in the pleasures of the world during the noontide of his own life. This triggers several stanzas of meditation on youth and age, with an elegantly riddling mini-allegory (with the man's heart as a hawk in pursuit of the pheasant of pleasure) leading to the realisation that pleasure and delight are fast tracks to the primrose path that leads to the everlasting bonfire:

> Liking is modir of synnes alle,   *desire is mother*
> And norischeth every wickid dede;   *nourishes; deed*
> In feele myscheves sche maketh to falle *in many a mischief she causes (a man)*
> Of sorowe sche dooth the daunce leede. *she leads the dance*
> This herte of youthe is hie of port,   *arrogant* (lit. *high*) *in bearing*
> And wildenes maketh him ofte to fle, *fly* (i.e. *like a hawk*)
> And ofte to falle in wickid sort;   *into wicked company*
> Thanne it is beste *revertere*. (81–88) *then it is best to 'turn again'*

---

[19] This poem survives in two versions: Duncan *LMELC*, No. 95 (the longer version), and Gray 1975, No. 80 (the shorter). For a similar poem on the refrain *Convertimini*, written by John Benet, priest of Harlington, Beds., from 1442/3 to 1471, see Robbins 1972.

By comparison with vernacular verse recorded from the thirteenth century, such fifteenth-century moral and penitential lyrics are likely to be characterised by more florid diction, greater stanzaic complexity, elaborate paraliturgical or scriptural allusions (as here, to Isaiah 44.22:'Return unto me for I have redeemed you') and/or displays of multilingual macaronic prowess.[20] But whereas these later poems address themselves to mixed or unspecified audiences of lay and clergy, men and women, earlier deployments of the conventions were often aimed at more restricted audiences. The body of moral, ascetic, and penitential verse and prose targeted at recluses and anchoresses, for example, sought to provide those enclosed, consecrated but often minimally literate souls, with materials to empower their religious feelings and to restrain their imaginations in the spartan and denuded contexts of their enclosure. The affective strategy of Thomas of Hales in his *Love-Ron* (Brown *XIII*, No. 43), written at the urging of a young woman dedicated to the service of God, deliberately constructs around a standard *ubi sunt* lament a series of skilfully deployed and mildly riddling stanzas that provide in their tight structure and formally balanced phrasing a cumulative demonstration of the ways in which the world is *al so the schadewe that glyt away* [like the shadow that glides away] (32):

Monnes luve nys buten o stunde;	*but momentary*
Nu he luveth, nu he is sad,	*weary*
Nu he cumeth, nu wile he funde,	*go*
Nu he is wroth, nu he is gled,	*angry; glad*
His luve is her and ek a-lunde,	*also elsewhere*
Nu he luveth sum that he er bed;	*someone whom previously he fought*
Nis ne never treowe i-funde –	*he is never found constant*
That him tristeth he is amed. (49–56)[21]	*trusts; crazy*

Each stanza (or, occasionally, a small group of stanzas) offers a complete meditative unit exploring the overthrow of worldly expectation.

Hwer is Paris and Heleyne	*where*
That weren so bright and feyre on bleo,	*fair of complexion*
Amadas and Dideyne,	
Tristram, Yseude and alle theo? . . . (65–8)	*all those*

Paris and Helen, Amadas and Edoyne, Tristram and Isoude – all legendary lovers – have passed away: *al is heore* [their] *hot iturnd to cold* (78). The reader is thus encouraged to seek consolation in contemplation of the Christ child, who is presented as the permanent embodiment of the secular virtues swept away by time. Thomas reveals his strategy in the peroration:

This rym, mayde, ich the sende	*maiden; thee*
Open and withute sel;	*seal*
Bidde ic that thu hit untrende	*I ask; unroll*
And leorny bute boke uych del. (193–6)	*learn every bit by heart*
	(lit. *without book*)

---

[20] See the late, previously unrecorded macaronic lyric *Spes mea in Deo est* edited by Griffiths 1995.

[21] See the discussion and bibliography for this poem in Fein 1998, 11–31.

The metaphorical (or perhaps literal) 'roll' on which is written the riddling poem or *run* (figured here as a letter-patent) is to be unrolled, displayed, interpreted and 'learned by heart' by the reader. Such poems may well have been designed to be taken to heart literally as well as spiritually. The relative simplicity of the paratactic syntax and predictable rhyme scheme and the prevalence of end-stopped lines would have made memorisation relatively simple. But in his deployment of standard transience tropes, Thomas has both the stylistic decorum and the stanzaic discipline to move his reader to the unconditional love of God. Working with a restricted palate of ideas and verbal colours, Thomas ensures that his anchoress (herself restricted in knowledge and in lifestyle) can inhabit an expansive imaginative world that is charged with the grandeur of God.[22]

While it is true that 'Middle English religious poets construct the illusion of private feelings, spontaneously expressed, as a powerful element in the didactic rhetoric of their verse' (Kuczynski 1995, 123), it is also true that they usually construct this illusion from a common stock of phrases, life circumstances and penitential or spiritual gestures. In doing so, they often turned to the Scriptures for inspiration and example:

> O vanyte of vanytes and all is vanite!
> Lo! how this werld is turnyd up and downe. (Brown XV, No. 151, 1–2)

The language of the Wisdom books of the Old Testament supplies a ground bass of regret for the transience of worldly joys which modulates into a stoical rejection of those fickle pleasures. In the persons of David and Job, occupying adjacent books in the Old Testament, the poets found dynamic, psychologically plausible, and dramatically expressed role models for the protagonists of their own verse. The moral and spiritual trajectories of both men took them through puzzlement, dismay, anger, grief, despair, resignation, patience in the face of tribulation (a key medieval virtue, often explored and emphasised) and eventually hope and faith in the benevolence of God.

The Book of Psalms was read by many medieval readers as a vivid psychodrama of David's relationship with God, from which they could select poems appropriate to their spiritual moods or needs. The deployment of selected psalms into various liturgical and para-liturgical groupings (such as the Hours of the Virgin or the Hours of the Cross) allowed particular aspects of that relationship to be foregrounded. They provided emotional paradigms for medieval users to follow, and generated virtual spiritual dramas in which they could participate vicariously, or to which they could assimilate the circumstances of their own lives.One of the most popular of these subgroupings was the Seven Penitential Psalms (6, 31, 37, 50, 101, 129, 142 in the medieval numbering) which dramatise in particular David's sense of sin and yearning for forgiveness. The Penitential Psalms reinforced the Church's pastoral emphasis on regular auric-

---

[22] A similar technique can be observed in the embedded lyrics in the prose epistles of Richard Rolle, whose commentary on the Psalter probably contributed to his sense of the efficacy of short verse, and in the lyrics attributed to his school. See especially Ogilvie-Thomson 1988, 28 (84–91), 50 (1–25).

ular confession by showing David's monologues moving towards the point at which his acknowledgement of his sins, his recognition of his powerlessness to redress them, and his passionate calls for mercy and forgiveness unleash the redemptive grace of God.

Individual psalms from the sequence were often alluded to or translated in moral and penitential poems (especially Psalm 50, one of the most explicitly penitential), and there are two English verse translations of the entire sequence.[23] The version by the Carmelite Richard Maidstone (d.1396), in the eight-line ballade stanza often used for such moral poems after about 1380, translates and glosses each verse of the psalms into a single stanza. The result is a sort of prototype sonnet sequence, a one-voiced conversation with an absent and inscrutable beloved. The poems work either as stand-alone lyrics or as part of a cumulative verse monodrama (selective or strategic reading in longer religious texts was increasingly being encouraged by the end of the fourteenth century).[24] The popular Psalm 50 is explored by Maidstone in terms of the examination of conscience required of penitents before they make their confession to the priest. He substantially expands the Latin to bring this aspect to the fore, invoking not only the Deadly Sins but also the affective language of lyrics on the Passion of Christ, linking his sufferings with mankind's sins:

> *Cor mundum crea in me, Deus, et spiritum rectum innova in visceribus meis.*
> God make In me my herte clene,
> Thi rightful goost in me thou newe,   *spirit; renew*
> Fro synnes seven thou make hit shene.   *clean*
> [Wher so thou go I may the sewe]   *follow thee*
> Alas! Thi turmente for tene   *on account of malice*
> Thi body blak, thi bones blewe,
> Mekeful lord, [thou] make it sene   *visible*
> [Within] my herte, that hidouse hewe.   (Edden 1990, stanza 59, cf. stanza 62)

The stanza disposes of the Latin text in the first two lines and then expatiates in a series of end-stopped sense units that lend themselves to reflection and meditation (the internalisation of the wounds of Christ *within my herte* is a classic meditative manoeuvre). Maidstone hammers home the penitential aspect of these psalms (his prologue says that he has translated them *For synne in man to be fordon* [destroyed]):

> But whenne we dedly synnes do,
> Thi righte us demeth doun to helle;   *justice condemns us*
> But whenne we ceese and con saye 'hoo!',   *'stop!'*
> Thi mercy is oure wasshynge welle.   (stanza 64, 509–12)

In his expansions he draws in contemporary transience motifs (like the Three Sorrowful Things in stanza 31) to increase the impact of his exposition. In Psalm

---

23 Kuczynski 1995 offers the fullest discussion to date of these materials and their influence. Thompson 1988 and Fein 1988–9 both discuss the same paraphrase of Psalm 50 from the London Thornton manuscript (BL MS Additional 31042), which uses the increasingly fashionable 12-line ballade stanza.

24 See Gillespie 1989, and the comments in *The Myroure of Oure Ladye* (Blunt 1873), 65–71.

142, Maidstone's elaboration of the original reconfigures David's cry to be released from the dark places of despair to relate to the need of sinful man for God's help to escape from his own recurrent fall into the slough of sinfulness:

> He put me in places derke to be
> As tho that of this world ben dede;   *as those*
> My goost was greved upon me,   *spirit*
> Astoneyed was myn herte of drede.
> In this myscheef I may me se,
> Whenne-ever I do a dedly ded;
> Therfore, Jesu, ful of pite   *compassion*
> My lif out of this angur lede. (stanza 109)   *this distress*

The psalms had long provided the soundtrack of Christian yearning. Patristic writings are saturated with them, and they formed the major part of the daily Office of monks and priests. Much of the core vocabulary of David's laments had influenced Latin meditations like the *Meditationes piissimae*. But to come across phrases like *my lyfdayes like the smoke / Han fayled and awaywarde hyed* [hastened away] (569–70), or *my boones wanten* [lack] *pees and wele / For synnes that me thus deface* (219–20) in this paraliturgical context probably had the effect for contemporary audiences of invoking the imagery associated with moral and penitential writing. Certainly the other verse account of these psalms, made by the Franciscan Thomas Brampton, is prefaced in both its versions by dramatically realised prologues that present the protagonist turning to the psalms in times of trouble:

> In wynter whan the wedir was cold
> I ros at mydnyght fro my rest
> And prayed to Jesu that he wold
> Be myn helpe for he myght best.
> In myn herte anon I kest   *reckoned*
> How I had synned and what degre.   (Kuczynski 1995, 127)

Brampton places his paraphrase explicitly in the context of the speaker's examination of his conscience, and the rough attempt at dramatising the time and setting surely reflects the tendency of moral lyrics from the later fourteenth century onwards to create fictional locations and putative circumstances for their explorations of their penitential motifs. The second version of the prologue is even more specific in its placing of the poem in the context of the protagonist's particular circumstances:

> As I lay in my bed
> And sikenes revid me of rest   *robbed*
> What maner life that I had led
> For to thynke me thoughte it best.   (Kuczynski 1995, 128)

Here the examination of conscience brought about by sickness and the fear of death vividly (if clumsily) relates the following paraphrase not only to the *ars moriendi* [art of dying] tradition but also to popular texts on the uses of tribulation as spurs to spiritual renewal. Brampton is maximising his potential audience, and the utility and applicability of his work, by carefully situating his protagonist in a setting recognisable from a number of sub-genres of moral and penitential writing.[25] Witty, powerful and original lyrics such as *Farewell this world! I take my leve for evere* (Duncan *LMELC*, No. 102) recognisably inhabit the same imaginative spaces as these longer paraphrases, and are part of the same poetic spectrum of dramatic and spiritual paradigms:

Speke soft, ye folk, for I am leyd aslepe!	*softly; laid asleep*
I have my dreme – in trust is moche treson –	*dream; much deception*
Fram dethes hold feyne wold I make a lepe,	*gladly would I; leap*
But my wysdom is turned to feble resoun. (15–18)	*feeble speculation*

The sufferings of Job also attracted the attention of the poets: *thynk on Jop* [Job] *that was so ryche* urges one Vernon lyric, *By a way wandryng as I went* (Brown *XIV*, No. 105, 41), subtly educing salient aspects of Job's experiences. Versions of parts of the Office of the Dead, sometimes called *the nyne lessons of the Dirige, whych Job made in hys tribulacioun lying on the donghyll* (Fein 1998, 308), were more commonly known as the *Pety Job* or by their refrain *Parce mihi domine* [Spare me, O Lord]. Designed, according to the colophon of one copy, *to stere synners to compunccioun* [to stir sinners to remorse and contrition] (Fein 1998, 308), the poem is a version of the matins service from the Office, reworked and paraphrased using the same complex and demanding twelve-line ballade stanza found in *Pearl* (another poem about death and bereavement, of course) and in the most elaborate of the Vernon lyrics. It is comparable to *Pearl* in scale and ambition, and like that poem it combines an intensity of local effect (encouraging single sections or stanzas to be reflected on, ruminated over or applied to a reader's own life) within an overarching narrative that incrementally pulls the poem forward. The sequence dramatises Job's psychological progress in the face of grief and tribulation and expresses his plight with real intensity, elegance and imagistic force:

My dayes Lorde passed are,	
And olde I am, I am no faunt.	*infant*
My thoughtes wandre wyde whare,	*far and wide*
For they ben, Lorde, full variaunte.	
Myne herte they grevyn wonder sare,	*grieve; sore*
For ever about hym they haunte;	*it they lurk*
Thys maketh me to drowpe and dare	*to be downcast and fearful*
That I am like a pore penaunte!	*penitent*
Though I be, Lorde, unsuffisaunte	*unworthy*
Any helpe to gete of The,	
Yet, for I am Thy creaunte,	*captive*
Lorde, *Parce mihi Domine*!	(Fein 1998, 325, stanza 40)

The three rhymes of the stanza are effectively handled here (especially the pointedly desperate *penaunte / unsuffisaunte*), with the syntactically and metrically

---

[25] The prose commentary on the Penitential Psalms translated from the French early in the fifteenth century by Dame Eleanor Hull also suggests the influence of moral and penitential verse in the lexical choices she makes: Barratt 1995, 11, 15, 24, 193.

varying position of the word *Lorde* serving to create the illusion of spontaneity, urgency and a touch of panic in the voice of the suppliant. Some of the vernacular expansions of the Latin text seem to be imbued with the language and images of the lyrics on transience:

> I renne forth fro rowe to rowe,   *hither and thither*
> Somtyme before, somtyme behynde
> I grope as man that ys full blynde,
> But though I stomble, Thow folowest me.
> A, Lord, Though I to The be unkynde,
> Yet, *Parce mihi domine*.   (Fein 1998, 317, 247–52)

Here the tension is between the blind futility of human effort and the reassurance offered by the presence of God. That man's frantic search for meaning leads him to lack direction and ultimately to stumble is nicely suggested by the initial refusal of the stanza to make onwards progress towards its resolution until the need for God's mercy is recognised. But by the end of the poem, Job's prayer for deliverance from the pain of hell enacts the faith and hope he has acquired in the serenity and order of its syntax and the stateliness of its rhetorical balancing of ideas:

> The londe of woo and of wrechednesse,
> Where ben mo peynes than tonge may telle,
> The londe of deth and of duresse,
> In wyche noon order may dwelle,
> The lond of wepyng and of drerynesse,
> And stynkyng sorow on to smelle!
> Now from that londe that cleped ys helle,
> Worthy Lord, rescue now Thow me,
> So that I maye ever with The dwelle
> Thorough *Parce mihi domine*.   (Fein 1998, 333, 675–84)

The alliterative descriptions of hell create verbal collocations (*woo / wrechednesse; deth / duresse*) and then the alliterative consonants are elegantly blended together and varied in the third description (*wepyng / drerynesse*), while the anaphora at the beginning of each pair of descriptive lines (*The londe of*) establishes a reassuring rhetorical pattern. Although hell is indeed a place *In wyche non order may dwelle*, the poem is enacting in its own form the control exercised over its entropy by the providential Lord to whom the poem's prayer is addressed. This is writing that is both rhetorically stylish and theologically subtle. Its confidence creates from the scriptural texts a powerful, recognisable and often awesome mental landscape which its readers are invited to enter into and traverse, applying it to their own lives as they do so. So effective were the readings from Job in providing voices for the fears and griefs of suffering humanity that the refrain *Parce mihi domine* was often reworked and re-presented in lyrics of yearning:

> Yowthe ys now fro me agon
> And age ys come me upon;

Now shall y say and pray anon,
Parce mihi domine.   (Patterson 1911, No. 34, 7–10)[26]

More fancifully, in 'The Bird with Four Feathers' (Brown *XIV*, No. 121, Brown's title), a lyric which sometimes occurs in manuscripts with the *Pety Job*, the refrain is ascribed to a bird encountered by another of our sporting protagonists. Opening (as many fifteenth-century lyrics do) in the manner of the *chanson d'aventure* –

> By a forest syde walking, as I went
> Disport to tak in o morning. (1–2) –

this lyric continues as a dialogue. In an elaborate didactic and allegorical schematisation,[27] the bird laments the loss of its feathers (youth, beauty, strength and riches) through the vicissitudes of fortune and his own carelessness.[28] This sketchily dramatised and somewhat implausible scenario (the bird has a wife and children, goods, cattle and a castle) causes the protagonist to reconsider his own priorities and to seek solace in Job's own cry:

> I sette me down up-on my knee,
> And thanked this bryd of here gode lore;   *for her good teaching*
> It thought me wele this word *Parce*   *it indeed seemed to me*
> Was bale and bote of gostly sore. (233–6)   *both the painful effect and the*
>   [*remedy of spiritual hurt*

V

Nowhere are these semi-dramatised settings more effectively deployed than in the collection of moral poems found in a separate quire at the end of the Vernon manuscript. This massive anthology of orthodox and traditional religious writings (largely mirrored in its sister, the Simeon manuscript) establishes a *de facto* canon of the range and styles of vernacular religious texts in circulation in the last quarter of the fourteenth century.[29] Its compendious contents provide for all the moral and spiritual needs of its potential reader, whether lay, nun or clerical.[30] The occurrence of several of the poems singly or in clusters in other manuscripts suggests that the Vernon compiler had access to good sources and an

26 The Vernon lyric *As I wandrede her bi weste* (Brown *XIV*, No. 107), although using the refrain *Ay merci, God, and graunt merci,* borrows much of its setting and psychology from the Job story. See below for further discussion of this lyric.

27 For a similar allegory, see *The Quatrefoil of Love* (Fein 1998) and the discussion and bibliography there and in Fein 1999.

28 See the useful discussion and detailed bibliography accompanying the text in Fein 1998, 255–68. The poem is mainly in the 12-line ballade stanza, but has a few 8-line ballade stanzas, creating different densities of verse in different parts of the text.

29 The most recent critical discussions are Burrow 1990, Thompson 1990 and, especially, Matsuda 1997. See Pearsall 1990 for a conspectus of recent research on the whole manuscript in the wake of the publication of the facsimile (Doyle 1987). On the canon-forming effects of the book, see Hanna 1997.

30 The medieval list of contents to the book describes the collection as *Salus anime* or *sowlehele*.

interest in including in his book a wide range of examples of moral and penitential verse.

Certainly the Vernon poems cover a wide range of the key themes typically
found in this kind of vernacular verse: death and judgment balanced by grace
and mercy; the importance of self-knowledge; false friendship; trust and truth;
estates satire and the social and spiritual responsibilities of the gentry; and,
more pointedly (and perhaps more topically) than in earlier verse, the magisterial teaching role of the clergy and the laity's duty to obey and to avoid speculation on matters of faith. So a scripturally derived poem like *In a pistel that Poul
wrought* (Brown *XIV*, No. 100), with its telling refrain *Uche mon oughte himself to
knowe*, can work out the implications of the highly formulaic images it invokes
in a series of tightly argued stanzaic syllogisms:

Knowe thi lyf, hit may not last,	
But as a blast blowth out thi breth, –	
Tote and bi another man tast –	*look; test*
Riht as a glentand glem hit geth.	*fleeting gleam; goes*
What is al that forth is past?	*all that has passed away*
Hit fareth as a fuir of heth;	*a heath fire*
This worldes good awey wol wast.	*waste*
For synnes seeknesse thi soule sleth,	*sickness*
And that is a ful delful deth;	*lamentable*
To save thi soule, ar thou be slowe,	*before; slain*
With thi maystrie medel thi meth,	*with your power combine moderation*
For uche mon oughte himself to knowe. (25–36)	

This stanza divides like one of Gerard Manley Hopkins' curtal sonnets: the first
seven lines set up a proposition that invites the audience to reflect on the truth of
the observations by directing their attention outwards to other men (*Tote* [look]),
reaching the semi-resolution of the conventional wastage of earthly riches. Then,
focussing inwards, the final five lines proceed to a penitential diagnosis of the
sinful state of the soul and prescribe moderation, humility and self-knowledge
as antidotes to the poison of the world.

Again, in *As I wandrede her bi weste* (Brown *XIV*, No. 107), a *chanson d'aventure*
setting, is used to allow the protagonist to eavesdrop on a man settling to rest
under a tree. The grieving man then pours out his heart in a passionate act of
contrition and confession, analysing his faults and sins in the hope of attaining a
state of patient humility. Its narrative strategy is reminiscent of longer penitential poems, like the *Speculum misericordie*, where a dying man, injured in a fall
from his horse in a similar romance-like setting, is visited by allegorical figures
who help him to reflect on his faults and to confess his sins in preparation for his
unexpected and untimely death.[31] The Vernon poem allows the audience to see
a good confession at first hand (something that penitential practice would not
normally have allowed), and provides a series of proforma prayers. The whole
quasi-sacramental process is presented in a mildly alliterative form that would
not have been difficult to memorise:

---

[31] On the *Speculum misericordie*, see Robbins 1939b. See also the similar motifs in the *Speculum Gy
de Warewyke* (Morrill 1898).

Graunt merci, God, of al thi yifte   *gifts*
Of wit and worschupe, weole and wo; *understanding and honour, joy and sorrow*
Into the, Lord, myn herte I lifte,   *unto thee*
Let never my dedes twynne us atwo.   *set us apart*
Merci that I have misdo,   *have mercy on what*
And sle me nought sodeynly!
Though Fortune wold be frend or fo,
Ay merci, God, and graunt merci! (17–24)

The writing in the Vernon lyrics is consistently sprightly, skilful, rhetorically controlled, and displays an unusual sense of literary architecture. But these lyrics are also fascinating for their creative engagement with the standard themes of moral poetry, and the ways in which their assemblage at the end of the manuscript offers (not necessarily intentionally) a pattern book or portfolio of the dominant styles and motifs of this kind of verse. For all the stanzaic artfulness and the witty playfulness of their refrains, there are few motifs in the lyrics collected in Vernon that can not be widely paralleled from other, earlier moral and penitential poems, or indeed from the didactic and meditative works found earlier in the manuscript.[32] But that, in a way, is the point. Vernon's lyrics place the abstract teachings found earlier in the manuscript into tightly realised and carefully argued verse scenarios. The very familiarity of the attitudes and aphorisms when encountered in skilfully developed fictional encounters allows access into that dramatised environment for an audience that is already competent in the clichés of contempt for the world. Nowhere is this more stylishly and impressively demonstrated than in *Whon men beoth muriest at heor mele* (Brown XIV, No. 101), which displays in its fifteen stanzas a virtuoso command of the motifs of earlier poems on transience and death. Here is a poet who can bend the stanza form to his artistic will, and build from his largely end-stopped lines a compelling and forceful sense of the inevitability of his argument as awesome in its way as the inevitability of the dissolution it is foretelling.

As the laity began, in the course of the fourteenth and fifteenth centuries, to become increasingly articulate in the presence of the deity, orthodox teaching sought to remind the faithful, in the face of increasing Lollard attacks on the office of priesthood, that the clergy provided an essential and valuable guide in the ways of spiritual and moral growth, as well as access to the key sacraments of Penance, the Eucharist and Extreme Unction (administered to the sick and dying). The empowerment the laity though vernacular religious texts to enable them to progress in their devotional and sacramental lives needed to be balanced against the danger of diminishing the centrality of the institutional Church (dismissed by the Lollards as corrupt and irrelevant, and open to trenchant criticism at a time of schism and disarray) or the intermediary sacramental functions of its clergy.[33] Vernon's lyrics embody important aspects of the politics of vernacular spiritual writing in this period. *In a chirche, ther I con knel*

---

[32] E.g. the verse *The Sayings of Saint Bernard* (Furnivall 1901, 511–22) or *A lytel sarmoun of good edificacioun* (Furnivall 1901, 476–8), which has the dramatised setting and 8-line stanzas of some of the lyrics at the end of the book.

[33] See Watson 1995 and 1999; Gillespie 1989 and 2004.

(Brown *XIV*, No. 96), for example, dramatises the expository and magisterial function of the clergy. The protagonist has been kneeling in church and, having enjoyed a choral service, he approaches a priest and courteously asks him to expound the significance of the anthem or hymn that is being sung. The priest gives a brief but effective and affective explanation of the incarnation and the Trinity (*For al the world in wo was wounde / Til that he crepte into ur kinne*, 27–8), before excusing himself to continue saying his service, explaining that he has said all he can about why *clerkes wyse / And holychirche* (37–8) praise God in this way. The protagonist leaves the church, determined not to forget what he has been told. He is now emboldened to voice the significance of the teaching he has received for secular lords and those involved in the administration of justice. *Deo gracias* [thanks be to God], he asserts, is a prayer suitable for all occasions and circumstances of life:

In mischef and in bonchef bothe,	*adversity; well-being*
That word is good to seye and synge,	
And not to wayle ne to bi wrothe,	*wail; be angry*
Thaugh al be naught at ure lykynge;	*to our liking*
For langour schal not ever lynge,	*languor; last*
And sum tyme pleasaunce wol overpas,	*come to an end*
But ay in hope of amendynge,	
I schal seye, 'Deo gracias'. (49–56)	

The poet uses the eight-line ballade stanza to navigate his way cooly and deliberately through the conventional encouragements to suffer misfortune with patience. The poem is in effect a mini courtesy book: the gentility of the exchange between the engaged and committed layman and equally dedicated priest observes careful social decorum, and the layman's willingness to let the priest return to his duties is matched by the priest's care to relate his words to the authority and traditional teachings of the church. This is an idealised exchange between *gentil* [courteous] and gentle speakers, deployed at a time when intrusive and increasingly speculative quizzing of the clergy was starting to be a problem (especially as the clergy were apparently not always well equipped to answer the questions put to them).[34]

The issue is further alluded to in *I wolde witen of sum wys wight* (Brown *XIV*, No. 106), a stylish and skilful deployment of traditional transience motifs derived from Ecclesiastes (Sitwell 1950), but here packaged neatly and effectively into the twelve-line stanza that marks out the most ambitious of these late fourteenthc-century lyrics, and topped off with the all-together-now refrain *This world fareth as a fantasye*. The opening stanza snappily lays out the suddenness of unexpected death:

I wolde witen of sum wys wight	*would like to know; wise person*
Witterly what this world were;	*truly what the nature of; might be*
Hit fareth as a foules flight,	*goes; bird's*
Now is hit henne, now is hit here,	*far off*

---

[34] See Brown *XV*, Nos 119–21; Greene Nos 334–48 and 366.

Ne be we never so muche of might,	*so great in strength*
Now be we on benche, nou be we on bere;	*now we are; bier*
And be we never so war and wight,	*vigilant and valiant*
Now be we sek, now beo we fere,	*sick; healthy*
Now is on proud withouten peere,	*one proud without equal*
Now is the selve i-set not by;	*the same person thought nothing of*
And whos wol alle thing hertly here,	*whoever*
This world fareth as a fantasy. (1–12)	*an illusion*

The *dramatis personae* of such poems always seem to be rich and powerful but, although the rural gentry and nobility no doubt made up a significant part of the secular market for these kinds of vernacular texts, it is more likely that the social calibration of these protagonists is partly indebted to the patrician tone of Ecclesiastes and the other wisdom books, and partly predicated on the traditional nobility of those destined to suffer the vicissitudes of Fortune's wheel in Boethian tragedy.

This poem, though, does much more than just polish up and repackage the usual paradoxes and oxymorons. The poet uses the vanity tropes of Ecclesiastes to launch an assault against *alle theos disputacions* that *Idelyche all us ocupye* (33–4):

Uche secte hopeth to be save,	*sect; saved*
Baldely bi heore bileeve;	*confidently according to their belief*
And uchon uppon God heo crave –.	*they*
Whi schulde God with hem him greve? (61–4)	*trouble himself with them*

On one level this is a conventional attack on futile and sectarian academic speculation (and perhaps the factionalised state of the church during the years of the Avignon papacy and the Great Schism). But in the circumstances of late fourteenth-century England it is hard not to expect that it would have had a more pointed resonance for members of an English church assailed with its own sects and theological strains. This lyric advocates a fideism apparently devoid of scepticism, and is representative of an important new strand in moral lyrics that seeks to discourage idle speculation and questioning and to encourage trust and faithful obedience to the teachings of the church:

Wharto wilne we forte knowe	*to what end do we wish*
The poyntes of Godes privete?	*the particulars; secret purposes*
More then him lustes forto schewe	*it pleases him (God); reveal*
We schulde not knowe in no degre . . .	
Of material mortualite	*material mortal matters*
Medle we and of no more maistrie.	*let us concern ourselves; greater knowledge*
The more we trace the Trinite	
The more we falle in fantasye. (85–8, 93–6)	

Some clergy clearly thought that the laity should be seen and not heard: *keep* [guard] *thy tongue* is a regular theme in lyrics after 1380.[35]

---

35 See, for example, Brown *XV*, Nos 180, 181 (*A lytell spark may set a towne afire* (22)), 182; Kail 1904, No. 4; and the macaronic proverb *Of a lyttil sparkyll commeth a great fire /De modica magnus*

VI

When the world is always a 'cherry fair',[36] when every life passes like a shadow, when truth is always in chains, when Fortune's wheel is always turning,[37] and the bier is waiting at the gate, how can such texts be said to be 'affiliated' to a particular moment in history? This is one of the key challenges for approaches that seek to explore the socio-literary practice of medieval poets.[38] The abuses of the age and the evils of the world may be much the same from generation to generation (and certainly the poetic checklists enumerating them are remarkably stable across the centuries). But every age may with some justification feel that those abuses are particularly applicable to their own times. Equally, laments concerning such matters are so generalised and prophetically vatic in their formulation that it is often left to contemporary readers to create a specific bridge to the particularities of their own history. This is one of the great imaginative strengths of moral poetry. Such poems combine maximum referentiality (in that they are always applicable to the age in which they are read) with maximum deniability (in that their commonplace nature allows their authors to hide behind the conventionality of their language as a defence against charges of *ad hominem* satire).[39] The obliquely angled but pointed morality tropes of Chaucer's *The Former Age*, *Truth* and *Fortune* have frustrated most attempts to relate them to specific contemporary events, though Chaucer does on occasion invoke named recipients. The excellence and courtly poise of Chaucer's moral lyrics make them important (and strikingly elegant and skilful) witnesses to the ways in which the themes and images of Boethian philosophy were assimilated into the genres of moral poetry. His *Lak of Stedfastnesse* (Benson, 654) situates itself as a Boethian complaint against the Evils of the Age, reflecting and reinforcing the end-stopped predictability of the genre:

> The world hath mad a permutacioun
> Fro right to wrong, fro trouthe to fikelnesse,
> That al is lost for lak of stedfastnesse. (19–21)

---

scintilla nascitur ignis in Dyboski 1907, 130, 33–4, and compare with Chaucer's use of the same trope in the *House of Fame*, 2075–80 (Benson, 372). Hoccleve unsurprisingly uses the same theme in his call for religious orthodoxy in *Remonstrance against Oldcastle*, 137–60. The Vernon Proverbs warn against being a maker of *newe tales* (Furnivall 1901, 566) in ways that resonate with the warnings against careless talk in Chaucer's *Manciple's Tale*. On this issue more generally, see Wallace 1997, chs 8 and 9.

36 For examples of this comparison in the Vernon lyrics, see Brown *XIV*, Nos 103, 108 and 120. For examples in Digby 102, see Kail 1904, Nos. 3 and 14. It is a proverbial commonplace, used by Hoccleve in his *Regement of Princes*, by John Audelay in his lyrics, in the *Speculum misericordie*, and in various carols (e.g. Greene Nos 365 and 371) and lyrics (e.g. Brown *XV*, No.149, *Farewell this world! I take my leve for evere*, and No. 159, a lament for the soul of Edward IV, which bridges the gap between the conventional and the contemporary).

37 See, for example, Brown *XIV*, Nos. 28, 42, 96 (49–56) and 99 (17–24); Brown *XV*, Nos 151, 165–70.

38 E.g. Barr 1994 and 2001; Strohm 1989, 1992 and 1998; Coote 2000.

39 See the interesting discussion on the historicity of complaint poetry in Newhauser 2000, especially his comment (in relation to Harley 2253) that 'we must be ready to admit into our habits of reading a literature in which context is pretext and what appear to be topical allusions are doorways to a universal realm' (204).

Its envoy to Richard II directs at the unstable monarch recognisable homiletic and lyric imperatives:

> Dred God, do law, love trouthe and worthinesse,
> And wed thy folk agein to stedfastnesse. (27–8)

Appropriately this lament against instability is delivered in verse that is itself showily steadfast in its deliberate onward progression. Chaucer's most frequently preserved lyric, *Truth* (Benson, 653) – tellingly called in some copies a 'balade de bon conseyl' – exhorts its recipient (probably Sir Philip de la Vache, a long-serving member of the royal household) to abandon the world by means of a cumbersome bilingual pun on the recipient's surname (Vache 'beast'):

That thee is sent, receyve in buxumnesse;	*what; submissively*
The wrastling for this world axeth a fal.	*wrestling; invites*
Her is non hoom, her nis but wildernesse;	*no home; is nothing but*
Forth pilgrim, forth! Forth, beste, out of thy stal! (15–18)	*onwards; beast*

It is probably the conventional nature of such sentiments that gave rise to the legend that Chaucer made this poem *on his deeth bedde* (Benson, 1084). In attributing it to an Old Man dispensing wisdom on the point of death, the legend is invoking a conventional lyrical context for the performance of such a poem, a context defined as much by the elegies of Maximian or *The Consolation of Philosophy* as by Chaucer's own life and times.[40]

But the collection of moral lyrics in Bodl. MS Digby 102 offers the challenge of social and political immediacy in a particularly acute form. Apparently written over the first twenty years or so of the fifteenth century (that is, during the reigns of Henry IV and Henry V), it has been suggested that some of these two dozen poems allude to identifiable and dateable parliamentary debates and to key issues of political concern to the country's legislators and moralists in the first two decades of Lancastrian rule. These identifications, however, are very fragile.[41] The other works in the manuscript (an incomplete C-text of *Piers Plowman*, Richard Maidstone's *Penitential Psalms*, the *Debate of the Body and Soul* and the *Lessons of the Dirige*) suggest its affinity with collections of moral and penitential verse. Yet all these texts also have the potential to carry political freight. The psalmist David was a king and ruler beset with guilt about his illegitimate acquisition of power (arguably like Henry IV); *Piers* affiliates itself both with the strand of Lollard polemic that read Langland as a proto-reformer and with Langland's own powerful and idiosyncratic stance on the traditions of moral and penitential verse; even the debate of Soul and Body is open to a reading of the body politic in microcosmic/macrocosmic relation to the human body, a trope also found in one of the Digby lyrics, *Whereof is mad al mankynde* (Kail 1904, No. 15).

If moral poetry is not susceptible of application to contemporary events, it

---

[40] The logical extension of this is the inclusion of similar motifs in epitaphs and grave verses: see King 1981.

[41] See Turville-Petre (below), 179–81.

has effectively lost its purpose.[42] In applying the great and unchanging truths of moral complaint to the particular (though obliquely invoked) circumstances of their own age, the Digby poems oscillate between a declamatory and satirical standpoint that seems fired by contemporary zeal, and a more routine and unfocussed invocation of moral generalisation. The poems, probably all by the same person, manifest an obsession with the themes of truth and *trouthe* betrayed;[43] with the power of *glosers* [deceivers] and flatterers to pervert true doctrine and good legislation; with the need for Reason, Will and Conscience to work together; with the tensions between Wit and Will; with the role of money and Meed [reward/bribery]; with the need for religion and sound doctrine (the author was probably a cleric himself); with the merits of keeping quiet and listening attentively (a major and perhaps newly prominent theme); and, more satirically, with the need to learn duplicity and double-talk to survive in public life. These themes are reminiscent of those commonly found in *Piers Plowman* and in what has been called 'the *Piers Plowman* tradition' (Barr, 1993), and all those poems can profitably be studied in the context of this kind of moral verse. Indeed the Digby poet's apparent links with the church, law and government in Westminster and London place him firmly in the milieu that provided the main readership of Langland's poem.

Typically the mainly eight-line stanzas in Digby 102 are built from accumulating couplet aphorisms leading towards a refracting refrain line:

In kyngdom what maketh debate,	*conflict*
Riche and pore both anoyyed?	
Yong conseil and prevey hate	*immature; secret*
And syngulere profit ys aspiyed,	*particular*
Highe and lowe men abyyed;	*subdued*
Echon wayte other for to kille.	
That kyngdom mot nede be strighed	*destroyed*
That leveth wit and worcheth by wille.	(Kail 1904, No. 5, 25–32)

In most respects this is little different from the lists of the Twelve Abuses widely circulating from the twelfth century onwards in Latin, French and English. But (as in the cognate field of political prophecy) such generality is both a defence (this is what happens in any badly regulated kingdom) and an accusation (this is all happening NOW). When adjacent poems appear to be alluding to specific debates in parliament, the balance tips in favour of accusation. The collection contains apparently innocuous poems on preparing for death (*Man knowe thy self*

---

42 A few Vernon lyrics do relate overtly to identifiable historical events, most notably one poem written in the aftermath of the 1382 earthquake, linking together the rising of the Commons in 1381, the great plague and the earthquake as signs of impending danger, and perhaps as a warning to the so-called 'earthquake synod' of 1382. Boethian poems on the fall of kings (including one apparently spoken by the soul of Edward IV) usually lack much specificity. The poem composed for William Waynflete c. 1451 (Wilson 1983) blends moral commonplace and contemporary political and clerical issues in an artful and oblique melange.

43 On the prevalence of this theme in fourteenth- and fifteenth-century literature, see Green 1999. For examples of this theme in Vernon, see Brown *XIV*, Nos 103, 108 and 120; in Digby 102, see Kail 1904, Nos 3, 4, 12 and 13. On truth and treason linked to penance and contrition, see Brown *XV*, No. 57.

and lerne to dye is the refrain of Kail 1904, No. 7) alongside exhortations to parliament to address the pressing needs of the country, or possible references to the coronation of Henry V in 1413 (*God save the kyng and kepe the croun* is the refrain of Kail 1904, No. 12). Some poems are more satirically pointed, almost technical in their legal register, yet still using the standard buzzwords and inversion techniques of moral verse:

In alle kyngdomes, here lawe is wryten;	*their; inviolable*
For mede ne drede they chaunge it nought.	*bribery nor fear*
In Engeland, as all men wyten,	*know*
Lawe, as best, is solde and bought.	*like a beast*
Eche yer newe lawe is wrought,	*made*
And clothe falsed in trouthe wede,	*and falsehood dressed in truth's*
Fern yer was lawe; now nes it nought.	*years ago [garments*
We ben newe fangyl, unstable in dede.	*eager for change*
	(Kail 1904, No. 13, 25–32)

This poem has a menacing inevitability in its syntactical, lexical and stanzaic development. Bad social and moral outcomes flow unstoppably from the failings of English lawmakers:

Therfore the fals the false fede,	
Til trouthe in preson be faste alyede,	*consigned*
And dampne trouthe for falsed dede. (102–4)	*truth is damned by false deeds*

The oppressively restricted lexis here surrounds Truth literally and figuratively with falsehood to create a nightmare snapshot of a radically disordered society. In *The herrere degre, the more wys* (Kail 1904, No. 14) this inevitability is again harnessed to create a sense of the moral slipperiness of high office or status:

The herrere degre, the more wys;	*wiser*
The gretter worschip, the noblere fame;	*honour*
The herrere degre, the more nys	*foolish*
The gretter foly, the more blame. (1–4)	

Two alternative trajectories for a man's career (good and bad) are syntactically indistinguishable and yoked together by rhyme (*wys/nys; fame/blame*). Only careful moral discrimination can separate them: *Eche man be war, er hym be wo.*

Such stylish obliquity relies for much of its effect on an audience competent to detect the subtle nuances that are being inflected on the surface of conventional sentiments and commonplace moral teachings. In the writings of Thomas Hoccleve (d.1426), also writing for a literary coterie of fellow civil servants, holders of public office, book lovers and scribes in Westminster and the City of London, we see that obliquity being deployed in more playful and virtuosic forms. The poem described in colophons as *La Male Regle de T. Hoccleve* precisely and deliberately collapses the political macrocosm into the personal microcosm.[44] It purports to provide his confession of ill-living and a penitential intent

---

44 Thornley 1967; Knapp 1999, who sees it as a poem that 'yokes together the political and penitential genres in such a way that they work at cross purposes' (371), and 2001.

to reform addressed in playful invocation to the God of Health who, after years
of overindulgence, has removed his grace from Hoccleve:

> Who may conpleyne thy disseverance   *lament; departure*
> Bettre than I that, of myn ignorance
> Unto seeknesse am knyt, thy mortel fo?
> Now can I knowe feeste fro penaunce,   *feasting*
> And whil I was with thee kowde I nat so.   (Ellis 2001, 20–4)

The vocabulary of moral and penitential poetry is being played with here: the
fear of death; the need for penance that has been left too late; the urgings to self-
knowledge; even the feast that so often provides the setting for dramatised
moral lyrics (cf. Vernon's *Whon men beoth muriest at her mele*, Brown *XIV*, No.
101): all these are subsumed into a 'complaint' form whose tongue is firmly in its
cheek. Yet, as the ambiguous colophon implies, the personal is here also the
political, and the poem is also about bad rule in a macropolitical sense. Its coded
allegory unfolds into a powerful complaint against the abuses of the age.
Hoccleve's use of the eight-line ballade stanza signals his engagement with
moral verse, as does his elaborately over-rhetorical manner with its apostrophes
and invocations of authority. But this stylistic playfulness does not mean that
Hoccleve was not taking the subject seriously. Indeed his invocation in *La Male
Regle* of Robert Holcot's commentary on the book of Wisdom (249–64) shows
how knowingly he is invoking the moral stereotypes of complaint poetry to
make his case for the need to return both the kingdom and himself to health.
Later stanzas strike a series of rhetorical postures that emulate the end-stopped
sense units of much moral and penitential verse:

> As for the more paart, youthe is rebel
> Unto reson and hatith hir doctryne;   *teaching*
> Regnynge which, it may nat stande wel
> Wth yowthe, as fer as wit can ymagyne.
> O yowthe, allas, why wilt thow nat enclyne
> And unto reuled resoun bowe thee,   *the rule of reason*
> Syn resoun is the verray streighte lyne   *true*
> That ledith folk vnto felicitee? (65–72)   *happiness*

As a poet, Hoccleve is himself the master of the *verray streighte line*, and the
linear sententiousness of moral poetry suits his own preference for verse with an
open weave and a lucid progression. But this stanza is surely flirting with
humour in its hectic name checks of the mental powers of mankind (reason, wit,
imagination); its dangling before the audience of words that carried a political
and religious charge in Hoccleve's own time (rebel, reigning, doctrine); and its
eventual subjugation of them to the rule of Reason in a scenario that will lead
directly to personal and political felicity. His syncopated version of the tropes of
moral and penitential poetry shows the extent to which he could assume his
audience's familiarity with them and their imaginative complicity in their
playful deployment here:

> O god, o helthe! unto thyn ordenance,
> Weleful lord, meekly submitte I me.   *blessed*

I am contryt and of ful repentance	*sorry; fully repentant*
That evere I swymmed in swich nycetee	*folly*
As was displesaunt to thy deitee.	*displeasing*
Now kythe on me thy mercy and thy grace,	*show to*
It sit a god been of his grace free.	*it befits; generous*
Foryeve and nevere wole I eft trespace. (401–8)	*forgive*

The language of this stanza could be parallelled in any number of straightforward vernacular English verse confession formularies from the Middle Ages.[45] But, as with Pandarus's administration of confession and penance to Troilus as he seeks to gain the favour of the God of Love (*Troilus and Criseyde*, I. 932–8), such parodies are a reminder of how far the language, gestures and attitudes taught by such moral and penitential verses had penetrated into the collective consciousness of medieval England.

---

[45] See, for example, the simple confessional poems printed in Patterson 1911, Nos 1–4, and those in Brown *XV*, Nos 137–45, which are more artful.

5

Middle English Religious Lyrics

CHRISTIANIA WHITEHEAD

Middle English texts rarely, if ever, exhibit degrees of textual stability and closure similar to literary texts of later periods. Yet, even by this reckoning, the Middle English religious lyrics are a singularly heterogeneous brood. Exemplifying many kinds of composition, from close translation to so-called originality, and serving a vast spectrum of devotional purposes, from doctrinal exposition to quasi-ecstatic fervour, they are also notable for their disconcerting instability of form – appearing with or without music, with or without illustration, with differently ordered stanzas, or with differing numbers of stanzas, in varying manuscript contexts. It is sometimes said, perhaps in a bid to recover some semblance of generic unity, that the religious lyrics speak with a particular kind of voice – personal, sincere, involved, immediate. Nonetheless, even this needs to be qualified by the recognition of the many different rhetorical and performative stances this voice can assume, and of the diversity of its acts of speech: Christ's speech from the cross, Mary's sorrowing speech as pietà, the loving or self-reproachful address of the lyric 'I', speaking for all devout believers, to mention but a few. This chapter attempts to negotiate this heterogeneity, capturing major themes, offering paradigms for reading, and interrogating some received patterns of reading in the light of recent religious scholarship. However, since none of these issues can be addressed with assurance without a preliminary understanding of the origins of the lyrics, and of their varying functions and readerships, we shall begin our discussion by laying a few contextual foundations.

Studies in the provenance of the most major manuscript collections of lyrics prior to 1350 have demonstrated that the Franciscan order played a decisive role in the introduction and development of the vernacular religious lyric within England, up until the mid-fourteenth century.[1] The reasons that dictated this involvement are readily apparent. Committed from their earliest foundation to pastoral outreach amongst the laity, and well-known for the lyrical cast of their

---

[1] By adding MSS Digby 86 and Cambridge, Trinity College B.14.39 (formerly ascribed by R. H. Robbins to the Dominicans) to the list of more established Franciscan manuscript miscellanies, MSS Digby 2, Oxford, Jesus College 29 and BL Harley 913, David Jeffrey argues that practically all of the early 'friars' miscellanies' of lyrics should be viewed as Franciscan productions (Jeffrey 1975, 203–7). In addition, in a recent essay, he also comments on the 'Franciscan' qualities of the important, early fourteenth-century poetry anthology, BL MS Harley 2253 (Jeffrey 2000). The extent of Franciscan influence on such manuscripts is, however, open to question: see Boffey (above), 7–8.

spirituality (an ardent lyric writer himself, Francis envisaged his followers as evangelists who would 'sing' men into the kingdom of heaven), the Franciscans appear to have viewed the vernacular lyrics as effective evangelical tools, utilising them within sermons to win the hearts and excite the emotions of those whom they addressed, as well as envisaging them as spurs to more personal and private devotion.[2]

Composed to serve this devotional and pastoral purpose, early Middle English religious lyrics are primarily informed by two textual traditions. On the one hand, some lyrics appropriate the metres and idioms of popular songs, adapting their romantic or convivial subject matters to more spiritual imperatives. The related lyrics, *The Way of Woman's Love* and *The Way of Christ's Love*, in BL MS Harley 2253, have traditionally been regarded in this light: the later conceived as a religious revision of the former.[3] However, the majority of the religious lyrics draw closely upon a much more learned background, improvising upon phrases derived from the liturgy or from the scriptural lessons associated with the major church festivals. Some of these lyrics are little more than verse translations or paraphrases of liturgical material, the lyric opus of the Franciscan theologian, William Herebert (c.1270–1333), contained in BL MS Additional 46919, serving as a case in point.[4] The majority of Herebert's lyrics consist of vernacular translations of Latin hymns or antiphons associated with specific seasons within the church calendar,[5] while several of the remainder, including Herebert's best-known work, *What ys he, thys lordling, that cometh vrom the vyht* (Gray 1975, No. 40), are vigorous, idiosyncratic versifications of passages from scripture associated with key feasts within the ecclesiastical year.[6] Lyrics by other writers engage with liturgical and scriptural material in looser and more creative ways. Some interweave liturgical Latin phrases with vernacular images and invocations to produce a macaronic effect, as in these lines from a lyric by the late fifteenth-century Franciscan, James Ryman:

> O emperesse, the emperoure
> > *Quem meruisti portare,*   *whom you were worthy to bear*
> Of heven and erthe hath made the floure: *made thee flower*
> > *Regina celi, letare!*   *queen of heaven, rejoice!*
>
> O quene of grace, the king of blisse
> > *Quem meruisti portare,*

2   One of the earliest attested Middle English Franciscan lyrics, the *Love-Ron* of the Franciscan friar, Thomas of Hales, written between 1234 and 1272, addresses a young woman in religious orders, recommending regular singing of the *love-ron* [love song] as a way of strengthening her dedication to chastity and her love-longing towards Christ. See Fein 1998, 32–8; also Gillespie (above), 79–80.

3   Brook, Nos 31, 32. For an alternative account of *The Way of Woman's Love* as an obliquely devotional poem addressed to the Virgin, see Jeffrey 1975, 213.

4   See Reimer 1987. Over half of the lyrics in the well-known preaching notebook of Friar John of Grimestone, NLS MS Advocates 18.7.21 (c.1372), are also direct translations of Latin texts.

5   For example, *Conditor alme siderum*, a translation of a ninth-century Advent hymn, and *Eterne rex altissime*, a translation of a fifth-century Ascension-tide hymn. Reimer 1987, 123–4, 130–1.

6   *What ys he, thys lordling* is a loose translation of Isaiah 63:1–7, a passage applied to the post-crucifixional appearance of Christ in the reading for Wednesday of Holy Week.

Hath made thy sete next unto his: seat / throne
   Regina celi, letare!

(Duncan *LMELC*, No. 52, 1–8)

In this instance, the Latin refrain is taken from the antiphon *Regina caeli laetare.*[7]
On other occasions, a single line from the liturgy or from scripture operates as a
springboard for more extensive vernacular reflection. In William Dunbar's *Hale,
sterne superne* (Duncan *LMELC*, No. 55), an aureate hymn in praise of the Virgin,
the opening line of the Angelic Salutation, *Ave Maria, gracia plena,* is repeated as
the ninth line of each stanza, situating Dunbar's extravagantly ornamental
evocations of Mary – e.g. *Bricht ball cristall, ros virginall* (79) – as a series of
exuberant and creative figurative variations upon a scriptural and liturgical
theme.[8]

   In addition to considering the textual traditions underlying the lyrics, it is also
necessary to take account of the social and textual environments within which they
originally appeared. We have already commented briefly upon the Franciscan
partiality for incorporating lyrics into their sermons. Siegfried Wenzel has identified a variety of purposes to which a lyric could be put within a homily – from
rendering its structural divisions, to warning or admonishing congregations, to
providing a memorable epitome of its main themes.[9] Wenzel also suggests that
many longer, more 'poetic' and more emotive Passion lyrics, that do not readily fit
this pedestrian bill, may possibly have been intended for use within Good Friday
homilies, when the traditional thematic structure of the sermon tended to be
replaced by a narration of the Passion, intersected by interpretative comments and
reflections.[10] Sermons and sermon handbooks played a considerable role in
shaping the early history of the Middle English religious lyric.[11]

   A significant number of religious lyrics (especially those in circulation prior
to 1375) evolved to meet pastoral and homiletic needs. However, alongside this
public function, it is also possible to uncover instances of lyric composition and
recitation in more closeted or individuated circumstances. The works of Richard
Rolle, the fourteenth-century Yorkshire hermit, provide an instance of the use of
lyrics in the service of far more sophisticated spiritual practices – as contributions to the act of contemplation.[12] Writing within a devotional tradition of
rhapsodic affectivity that makes pronounced use of the spiritual senses, Rolle
frequently describes his mystical experiences by utilising the vocabulary of
melody and song. His readiness to perceive an affinity between rhythm and
ecstasy presumably underlies his decision to couch many of his own written

---

[7] Another well-known example is the unusually abstract carol *Ther is no rose of swych vertu*
     (Duncan *LMELC*, No. 46), which incorporates a number of Latin phrases from the
     twelfth-century sequence, *Laetabundus exsultet fidelis chorus.*
[8] For a detailed recent analysis of this poem, see Gray 2001.
[9] John of Grimestone's alphabetical handbook and the anonymous handbook, *Fasciculus
     Morum,* are amongst the best-known examples of Franciscan preaching manuals that incor-
     porate considerable numbers of vernacular lyrics.
[10] Wenzel 1986, 146–51. Less convincingly, Wenzel also argues that nativity lullabies, such as
     the ones in John of Grimestone's preaching notebook, may also have played some part in
     Good Friday sermons.
[11] See further Fletcher (below), 190–209.
[12] For an account of a more mystical English lyric tradition, see Gray 1997.

meditations in lyric metre, suggesting that he regarded them as earthly reflections of heavenly sound. It also seems likely that it influenced his decision to provide his female disciples with a number of *cantus amoris* [songs of love] for *syngand gastly . . . noght bodyly cryand wyth mouth . . . when thou covaytes hys [Jhesu] comyng and thi gangyng*,[13] indicating that he viewed this practice of interiorised song as an effective way of initiating and stimulating contemplative experience.

Lyrics could play a part in facilitating contemplation. Yet, at the other end of the spectrum, particularly in the fifteenth century, it is also possible to find many examples of occasions when they were read or privately recited with far more mechanical and instrumental ends in mind. It can come as a shock to realise that the starkly powerful fifteenth-century lyric, *Wofully araide* (Duncan *LMELC*, No. 71), in which the crucified Christ presents his violated body as a reproach to mankind, is accompanied in one manuscript (BL MS Harley 4012, fol. 109r) by a rubric specifying the number of years of relief from purgatory that result from its recitation. Similarly, Lydgate's lyric, *The Dolerous Pyte of Crystes Passioun* (MacCracken 1911a, I, No. 47), which seems to have been designed to work in conjunction with an actual *imago pietatis* (an image of Christ presenting his wounds), but which also effectively reiterates that image through words, closes with a stanza promising thousands of years of purgatorial remission to believers who develop a daily devotion to this *pyte* [piteous image]. Other lyrics set great store upon the protective and beneficent power of certain words and phrases, pondering Latin tags extracted from their original scriptural or liturgical context with a naïve admiration that borders upon awe. In one of the Vernon lyrics, *In a chirche, ther I con knel* (Brown *XIV*, No. 96), the affectedly simple narrator describes how, having encountered the phrase *Deo gracias* in the course of the Mass and ascertained its meaning from a *selk . . . clud* clerk, by dint of reverential private repetition (*twenti tymes I con say*) the words began to assume a kind of talismanic power for him: *In mischief* [adversity] *and in bonchef* [well-being] *bothe, / That word is good to seye and synge* (43, 49–50).[14]

Rolle intended his spiritual songs for a coterie of nuns and anchoresses, and it seems probable that the Vernon manuscript was primarily compiled with an audience of nuns in mind (Riddy 1993, 106). However, by the fifteenth and early sixteenth century, in addition to their continued voicing in sermons, it is important to note the extent to which religious lyrics were also beginning to be used privately by devout middle- and upper-class laypeople to support personal daily programmes of meditation and devotion. Alexandra Barratt has drawn attention to the close links between the devotions and prayers of the primer – that most popular of late medieval, middle-class possessions – and the contents of many fifteenth-century passion lyrics,[15] suggesting that these lyrics may well have been intended to operate within the same devotional setting. More recently, Eamon Duffy has remarked upon the way in which verse translations

---

[13] Richard Rolle, *The Form of Living* (in Allen 1931, 106–7, lines 65–7, 94–5).

[14] For additional examples of poems enclosing authoritative written tags or *tituli*, see Boffey 1997, 142–4.

[15] Barrett 1975. For a recent, detailed account of the use of the primer in fifteenth-century England, see also Duffy 1992, chs 6–8.

and paraphrases of prayers from the primer, together with other associated devotional poems, were frequently copied directly into its margins and flyleaves by various lay users, effectively expanding it to encompass an additional range of vernacular devotions (Duffy 1992, 224). The religious lyrics framed the devotions of the primer. In addition, they were also copied into miscellaneous commonplace books, a further demonstration of middle-class use and possession. The best-known of such books, Oxford, Balliol College MS 354, compiled by Richard Hill, an early sixteenth-century London grocer, contains upward of eighty religious and moral lyrics, copied in amongst other literary, domestic, and proverbial items.[16]

What was it about the spiritual tone of these lyrics that gave them such widespread appeal? In order to answer this question satisfactorily it is necessary to devote some attention to the influential tradition of affective piety that dominated many areas of devotional practice from the twelfth century up until the Reformation. Developed initially within the houses of 'new' religious orders such as the Cistercian order, and expounded with greatest eloquence by theologians such as Anselm, Bernard, and William of St Thierry, affective piety evolved as a practice in which religious practitioners were encouraged to show devotion to Christ through the prayerful engagement of the emotions or 'affections', rather than the intellect. In order to stimulate these 'affections' successfully, emphasis was generally placed upon the manhood of Christ, and practitioners were exhorted to use their imaginations, together with the gospel accounts, to develop a detailed mental picture of his humanity. Their consequent meditative response to this mental image could assume a variety of forms. Practitioners were frequently encouraged to develop an intimate and informal response by drawing upon their memories of familial and romantic relationships, and relating to Christ as to a son, brother, father, or bridegroom.[17] On other occasions, as we shall explore in more detail later in this chapter, they were encouraged to empathise with the experiences and sufferings of Christ by pursuing more direct forms of identification. However, whatever the form of identification employed, in all cases affective empathy was judged to facilitate repentance and moral reformation, and, as such, was invariably envisaged as a salvatory mental stratagem.

Religious practitioners were encouraged to sift through the gospels in their search for the narrative information necessary to build a detailed meditative image of Christ. In addition, as a way of resolving the problems posed by the gospels' numerous narrative lacunae and their affective deficiencies, they also began to be provided with more emotive and closely focussed accounts of episodes from the life of Christ, in particular the Passion, in thirteenth-century texts such as Edmund of Abingdon's *Speculum ecclesiae*, Bonaventure's *Lignum vitae*, James of Milan's *Stimulus amoris*, and Jacobus de Voragine's *Legenda aurea*. The accounts pioneered by these writers were extended and systematised in the

---

[16] Dyboski 1908. A table of the manuscript's contents is given on xxxiv–lix.

[17] One of the most famous of the vernacular lyrics, *In the vaile of restles mynd* (Gray 1975, No. 43), experiments with a number of gendered and relational modes, evoking Christ as a bridegroom and a mother.

course of the fourteenth century in texts such as Ludolf of Saxony's *Vita Christi* and the enormously influential pseudo-Bonaventuran *Meditationes vitae Christi*.[18] Finally, several of these texts, most notably the *Meditationes* and the *Stimulus amoris*, were translated into Middle English in the late fourteenth and early fifteenth centuries,[19] bringing carefully monitored versions of the emotional intensity of the affective regime within direct reach of the lay middle class.[20]

As stated above, many of these texts supply verisimilar details absent from the gospels – the colour of Christ's body on the cross, the climatic conditions at the time of the nativity, the precise wording of Christ's prayer in the Garden of Gethsemane. In addition, they also take advantage of the circumstances of affective meditation to diminish spatio-temporal difference, exhorting the meditator to imagine himself present as an observer, or even as an active participant, in a variety of gospel settings. In the chapter upon Christ's passion in his *Mirror of the Blessed Life of Jesus Christ*, Love repeatedly invites the meditator to 'see' the parts of the passion process as events within a contemplative and ahistorical 'present':

> Now with inwarde compassion behold him here . . . so passyng faire a yonge manne, most innocent & most lovely in that maner alle to rent, & wondet, & alle blody nakede.
>
> (Sargent 1992, 173)

Later, towards the close of the chapter, after the Virgin and disciples have finally departed from Christ's tomb, he/she is encouraged to pursue a yet more participatory role:

> And thou also by deuoute ymaginacion as thou were there bodily present, confort oure lady & that felawshipe praiyng hem to ete sumwhat.
>
> (Sargent 1992, 190)

In many instances, it is quite valid to view the religious lyrics as a series of 'stills' from this meditative tradition of gospel animation, isolating brief passages from the narrative of Christ's life and recasting them via rhyme and metre into a number of relatively self-contained devotional units. The well-known Harley lyric, *Stond wel, moder, under rode* (Duncan *MEL*, No. 91),[21] depicting a tense, unresolved dialogue between Christ and Mary at the foot of the cross, serves as an example of this type of excerpted conversation, as does *A sory beverage it is* (Duncan *MEL*, No. 98), an unframed lyric elaboration of Christ's prayer in the Garden of Gethsemane, and the version of the lyric *As Reson hath rulyd my recles mynde* in MS Harley 3954, fol. 90a, in which the meditator acts to relieve the

---

18 For supplementary examples of affective narrations of this kind within the Middle English mystical tradition, see the two passion meditations of Richard Rolle, and the passion 'showings' described in Julian of Norwich's *Revelation of Love*.

19 The *Meditationes* and the *Stimulus amoris* as Nicholas Love's *Mirror of the Blessed Life of Jesus Christ* (Sargent 1992) and *The Prickynge of Love* (Kane 1983), respectively.

20 For recent accounts of the way in which Nicholas Love adapted the *Meditationes* to oppose Lollardy, support ecclesiastical practice, and circumscribe the workings of the imagination, see Sargent 1992, xliv–lviii, Beckwith 1993, 64–70, and Renevey 2000, 202–4.

21 This lyric bears a relation to an earlier Latin sequence, *Stabat iuxta Christi crucem*.

Virgin's grief after the crucifixion by attempting to revive her from a swoon.[22] On other occasions, this tradition is used to regulate the tone and reception of more ambitious narratives, such as the fifteenth-century lyric, *Brother, abyde, I the desire and pray* (Duncan *LMELC*, No. 72), which relates the entire history of Christ's life, from birth up until death.

Identifying the tradition of affective meditation upon Christ's humanity, then, as the key devotional context underlying the content and expression of many religious lyrics, the remainder of this chapter will be dedicated to showing the various forms that affectivity can take in different categories of lyrics, and to a closer investigation of the meditational tools of image, memory and identification, by which emotional involvement with Christ is initiated and maintained. It seems appropriate to begin with a brief discussion of the nativity lyrics. Lyrics utilising the nativity as their primary meditational focus emerge comparatively late within the Middle English devotional corpus, making their first recorded appearances in John of Grimestone's preaching notebook of 1372.[23] Nonetheless, despite their rapid rise to popularity in the decades which follow, and in the fifteenth century, it is necessary to point out that the majority of these lyrics are technically 'carols', a form generally designed for group singing in settings of public celebration or conviviality rather than for private meditation.[24] The public context of much carol singing appears to have fostered an objective, relatively impersonal approach to the subject of the nativity. However, on occasion, particularly in the earlier lyrics, it is also possible to see glimpses of a more affective and empathetic concern. Attention is repeatedly focussed upon the intimate lyric exchange between mother and child, as Mary lulls her child to sleep, and upon her concern to protect her newborn from the hardships of the physical environment, engaging the sympathetic understanding of the parenting laity. The pathos of juxtaposing Christ's birth with the anguish of his subsequent death – whether anticipated by the Christ-child in the cradle, or helplessly foreseen by the narrator – is also exploited, as is, upon occasion, the gruelling pathos inherent in Mary's painful ignorance of what the future holds for her son.[25]

On other occasions, affectivity is exchanged for ingenuity, and the lullaby to the Christ-child is used to view familiar events from a new perspective, or to illustrate doctrinal symmetries. In *As I lay upon a night* (Duncan *MEL*, No. 81), Mary responds to her child's request for a song by relaying the events of the Annunciation, ingeniously superimposing two key moments in salvation history, while in *Lullay, lullay, litel child* (Duncan *MEL*, No. 107), the Grimestone lullaby in which a repentant Eve sings to the Christ-child, acknowledging his

22 Furnivall 1866, 238–42, lines 7–12, cited in Woolf, 262. For an account of a participatory response to the events of the passion narrative which threatens to get out of hand, see Renevey 2000, 205–8.

23 However, Karen Saupe cites the use made of the nativity in earlier lyrics upon the Five Joys of Mary. She also links late fourteenth-century interest in the nativity as a distinct subject to the emergence of the Middle English Mysteries. Saupe 1998, 22.

24 For fuller information on the form, purpose and origins of the medieval carol, see Woolf, 383–8, Greene, xxi–clxxii, and Reichl (below), 150–70.

25 The fifteenth-century lullaby *This endrys nyght* (Duncan *LMELC*, No. 66), in which the Christ-child's increasingly disturbing revelations of his future fate are intertwined with Mary's placid and unregarding lullaby refrain, serves as an example of this pathos.

birth as the solution to her transgression, scriptural time is collapsed on a yet more dramatic scale, transposing both protagonists into a purely textual space of penitential interaction, outside linear time.

> But for my sinne I wot it is   *only; I know*
> That Goddes sone suffreth this,
> Merci lord, I have do mis,   *done wrong*
> Y-wis I wile no more. (8–11)   *certainly*

Several later nativity lyrics extend this movement towards temporal abstraction. *Ther is no rose of swych vertu* (Duncan *LMELC*, No. 46) fractures the nativity into a series of compressed and haunting variations upon a single metaphor (Mary as rose), subjecting this metaphor to ever more severe degrees of conceptual strain: *In this rose conteyned was / Heven and erthe in lytyl space* (7–8). *I passed thoru a garden grene* (Duncan *LMELC*, No. 63) transforms the events of the nativity by imagining them in a wholly different way, transposing the various key players into the forest of courtly romance and reassembling them along a linear route as goals of questing endeavour. Thus, as the narrator proceeds through this wood he encounters first of all (line 5) *a mayden bryght off hew* (a romance substitution for the Virgin), then a group of shepherds, and finally, *threo commely kynges* (34), all singing the refrain *verbum caro factum est* (8, etc.). The effort of generic translation required to convert these forest voices back into participants in the traditional tableau of the nativity may be correlated with the act of linguistic translation required to decode the nature of the event that has generated all these voices (the word made flesh). Such efforts of interpretation please the literary and linguistic intellect, while the poetry that imposes them simultaneously exhibits a poise and creativity that offers its own satisfaction. Nevertheless, it remains a world away from the loving imagination of the crib found within 'Bonaventuran' meditational texts.

Alongside their experimentation with different forms of affectivity and ingenuity, many of the nativity lyrics are also notable for their self-reflexive concern with the act of singing. Perpetuating the contemplative dictum that devotional song acts both as a 'likeness' of heavenly melody, and as an avenue facilitating participation in it,[26] albeit at a far simpler register, a number of lyrics devotes considerable space to valorising their own melodic voice. They achieve this by foregrounding the shepherds' song as a reflection of heavenly song, and as an exemplary response to the incarnation, implicitly inferring that their own lyric resumé of the nativity carries equivalent power.[27] If singing holds such exemplary status and carries such salvatory implications, small wonder then, that the most frequent form of anxiety or crisis in the nativity lyrics concerns moments where singing threatens to break down, as with Mary, cradling the infant Jesus (*Whan I thenke of thy mischeef, / me list wel litel singe*, Duncan *MEL*, No. 82, 15–16) or with the speaker in the carol *The shepherd upon a hill he satt* (Duncan *LMELC*,

---

[26] See the earlier discussion of Richard Rolle.
[27] For example, *I saw a fair maiden* (Duncan *MEL*, No. 80), *When Cryst was born of Mary fre* (Duncan *LMELC*, No. 58), and *Abowt the fyld thei pyped full right* (Duncan *LMELC*, No. 60).

No. 59) who questions his emotional ability to live up to the music of Joly Wat the shepherd's rapturous account of the nativity:

> 'Can I not syng but 'hoy',
> Whan the joly sheperd made so mych joy?' (1–2)

While the nativity lyrics retain affectivity as a tonal option alongside other types of convivial or ingenious expression, it assumes pride of place once we turn to the crucifixion. The change in attitude towards the crucifixion that takes place in the course of the twelfth century, and the reasons that motivate that change, are so widely known that they require little repetition here. Consequently, it is probably sufficient to say that, while pre-twelfth-century versions of the crucifixion portray the event, in more impersonal terms, as the occasion of Christ's heroic triumph over the devil,[28] changes in the doctrine of atonement developed during the twelfth century, taken in conjunction with the affective emphases of Anselm and Bernard, gradually engender a revised understanding, in which Christ's death is interpreted as the supreme expression of his love for mankind, demanding an equivalent response of love in return.[29] On occasion, this understanding is developed very literally, as in the Bernardine comment in the Legenda aurea, in which Christ's outstretched arms and bowed head upon the cross are interpreted as passionate gestures:

Uidelicet caput inclinatum ad osculum, brachia extensa ad amplexum, manus perforatas ad largiendum, latus apertum ad diligendum, pedum affixionem ad nobiscum commanendum, corporis extensionem ad se totum nobis impendendum.[30]

A devotional commonplace, vernacular versions of this comment reappear in several religious lyrics.[31] On other occasions, the erotic possibilities of this love are developed by drawing upon a succession of sensuous images from the Song of Songs,[32] painting the love expressed by Christ on the cross and returned by the devout onlooker as a type of nuptial encounter. Thus, in Alas! Alas! Wel evel I sped! (Duncan MEL, No. 71), the bridegroom who stands outside the door and knocks in the Song of Songs 5:2 is reconfigured as the crucified Christ, suing for

---

[28] This general perception may require some fine-tuning in the light of Bennett's disclosure of occasional images of a 'suffering and dejected Christ' in pre-conquest English iconography. Bennett 1982, 32–3.
[29] For a seminal discussion of this shift as a background to vernacular passion lyrics, see Woolf, 21–7. The Grimestone lyric, Love me broughte (Duncan MEL, No. 70), offers a powerful poetic synopsis of this understanding, couched in the voice of Christ: Love me slow, / And love me drow, / And love me leyde on bere (7–9).
[30] Maggioni 1998, 346. 'The head bowed to kiss, the arms outstretched to embrace, the hands pierced to pour out gifts, the side opened for love, the feet held fast to keep him with us, his body stretched to give himself wholly to us' (Ryan 1993, I, 210).
[31] E.g. In the vaile of restles mynd (Gray 1975, No. 43, 70) and Swet Jesu, now wol I synge (Horstmann 1896, II, 15, lines 181–4), quoted in Gray 1975, 126–7.
[32] In the Middle Ages, the Song of Songs was commonly read as an allegory of Christ's love for the church, for the soul, or, upon occasion, for Mary. The commentaries of Origen and Bernard of Clairvaux offer particularly influential readings of this kind. For two informative recent accounts of ways of reading the Song of Songs in the Middle Ages, see Astell 1990, and Renevey 2001.

entry into man's soul but excluded by the architectural impediment of human sin. While in *In the vaile of restles mynd* (Gray 1975, No. 43), the wound in Christ's side is pictured in lines 58–9 as a nuptial bedchamber (*Loke in me, how wyde a wound is here! – / This is hyr chamber*) made available with patient persistence to his feckless spouse: *Now rynne she awayward, now cummyth she narre* (75).[33]

Although the Song of Songs remains the dominant textual resource for amorous expositions of the crucifixion, it is also necessary to take note of the important body of religious lyrics which express love by exploiting the terms and dramatic conventions of *fin' amour*. Developed initially in Latin and vernacular writings designed for anchoresses and women in religious orders,[34] this generic exploitation subsequently moves into lyric verse, using the same *topoi* to shape (and gender) the spiritual self-perception of a far more disparate devotional audience. The religious lyrics of MS Harley 2253 provide several good illustrations of this kind of 'mixed' writing. *Now I se blosme sprynge* (Duncan *MEL*, No. 69) prefaces a self-critical address to Jesus, *lemman softe* [gentle lover], with a nature opening, the conventional signal of a romance theme in secular texts, while *As I me rod this ender day* (Duncan *MEL*, No. 105) employs a *chanson d'aventure* opening – the speaker rides out by a green wood, his heart entirely set on a maiden *swete and fre of blod* (7) – before gradually revealing that the maiden in question is none other than the Virgin.[35] Some of the best lyrics of this type leave the transference from secular to sacred unstated from start to finish, as in the powerful little piece *At a sprynge-wel under a thorn* (Duncan *LMELC*, No. 48), originally quoted within a Latin homily, in which it is left to the reader (and homilist) to infer that the maid in love's bonds who stands at the well must be Mary, witnessing the stream of Christ's blood coursing from beneath his crown of thorns.[36] In general, it is true to say that lyrics within this tradition aim to infuse devotion to Christ and his mother with the appeal and allure of the world of courtly romance, whilst implicitly contrasting the value systems of the two. Nonetheless, there are odd occasions when the appropriation of the terms of *fin'*

33 Both Suzanne Greer Fein and Ann Astell comment interestingly on the shifting gender roles in this lyric. Although Christ is initially presented as a sorrowing male lover, he is increasingly feminised: laying out his body as 'enticing bait', languishing like a bride, and opening his body to be entered. Fein 1998, 58–60, Astell 1990, 146–54. In addition, Karin Boklund-Lagopoulou has written interestingly upon the way in which the entry into Christ's wound also acts as a return to the womb. Boklund-Lagopoulou 2000, 147–8.

34 In such textual vicinities, the devout female addressee is repeatedly constructed as the mistress of a great king or chivalric knight (Christ, by implication). Good examples of this construction occur throughout *Ancrene Wisse*, an early thirteenth-century vernacular treatise addressed to anchoresses, *De doctrina cordis*, a thirteenth-century Latin devotional treatise by the Dominican, Hugh of St Cher, addressed to nuns, and the *Love-Ron* of Thomas of Hales, a late thirteenth-century Franciscan lyric addressed to a nun, extolling the virtue of virginity.

35 For a recent discussion of the Harley religious lyrics, see Kuczynski 2000. Other lyrics use similar conventions in an attempt to add a romance frisson to decidedly *unromantic* church-controlled penitential practices, for example, the Vernon lyric, *Merci God and graunt Merci* (Brown *XIV*, No. 107), in which the voice of exemplary confession is transposed into a forest setting.

36 The 'Corpus Christi' carol, *He bare hym up, he bare hym down* (Duncan *LMELC*, No. 79), remains similarly opaque. In this instance, the image of the pietà is reconfigured as a maiden weeping at the bedside of a bleeding knight.

amour can threaten to get out of hand, leaving the reader uncertain whether contrast or continuation is implied.[37]

The assumption that Christ's self-sacrificial love deserves nothing less than man's unconditional love in return, engendered out of 'feeling' for his sufferings, frequently produces a poetics of anxiety, characterised by declarations of pronounced inadequacy, that is arguably more evident in these lyrics for meditators of mixed ability and dedication than in monastic devotional literature. Lyric speakers ponder their ability to 'feel' adequately, or desperately enquire how they are to make themselves love, generating utterances centred around the anatomisation of their spiritual anxiety. Thus, in lyrics such as *Now I se blosme sprynge* (Duncan MEL, No. 69), the penitential speaker explores the gap between exemplary sensitivity to Christ's suffering, and his own affective impotence:

> Wel oughte myn herte, . . .
> Syk and sory be.
> A way! That I ne can
> To Him turne al my thought . . .
> Of love ne can I nought! (28, 30–2, 37)[38]

Likewise, in the well-known lyric *Whan Ich se on rode* (Duncan MEL, No. 87), the speaker's ability to respond to the cross is left caught upon a knife-edge of perpetualised irresolution:

> Whan Ich se on rode
> Jhesu mi lemman . . .
> Wel ow Ich to wepen . . .
> Yif Ich of love can,
> Yif Ich of love can,
> Yif Ich of love can. (1–2, 8, 10–12)

The final repetitions can be read as a series of increasingly frantic and inconclusive attempts to move the speaker's devotional position from the contingent (*Yif Ich . . . can*) to the affirmative (*Ich . . . can*).

Other devotional texts acknowledge that the solution to this problem of 'feeling' lies outside their grasp, and bounce the initiative away from the meditator back towards the divine addressee. Julian of Norwich includes a wish for *the wound of willfull longing to God* within one of the three formal petitions that she puts to God at the beginning of her *Revelation* (Glasscoe 1993, 3). In like fashion, the popular Latin hymn, *Stabat mater*, contains repeated assertions of the will to feeling: 'make me feel . . . make me mourn with you . . . make me weep lovingly with you'.[39] While, in most cases, the religious lyrics confine their anxieties

---

[37] It is possible to read the mannered fifteenth-century lyric, *Goe, lytyll byll* (Duncan LMELC, No. 51), a lyric to the Virgin in the form of the secular love epistle, in this light.

[38] The hermit, Richard Rolle, participates avidly in this affective anxiety, repeatedly lamenting his inability to respond 'feelingly' to the passion narrative and castigating *my sory herte . . . hardere than the stonys that clovyn at thi deth, it may not of thi passyoun a lytel poynt fele* (*Meditations on the Passion I*, in Allen 1931, 26, lines 238–40).

[39] *Me sentire . . . fac, ut tecum lugeam . . . Fac me tecum pie flere* (Blume and Bannister 1915, 312–18), quoted and translated in Duffy 1992, 259.

about feeling to a series of fervent petitions, one or two more assured and didactic lyrics go so far as to dramatise a possible solution. The fifteenth-century lyric, *Sodenly afraide* (Duncan *LMELC*, No. 74), describes a dream vision of a pietà (that most popular of late medieval devotional images, a representation of the grieving Virgin holding the dead body of Christ upon her knees) in which Mary addresses the visionary to propose her passionate maternal grief as a solution to his affective shortcomings:

> I said I cowd nòt wepe,
>   I was so harde hartid . . .
>   she seid . . .
>   'Who cannot wepe,
>   may lern at me.' (13, 20–1)

The lyric author commandeers the voice of Mary to define and authorise the redemptive capability of the pietà: even the hard-hearted cannot but be moved by this depiction of Mary's sorrow. Nonetheless, at the same time, his over-emphatic concern to defend the authority of this perception – he repeatedly reassures his audience that he relates Mary's words exactly as spoken in his vision (lines 10, 20, 30) – arguably betrays the comparatively recent character of this particular devotion.

It is possible to 'learn' feeling by viewing the image of the weeping mother. More broadly, it is important to underline the centrality of the act of seeing to the affective programme of the religious lyrics, and to late medieval devotional texts in general. Love's *Mirror* contains repeated exhortations to 'behold' details from the narrative of Christ's life, referring not to physical sight, but to the faculty of inner or imaginative sight, coupled with compassion, termed by Love, Rolle, and other writers, 'the eye of the heart'.[40]

> Thou maiht beholde with inwarde compassion how he wipeth his bodye . . .
> Beholde nowe . . . the grete pacience of oure lorde . . . And also beholde his
> modere & hese other frendes. (Sargent 1992, 166, 21–2; 170, 18–19, 24)

Several of the lyrics, in particular those based upon the 'Reproaches' or *Improperia* of the Good Friday liturgy,[41] take this process of exhortation a step further by making it appear to originate with Christ himself. In the sub-genre of Passion lyrics generally referred to as the 'Complaints of Christ', Christ speaks from the cross to commend the sight of his broken body and, frequently, to draw attention to his five wounds, in particular, the wound in his side: *Lo, here my hert!* (Gray 1975, No. 26(b), 6).

Given that the recommendation to view or to behold occurs with such persistent regularity, it is necessary to enquire *why* there should have been this preoccupation with seeing, and also to investigate the different types of 'seeing' that

---

[40] Sargent 1992, 162, line 27. W. F. Pollard discusses the pseudo-Dionysian notion of the three 'eyes' of flesh, reason, and contemplation, its re-emergence in Cistercian and Victorine spiritual writing, and relevance to Rolle (Pollard 1997). See also the lines in the Harley lyric, *I sike al when I singe* (Duncan *MEL*, No. 94): *Whan Ich Him biholde / With eye and herte bo* (21–2).

[41] These reproaches are based in turn upon Lam. 1:12 *O vos omnes*.

the lyrics explore. Quite apart from the fact that most uneducated people's experience of the life of Christ was conducted as a series of sights – wall paintings,
stained glass, and the brief visual tableaux of the mystery cycles constituted the
libri laicorum, the books of the laity – it is also the case that, from the twelfth
century onwards, the imagination began to be accorded a distinct and systematic role in spiritual formation within a monastic and canonical milieu,[42] and
that, by the fourteenth century, images and sights were also held to have
unprecedented power to arouse the emotions, effectively enabling the viewer to
'feel', and by 'feeling' to resolve upon a programme of personal moral reform.[43]
O man unkynde (Duncan *LMELC*, No. 70), a fifteenth-century lyric in which
Christ's familiar exhortation to see his pierced body gives rise to an exemplary
human response –

Therfore fro synne	*from*
I hope to blynne	*to desist*
And grefe no more (22–4) –	*grieve (thee)*

epitomises this process from sight to reformatory resolve, while the late
thirteenth-century lyric, *I sike al when I singe* (Duncan *MEL*, No. 94), pursues a
train of reasoning that has much in common with many of the nativity lyrics,
identifying the inward 'sight' of the passion as a source of affective song, and
investigating those moments of visual crisis where singing threatens to break
down, or, more alarmingly still, where seeing fails to procure the expected reformation:

Allas that men ben wode! –	*mad*
Biholden on the rode	*(they) look upon the cross*
And sellen (Ich ly nought)	*sell; lie not*
Her soules into sin	
For any worldes win. (55–9)	*any worldly pleasure*

Interestingly, this lyric presents and approves a mode of seeing that is a 'seeing
through tears' – *When Ich with wepinge, / Biholde upon the tre* (3–4) – identifying
this blurred or problematic sight as devotionally exemplary. The renewal of this
specialised sight of Christ's bleeding body, both verse by verse within the lyric
and day by day (*wel ofte*) within the personal meditations of the lyric persona, a
renewal that can seem stultifying or morbid in its refusal to move on from the
image of dying pain, whips both sight and song up into a state of fevered intensity and rhetorical fervour that imbues the crucifixion with a feeling of horrifying excess and verisimilitude:

---

[42] See, for example, the *Benjamin minor* and *Benjamin major* of Richard of St Victor where the
exercise of the imagination is identified as a necessary early stage in the contemplative ascent
of the mind. *PL* 196. 1–192. For important recent discussions of Victorine theories of the imagination see Zinn 1979, 1–49, and Renevey 2001, 9–17.

[43] The fifteenth-century orthodox dialogue, *Dives and Pauper*, provides an excellent summary of
this belief. To Dives' question regarding the utility of images, Pauper replies: *they been
ordeynyd to steryn manys mende* [mind] *to thynkyn of Cristys incarnacioun . . . Also they been
ordeynyd to steryn mannys affeccioun and his herte to deuocioun* (Barnum 1976, I, 82).

The nailes ben al to stronge,	*too*
The smith is al to sleye,	*skilful*
Thou bledest al to longe,	
The tre is al to heye.	
The stones waxen wete. (41–5)	

Alongside these relatively conventional modes of seeing, a number of lyrics and devotional texts also explore more indirect or unexpected perspectives. Several lyrics modestly channel their vision of the crucifixion through Mary's suffering eyes. Rather than viewing the cross directly, they look upon her looking, presumably taking their cue for feeling from the contemplation of her supremely sensitised gaze.[44] Sarah Stanbury has commented upon the way in which the unprecedented assertiveness and directness of Mary's feminine gaze are, by this means, transformed into spectacle. Nonetheless, she writes, it would be 'reductive . . . to argue that her gaze is simply defeated or mastered by patriarchal lines of sight' (Stanbury 1991, 1090). Rather, Mary's ability to transfix and control Christ's body with her suffering gaze,[45] taken in conjunction with the meditator's frequent wish to become the object of her protective gaze,[46] attests to the undiminished 'power of that look' (Stanbury 1991, 1090). Occasionally, the trope of the mediated gaze is used to different effect. By contrast with the expansive, relatively self-assured gaze of many of the religious lyrics, Julian of Norwich describes how she lacks the confidence to look *beyond* Christ's face except by following the direction of his gaze – towards his heart, towards his mother – shaping and authorising her own seeing through an act of intimate, yet effacing, visual identification with Christ (Glasscoe 1993, 35–6).

In addition to registering mediated visions, several devotional writers also explore moments where the act of seeing is subjected to strain. Helen Phillips discusses how, while it remains easy to see Christ's body, it is often very hard to see Mary's. All eyes or, more precisely, only eyes (indeed, only eyes in so far as they look upon Christ), the rest of her body is either left unrealised or translated into a series of rapidly changing, compound, erudite metaphors that 'resist fully satisfactory realistic visualization' (Phillips 2000, 85). On other occasions, the thing that we are asked to see proves visually inaccessible. In *O man unkynde* (Gray 1975, No. 26(b)), Christ's commonplace exhortation, *Lo, here my hert!* (6), for all its apparent simplicity, actually necessitates an abrupt hermeneutic shift, since 'seeing' Christ's heart entails extracting it from the realist context of the crucifixion that determines most acts of seeing, and resituating it in a symbolic or emblematic context.[47] In more instances still, the act of seeing becomes the

---

[44] See, for example, *Jesu Cristes milde moder* (Duncan MEL, No. 90).

[45] Stanbury discusses this transfixing gaze in relation to the well-known crucifixion dialogue lyric, *Stond wel, moder, under rode* (Duncan MEL, No. 91). See also Stanbury (below), 237–41.

[46] See, for example, lines 13–14 of *Levedie, Ich thonke thee* (Duncan MEL, No. 74).

[47] Although 'seeing' Christ's heart is necessarily a symbolic action, that of focussing on what the heart stands for and not literally on the physical organ, the emphasis on devotion to the Sacred Heart in the fifteenth century did give rise to pictorial, emblematic representations of Christ's heart. A drawing of a heart replaces the word *hert* in the version of this poem found in Bodl. MS Tanner 407, and, in BL MS Additional 37049, the text is accompanied by a representation of Christ offering to man an image of his wounded heart. See Woolf, Plate 1 (opposite p. 186), and Gray, Plate 2 (opposite p. 23).

occasion for displays of penitential defiance or fascinated optical analysis. Rolle refuses to look on Christ's wound, even via the mediated vision of Mary, through a personal sense of moral unworthiness. Instead, he petitions to be allowed to see Christ through the eyes of the thief hanging alongside, or from the vantage point of hell.[48] Julian, equally penitential, doesn't dare to stop looking (Glasscoe 1993, 28). Yet, it would be wrong to assume that her transfixed gaze necessarily results in a unified sight. Rather, earlier in her account of her revelations, Julian records how she operates two kinds of spiritual sight to obtain a simultaneous vision of two different details from the crucifixion scene: she gazes devoutly upon Mary with her *ghostly sight*, while, with her *bodyly sight*, she views Christ's continuously bleeding brow (Glasscoe 1993, 10).

In thirteenth- and fourteenth-century lyrics, the meditator is generally encouraged to 'see' directly, depending solely upon the visualising capacity of the written word and the resources of his imagination to engineer a mental picture of the crucifixion scene (Woolf, 203). By the fifteenth century, an actual devotional artefact of some type – a statue, crucifix, or illustration within a book – is frequently proposed as a supplementary tool, encouraging the meditator to nurture his or her mental sight *by way of* an actual image. The well-known fifteenth-century lyric, *In a tabernacle of a toure* (Gray 1975, No. 61), frames a spiritual vision of Mary as *mediatrix* with an opening in which the narrator ponders a statue of Mary mounted within the niche of a tower. Similarly, Dunbar's poem, *Amang thir freiris within ane cloister* (Kinsley 1958, No. 2), a powerful vision of the Passion narrative, is springboarded by a programme of paternosters before a crucifix within a Franciscan oratory. Lydgate traces this movement from devotional artefact to the visualising imagination in several lyrics, suggesting that he regarded it as a valuable route into meditation. However, on occasion, he also allows more literary preoccupations to intrude – appropriating the Chaucerian trope of finding inspirational material within a book after a sleepless night to explain how he lights upon the image of a pietà, and subsequently responding to that image in terms that have more than a hint of aesthetic appreciation intermingled with their affectivity: *With weepyng eyen, and cheer most lamentable: / Though the proporcioun by crafft was agreable.*[49] Dunbar and Lydgate both negotiate the transition from artefact to vision with literary competence. However, in general, it is possible to read the fifteenth-century resort to secondary images as a move tending towards caution rather than creativity. For, whether these actual images are encountered publicly (in the course of church attendance or, routinely, within a fraternal or monastic setting) or more privately (within a domestic book of personal devotion, such as a primer), in all cases, their recommendation as meditational aids or prerequisites would appear to have the effect of ensuring that visualisation of the passion remains closely linked to officially sanctioned images encountered in orthodox textual or architectural locations.

Our seeing may commence with our physical eyes, or it may solely engage the eyes of our heart. Yet in either case it is necessary to ask what is to be seen? As with many courtly lyrics, the body remains central. However, whereas the

---

[48] Rolle, *Meditations on the Passion I* (in Allen 1931, 26–7, lines 251–65).
[49] *The Fifteen Joys and Sorrows of Mary* (MacCracken 1911a, I, 268, lines 11–12).

courtly lyrics and associated romance texts tend to concentrate a 'male' stare upon a female body that is physically perfect and alluring, the religious lyrics transfer the tags of perfection and allurement to the sight of the bruised and violated male body, and position the reader within a mode of intimate and amorous seeing that is often, by implication, feminine (Astell 1990, 138). As part of this strategy of inversion, the review of the bodily members frequently takes place via a process of antithesis.[50] In *Jesus doth him bymene* (Gray 1975, No. 30), the stretched limbs and torn flesh of Christ's crucifixional body are contrasted with the postures and fashionable clothes of a young gallant, recasting the courtly body as culpably superficial, while in *O alle women that ever were borne* (Gray 1975, No. 25), Mary presents Christ's crucifixional body to an audience of mothers, inciting pathos by beseeching them to compare the torn members of her son with the healthy bodies of their own children.

In some of the most effective lyrics, even these comparisons and ramifications are cut away, and we are presented with a simple description of the body whose power derives precisely from its unimpeded physicality. Some of the best examples of this presentation occur in the various Middle English lyric versions of the *Candet nudatum pectus*, a short description of Christ's body, which originally appeared in the course of a longer Latin meditation by John of Fécamp.[51] These versions, which exemplify the late medieval propensity to extract especially memorable or visual passages from longer works designed for a monastic clientele and circulate them independently, and which variously perform as self-contained lyrics or as insets within longer texts,[52] focus solely upon the colours of Christ's body and its spatial co-ordinates –

Whyt was hys naked brest	*white*
And red of blod hys syde,	
Bleyk was His fair andléd,	*pale; fair face*
His woundes dep and wide,	
And hys armes y-streight,	*stretched*
Hey upon the rode;	*high; cross*
On fif stredes on His body	*five places*
The stremes ran o blode – [53]	

creating a verbal image designed to 'fix the complete attention of the meditator' in a way 'comparable to that of the graphic image'.[54] Here, colour dominates the description. However, in many instances, it is the *liquidity* of the body, awash with life-giving blood, or, conversely, its gradual dehydration, that is singled

---

[50] For an account of antithesis in the lyric complaints of Mary, see Keiser 1985.

[51] The differences between the various vernacular versions, and between the vernacular versions and the original Latin text, are ably discussed by Copeland 1984.

[52] Richard Rolle inserts slightly different versions of the *Candet* into two longer religious lyrics, *A Song of Love-longing to Jesus* (37–40), and the *Meditacio de passione Christi* (227–30), itself inset within his prose treatise, *Ego dormio* (Allen 1931, 42–3, 68).

[53] Duncan *MEL*, No. 85. For a variant version, see Duncan *MEL*, No. 86.

[54] Copeland 1984, 73. Copeland argues that since the English poets have 'no available native verse equivalents . . . they realise their material largely through the structures associated with iconographic design' (76).

out for comment.[55] Sometimes, the vision remains relatively panoramic – we see
Mary and John at the foot of the cross, or are shown the meteorological disruption associated with the death of Christ.[56] At other times, the field of vision
narrows until it becomes concentrated upon a single microscopic point – a tear
in Christ's eye, or a drop of his blood.[57] In many of the evocations, in order to
work the affections to requisite heights of empassioned empathy, the body and
its details remain momentarily devoid of theological meaning, in particular, of
any knowledge of the resurrection.[58] However, Sarah Beckwith and David Aers
have shown that, even when viewed through this apparently artless lens, the
crucifixional body is never unideological. In one of the most interesting recent
trends in cultural criticism of the late middle ages, they develop a reading of
Christ's body that restores neglected societal meanings – we are all members of
the body of Christ (1 Corinthians 12: 12–31) – speculating that the emphasis
upon the torn body in the late fourteenth and early fifteenth century may well
reflect anxiety regarding the 'dismemberment' of traditional communities.[59]

Having seen the body, it is next necessary to attempt to feel what it feels. We
have already discussed occasions where the perceived failure to meet with this
demand generates a poetics of anxiety. It is now necessary to investigate the
way in which this exhortation to feel impels the meditator along an affective
path that is designed to culminate in profound identification. Frequently, in
order to effect this salvatory identification, the meditator is invited to view his
sensations of sorrow and compassion for Christ's suffering as a wound that
replicates, either the physical wound in Christ's side, or Mary's psychological
wound of maternal anguish: 'And a sword will pierce your own soul also'.[60] On
other occasions, the meditator's wound is given less to do with sorrowful feeling
than with the simple practice of 'thinking on' the passion, and of bringing it to
repeated awareness:

> And evermore in hert myn
> Let thi passion fastned be,
> As was the spere into thyn
> When thow suffredest deth for me.
>
> (Gray 1975, No. 53(a), 5–9)

Many lyrics move towards a concise, even aphoristic, moment of identification.
Few anatomise its characteristics particularly closely. Consequently, it is informative to examine a lyric such as William Dunbar's *Amang thir freiris within ane
cloister* (Kinsley 1958, No. 2), in which the parallels between the lyric's poetic

---

[55] Julian, for example, paints a panoramic picture of Christ's body hung out to dry upon the
cross (Glasscoe 1993, 24–5).

[56] See, for example, Duncan *MEL*, Nos. 87, 89; Kinsley 1958, No. 2, 83–6.

[57] See *Lovely ter of lovely eye* (Duncan *MEL*, No. 93), and Julian's focus upon individual drops of
blood in her *Revelation* (Glasscoe 1993, 10–11).

[58] Julian is perhaps exceptional in the joy she detects in Christ's face as he nears death: *Sodenly, I
beholdyng in the same crosse, he chongyd his blissfull chere* (Glasscoe 1993, 31).

[59] Beckwith 1993, 22–44; Aers and Staley 1996, 265.

[60] Luke 2:35. Rolle declares *woundys of reuthe is al my desyr* (*Meditations on the Passion I*, Allen
1931, 23), while Lydgate prays that Mary's sorrows may pierce his heart with compassion
(*The Fifteen Joys and Sorrows of Mary*, MacCracken 1911a, I, 274, lines 176–82).

persona and the crucified Christ are set out in more extensive detail.[61] The first half of this unusually lengthy lyric provides an unexceptional narrative of the process of the crucifixion couched as a detailed linear sequence in accordance with pseudo-Bonaventure's *Meditationes* and related texts, while the second half abandons this linear approach for a personification allegory in which the first-person persona finds himself assailed and buffeted by the personifications of Compassion, Contrition, Pity etc., and exhorted to use these and other person-ifications to prepare his soul as a metaphorical sepulchre for the dead Christ. Effectively, the second half depicts in allegorical terms the exemplary response of contrition and reform that ideally follows upon devout contemplation of the passion narrative. In other words, the second half is a psychological dramatis-ation of how we ought to respond to the first half. However, alongside this rela-tion of cause and effect, we are also given the sense that the lyric speaker is formulating the stages of this exemplary response in such a way as to give them a metaphorical *equivalence* to Christ's passion experience. Some of that sense arises, in the first instance, from several of the verbs that Dunbar uses to describe the onset of these penitential personifications: the lyric speaker is buffeted, oppressed and accused by the personifications in a way that meta-phorically replicates the earlier description of Christ's buffeting and scourging. In addition, the lyric speaker's final sensations of terror at the thought of Christ's death – *The erde did trymmill quhair I lay* (138) – bring the perturbation of his soul into a relation of identity with the earlier description of the seismological distur-bance upon Calvary: *The erde did trimmill, the stanis claif* (83). Responding with contrition, compassion, and pity, and experiencing these sensations as painful moral assaults, the lyric speaker posits an identity with Christ. However, it can be argued that his interest in schematising the stages of this response and in shaping them as parallels to the passion process, overtakes his selfless spectation of the cross such that, in the second half of the lyric, the focus upon Christ's violated body is displaced in favour of more earthbound and peniten-tially self-centred considerations.

Sometimes the movement of identification within the lyrics is couched in distinctly performative terms.[62] One puts on the suffering body of Christ as one might put on a costume: *I wolde be clad in Cristes skyn, / That ran so longe on blode* (Duncan *MEL*, No. 96, 3–4). Wounds are conceived as blackly ingenious garments: *This blody surcote she hath on me set . . . Thes gloves were given me . . . rede and wan, / Embroudred with blode* (Duncan *MEL*, No. 73, 28, 42–4).[63] At other times, the movement of identification is represented as a movement of mutual indwelling or sexual fusion, as discussed earlier. Meditators are invited to enter Christ's body via the wound in his side, to sleep within his heart, or to feast on what they encounter there.[64] On such occasions, it is easy to see that this meditational fusion with, or absorption into, the body of Christ may have disconcerting consequences for the ecclesiastical regulation of access to Christ's

---

[61] For a comparable reading of this lyric, see Bennett 1982, 121–4.
[62] See Beckwith 1993, 61; Beckwith 1992, and Gibson Murray 1989.
[63] See also Duncan *LMELC*, No. 71, lines 1–6.
[64] E.g. Duncan *MEL*, No. 96, 5–6 and No. 73, 57–60, 105–11.

body at the eucharist, offering as it does an alternative, wholly interiorised, method of communion. Beckwith has investigated the way in which the orthodox meditational text, Love's *Mirror*, composed in the wake of Arundel's *Constitutions*, goes out of its way to assuage this concern, linking the phases of private meditation to phases of liturgical time, providing inoffensive answers to the visual and imaginative questions that the text raises, and appending additional material on the centrality of the eucharistic sacrament that is absent from its Latin source.[65] Work remains to be done on the positioning of recommendations to identification within the religious lyrics in relation to these fifteenth-century debates and concerns. However, in general, it seems fair to comment that while some pursue empathetic devotion to an openly eucharistic conclusion – *Bowe thu doun to the brinke / And mekely taste of the welle* (Duncan *LMELC*, No. 78, 7–8) – others invite the meditator to construct sophisticated fantasies of intimacy and absorption that bear no overt connection to sacramental practice.

We need to see. We need to identify with what we see. And, thirdly, we need to remember. A lyric in a fifteenth-century manuscript opens, *O Jesu, lett me never forgett thy byttur passion* (Gray 1975, No. 52, 1); another, written in a Rolle-like rhapsodic idiom, beseeches, *The mynde* [memory] *of this myrour thou lat me noght mysse* (Gray 1975, No. 19, 26); while a third, voiced by Christ, which exploits the metaphor of the lover-knight, exhorts the meditator, *take myne armes pryvely / And do tham in thi tresory* (Duncan *MEL*, No. 102, 7–8), the 'treasury' or *thesaurus* serving as a commonplace classical and medieval metaphor for the faculty of the memory.[66] In addition to its representation as a mental storehouse for valuables, classical discussions of memory also frequently picture the faculty as a malleable surface upon which sense impressions can be inscribed or engraved – the image of a wax writing tablet and stylus is often used. Lydgate's devotional lyrics repeatedly employ memorial images of this variety. Thus, in *The Dolerous Pyte of Crystes Passioun* (MacCracken 1911a, I, No. 47), he writes, referring to the *imago pietatis*,

> Set this lyknesse in your remembraunce,
> Enprenteth it in your Inward sight . . .
> Grave this triumphe depe in your memorie. (9–10, 43)[67]

While the exhortation to remember texts or pictures of the passion has an obvious salience within a religious culture in which such things are far less readily privately accessible, in order fully to appreciate the reasons for this emphatic weight, it is also necessary to be aware of the classical and medieval association of memory with virtue.[68] To elaborate: Cicero's definition of memory as one of the parts of the virtue of prudence was revived and extended by Dominican theologians during the Middle Ages (Hubbell 1949, Bk. 2, ch. 53,

---

[65] Beckwith 1993, 64–70; Renevey 2000, 204.

[66] See St Augustine's famous reference to the treasure-house of the memory in his *Confessions* (O'Donnell 1992, I, Bk. 10, ch. 8).

[67] For a useful discussion of Lydgate's interest in 'remembering', see Boffey 1997, 137–9.

[68] Definitive accounts of classical and medieval memory can be found in Yates 1966, Carruthers 1990, and Coleman 1992.

159–60), engendering a general perception that continually recalling an act of superlative virtue, such as the self-sacrifice of the crucifixion, carried high moral value, since it could enable the 'remembering' Christian to establish a similar practice of virtue in his or her own life. This perception, taken in conjunction with the fact that, from Aristotle onwards, the visual memory was widely viewed as the surest and most superior mode of recollection, may well provide us with an important additional explanation for the emphasis placed upon the act of seeing within the religious lyrics as a whole. The sight of the crucifixion was considered the surest way to form a reliable and vivid 'memory' of it.

In addition to either exhorting the meditator to remember, or actually providing him or her with an authorised 'memory' of the passion, it is also possible to read many of the religious lyrics as contributions to simpler and more mechanistic mnemonic programmes. It is well known that the friars, in particular, the Dominicans, experimented with a wide range of mnemonic aids to improve the effectiveness of their homiletic and catechetical outreach to the laity, from the early thirteenth century onwards. These aids included numerical and alphabetical lists, rhymes and jingles, and references to schematic visual images, such as trees, plants, or buildings, around which the central tenets of the Christian life could be organised, differentiated and anatomised. Many of the religious lyrics are best understood as versifications of one or more of these mnemonic learning schemes. Thus, lyrics listing the five joys of the Virgin or, in Lydgate's more complex case, her fifteen joys and sorrows, should be viewed as a poetic elaboration upon the mnemonic device of the numerical list, sacrificing the narrative continuity of the Virgin's experience to service an elementary learning programme, and reformulating it as a sequence of emotionally oppositional stanzaic snapshots.[69] The fifteenth-century carol, *Lyth and lysten, both old and yyng* (Duncan *LMELC*, No. 47), takes this one step further by linking each of Mary's five joys with the five branches of a rose bush. The equation celebrates Mary as mystic rose, yet simultaneously evokes the rather more pedestrian scholastic schema of the teaching tree, frequently used in sermons and didactic compilations to map the relation between different areas of Christian practice, or to anatomise the vices and virtues.[70] Another fifteenth-century lyric, *Away, feynt lufe, full of varyaunce!* (Gray 1975, No. 57), provides a similar schema with an additional alphabetical dimension by linking each of the letters of Mary's (Maria's) name to the five petals of a cinquefoil, and then linking these in turn with female prefigurations of Mary from the Old Testament, and gemstones of assorted virtues. The lyric enriches and extends the meditator's imaginative contemplation of Mary by providing her with additional courtly, intertextual and symbolic resonances, and enacts a simple artificial memory technique, relating letters and numbers, to ensure that these additional items will not become confused.[71] Lyrics based around mnemonic schemes of what-

---

[69] See MacCracken 1911a, I, No. 51.

[70] See the tree of vices in *The Book of Vices and Virtues* (Francis 1942, 13–68), the tree diagrams in *The Desert of Religion*, discussed by Mc Govern-Mouron 1996, I, 39–57, and the tree diagrams in the *Speculum theologie* (reproduced in Sandler 1983, pls 8, 9, 14).

[71] Chaucer's *ABC* (Benson, 637–40), a translation of a Marian prayer by Guillaume de Deguileville, provides an additional example of a similar device.

ever type intrigue through their ingenuity. However, it can be argued that this ingenuity tends to inhibit emotional engagement, confining the lyric recipient within a set of relatively technological devotional responses.

Having explored various lyrics of the nativity and crucifixion, under the headings of vision, identification, and memory, it is now time, finally, to turn our attention more directly upon Mary, and upon those lyrics that explore her New Testament and doctrinal experience. We have already touched on the way in which certain lyrics mediate the crucifixion through Mary's sight and through Mary's pain, identifying that sight and that pain as exemplary for mourners (Woolf, 241; Keiser 1985, 168–9, 174). As with so much in the canon of Middle English religious verse, many of these lyrics take their lead from an earlier Latinate tradition of monastic meditation, specifically the Pseudo-Anselmian *Dialogus beatae Mariae et Anselmi de passione Domini* (*PL* 159, 271–90) and the pseudo-Bernardine *Liber de passione Christi et doloribus et planctibus matris eius* (*PL* 182, 1133–42), which both devote extensive attention to scrutinising Mary's reactions. These meditations and the lyrics that follow them develop the devotional idea, again already touched upon, that Mary's psychological passion in some way parallels or even aggravates Christ's physical passion. The idea is well conveyed in the late thirteenth-century sequence, *Stond wel, moder, under rode* (Duncan *MEL*, No. 91), which alternates these two differing modes of anguish, linking them in a symbiotic relationship in which the sight of Mary's stubborn and persistent grief seems to move Christ to ever more intense sensations of filial agony: *Moder, merci! Let me deyen* (31).[72] As such, Mary's grief may be exemplary, yet it can also be obstreperous. Here, for example, it serves as a contestive affective focus, deflecting attention from the cross, or at least resituating it as subsidiary to a tense negotiation in which the complexities of mother-son psychology predominate. On occasion, Mary's grief pushes still further. Somewhat similar to the way in which Margery Kempe occasionally attempts to wrest the main female role from Mary in her participatory visualisations of the passion narrative (Renevey 2000, 207–8), it is not uncommon for Mary to intrude herself very physically into the vocational activity of her son. In *Stond wel, moder, under rode*, she pleads *Let me deyen thee biforen* (36), while in *Why have ye no routhe on my child?* (Duncan *MEL*, No. 92) she demands:

> Tak doun o rode my derworth child,   *from the cross*
> Or prik me o rode with my derling! (3–4)   *nail me on the cross*

Mary's efforts to undergo a substitutionary death for her child re-nuance the meaning of the passion so that, as well as exemplifying a faintly impersonal male love for mankind, it is also made to exemplify a sharply personal maternal sacrifice. Such nuances feminise and 'parentalise' the work of the passion, providing women readers and married and parental readers with clear opportunities for identification, even though the substitution that Mary proposes remains hypothetical and unfulfilled.

---

[72] An account of the tense relationship enacted in this lyric is given in Stanbury 1991, 1087–9. See also Stanbury (below), 237–41.

As well as being considered a parallel passion, Mary's pain at the cross is also often interpreted as a completion of her humanity. Several crucifixion lyrics develop the idea that this pain replicates the pain Mary allegedly failed to experience during childbirth,[73] fusing the nativity with the crucifixion, and constructing the latter as a site of spiritual birth or rebirth. In such readings, the crucifixion acts to facilitate Mary's understanding of the experience of child-bearing women, giving her new reserves of sympathy and, presumably, a new eagerness of intercessory involvement.[74] Once again, the crucifixion is structured with the parenting lay community in mind, although in the process the normal axes of empathy are reversed. Instead of the meditator being exhorted to identify himself with the physical or psychological pain of Christ or Mary, she or he is shown a scenario in which the crucifixion completes the empathetic capacity of its main female protagonist.

We can sum up some of the preceding points by saying that the lyrics use Mary to construct the crucifixion as a 'motherly' experience and to communicate convincingly with a readership of mothers and parents.[75] However, once we move to the final scenes in the drama of Mary's life history – her assumption into heaven and heavenly coronation, scenes which attract particular devotional attention during the fifteenth century – her construction changes entirely, and her representation as 'mother' is exchanged for a set of far less 'human', more remote and reverential characteristics. Despite their late date, the lyrics of the assumption and coronation, which celebrate Mary for her regal power, moral invincibility, and virginal intactness, are probably best viewed as updated, elaborated versions of a much earlier discourse of Marian invocation, developed in the eleventh and twelfth centuries within a largely monastic milieu.[76] As such, they completely bypass the muted acknowledgement of the bodily presence of Mary developed in the nativity and crucifixion lyrics,[77] stringing together long sequences of Marian titles derived from antiphons and Latin hymns that maintain her at a level of unbroken, continually changing metaphor (Phillips 2000; Boklund-Lagopoulou 2000, 139). Lydgate's Marian poems offer many well-controlled examples of this practice, invoking Mary successively as *sterne of the see, rote of holynesse, closet clennest of chastyte, closid gardeyn* and *cristallyn welle of clennesse*,[78] while other lyrics combine stray images from scripture, read through the lenses of patristic exegesis, to create more convoluted titles: *launtern of odour*.[79] Heavily abstract and intellectually complex, these rapidly shifting meta-

---

73 See, for example, *Stond wel, moder, under rode* (Duncan MEL, No. 91, 37–42).
74 E.g. see Duncan MEL, No. 91, 43–8.
75 This construction can be contrasted with twelfth- and early thirteenth-century texts, such as the *Ancrene Wisse*, in which the restrictiveness of the cross and sepulchre is likened to the restrictiveness of an anchorhold. In other words, the passion is constructed for meditators practising dedicated and virginal lifestyles.
76 See Graef 1963, I, 210–64; Clayton 1990, 88–9; Whitehead 2000, 114–16.
77 Mary is given a bodily presence in so far as she gazes at Christ, sings to him, feeds and warms him with her body.
78 Lydgate, *Ballade at the Reverence of Our Lady, Qwene of Mercy* (MacCracken 1911a, I, 255–6, lines 23, 29, 34, 36–7). See also similar invocations in *To Mary, the Queen of Heaven*, *Ave Regina Celorum*, and *Ave, Jesse Virgula!* (MacCracken 1911a, I, 284–7, 291–2, 299–304).
79 Brown XV, No. 35, 2, quoted in Phillips 2000, 85.

phors inspire admiration and reverence in the lyric reader, yet they fail to make much connection with human experience. In addition, Helen Phillips has commented upon the way in which, by contrast with the visual realism of the crucifixion lyrics, many of these images actually present severe visual difficulties. How, for example, is one to visualise a *launtern of odour*?[80] The use of aureate and macaronic language aggravates further this sense of mystifying incomprehension:

> Oleum effusum, to languentes medsyne –   *oil poured out, medicine to the faint*
> O Maria by denominacioun! –   *by name*
> Fulgent as the beame celestyne,   *resplendent as the heavenly beam*
> Called unto hir coronacioun.
>
> (Duncan *LMELC*, No. 54, 17–20)

Thus, on the occasions when these lyrics are intended for lay use, as they very often are in the fifteenth century, all these factors combine to leave the lyric reader effectively subordinated, hampered by a sense of visual disability and intellectual inferiority.

Why does the Marian lyric of the assumption and heavenly coronation move in this direction? Why is there this sudden shift towards ornamentalism and intellectual difficulty, following after the intimate closeness of many crucifixion lyrics (*I wolde be clad in Cristes skyn*, Duncan *MEL*, No. 96, 3), and how ought we to evaluate it? Opinions upon this question have differed over the years. On the one hand, of course, opting for sequences of images can be construed as the only realistic linguistic response to a celestial event that remains morally and intellectually wholly inaccessible. Nonetheless, traditional critical opinion has often tended to deplore this solution, condemning the reliance upon ornament as decadent and excessive (Woolf, 300–1). Set against this, Douglas Gray takes a notably more positive approach, locating the baroque tendencies of these lyrics within a fifteenth-century literary milieu that 'prizes intricate ornament, rhetorical display and elaborate musical patterns' (Gray 2001, 207).[81] As well as vindicating the ornamental emphases of these lyrics, Gray also provides a positive assessment of the fifteenth-century fascination with Mary's heavenly apotheosis, terming it an example of 'Christian humanism' (Gray 2001, 198). However, Helen Phillips, writing on the same topic, views lyric representations of this apotheosis and its apparent empowerment of Mary with a far more ambivalent eye. Remarking that Mary's translation into awe-inspiring metaphorical sequences comes at the expense of her bodily unity, attributing 'hyperbolic power' to her, but in fact 'deflecting attention onto other objects' (Phillips 2000, 86), she goes on to point out that this representation of Mary's incomprehensible heavenly power is in fact far more controlled and bounded than might at first appear, relying as it does upon a succession of compound biblical and liturgical metaphors that can only be fully translated by members of clergy with scholarly

---

[80] Phillips 2000, 85. William Dunbar remarks tellingly, in his *Hale, sterne superne* (Duncan *LMELC*, No. 55): *Haile, schene unseyne with carnale eyne* (39).

[81] Gray's contextualisation encompasses a number of fifteenth-century French 'rhétoriqueur' poems to Mary.

access to scripture and its commentaries (Phillips 2000, 99). In other words, the very terms by which Mary's female empowerment is depicted have the decidedly less enabling effect of delivering her back safely into the hands of the ecclesiastical establishment. We can empathise with Mary the bereaved mother as much as we please. But Mary, heaven's queen, is held away from us, fractured into a series of unlike objects that impede unity, and maintained at a level of textual erudition that renders her safely incomprehensible to the women she might have been expected to empower.

Our readings of Middle English religious lyrics today continue to remain fundamentally informed by the ground-breaking scholarship of the mid-twentieth century. Carleton Brown's editions in the twenties and thirties, and the authoritative analyses of Rosemary Woolf and Douglas Gray in the late sixties and early seventies, have, to some degree, discouraged further large-scale studies of the religious lyrics other than to explore further their links with Franciscan spirituality and with the practice of preaching (Jeffrey 1975; Wenzel 1986). During the last couple of decades, scholarship upon the lyrics has remained, for the most part, small-scale, represented by essays and articles which offer close readings of single lyrics from a particular ideological angle, or which bring to light some previously overlooked lyric text or variant version.[82] Several potentially promising new directions of exploration have emerged from amongst these articles; in particular, a new sensitivity to the manuscript context of the religious lyrics,[83] and an acknowledgement of the complexity of their gender strategies.[84] Perhaps the time is ripe for a new large-scale study foregrounding one or more of these issues. However, I would also venture to suggest, in line with some of my own interpretative emphases in this essay, that the religious lyrics could also benefit from a reconsideration in the light of recent developments in the scholarship of affective spirituality and of the Middle English mystical tradition: in particular, ongoing research into meditational optics, identificatory practices, and the ethics of remembering. Attention to these areas may well bring new dimensions to our appreciation of these poems. Nonetheless, as a final counterbalance to these various interpretative options, and rather in opposition to the general consensus upon their functionalism, I would like to close by applauding the continuing enigma, compressed power, and hermeneutic defiance of some of our finest lyrics, and by voicing a plea that we not ignore the validity of their contemporary aesthetic appeal:

> Lulley, lulley; lully, lulley;
> The fawcon hath born my mak away.
>
> (Duncan *LMELC*, No. 79, 1–2)

---

[82] For a comprehensive survey of such articles, see Greentree 2001.
[83] See Boffey (above), 1–18.
[84] See Astell 1990, Stanbury 1991, Phillips 2000, and Boklund-Lagopoulou 2000.

6

Middle English Courtly Lyrics: Chaucer to Henry VIII

DOUGLAS GRAY

The late Middle English courtly lyrics are less well known and less esteemed than their devotional counterparts, and still are often dismissed as flat, conventional, and repetitious.[1] Some are, but many more, when examined closely in their cultural and historical contexts, become much more interesting works, while a number show poetic and imaginative talents of a high order. The adjective 'courtly' applied to these poems cannot be defined in an absolute sense. It suggests, rightly, that they are essentially literary works, sometimes self-consciously so, written by those who belonged to or moved in the world of the 'court' – whether of kings, the high nobility or the lesser gentry – or written for the entertainment and instruction of those who did. But as we shall see, the category is not always self-contained or clearly demarcated. In particular, it is misleading to present the 'courtly lyric' as something totally separate from or opposed to the 'popular lyric'. The literary evidence seems rather to suggest that 'courtly' and 'popular' should be seen as the polar extremes of a continuum. There seems to be much interaction: a song of popular origin may find its way into a courtly manuscript or setting; a poem of courtly origin may end up as a popular song or ballad.

Most readers will derive their idea of a courtly setting from reproductions of splendid scenes from early fifteenth-century French manuscripts, such as the New Year feast of Jean, Duc de Berry, as painted for his *Très riches heures* by the brothers Limbourg.[2] The entertainments of the English nobility and royalty probably looked slightly less splendid and opulent – and we will need to extend our idea of a courtly setting beyond the palaces of those in the highest level of society to include the festivities and social gatherings in the country houses of England. But there is no doubt that the tradition of courtly lyric inherited by Chaucer and developed by him and his successors was primarily a French one, although, as in other areas of English cultural history (in art and architecture as well as in literature), reception and adaptation were by no means slavish imitation.

The French tradition was a long one, reaching from the twelfth-century troubadours to the 'rhétoriqueurs' of the late fifteenth and early sixteenth centuries.

[1] Notable exceptions are Stevens 1961 and Boffey 1985.
[2] Frequently reproduced, e.g. in Trapp, Gray, and Boffey 2002.

Of particular significance in our period was the heritage of the first part of the *Roman de la Rose* written by Guillaume de Lorris in the thirteenth century, an allegorical poem in which, he says proudly, 'the whole art of love is contained' (Horgan 1994). It certainly turned out to be one of the most influential books of the Middle Ages. The poem opens with a young man aged twenty falling asleep and dreaming. In his dream he is admitted to the enclosed garden of Mirth, and becomes the liegeman of the God of Love. He is instructed in Love's command-ments, and also learns the pains of love. In an elegant psychological allegory, dynamic personifications of mental states – some sympathetic and helpful towards the dreamer and Love, like Fair Welcome; others totally hostile, like the ugly figure of Daunger (Disdain, Rebuff) with his club – scheme and contend. It is a precursor of the later French *carte du tendre* or 'map of love', an allegorical landscape of the progress (and setbacks) of young love. For all its courtly formality, the pattern of love and desire is still very recognisable: an aspiring young male lover can still recognise 'Daunger' in a lady's glance. Its paradise of intense delight, its idealised love and its graceful young servants (this is certainly no country for old men) continued to entrance later writers, and we find the personified figures of the poem (Hope, Shame, Jealousy, Reason, Cour-tesy, Pity, etc.) appearing again and again in courtly narrative and courtly lyric.

Some excellent English examples of the many literary works which attempt to evoke the glories and the miseries of the lover's life are found among the fifteenth-century poems formerly attributed to Chaucer, such as *The Floure and the Leafe*. The tone is often a mixture of 'game' (sometimes dream fantasy, some-times a hint of Ovidian detachment) and 'earnest' in the (usually, though not always) serious advice and instruction to lovers. This is not confined to litera-ture, but was found in the pastimes of noble life. At the beginning of the fifteenth century there are records of an actual *cour amoureuse* at the French court. Mass was to be said on St Valentine's Day, followed by a meal and 'joieuse recreation et amoureuse conversacion'. Poems were to be read to the ladies, who were to judge them. Penalties could be imposed: anyone who made a *complainte*, *balade* or *rondeau* 'au deshonneur, reproche, amenissement ou blame' of ladies would be driven from 'toutes gracieuses assemblees et compaignies de dames et demoiselles'.[3] No such records survive in England, but literary evidence suggests some similar courtly games and perhaps competi-tions, and the general pattern of ideas was certainly familiar. This 'play world' was a mirror of courtly society: Cupid and Venus were powerful lords, and could rightly have their statutes, courts and courtiers (as in the English poem *The Court of Love*). But they were also gods, and the doctrines, language and practices of contemporary religion could be adapted or parodied (as in the English *Lovers' Mass* or the *Confessio Amantis* of Gower).

'Joieuse recreation et amoureuse conversation' could include discussion and debate concerning the dilemmas, problems and questions of love. This had early established itself as part of the tradition, and became widespread in European literature. There was plenty of scope for this in *Roman de la Rose*, especially in the

---

3   Piaget 1891 and 1902. See Stevens 1961, 164–7.

continuation of the poem by the self-consciously intellectual Jean de Meun. Questions of love continued to be debated in narrative *dits* and collections of poems. In the fifteenth century in France there was a full-scale debate on the *Roman de la Rose* itself, sparked by the real or supposed anti-feminist views of Jean de Meun. To this, the 'querelle de la Rose', a number of eminent writers made contributions, and it finds echoes in England – most obviously in Hoccleve's adaptation of Christine de Pisan in *The Letter of Cupid*, and the translation by Roos of Chartier's *La Belle Dame sans Merci*.

The influence of this extensive and varied French tradition remained strong in England throughout our period. Connections between England and France continued up to and beyond the end of the Hundred Years War. They were both literary (Chaucer translated Graunson, 'flour of hem that make in Fraunce', was praised by Deschamps, knew also the work of Machaut and Froissart, and was inspired by both parts of the *Roman de la Rose*) and personal: Froissart visited England, Charles d'Orléans was prisoner there. Lydgate says he visited Paris and saw the Dance of Death painted there – this would be in the period of the English occupation under the regent John, Duke of Bedford, a patron and collector of French painting. There were political marriages. Other contacts were more purely literary; some of the works of Christine de Pisan were known in England, as were those of Alain Chartier. French lyrics remained popular in England. Indeed, Julia Boffey remarks that 'English readers seem to have valued lyrics *as reading matter* only if they were either in French, or had strong French connections', pointing out also that the manuscripts copied by the indefatigable scribe John Shirley contain more courtly love lyrics in French than in English.[4] Two sumptuous manuscripts of French lyrics survive in English libraries: BL MS Harley 4431, containing lyrics by Christine de Pisan, which seems to have been acquired by Bedford, and BL MS Royal 16. F. ii, from the beginning of the sixteenth century, containing those of Charles d'Orléans, which was prepared for Arthur, Prince of Wales.

Although the English lyrics are deeply indebted to this French tradition, there are some marked differences. These are most obvious in the nature of the manuscripts in which they survive, and what these may reveal about patronage and their social contexts. They cannot match the splendid French collections of lyrics, nor do they usually seem destined for great patrons, great princes or courtiers. Even the Tudor songbooks associated with Henry VIII's court, are, as Boffey suggests, probably immediately designed 'more for the use of the singing-men of the Chapel Royal – clerks – than for that of illustrious courtiers, or of the king himself' (Boffey 1983, 11) – though they would presumably be the audience at any performance. Many are quite humble productions. Boffey has shown that a large proportion of the surviving English courtly lyrics are actually in manuscripts compiled by clergy. A Premonstratensian canon, John Gysborn, for instance, included one, *Grevus ys my sorowe / Both evyne and morrow* (Robbins *Sec.*, No. 206), in his personal (and largely religious) anthology, BL MS Sloane 1584.[5] Nor are they – with the notable exception of the English lyrics of Charles

---

4   Boffey 1983, 6. On Shirley, see Connolly 1998.
5   Boffey 1985, 129; Boffey 1983, 11.

d'Orléans in BL MS Harley 682 – elaborate, carefully organised anthologies or series of lyrics like a number of the French examples. More characteristically they appear separately or in small groups in what are at best somewhat miscellaneous collections. Some manuscripts containing them, like the early Chaucerian manuscripts, Bodl. MS Fairfax 16 and CUL MS Gg. 4. 27, are carefully produced, and certainly suggest an elegant context. And some lyrics, no doubt, could have been read or sung to a high courtly group like that depicted in the famous 'Troilus Frontispiece' in a manuscript in the Parker Library at Corpus Christi College, Cambridge[6] – although such an audience might still in real life have preferred French lyrics. Some English examples are attributed (perhaps with varying degrees of accuracy) to members of the highest nobility – the French Duke Charles d'Orléans, the English Earl of Warwick and Duke of Suffolk, even Henry VIII – but others are certainly the work of members of the gentry – the men and women of the Findern family, or Humfrey Newton esquire.

The English courtly lyrics seem to have been put to a variety of uses, so much so that they have been said to have a 'chameleon-like nature' (Boffey 1983, 14). Entertainment, both private and public, was certainly one. Sometimes it was probably very public – even, as C. S. Lewis suggested of Wyatt's songs, 'a little music after supper', in an atmosphere in which 'all the confessional or autobiographical tone' falls away: 'the song is still passionate: but the passion is distanced and generalized by being sung'.[7] Yet we should not exaggerate the role of music: outside the Tudor 'song books' it is rare to find musical notation accompanying the texts.[8] This, in some cases, may suggest that the music was so well known that it did not need to be recorded; often, however, it may be taken as an indication that the texts were primarily intended to be read rather than sung. On the other hand we can find instances in which a poem which looks rather thin and undistinguished on the page can be heightened and transformed by a musical setting.

Other lyrics may have had a role in the festivities and games of court or household – Mayings, festive games and revels, exchanges of gifts, etc. It seems that quite often, like their religious counterparts, the secular courtly lyrics could have a practical purpose – here in the rituals of courtship, the 'game of love'.[9] They might be presented to ladies as expressions of devotion, or given with gifts or emblems (like a 'truelove'). Thus, one rhyme royal stanza addresses a ring:

> Goo, lytell ryng, to that ylke swete   *same sweet one*
> That hath my hert in hyr demaeyne,   *possession*
> And loke you knell doune at hyr fete
> Besechying her she wold not dysdayene
> On hur smalle fyngerys the to streyne;   *thee*
> Than I wyll you say boldly:
> 'My master wold that he wer I.'   (Robbins *Sec.*, No. 95)

6 Reproduced, for example, in Loomis 1965, fig. 68.
7 Lewis 1954, 230. See also Boffey 1983, 10–11.
8 See Boffey 1985, 87–112.
9 Stevens 1961, 154–202.

The use of rings as speaking objects and as messengers is implied in some ring inscriptions: *Most in mynd and yn myn herrt / Lothest from you fer to deparrt* (Evans 1931, xv). Yet once more it is important not to exaggerate the importance of the 'game of love'. This ring-verse is clear enough, but we have to admit that in many cases we cannot tell if the lyrics, though they may have possibly been used as 'moves' in this game, were originally composed with that in mind. Many may have simply been composed – and collected – for the entertainment of a private individual. One rather good lyric can illustrate the difficulty of fixing a single 'context' or a 'use' with certainty:

> Go hert, hurt with adversité,   *heart*
> And let my lady thi wondis see,   *wounds*
> And sey hir this, as y say the: *say this to her; to thee*
> 'Farwel my joy, and welcom peyne,   *pain*
> Til y se my lady agayne.'   *until*
>   (Duncan *LMELC*, No. 23)[10]

Like the ring-verse above, it uses the device of prosopopoeia, though this messenger speaks with a more melancholy tone. The central image may remind us of a poem of Charles d'Orléans (*Go forth myn hert with my lady*, Arn 1994, Appendix 1, No. 2), in which the lover sends his heart to his lady as her servant, while he remains as a body without a heart. Perhaps too, as Thomas Duncan has suggested, there may be (in the manner of the 'religion of love') an underlying allusion to the wounded heart of Christ which he presents to mankind (Duncan *LMELC*, xxiv). The language is simple and elegant, and the poem reads as if it could easily be used (perhaps given with an emblem or an image of a heart) as a 'move' in the 'game of love'. Yet in the only manuscript in which it survives it is accompanied by its music,[11] and indeed, in performance, it is both elegant and passionate. An obvious conclusion would be that such lyrics could be put to more than one single use, private or public. And, as T. S. Eliot remarked, 'a good love poem, though it may be addressed to one person, is always meant to be overheard by other people.'[12]

When we look more closely at the characteristics of individual English lyrics we can see a closeness to the French tradition (notably in metrical forms, vocabulary and ideas) but also some independent variations and emphases. There is a preference for a few favourite French forms which are found again and again. Of these, the most popular is the *ballade*, which allowed space for a more elaborate poetic 'argument' than some other forms. Strictly, it consisted of three seven- or eight-line stanzas, each using the same rhymes throughout, and ending up with the same line as a refrain, and usually concluded with an 'envoy' addressed to a

---

[10] For the topic of sending the heart, cf. *Go forth myn hert with my lady* by Charles D'Orléans, Duncan *LMELC*, No. 9.
[11] Bodl. MS Ashmole 191; see below, p. 141. Part IV of the MS contains 'alchemical and astrological material in English and Latin with some English songs' (Boffey 1985, 195). All six poems (Robbins, *Sec.*, Nos 152–6 and 171) have music, but that one of them (171) also appears in the Findern MS (see below, p. 143) which suggests that this too may not have been the only or the original 'context'.
[12] *On Poetry and Poets*, quoted by Duncan, *LMELC*, xxv.

prince, a lady, or another person – but there were variations. The *roundel* or *rondeau*, probably originally a dance form, repeated the opening lines in whole or in part as a refrain after further groups of lines, and again, complete, at the end. Less common was the more complicated – and flexible – *virelai*, which often consists of stanzas of short lines with two rhymes, the second of which becomes the first and chief rhyme of the following stanza – though there are variations in which this 'tail-rhyme' is not carried forward.

There are other, less 'fixed' forms like the 'complaint' (or lament) or the 'epistle'. Both are common: the verse epistle in particular seems to have become especially popular in the fifteenth century. There are examples of the elegant and witty 'begging letter'. Much more frequent are 'epistles' devoted to the pleas of lovers or their protestations of devotion. These are sometimes simply lyrics with rather general pleas or messages or laments; others, however, use the characteristic formulae of a contemporary English letter (as Chaucer had done in the 'Letter of Troilus' in Book V of his poem).[13]

Some of the characteristics, and the possibilities, may be illustrated from an excellent pair in Bodl. MS Fairfax 16, often attributed to Suffolk (though doubts have been expressed about his authorship). One, *Myn hert ys set, and all myn hole entent* (Robbins *Sec.*, No. 188), with a significantly general rubric, 'How the lover is sette to serve the floure', expresses the poet's determination to serve 'this flower' faithfully, and for her sake to serve all other ladies. Since Chaucer, *off poetry y-namyd worthiest*, is dead, the poet requests Lydgate, the monk of Bury, to *enlumyne his pen*, with a gracious compliment: *For thy connyng* [skill] *ys syche, and eke* [also] *thy grace, / After Chaucer to occupye his place*. But then the poem becomes a defence of love and of ladies, *wher-as ye say that love ys but dotage*. The switch from 'thou' to the polite plural seems deliberate: it sounds as if the poet is wittily reproving the monk's views on women. The true doctrine is firmly put to him: every man that has *a good corage* [heart] */ Must lover be – thys wold I that ye knew: / Who lovyth wel all vertu will hym sew* [follow]. As for the idea that women's *trouthe* [faithfulness] does not last, that they should not be trusted, that they are unsteadfast, God forbid that everything that clerks write should be true. With an exclamation, and another switch to the familiar (and mockingly inferior?) 'thou' – *A fye! For schame! O thou envyous man!* – the offender is cast as accused in the court of love. Knock on thy breast and repent, he is told: *O thou unhappy man, go hyde thy face!* If thou art wise do not appear in person, but let thy attorney plead, and see if he can excuse thy negligence. The letter ends firmly (reminding us that it is a letter – it has once earlier been called a 'bill'), and with mock severity: *Have mynde of this, for now I wryte no more!* This lively *jeu d'esprit* is a contribution to the ongoing 'querelle des femmes', and very probably to the entertainment of a coterie.

The other poem, *Myn hertys joy, and all myn hole plesaunce* (Duncan *LMELC*, No. 11), is a straightforward love lyric, smooth and elegant. But here the fiction of the letter is much more strongly emphasised – from *Besechyng yow thys lytell byll* [little letter] *and I / May hertly, wyth symplesse and drede* [simplicity and reverence], */ Be recomawndyd to your goodlyhede* [excellence] (5–7), through a number of

---

13 See Davis 1965.

contemporary epistolary formulae (if you want to know how I am, I am in good health *as of body* but *treuly not in hert* nor will I be until I see you, or *I wryte to yow no more for lak of space*). The poet beseeches the Trinity to guard and protect her. And he even works in the date: *Go lytill byll, and say thou were wyth me / Of verey trouth, as thou canst wele remembre, / At myn uprist, the fyft day of Decembre* (19–21). These same formulae can be seen in the well-known Valentine letter of Margery Brews to John Paston III in 1477, in which she slips into courtly verse:

> And yf it please yowe to here of my welfare, I am not in good heele of body ner of herte, nor shall be tyll I here from yowe
> > For ther wottys no creature what peyn that I endure,
> > And for to be deede, I dare it not dyscure . . .   *reveal*

and ends *No more to yowe at this tyme, but the Holy Trinity hafe yowe in kepying.*[14]

A number of the writers profess (with more or less traditional modesty) the inadequacy of their eloquence (*all* [although] *can y not well endite; greting hir . . . in termes rud, but yit with esperaunce*, etc.). Some of their epistles – like other English courtly lyrics – are somewhat rough and amateurish, and many are uneven in style, but many are gracious and pleasing, like the 'Suffolk' poems quoted above. And there can be something touching about a self-conscious attempt at eloquence:

> Now and y were as prest of flight   *as swift of flight*
> As ever was faucon tyl his pray,   *falcon to*
> Y wolde then with all my myght
> To speke with you onys a day.   *once*
>
> Y may wryte no more a dele,   *no further*
> For of no leyser sykerly;   *certainly*
> But ofte-tymes y grete you wel
> As sterris sitten on the skye;
> And more often by a thousand part
> Then ony clerke may wryte with inke,
> Or eny man can pryve by art,   *prove*
> Or mouthe speke, or hert thinke!   (Robbins *Sec.*, No. 197, 37–48)

One of the most pleasingly intricate examples is a pair of macaronic letters, care-fully composed (by the same poet, probably?) in lines of English, French and Latin.[15] Both begin with appropriate 'headings' ('De Amico ad Amicam' and 'Responcio'), appropriate opening lines (*A celuy que pluys eyme en mounde* and *A soun treschere et special*), and excite admiration for their fine craftsmanship while at the same time managing to involve the reader in the lovers' situation. The man laments and pleads:

> Ma tresduce et tresamé,   *my most sweet and most beloved*
> Nyght and day for love of the   *thee*
> > Suspiro.   *I sigh*

---

14 Davis 1971, 662, No. 415.
15 Duncan *LMELC*, Nos 12 and 13; see Boffey 1983, 12–13.

Soyez permanent et leal,	*be constant and faithful*
Love me so that I it fele,	
Requiro.	*I ask*
	(Duncan *LMELC*, No. 12, 13–18)

The lady responds:

Vous estes ma mort et ma vye,	*are my death and my life*
I pray yow, for youre curteysye,	
Amate;	*love me*
Cestes maundés, jeo vous pry	*this letter, I pray you*
In youre herte steadfastily	
Notate.	*inscribe*
	(Duncan *LMELC*, No. 13, 49–54)

These two poems, artful and passionate, remind us of a duet in early opera. In the midst of such a display of technique, simple English words (like *sweeting* [sweet one]) and the familiar topics of letters, both implicit and explicit (*I am right in good heele*; *Pur vostre amur, allas, allas / I am werse than I was*), reinforce the emotion.

A concern (sometimes a self-conscious concern) with eloquence is common among the writers of courtly lyrics. Some achieve this primarily by the use of a smooth and easy syntax and a generally simple vocabulary. Only a few attempt a deliberate ornamentation of style, sometimes using learned or 'aureate' diction deriving from Lydgate and later poets, and later perhaps influenced by some of the French *rhétoriqueurs*. It is clear that for the most part we are dealing with a formal and traditional type of poetry which uses conventional forms, conventional (almost formulaic) language, and conventional images and ideas. The art of the poet is less in the direct outpouring of a distinctive personal passion than in expressing emotion through the skilful use of traditional style and material. We have already seen examples where poems express what seems to be 'genuine feeling'. It would be very rash to claim that such poems never arose from personal experience, but even more rash to suppose that they always did. Experience, whether personal or imaginatively conceived, is transformed by as well as mediated through the poet's art. His individuality can be discerned from the particular treatment of the traditional matter and style. Perhaps the audience took pleasure in familiar forms and material, and also in detecting smaller or greater variations (in the manner of a musical composition). The poet's art of composition and transformation was partly a demonstration of his talent, and sometimes also had an element of self-conscious 'game'. The courtly lyric in both French and English had developed a vocabulary of almost technical terms or 'termes clefs', words which constant repetition had endowed with a cluster of special resonances – the great oppositions of the lover's life, joy or sorrow, the qualities derived from the French psychological allegory, and a host of others – 'service', 'longing', etc. Even 'eye' or 'heart' may carry a special 'charge'. These can be used straightforwardly, or sometimes with a certain ambiguity.

Such terms embody the main themes and topics of the love lyric. It generally prefers to concentrate on the agonies of the lover's life – partings and separations, 'daunger' and rejection – rather than the joys of love consummated. The lover will dream of his lady (*but when I wakyde, ye were a-wey*) or wish that he were a *bird invisible . . . With my wynges that y might flussh* [fly] / *Pryvyly to you, suetyng fre* [noble beloved] – but *Alas, yit wissh helpeth me nought.*[16] There are many celebrations and descriptions of the lady's beauty, but usually joy is mingled with sorrow. In the lyric *Grevus ys my sorowe* (Robbins *Sec.*, No. 206) which Gysborn put in his book, a lady laments that she is killed by 'unkindness'. The reader of such poems may recall the old music-hall song: 'This high-class music is a little melancholy / But it's always so refined'. Indeed, a number of English poets, like their French counterparts, seem to relish exquisite melancholy.[17]

Love is the central subject of courtly lyric, but it is not the only one. The lyrics provide entertainment, but also, in the widest sense, instruction – and not simply instruction in the art of love or the duties of lovers, as in 'The Ten Commandments of Love' in Bodl. MS Fairfax 16, which, if observed, mean that *Daunger and unkindness bin oppressed* (Robbins *Sec.*, No. 177, 12). A number of poems have a distinct if general moral emphasis. This seems to accord with a widespread taste for works of moral advice. Interestingly, it has been suggested that the order of the French poems of Charles d'Orléans in BL MS Royal 16. F. ii, made for the English prince Arthur, was adjusted in order to impress upon him the joys of married love.[18] Chaucer's philosophical and moral lyrics seem to have been as popular as his love lyrics, and do not seem to have been explicitly differentiated from them (Boffey 1985, 12). Just as the term 'courtly' has to expand in England to encompass gentry, landowners and their manor houses, so do style and subject: courtly lyric can encompass popular songs used for courtly entertainment and moral proverbial instruction or meditation, like the rhetorical and proverbial *The worlde so wide, the aire so remuable* (Duncan *LMELC*, No. 93) attributed to Squire Halsham. We have already encountered ring inscriptions and mottoes. There are even graffiti: in Duxford Church someone inscribed what seems to be a lover's anagram: *With wiel* [happiness] *my herte is wa* [sorrowful], / *And closed ys with care;* / *L and S sekurly* [truly] / *Cause me to sygh* [sigh] *full sar* [sorely] (Robbins *Sec.*, No. 145, 1–4); at Landewade there is what is apparently the opening of a 'farewell' lyric: *Fare well all clene melawdy* [melody] / *Fare well all ladyes and . . .*[19] Perhaps we might be permitted to place on one edge of this varied and not very clearly defined genre some of the moral and instructional verses on walls or tapestries.[20] We can certainly place on another edge a number of parodies or mock-courtly poems. Within the main stream of the tradition were poems which admitted the disappointments and bitterness which love can bring. Moreover, the pure intensity of passion and the exquisite melan-

---

16   Robbins *Sec.*, No. 200, 8, and No. 205, 58–60, 64.
17   Kilbansky, Panofsky and Saxl 1965, 217–27.
18   Boffey 1983, 3. See Fox 1973, Introduction. On the manuscript see Boffey 1985, 37–40, 75–6, 115, 137–9.
19   See Pritchard 1967, 54, fig. 73.
20   See Gray, 47–8. A letter to Wolsey asks for Alexander Barclay to 'devise histories and convenient reasons to florisshe the buildings and banket house' for the Field of Cloth of Gold. Thomas More in his youth devised 'nyne pageauntes and verses over' in his father's house in London. Later, William Bulleyne (1564) speaks of 'faire clothes with pleasaunte borders upon the same with many wise sayings paynted upon them' (*Archeological Journal* 92 (1935), 247).

choly of the high courtly tradition can sometimes hover on the brink of self-parody: not surprisingly some poets enjoy making the conventional language and forms tremble a little, and others enjoy turning the fragile world of love upside down.[21]

Our survey begins with Chaucer – and what a spectacular beginning it is. His acknowledged pre-eminence as a narrative poet has sometimes made us forget that he was also a most distinguished lyric poet. He also seems to have been a prolific one – although much has probably been lost. In a 'court of love' situation in the Prologue to *The Legend of Good Women*, Alceste, defending him against the God of Love, who had complained about his Criseyde (*that maketh men to women lesse triste* [trust]) and his translation of the *Roman de la Rose* (*that is an heresye ayeins my lawe*), says that Chaucer has written *many an ympne* [song, poem] *for your halydayes, / That highten balades, roundels, virelayes* (Benson, *The Legend of Good Women*, F, lines 423–4). These were probably similar to what he called in a rather different penitential context in his 'Retracciouns' *many a song and many a lecherous lay*. His friend Gower says that in his youth Chaucer composed *ditees and songes glade*. Perhaps some, like Gower's, were written in French. In modern editions his lyrics or 'Short Poems' are often accompanied by a few more dubious contenders, 'poems not ascribed to Chaucer in the Manuscripts'. It has been argued that one or more of these may actually be his, but in such a traditional genre arguments based on internal stylistic evidence are difficult to sustain. *Merciles Beaute*, a skilful triple roundel, which uses the traditional topics of French love lyric, has been called 'thoroughly Chaucerian'. It has a bold dramatic opening – *Your yen two wol slee me sodenly* – but roundels quite often do. Yet it is certainly tempting to call lines like *Sin I fro Love escaped am so fat, / I never thenk to ben in his prison lene* (27–8) 'Chaucerian', whether they really come from his pen or not.

Those lyrics which can be more confidently ascribed to Chaucer reveal a willingness to experiment with form and technique (most strikingly, perhaps, in *A Complaint to his Lady* where Dante's *terza rima* seems to appear for the first time in English). They also show a notable variety in topic and tone, ranging from the satirical address to Adam his own scribe or the witty *Complaint to his Purse* (in which the purse becomes his *lady dere* and the subject of a mock love complaint) to poems more straightforwardly in the high courtly tradition, as the ballade *Womanly Noblesse* or *The Complaint unto Pity*, in which the poet who has long sought Pity finds her dead *and buried in an herte*, surrounded by figures such as Bounté and Jolyté, but all *confedered* [allied] by the bonds of Cruelty, the foe of Pity – an elegant and graceful excursion into the world of French love-allegory. The ballade addressed to Rosemounde, however, has some characteristic self-deprecating comedy: the poet compares himself to a pike steeped in galantine (sauce), and identifies himself as *trewe Tristam the secounde* as he burns in *an amorous plesaunce*.

Chaucer was especially fond of the 'philosophical' lyric of ideas, often ideas

---

21 Stevens 1961, 220: 'the intense idealisms of courtly love were bound to produce . . . intense disillusions'; see also 220–4. This strand is found throughout the tradition, from the troubadours on.

which engaged him deeply in his longer works. These include the ballades *Fortune* and *Gentilesse*. *Lak of Stedfastnesse* is a 'lament upon the times' – stability has gone; everything is turned upside down because of bribery and wilfulness – with the gloomy refrain *Al is lost for lak of stedfastnesse*. The topic is traditional, but many readers have sensed a more personal feeling here; the scribe Shirley says Chaucer wrote it in his last years. Similarly, *The Former Age*, based on Boethius, describing the happy life of those who lived simply and innocently in the 'first age' before covetousness first brought sorrow, and contrasting it with the effete and corrupt present age, gives eloquent expression to traditional ideas, but Chaucer's ending (*For in oure dayes nis but covetyse, / Doublenesse and tresoun, and envye, / Poyson, manslawhtre, and mordre in sondry wyse*) is remarkably vehement and suggests he may have been thinking of events in his own day – possibly in the last years of the reign of Richard II. *Truth* is a very impressive example of the 'philosophical' lyric – and that many copies of it survive may suggest a contemporary popularity. Shirley calls it 'Ballade that Chaucer made on his deeth bedde', but this may well be over-romantic: in other manuscripts it is entitled *Balade de bon Conseyl*. It consists of a series of urgent imperatives, beginning *Flee fro the press and dwelle with sothfastnesse*, transforming semi-proverbial topics of moderation and philosophical detachment from the pressures of the world into a powerful argument. Here the refrain *And trouthe thee shal delivere, it is no drede* brings a note of hope and consolation. It is addressed to 'Vache', probably Sir Philip de la Vache, a courtier, and combines sympathetic, firm advice and a familiar tone. Vache is identified not only with a 'pilgrim' but with a 'beast' in a stall – in what seems to be an outrageous pun on his name.

Very distinctive are a couple of verse epistles to his friends, in which, it has plausibly been suggested (Norton-Smith 1966a), he may be imitating the easy urbane and conversational tone of the Horatian epistle in a way that no contemporary or fifteenth-century English lyric poet does. His 'envoy' or verse letter to Bukton is relaxed and witty. Chaucer has promised to talk of the *sorwe and woo that is in marriage*. He will not say (he says) that it is the chain of Satan at which the devil continually gnaws, but he will dare to say that if he were out of his pain he would never wish to be bound again. Similar thoughts follow, expressed with mock caution, light-heartedly playing with various 'authorities' (including Holy Writ) and traditional images of marriage as a chain and a prison. Bukton is advised to read the *Wife of Bath*. That to Scogan jokingly suggests that since Scogan has not been faithful in an affair, Venus is weeping so copiously that all will be drowned by her tears, and Cupid will take revenge on all those *that ben hoor* [grey] *and rounde of shap*.

Chaucer's knowledge of the lyric tradition and the uses to which it could be put is evident in his other poems. He imagines Absolon singing a song of love-pleading outside Alison's house in the *Miller's Tale*, and, in the *Merchant's Tale*, the squire Damian composing for May a letter *In manere of a compleynt or a lay* which he slips into her hand – both clearly 'moves' in the game of love. In his own narratives he makes superb use of lyrics. In the *Book of the Duchess* a 'lay' changes the intellectual direction of the poem. In the Prologue to the *Legend of Good Women* the fine, confidently written ballade, *Hyd, Absolon, thy gilte tresses clere*, heralds the arrival of the beautiful Alceste and her maidens. The splendid roundel, *Now welcome, somer, with thy sonne softe*, sung by birds *to don Nature honour and pleasaunce* at their departing in the *Parliament of Fowls* is a magnificent celebration of spring and brings the poem to a joyous conclusion. *Troilus and Criseyde* contains a number of lyrics carefully placed in the mouths of characters at dramatic points. A sonnet of Petrarch appears for the first time in English in the song of Troilus smitten by love – *If no love is, O God, what fele I so?* – in the first book.[22] It is carefully fitted to the emotional moment, the character of Troilus, and the larger philosophical questions raised by the poem. Antigone's 'Trojan song' of ideal love in Book II provides an answer to Criseyde's worry that love may prove *the moste stormy lyf*, moves her, and leads on to the song of the nightingale and the dream of the eagle. Near to the end of the third book, Troilus (appropriately) sings a Boethian song on the cosmic power of love, ending with a characteristically 'gentil' prayer that even those with *hertes colde* should be encircled in the bond of love. In the final book, Troilus alone in Troy and desperately yearning for Criseyde, sings with 'soft voice' a single despairing stanza:

> O sterre, of which I lost have al the light,
> With herte soor wel oughte I to biwaille
> That evere derk in torment, nyght by nyght,
> Toward my deth with wynd in steere I saille;   *ustern, ul my back*
> For which the tenthe nyght, if that I faille   *I lack*
> The gydyng of thi bemes bright an houre,
> My ship and me Caribdis wol devoure.   (*Troilus*, V, 638–44)

None of Chaucer's English successors can match this variety and sophistication, but their efforts are far from uninteresting. An early testimony to the poet and his philosophical lyrics is to be found in the *Moral Balade* (1406 or 1407?) by his friend Henry Scogan (c.1361–1407), a Norfolk gentleman who became tutor to the four sons (*My noble sones, and eek my lordes dere*) of Henry IV,[23] who may have been the recipients – according to Shirley, at a supper of a meeting of merchants in the Vintry at the house of Lewis John. Scogan calls it a 'litel tretys', 'writen with myn owne hand full rudely'. In his age he laments that in his misspent youth he cherished vices rather than virtues: this 'complaint' is to warn his royal pupils and to urge them to follow virtue, for lordship without virtue cannot endure. He cites Chaucer's views on true nobility (*vertuous noblesse / Cometh not to you by way of auncestrye*), and quotes (*And of this thing herke how my mayster seyd*) his ballade of *Gentilesse*. Lords nowadays do not wish to hear about virtue, and act like a ship without *governaunce*, but *vertuous noblenesse / Roted in youthe, and with good perseveraunce, / Dryveth away al vyce and wrecchednesse*. He gives examples of virtuous heroes of humble origin, and of those of noble birth who fell because of vice.

---

22 The first 'Canticus Troili' is found separately in a number of manuscripts (as is the 'Complaint of Anelida', from *Anelida and Arcite'*. See Boffey 1985, 72.

23 Text in Skeat 1897, 237–44. Chaucer's *Gentilesse* is perhaps also echoed in *A Ballade of good Counsel* (*Sen trew vertew encressis dignytee, Index* 3151), formerly associated with James I of Scotland; see Lawson 1910, 102–3.

Another example of an apparent English liking for lyrics of good counsel in the courtly mode is to be found in Gower's lyrics. Gower himself left in *In Praise of Peace* (Macaulay 1901, 481–92), a long English lyric addressed to Henry IV, an eloquent work on a favourite theme: *With pees stant* [stands] *every creature in reste, / Withoute pees ther may no lyf be glad – / Werre is moder of the wronges alle*. It is a poem of advice to a prince, emphasising the need for *pité*. Gower's sequence of French ballades, *Traitié pour essempler les amantz marietz*, written at the end of the fourteenth century, was translated into English in the early fifteenth century by one Quixley (MacCracken 1908–9, 33–50), apparently from Yorkshire, as a 'litel tretice' (of just over 400 lines) on the 'meschef . . . of avoutrie [adultery]'. Hardly inspiring yet nevertheless interesting, this, like its original, is a strongly moral work. It exemplifies the continuing relationship of the French and English lyric and shows considerable care in translation (Quixley even follows the French syllabic metrical pattern). An early example in English of an organised series of ballades in the French manner, Quixley's version reproduces Gower's arguments and exposition with clarity of style and syntax. It celebrates the ideal marriage of two persons in unity. This is Gower's ideal of 'honest love' that we find in the *Confessio Amantis* – *Honeste love, that to trowth dooth obeisance, / Maketh marriages goode and ryalle* (Ballade 4). The moral message is continued and emphasised through the repeated refrain in each ballade which also gives a strong sense of unity to the whole (*A mans trowth to breke it is not honeste, Gret peril it is to breke a mans spousaille, Broken wedloke god will venge and despise, Horrible is the synne of avoutrie*, etc.), while exempla demonstrate the disasters which follow the lack of *trouthe*.

Two better known English poets of the earlier fifteenth century, both admirers of Chaucer, also wrote a number of courtly lyrics. Thomas Hoccleve (d.1426), clerk of the Privy Seal, was a Londoner with literary tastes who almost certainly knew Chaucer, and who was in touch with French literary culture. His shorter poems include a number of well-written occasional pieces, ballades addressed to Prince Henry (for whom he wrote his long poem of advice, *The Regement of Princes* (1410–13), and who, in 1413, became King Henry V), and presentation poems to John Lancaster, later Duke of Bedford, and to Edward Duke of York. The 'public' poems to Henry praise him for his defence of the faith against heresy; one exhorts the king to continue as *Piler of our feith, and werreyour/ Ageyn the heresyes bitter galle* and to *Hold up Cristes baner; lat it nat falle!*[24] More attractive to modern tastes are his petitions for money, like the ballade and roundel addressed to Master Henry Somer, Under-Treasurer (1408–10), which wittily puns on the recipient's name, Summer, and plays on its seasonal implications (*Hastith our hervest* [harvest], *as soone as yee may*) in a rather Chaucerian manner.[25] Another is a set of three roundels addressed to Lady Money, the last of which, *La commendacion de ma dame*, after he has been rejected, is a tour de force of a different kind. A mock description of the lady's beauty, a

24 Mitchell and Doyle 1970, Nos 5 and 6.
25 Mitchell and Doyle 1970, No. 13. Another merry lyric (?1421), again addressed to Somer, now Chancellor, concerns a meeting of a Temple dining club, the *court of Good Company*, Mitchell and Doyle 1970, No. 17.

splendid reversal of the traditional rhetorical topics, becomes an equally rhetorical presentation of ugliness. Her forehead is gold, her brows like to *dym reed* [red] *coral*, her eyes glitter like jet; she has baggy cheeks and large jaws; her nose is a roof to keep out the rain, her chin can hardly be seen, and her comely body is shaped like a football. It is all done with great panache and a self-conscious metrical skill – the whole poem has only two rhymes.

John Lydgate, Benedictine monk of Bury St Edmunds (d.1449/50), a prolific writer, left a number of courtly lyrics which are polished and confident in their handling of traditional matter. They also show an interesting variety. His smoothness and skill can be seen in one, which, according to the rubric, he 'wrote at the request of a squyer that served in loves court':

Freshe lusty beaute, joined with gentylesse,	*delightful beauty; graciousness*
Demure appert, glad chere with gouvernaunce,	*reserved, honest, in manner*
Yche thing demenid by avysinesse,	*ruled by discretion [pleasing and poised*
Prudent of speeche, wisdam of dalyaunce,	*wise in conversation*
Gentylesse, with womanly plesaunce,	
Hevenly eyeghen, aungellyk of visage;	*eyes; angelic*
Al this hathe nature sette in youre ymage.	

(MacCracken 1934, 379–81, lines 1–7)

It would make a nice, conventional 'move' in the game of love (though its listing of fourteen ancient heroines and exemplars of virtue might not persuade a modern lady). Another, 'a balade sayde by a gentil-womman whiche loved a man of gret estate' (MacCracken 1934, 418–20), illustrates his gift for the evocation of pathos, which he may have learned from the *Legend of Good Women*, the *Anelida*, and other works of Chaucer:

Allas! I wooful creature,	
Lyving betweene hope and dreed,	
Howe might I the woo endure,	
In tendrenesse of wommanhede,	*tenderness*
In langoure ay my lyff to lede,	*sorrow*
And sette myn hert in suche a place,	
Wher as I, be liklyhede,	*in likelihood*
Am ever unlike to stonde in grace! (1–8)	

Her lament contains a touching social narrative, like a gentler, less passionate version of one of the *Heroides*. There is, she says, such a difference between us that Daunger has brought me into great distress – and yet though I never attain my desire, I shall love him best. In our childhood we gathered flowers, and Love gave me *a knotte in hert of remembraunce* which cannot be unbound. He is my chosen knight, and (unknown to him) has been from my tender youth. In another lyric (MacCracken 1934, 424–7), the poet finds that at New Year the only gift that he can give is his heart:

And as I stoode myself alloone, upon the Nuwe Yere night,
I prayed unto the frosty moone, with hir pale light,
    To go and recomaunde me unto my lady dere.

And early on the nexst morowe, kneling in my cloos,   *cloister*
I prayed eke the shene sonne, the houre whane he aroos,   *bright*
    To gon also and sey the same in his bemys clere.

But tho ther came a clowdy thought, and gan myn hert assayle,
And sayde me, howe my servyce ther me shoulde not avayle,
    Til my lady mercylesse me hade brought on beer . . . (12–20) *bier*

He sends forth his 'little song' and his heart: *Go forthe, hert, and be right glad with hir to abyde, / And wayt upon hir day or night* (57–8). It is all highly traditional, but genuinely eloquent.

Others are short satirical pieces or poems of general, often proverbial, advice: poems on moderation, on peace, on contraries existing together. Also, like Hoccleve, Lydgate writes occasional poems: a ballade for Henry VI in the year of his coronation, which combines celebration with advice, or a (rather long-winded) poem on the gift of an eagle to the king. Like Chaucer and Hoccleve before him, he writes a 'begging poem', the *Letter to Gloucester* (Duke Humfrey, the king's uncle) lamenting that his purse is fallen sick (*his guttys wer out-shake*) and has had no help from leeches or apothecaries. In more familiar vein he wrote his elegant propemticon (a poem wishing a friend a safe voyage) for Thomas Chaucer, the poet's son (?1414): his friends must remember him and say every day, *Saint Julyan, our joye and al our glorye, / Come hoom ageyne, lyche as we desire, / To suppowaylen* [support] *al the hole shyre* 68–70) – a nice compliment with an allusion to his father's Franklin.[26]

Although these post-Chaucerian English poets can write competent and polished lyrics, the finest lyric poet in the England of their day was a Frenchman living among them, Charles d'Orléans (1394–1465), who was captured at Agincourt in 1415, and held by the English until his release and return to France in 1440. The great majority of the English poems attributed to him survive in MS Harley 682 in the British Library.[27] This contains over two hundred English lyrics, most of which correspond to French poems known to be by him. The question of the authorship of these English poems and their relationship to the French has been long and fiercely discussed.[28] Absolute certainty seems to be impossible, but the overwhelming probability is that the poems are not the work of an English translator but of the Duke himself. He spent 25 years in England: René of Anjou later remarked that he had stayed there so long that he had learnt the language. Occasional syntactical and metrical oddities could well suggest the work of a non-native speaker of English.[29] During his long captivity, Charles was moved from London to other places in a kind of house arrest: in its later

26 Norton-Smith 1966b, No. 2, 68–70. *Saint Julyan* was the patron saint of hospitality and *Seint Julian he was in his contree* was Chaucer's description of his generous Franklin (*CT* I, 340).
27 Some English poems are found in other manuscripts, including a Paris manuscript which is an autograph of Charles. All are contained in Arn 1994, from which quotations here are taken (though with some changes in punctuation). Line numbers are those of the entire sequence. Quotations from corresponding French poems are from Champion 1923 with individual line numbering for each poem.
28 Full references are given by Arn 1994, by Steele in Steele and Day 1941, I, and, more succinctly, in Duncan *LMELC*, 183–4. See also Arn 2000.
29 See Duncan *LMELC*, 186–7.

stages he spent some time under the 'guard' of the Duke of Suffolk (who had himself spent some time in French captivity earlier), a man of literary interests and the husband of Alice Chaucer, the daughter of Thomas, the poet's son. Charles's knowledge of English writing and literary traditions probably began earlier: it is clear that he had read Chaucer and Gower.[30] Charles was thoroughly at home in the French literary tradition, familiar with the work of contemporary writers such as Christine de Pisan (one of whose poems he adapted) as well as those of earlier periods. He was born into the highest nobility, to a family of power, and vast wealth – and of considerable sophistication. He possessed an extensive library, and after his return to France became himself a noted patron of letters in his court at Blois, which was briefly visited by the other outstanding poet of fifteenth-century France, François Villon.

The English poems of MS Harley 682 form an organised series of love poems (very much in the French manner), amounting to about 6,500 lines in all. It consists of two sequences with a connecting central section. The first has a formal allegorical narrative introduction[31] in which the poet is enrolled as a servant of Love, followed by a series of ballades addressed to Lady Beauty and concerned with his love and courtship of her. Lady Beauty dies, and the lover in despair renounces Love. There follows a series of songs and rondeaux called a 'Jubilee' – a 'banquet of song and dance' – intended as a kind of interlude. Then comes the second sequence: Venus and Fortune appear, and the poet is introduced to a second lady. This romance is cut short by Charles's enforced departure. The non-lyrical allegorical 'link' passages contain some good writing, as in the account of his memories of his dead love, or the description of Venus emerging from the sea.

In the shorter poems we hear the voice of a real lyric poet. Again and again we are struck by a vigorous opening – *How, how, myn hert! Opyn the gate of Thought / And resceyve into the a swete present / The which my bestbilovyd hath to thee brought!* (Ballade 34, 1222–24) – which dramatically imitates the speaking voice and creates the 'situation' of the lyric. The poet defiantly challenges Daunger – *A, Daunger, here y cast to the my glove / And thee appele* [accuse], *o Traytoure, of treason / Tofore the hy and myghti God of Love* (Ballade 44, 1548–50) – and querulously questions Hope: *What menyst thou, Hope? Dost thou me skoffe and skorne? / For wordis moche thou hast, and flateryng!* (Ballade 52, 1811–12). Such openings give us an instant entry into the emotional scene. In the course of a ballade he will pose a sad and bitterly incredulous question: *Allas! How evyr kouthe* [knew] *the God of Kynde / A body shape so fayre and so goodly / And in it sett so hard an hert unkynde?* (Ballade 91, 5520–21, in the second sequence); or violently reprove a deity:

---

30 His younger brother, Jean d'Angoulême, who spent even more time in English captivity, possessed a manuscript of *The Canterbury Tales* which he annotated himself.

31 The beginning of the English text is apparently lost. It begins in the 'Introduction' with the gods Cupid and Venus issuing a letter patent, which admits the *duk that folkis calle / Of Orlyaunce* as their servant. That we are in a high courtly world is made clear by Cupid's instructions to the new servant on the winning of a lady's favour: *gentil must be wonne with gentiles*, a merchant's wife by gifts, but *a cherlis doughtir dawbid in clay* by *strokis grete, not tippe nor tapp, do way!* On attempts to identify Lady Beauty with a real person, see Arn 1994, 134 and Boffey 1985, 64.

O fy, Fortune, fy thi dissayt and skorne,   *deceptiveness*
For all thi fraude, retorne yet wilfully,   *deceit; turn (your wheel)of your own*
That woldist ay eche wele were sone forlorne.   *you who; happiness; lost   [free will*
Iwis, [s]coffer, yet art thou no thing ny   *certainly; not even close*
Me to disseyve, for clene y the defy!   *to being able to deceive me*
                                        (Ballade 118, 6420–24).

In another dramatic situation (Ballade 37) he finds his heart in the company of
Hope, who comforts him (with a nicely colloquial phrase): '*O hert, be glad, for y
good tidyng brynge! / So now, let se, pluk up thi lustyhed*' (1313–14). Such phrases
(and there are a number of them: in one roundel, Roundel 5, he hopes to have
more joy then ther be stichis in my shert) invigorate all the traditional topics that he
uses.

The power and energy of his writing are everywhere apparent. Ballade 47
produces a genuine sense of excitement in its conversational style:

Welcome and yit more welcome, bi this light,
O Fresshe Tidyngis, unto myn hert are ye!
Say me, hast thou had of my ladi sight?
Come telle me sumwhat of hir, now lat see,
As bi thi trouthe how thynkist, is she not she   *is she not the one*
(She was when last we partid compane),
Which plesid hir say (to bring me out of woo,   *who was pleased to say*
Tredyng my foot, and that so pratily),
'Teys yow to whom y love am and no moo'. (1658–66)   '*It is you whose love I
                                                        [am and no one else's*'

Compared with the French version – *Pour m'oster de merencolie, / M'escrivy
amoureusement: / 'C'estes vous de qui suis amye*' (Ballade 39, 7–9) – this is more
'talkative' and more familiar: the treading on the foot and the spoken message
are only in the English. Sometimes his more expansive English lines sound more
'romantic' than the French, as in *In at the wyndowes of my derkid eyen* (Ballade 45,
1608) compared with *Par les fenestres de mes yeulx*.

Nevertheless Charles uses his English 'roughness'[32] self-consciously – in an
epistle, like his English contemporaries, he apologises for his *ruggid fowle langage*
(line 6149) – and to good effect. He likes abrupt questions and ejaculations:
*Retorne, for shame, retorne, retorne, ageyne! / Hye not to fast, parde, ye gon amys! / . . .
I put yowre silf to be my juge, ywis,/ When ye are – where? – now where as ye shulde be*

---

[32] It is frequently pointed out that Charles's English versions are often rougher and more vivid
than his French. He certainly does seem to have been very responsive to English style, but it
would be rash to claim a kind of essential 'Englishness' here (he would certainly not have
approved of being thought of as an honorary Englishman!). A number of practical considerations need to be noted. There is the question of genre – in French much of Villon's poetry is
'vivid' in a way that Charles's is not. Moreover, the ten-syllable line he chose instead of the
eight-syllable line he uses in his French ballades firstly offered him more scope (as it had done
for Chaucer) and secondly required more words – which can produce vivid details or adjectives, but also sometimes fillers, or loose connectives. The 'order' of the versions has been as
hotly debated as has the question of the authorship of the English. It seems to this reader
(though not everyone would agree) that the French collection of poems *as we have it now* is a
polished work of art, which feels like a final revised version.

(Ballade 119, 6448–49, 6454–55). Sometimes his deliberate interruptions – *Half in dispeyre – not half, but clene dispeyrid, / I take my leue of Love for onys and ay* (Ballade 108, 6101–02) – can become an 'echoic' technique, as it does in Ballade 100 to emphasise the poet's sorrow:

> Who is the cause herof then? Is hit ye?
> Ye? Nay, it is my freel hert!   *timid*
> Hert? Nay, my fonnyd love, parde!   *foolish*
> Love? Nay, my rakill lookis stert!   *bold impetuous glances*
> Lokis? Nay, for this y may advert . . . (5876–80) *observe*

Just as confident is his use of the techniques of formal rhetoric. He will use figures of balance, puns and paradox – especially for the traditional paradoxes of love, as (here emotionally heightened by the death of this lady):

> For dedy lijf, my lyvy deth y wite;   *death-like; my living death I blame*
> For ese of payne, in payne of ese y dye;   *ease of pain*
> For lengthe of woo, woo lengtith me so lite *for the prolongation of my woe, woe*
> That quyk y dyc, and yet as ded lyue y,   *living [prolongs my life very little*
>   (Ballade 60, 2082–85)

or in Ballade 99, where they are introduced by a powerful first stanza:

> With axcesse shake, forsekid, and forfaynt,   *shaken with lovesickness, made*
> The poore karkes so enfeblisshid is,   *[utterly ill and exhausted*
> The hert in woo torswelt and so attaynt   *agonised; worn out*
> That even a deth it is to lyve as this,
>
> . . .
>
> For all my joy is turnyd to hevynes,
> Myn ese in harme, my wele in woo,
> Mi hope in drede, in dowt my sikirnes . . . (5840–43, 5848–50)

So, like Chaucer's Man in Black, he can say: *Sorow is y and y am he*. He is especially fond of figures of emphasis: *Hadde y hertis a thousand, thousand score, / Alle shulde thei thanke yow, myn owen ladi dere, / For yowre promys . . .* (Ballade 109, 6171–73). Anaphora (not just of the traditional 'Welcome' or 'Farewell') is sometimes very eloquently used, especially in the group of elegiac ballades. One, Ballade 59, is a tour de force with every line beginning with *Alone*:

> Alone am y and wille to be alone,
> Alone, withouten plesere or gladness,
> Alone in care, to sighe and grone,
> [Alone], to wayle the deth of my maystres,
> Alone, which sorrow will me nevyr cesse . . . (2054–58)

Another, Ballade 58, uses exclamations and questions:

> A, wooful hert, whos sorrow kan not cesse,
> Round with hir deth thou shulde have tan thi bere   *at once*
>
> . . .
>
> O myghti God, what am y, quyk or deed?

Nay, certis, deed, this am y verry sewre
For, fele y plesere, ioy, nor lustihed?
Wo worthe the fate of my mysaventure!
Nought lak y now but clothe my sepulture.   *but to prepare my grave*
                                                   (2030–31, 2034–38)

Often the emotion is conveyed perfectly through the formal rhetoric:

Allas, Deth, who made thee so hardy
To take away the most nobill princesse,
Which comfort was of my lijf and body
Mi wele, my joy, my plesere and ricchesse?   *happiness*
                                                    (Ballade 57, 1994–97))

Sometimes he tries for a more consciously 'enamelled' effect:

Whan fresshe Phebus, day of Seynt Valentyne,   *on St Valentine's day*
Had whirlid up his golden chare aloft,   *swiftly driven; chariot*
The burnyd bemys of it gan to shyne   *radiant beams*
In al my chamber where y slepid soft . . . (Ballade 72, 2455–58)

This Valentine ballade, like others, gives a glimpse of the rituals of courtly life and demonstrates the easy use of allegory: Phebus wakes him from the sleep of Hevynes [sadness] on his hard bed of Newous Thought [painful thought]. The allegorical landscape of love, a worthy descendant of the *Romance of the Rose*, is established at the beginning of the work, and its figures appear throughout: Love, Fortune and Deth (qualities whose names are 'key-terms' in the courtly tradition), Hevynes, Thought (usually mournful, but there is also Swete Thought) etc., the Lover's foes, Refuse, Daunger, Drede, Payne and Disdayne, his friends, Pite, Hope, Mercy, Trouthe, Gladsum Desire, Plesaunce and others, and some nice minor characters, Wikkid Speche, Swete Remembraunce, or the secretary of the God of Love called Promys Playne. They are all deployed in various scenes, sometimes martial:

O Stedfast Truthe, displaye thi baner!
Support my right, y pray the hertily,
And fresshe assayle this newe and strong Fronter   *fortress*
Of Thought and Woo . . . (Ballade 25, 944–47)

The castle of the heart is besieged by Daunger *with his allyaunce* (Roundel 18). More elaborately, in Ballade 50, the castle of his heart, *the Hold of Gret Plesaunce. / Stondyng upon the Roche of Espeyraunce*, defended against Daunger *and all his rude puysshaunce*, is victualled with Comfort, and its towers are called Fyaunce-to-haue-socoure-and-that-right-hastily [Trust-to-have-help-and-that-right-soon], Remembraunce, and Stedfast Desyraunce.[33] Elsewhere on the *carte du tendre* we find an *auncient, oold manar* called the Castle of No Care (in the French, Non-chaloir), and the Prisoun of Grevous Displesaunce.

---

[33] Earlier (Ballade 43), his 'poor heart' has become a *hermyte / In hermytage of Thoughtful Fantase.*

Charles moves with especial ease in this mysterious allegorical landscape. After the death of his lady he evokes the solemn religion of love:

> I have the obit of my lady dere   *funeral rites*
> Made in the Chirche of Love full solempnely
> And for hir sowle the service and prayere,
> In thought waylyng, have songe hit hevyly,
> The torchis sett of Sighis pitously   *the torches of sighs*
> Which [were] with Sorow sett aflame;   *set aflame with sorrow*
> The toumbe is made als to the same
> Of karfull cry depayntid all with teeris.
> The which richely is write abowt
> That here, lo, lith withouten dowt
> The hool tresoure of all worldly blys. (Ballade 67, 2297–2307)

Ballade 70 has a haunting 'romantic' setting:

> In the Forest of Noyous Hevynes
> As y went wandering in the moneth of May
> I mette of Love the myghti gret Goddes,
> Which axid me whithir y was away.   *asked me where I was going*
> I hir answerid, 'As Fortune doth convey,   *guide*
> As oon exylid from joy, al be me loth,   *though I do not wish (it)*
> That passyng well all folke me clepyn may
> "The man forlost that wot not where he goth." '   (2395–2402)

Poems like this are convincing proof that he is a master of exquisite poetic melancholy. But though the poetry is always refined, it is not always so melancholy. There is an element of 'game' in many of the ballades, and of vitality and high-spiritedness in many more. In particular, the poems and roundels of the 'Jubilee' often have an infectious joyousness. Charles's metrical skill is evident enough in the ballades but the roundels show a very remarkable talent: with apparent ease he achieves a genuinely 'rounded' finish that is often intensely pleasing.

There is a 'game' here too. He challenges lovers to put a value on the lady – *Is she not full of all goodly manere, / The which y love in my most feithful wise? / . . . Ye lovers, now how say yow? lete us here – / What is she worth? Let se, sett to a prise!* (Roundel 4, 3180–81, 3184–85) – and warns them of the peril of looking at her beauty:

> Bewar! y rede yow, loke here not upon   *I advise you; her*
> The goodly fayre that y love feithfully!
> For ye shall lese yowre hert even sodaynly
> If so be that ye cast her lokyng on,   *cast a glance at her*
>
> Wherfore, but ye lust gefe yowre hert anoon,   *unless you with to give*
> Shette up yowre eyen and close hem wel surely.   *shut*
>   Bewar! y rede yow, loke here not upon
>   The goodly fayre that y love feithfully . . .   (Roundel 22, 3447–54)

If many of Charles's poems remind us of Chaucer, others, like the punning poem on the hunt of love –

The mede is flowe, the grace is goon,	*meadow / favour has vanished*
The hert is chaungid from his place,	*hart / heart*
Where y had wende hem be, he nas,	*thought he was*
Thus Myrthe and y are comen foon –	*become foes*

(Roundel 54, 1–4)

encourage us to look forward to Tudor songs and the poetry of Wyatt. All in all these lyrics represent one of the finest poetic achievements of the fifteenth century.

Among those lyrics which sometimes recall Charles d'Orléans, a set of English pieces in Bodl. MS Fairfax 16 (c.1450) has been attributed to his guardian the Duke of Suffolk – an attribution not universally accepted (one of them is certainly by Charles d'Orléans).[34] Shirley attributed a number of French poems in another manuscript to Suffolk 'whilst he was prisoner in France' but the authenticity of this too has been strongly questioned.[35] Yet, whoever the authors may have been, the English poems are talented and interesting. Complaint and epistle often overlap, in the tradition of the *Heroides* and Chaucer's *Legend of Good Women* (alluded to as the 'Legend of Cupid's Saints'). Two of the letters have been discussed above (pp. 125–6): others are direct and simple. A sombre complaint begins:

> O wofull hert profound in gret duresse
> Which canst not playn nor opyn thy dysese,
> But frete thy-selfe with care and hevynesse,
> Ay full of thought thy sorous to encresse,
> No wondir though thou be not wele at ese,
> When [th]ou so far art out of her presence,
> To whom thou must do servyse and reverence. (No. 7, 1–7)

Another, *Walking allon, of wyt full desolat, / In my sp[y]rytes tormented to and fro, / And with myself fallyng at gret debat . . .*, evoking the divided and tormented emotions of the lover, ends with a humble prayer to the God of Love. Everywhere we find careful and smooth syntax, and a simple eloquence: *Ryght goodly fayr, the gentylest in dede, / I yowe require, as her that I love best, / Relese my payn, and set myn hert in rest.* John Norton-Smith has plausibly suggested that these poems are organised as a unified series, with an 'autobiographical' introduction, and that the simple unornamented style of the complaints is deliberately intended to give the impression of 'spontaneously uttered sentiment'.[36]

---

[34] See the facsimile edition of Bodl. MS Fairfax 16, with introduction by Norton-Smith 1979. *O thou, fortune, whyche hast the governaunce / Of all thynges kindly* is by Charles d'Orléans, see Arn 1994, 386–7. For the attribution of the poems to Suffolk, see MacCracken 1911b, 142–80. For arguments against, see Norton-Smith 1979 and 1974, 20–21, and Boffey 1985, 65–6, 76 (who sees him as perhaps a 'transmitter' of lyrics rather than an author). See also Pearsall 2000. Jansen 1989 argues that there is no internal evidence that the English poems of MS Harley 682 and Fairfax are by the same person. Both Norton-Smith and Boffey recognised similarities with Charles, and the first of the epistles discussed above (p. 125) seems to me to be 'in his manner'.

[35] See Boffey 1988, 135–46 (especially 141–2).

[36] Norton-Smith 1974, 21. One other poem in the collection (*Index* 2182) is found in a (re-arranged?) version in the later manuscript Lambeth 306.

Another English nobleman was singled out by Shirley as a writer: Richard Beauchamp, Earl of Warwick (d.1439) is said to have made a poem beginning *I can not half the woo compleyne / That dothe my woful hert streyne / With bisy thought and grevous payne . . .*, a rare example of a virelai.[37] This attribution needs to be taken seriously, for Shirley had spent years in the service of this 'flower of chivalry'. Sadly the poem is competent rather than inspired.

Manuscripts from the latter half of the century preserve a large mass of anonymous lyrics. Again we find the favourite forms and topics – letters, complaints, poems praising the lady's beauty, often long and conventional – and, similarly, farewells to the mistress, with anaphora for very many lines, without the rhetorical power of a Charles d'Orléans.[38] Yet there is some variety. The songs of Bodl. MS Ashmole 191 include some eloquent examples of the traditional melancholy:

> Alas, departing ys ground of woo –   *parting*
> Other songe can y not synge.
> But why part y my lady fro,
> Syth love was caus of our metyng? . . .   *since*
>   (Duncan *LMELC*, No. 25, 1–4)

alongside an expression of a more carefree attitude to love: *Luf wil I with variance, / Because y drede of repentance . . .* (Duncan *LMELC*, No. 38, 1–2).[39]

A vehement and scornful dismissal of the lady (which surely would have aroused the God of Love's ire) is defiantly expressed in a high-spirited song in another manuscript: *Welcome to ye when ye goo, / And fare-wel when ye come!* (Robbins *Sec.*, No. 174).[40] A more ambitious exercise in this vein is a pair of mocking letters supposed to be exchanged by a lady and her lover.[41] Hers is addressed *To my trew love and able – / as the wedyr-cok he is stable* . . . With gleeful abuse she describes his *manly visage* (*your forehed, mouth, and nose so flatte, / In short conclusyon, best lykened to an hare / Of alle lyvyng thynges, save only a catte*), his general appearance (*your Garmentes upon you ful gayly they hynge / As it were an olde gose had a broke wynge*), and physique. A woman should be hanged if she chose such a mate *or onys woold lyft up here hole* [private parts] *for youre sake*. The lover replies *To you dere herte, variant and mutable, / Lyke to Carybdis which is unstable.* He is rather more pompous and 'literary' (*The ynglysch of Chaucere was nat in your mynd / Ne Tullyus termys with so gret eloquence . . .*), but excitedly produces a 'blazon' of grotesque ugliness which makes us think of Skelton:

> . . . your grete hede and your forhed round,
>   Wyth staryng eyen, visage large & huge,   *eyes*
>   And eyther of youre pappys like a water-bowge.   *skin water-bottle*

---

[37] MacCracken 1907, 597–607. See Boffey 1985, 15–16. For another competent (anonymous) virelai from a later manuscript see Robbins *Sec.*, No 173 (and note).
[38] See, for instance, Robbins *Sec.*, Nos. 203–5 (No. 202 is a more succinct example).
[39] See above, p. 124 and note. *Luf wil I with variance* deserves to be paired with *Love woll I withoute eny variaunce* from Ashmole 1393 – as it is in Duncan *LMELC*, Nos 37, 38.
[40] With music in manuscript.
[41] Robbins *Sec.*, Nos 208, 209.

Youre camusyd nose, with nose-thryllys brode,   *snub; nostrils*
    Unto the chyrch a noble instrument
To quenche tapers brennyng afore the roode . . .

                                        (Robbins *Sec.*, No. 209, 19–24)

These two epistles come from Bodl. MS Rawlinson poet. 36, a manuscript in which among some more straightforwardly courtly lyrics one lament stands out as an unusual and rather haunting example:

Iwyss, iwyss, I remembre me   *indeed*
Wheroff, in trowth, of tyme ipast . . .   *of what, in truth*
A, I counsel yow, lett that be –   *ah*
For all prevys but fantesyes at last.   *proves*
Why is love no more stedfast?
Now in trowth what remedy?
Prese forth, in youth be not agast,   *press*
Why plesyth not age with novelry?   *the new*   (Robbins *Sec.*, No. 175)[42]

    A number of poets manage to give the complaints of abandoned or slighted lovers some intriguing variations. In one, beginning *Alas, how schale my hert be lyght, / Wyth dart of love when hyt ys slayn . . .*, the lover dare not look or approach, but declares earnestly *yette wyl y love you privyly* (Robbins *Sec.*, No. 162).[43] A carol, *Whylome I present was with my soffreyne* (Greene, No. 439), with the repeated burden

For pency[f]nesse and grett distresse
    I am full woo;
Destitute from al refute,   *refuge*
    Alone I goo,

is the passionate complaint of a banished lady, which essays a higher style.[44] Modern readers would probably prefer a more direct love-complaint from earlier in the century:

The man that I loved altherbest   *best of all*
In al thys contré, est other west,   *country*
To me he ys a strange gest;
    What wonder est thow I be woo? (Greene, No. 451, stanza 1)[45]

A despairing male lover in a lyric in Aberystwyth, National Library of Wales MS Porkington 10 (Robbins *Sec.*, No. 134) declares, *Into unkouthe* [unknown] *londes I woll wende* (28), and – rather more originally – that he will write a letter, wind it round his head and wear it until the lady herself will unbind it. Another, in a love-letter, tells his lady, *yfe ye say me nay . . . By cryst, my-selfe I wyll for-doo* [destroy] */ And be-com schall I a gray frere* [friar] */ And nevere womman to draw nere*

---

42 Robbins entitles this lyric 'Age and Love'; cf. Nos 159, 192.
43 From MS Peniarth 26.
44 See note to Greene, No. 439.
45 This is an interesting example of the 'adaptation' of a lyric; another hand has written in feminine pronouns between the lines.

(Robbins *Sec.*, No. 195, 17–19).[46] A stronger threat to a heartless mistress comes from a lover in a poem in Cambridge, Trinity College MS R13.9 (Robbins *Sec.*, No. 138).[47] After describing a sad little scene –

> Ful sore hit greveth me when I by yow sate
> And say other better belovyd than I,   *saw*
> And ye in your armes so truly hym knyt,   *embrace*
> And I lyke a syphyr syt yow by – (9–12)   *cipher*

he at least has something to say for himself: others may be *of body both gret and strong / And semelokyr* [more pleasing] *men* (13–14) than he is, yet with wisdom he hopes to live as merrily as they (an opinion supported by Cato). And indeed if she does not relent and he should die for her sake, as he is like to, she shall not escape the pains of hell.

From the end of the century come two fascinating collections, both of which take us into the world of the provincial gentry. One, called the 'Findern Manuscript' from its connection with the Findern family in Derbyshire, contains, besides extracts from Chaucer, Gower, Hoccleve and Lydgate, over twenty lyrics, written by a number of scribes, some of them women. It has been convincingly suggested that a number of these may well have been the authors as well as the scribes.[48] The literary quality is uneven, but some of the poems are excellent, as this, on the sorrow of love:

> This ys no lyf, alas, that y do lede,   *lead*
> It is but deth as yn lyves lyckenese,   *in life's likeness*
> Endeles sorow assured owte of drede,   *guaranteed without doubt*
> Past all despeyre and owte of all gladenesse, *beyond all despair; devoid of all*
> Thus well y wote y am remedylesse,   *I know I am without remedy*
> For me nothing may comforte nor amende
> Tyl deith come forthe and make of me an ende. (Duncan *LMELC*, No. 28)

This is powerful writing whether by a man or a woman. In a carol (with the burden *Whoso lyst to love, / God send hym right good spede*) a male lover recalls his love was happy love, until one day there was *a gret affray* and *she bade me walkke forth on my way*. She would not tell him the reason; he is sure that he has done nothing wrong. His heart bleeds for sorrow – should he let her go? No, he will love her in the hope that *withyne short spase / She will me take agayne to grace* (Greene, No. 442). In another lively carol (Greene, No. 469), with the burden *Up, son and mery wether, / Somer draweth nere*, the speaker seems to be a woman who has escaped from the bond of *that wyckid creature* (a man? the God of Love?), and happily concludes:

> Now may Y ete, drynke, and play,
> Walke up and doune fro day to day

---

[46] On the manuscript see Kurvinen 1953.
[47] On this later fifteenth-century manuscript see Boffey 1985, 17–19.
[48] CUL MS Ff.1.6; the hands range from the mid-fifteenth century to the sixteenth. Facsimile edition, Beadle and Owen 1977. See Robbins 1954; Sarah McNamer 1991 (with full references to earlier bibliographical discussions of the manuscript).

And herkyn what this lovers say,
    And laugh at there maner. (Stanza 5)

There is less gaiety in another poem, *Whatso men sayn* (Duncan *LMELC*, No. 39):

What so men seyn,
Love is no peyn
To them, serteyn,   *certainly*
    Butt varians (1–4)   *inconstancy*

– and not only *varians* but also *doubleness* [duplicity] and *newfangellnys* [pursuit of novelty]. This female speaker (very likely the author) makes us think of the bitterness we sometimes find in Wyatt.

The other collection is the work of Humfrey Newton (1466–1536), a member of the Cheshire gentry, a man of literary tastes, and himself a minor poet.[49] In his commonplace-book he includes a number of poems, including one alliterative poem which may contain echoes of *Sir Gawain and the Green Knight*, a work from this general area, and a copy of the *ABC of Aristotle*: 'These byn gode proverbis to set in the bordere of the halle' – as such proverbs sometimes were. His own poems are filled with conventional topics and formulaic phraseology, but they can have a rather attractive awkwardness:

Her hert I wold I had, i-wis,
Unto the tyme I gaf it again;
My hert is loken withinne her chest –
Forsothe I wold sho knew my payn.
Ruthe it were to here me complayne!   *pity; hear me lament*
Ey, therfore, my swete and my swetenge,   *ah*
Y pray you remembre me in youre slepynge. (Robbins 1950, No. 4)[50]

Not surpringly for a Cheshire writer he likes alliteration: *and how she* [Venus] *keght* [caught] *me with a croke* [hook] *for to love a mey, / I shall telle yo titely* [immediately] . . .[51] He also occasionally attempts a higher style.[52] In a more unusual farewell poem (Robbins 1950, No. 11), a lady laments: *now, my luf, I most nedes sesse* [end], */ And tak me to hym that me has tan* [taken]. She counsels the lover to take another, and gives him a token in remembrance. *Send me one*, she says, *and I shall kepe for old qwayntenance*. Among Newton's better lyrics are two simple familiar epistles. One opens very directly –

I pray you, M, to me be tru,
For I will be tru as longe as I lif;
I wil not change you for old ne newe,
Ne neuer lof other whiles that I lif . . . –   *love another*

49 Bodl. MS Lat. misc.c.66. See Robbins 1950; Boffey 1985, 23–4 (who notes that names and acrostics – MARGARET, ELIN – 'hint at some kind of primitive sequence').
50 Note the acrostic in this stanza with the initial letters of the lines giving the name 'HUMFREY'.
51 Robbins, Poem 6, 13–14. Cf. Poem 5.
52 As in Poem 10. In 13 he is carried away: *Ye are my emperice – make me an emperoure! / Ye are my qwene – mak me a kynge! / Ye are my lady – mak me a lord of honour! / Ye are my mastres, my dere, and my swetynge!*

and ends: *Sithen as we may not togeder spek, / Be writynge we shal oure hertes breke.*[53]
The other, *Go, litull bill, and command me hertely / Unto her that I call my trulof and lady*, reminds her that she saw him in church, once when an old woman was sitting beside her, and again when she came with a gentlewoman, and

Thay kneled bothe on the flore	*floor*
And fast thay did piter-pater –	
I hope thay said matens togeder!	*I expect they said matins*
Yet ones or twyes, at the lest,	*once or twice at least*
She did on me her ee kest;	*cast her eye*
Then went I forthe prevely	*I went out unobtrusively*
And haylsed on thaym curtesly.	*and greeted them courteously*
	(Duncan *LMELC*, No. 15, 14–20)

These little scenes may seem far removed from the world of the high courtly lyric, but they are – humbly and rather charmingly – related to it.[54]

Early sixteenth-century manuscripts produce lyrics which search for a more ample eloquence, sometimes linking (as Dunbar did more flamboyantly) simple familiar language with a 'golden' vocabulary as in *O Excelent suffereigne, most seemly to see* (Robbins *Sec.*, No. 130):

Wherefore I pray God, or that I begynne,	*before*
That my simple wryttyng doo yow not dyspleyse;	
For I am nott to blame that I doo yow prease,	*praise*
O rubycounde roose, o lyllye most delycyouse,	
Splendant in bewtye as a dyamond most precyouse	
In syght,	
Your bryght fulgent face,	
Replete full of grace,	
And your goodly pace,	
Makethe my herte lyght. (39–48)	

This comes from Bodl. MS Rawlinson C. 813, an interesting collection of poems, some of which seem to have echoes of, or are literary reworkings of earlier works by poets such as Chaucer or contemporary writers like Stephen Hawes.[55]

A poem from another manuscript, in short lines and in a 'singing' metrical form like the French virelai –

O mestres, whye	*why*
Owtecaste am I	
All utterly	
From your pleasaunce,	*pleasure*
Sythe ye and I	*since*
Or thys, truly,	*before this*
Famyliarly	
Have have pastaunce . . . – .	*have passed our time*
	(Duncan *LMELC*, No. 36, 1–8)

---

[53] Poem 12; Robbins *Sec.*, No. 193.
[54] The parish church seems to take the place of the temple of Palladion in *Troilus*. In Poem 17, 10–13, the lover confesses: *When that I into the kirke come / My matens I wold say verray fayn, / When I you se then are thay don – / Forsothe I wold ye knew my payn!*

may introduce what are perhaps the most pleasing courtly lyrics of this late period, those contained (along with religious lyrics, satirical, political and humorous pieces) in three early sixteenth-century songbooks: the 'Fayrfax' MS (c.1500), 'Henry VIII's MS' (?c.1515), so called because in it thirty-one pieces are ascribed to the young king, and 'Ritson's MS' (perhaps in use from 1470–1520), once in the possession of the late eighteenth-century antiquary Joseph Ritson.[56] 'Freshness' is a word often used in praise of these songs, and indeed the best have a vivacity and simplicity (the products of art rather than nature) enhanced by skilful musical settings. Yet it should not obscure the fact that they are still using traditional themes and topics such as the praise of the lady or the lover's lament, as in:

> Complayne I may wherevyr I go,
> Syth I have done my besy payne   *made my constant effort*
> To love her best and no mo   *no other*
> And she me takyth in gret disdayne . . . *holds me in great disdain*
>   (Stevens 1961, 365)

Interestingly, although performed in a high courtly setting,[57] a number seem to be adaptations of popular songs (demonstrating that the boundary between 'courtly' and 'popular' lyric was often a fluid one) – as perhaps the little dialogue which begins:

> A Robyn,
> Gentyl Robyn,
> Tel me how thy lemman doth,   *sweetheart*
> And thow shal know of myne. (Duncan *LMELC*, No. 32, 1–4),

or a carol (attributed to the king) with the burden:

> Grene growith the holy,
> So doth the ivé,
> Thow winter blastys blow never so hye,
> Grene growith the holy. (Stevens 1961, 398–9)

Here the evergreen holly symbolizes the lover's steadfastness.

There is considerable variety. Poems range from a devotion to love as the source of noble acts – *For love enforceth all nobyle kyndes* [strengthens all noble natures], / *And dysdayne dyscorages all gentyl myndes* (Duncan *LMELC*, No. 31, 3–4) – to bawdy double-entendres as in 'hunting' lyrics like *Blow thi horne, hunter, and blow thi horne on hye!* (Duncan *LMELC*, No. 35). The mood is not always one of youthful *joi de vivre* and 'pastime with good company': there is some melancholy, and even a denial of love: *Love I deny; / Hyt ys foly / To love vaynly: / This do I prove* (Stevens 1961, 342). We have learnt to expect considerable

---

[55] See Padelford, 1908. On the manuscript see Boffey 1985, 26–27 (on reworkings, 70, 72, 78).

[56] See Stevens 1961, 3–7. 'Fayrfax' is the composer Dr Robert Fayrfax.

[57] One carol, *Whilles lyve or breth is in my brest/ My soverayne lord I shall love best* (Stevens 1961, 405–6), has a lady praising her lord's skill and handsome appearance as he jousts for her at a tournament: it seems likely that the figures represent Queen Catherine and Henry.

variations in attitude in the courtly tradition, so that it should not occasion surprise, though it is a moment of delight, to find a carol which brings back the world of the *Romance of the Rose*, *The knight knokett at the castell gate* (Duncan *LMELC*, No. 34). Here the portress is *Strangenes*, and the knight announces himself as *Desyre*; he must prepare a *byll* [petition], *Kyndnes* will bear it, and *Pyty* promises to be present – *but how thay dyd we cannott say – / We left them ther and went ower way.*

By this time the effects of some significant cultural changes were beginning to become evident, most obviously the spread of the newer Italian humanism associated with the name of Petrarch, and the results of the invention of printing. Of the well-known poets of the period, Skelton (?1460–1529) belongs to the older tradition of 'medieval humanism' as found in Chaucer, Gower and Lydgate rather than to that developing in the circle of More and Erasmus, but he has the distinction of seeing some of his lyrics in print in *Dyvers baletlys and dyties solacyous devised by Master Skelton Laureat*,[58] the first surviving printed collection of secular lyrics in English, a small booklet containing five poems printed by Rastell in the late 1520s just before the poet's death. (Many more ambitions and impressive examples of printed collections were, of course, to appear in the following centuries, but it should be remembered that the circulation of lyrics in manuscript still remained of primary importance in the sixteenth and seventeenth centuries.) The poems themselves in Rastell's collection almost certainly come from an earlier period in Skelton's career (?c.1495–1500).[59] They are 'solacyous' in that they give pleasure, mixing 'game' with 'ernest' in the manner of some of the lyric collections we have encountered. *My darling dere, my daysy floure* concerns the deception of a man by a prostitute. In *The auncient acquaintance, muday, between us twayn* Skelton begins gravely as if to introduce a love-lyric recalling her *goodly port* and *bewteous visage*, but the tone changes abruptly and it becomes a scurrilous and suggestive account of their behaviour culminating in a wildly unruly scene. Like the first poem it ends with a warning. The following poem, *Knolege, acquaintance, resort, favour, with grace*, is straightforwardly courtly, a panegyric of 'Kateryn' (whose name is revealed in an acrostic) which blends learned and aureate diction with deliberately simple words: *Open myne hart*, and you will see *how there nys thynge that I covet so fayne / As to embrace you in myne armys twayne*; he has *gravyd her within the secret wall / Of my trew hert, to love her best of all!* In another, proverbial verses in Latin and English urgently and anxiously warn against Fortune's *double cast* [stroke] and the dangers lurking. The final poem, written *at the instance of a nobyll lady*, is an eloquent courtly lyric on a traditional topic, with, again, an undertone of anxiety and unease:

Go, pytous hart, rasyd with dedly wo,	*lacerated*
Persyd with payn, bleding with wondes smart,	*painful*
Bewayle thy fortune, with vanys wan and blo.	*dark and leaden-coloured veins*
O Fortune unfriendly, Fortune unkynde thow art,	

---

58 See Boffey 1985, 30, 80–1.
59 Texts in Scattergood 1983a, 41–46.

To be so cruell and so overthwart,   *perverse*
To suffer me so carefull to endure,   *sorrowfull*
That wher I love best I dare not dyscure! (1–7)   *reveal*

In the *Garlande or Chapelet of Laurell* (printed in 1523, but probably in the making from c.1495), Skelton is instructed by *Occupaation* to commend *these ladies and gentlewomen* who have been set to work on a *cronell* [garland] *of lawrell with verduris* [green herbs] *light and darke* for him. He produces lyrics praising all eleven, carefully arranged according to rank, and in appropriate form and style (Scattergood 1983a, 335–43). The first, to the Countess of Surrey, is a learned ballade, *So shall your name endure perpetually.* The others vary in tone. Lady Mirriell Howarde is addressed more familiarly: *Mi litell lady I may not leve behinde, / But to you servyce nedis now I must.* Margery Wentworthe's begins with a play on her name: *With margerain jentyll* [fine marjoram] */ the flower of goodlyhede, / Enbrowdred* [embroidered] *the mantill / Is of your maydenhede.* Margaret Hussey is addressed as *Mirry Margaret, / As mydsomer flower, / Jentill as fawcoun* [falcon] */ Or hawke of the towre* [soaring hawk]. It is a remarkable tour de force. Skelton is justly renowned for his satirical writing, but even there he shows himself to be in touch with the range of the late medieval lyric; he quotes snatches from popular songs, and will suddenly move from invective into unexpected lyrical passages.

More complex as a lyric poet is a nobleman of the following generation, when the Henrician court had become an even more slippery place, Sir Thomas Wyatt (c.1503–1542) who must bring this survey to its end. For lack of space I make only a simple point. He is a very significant figure in the history of the English lyric, but his work does not represent a complete break with the past. In his English songs and 'balets' (as against his translations) he is very close to the tradition of medieval lyric that I have described. Some of his songs are almost indistinguishable from those of the fifteenth century; others treat exactly the same topics with greater power and eloquence:

> And wylt thow leve me thus,
> And have nomore pyttye
> Of hym that lovythe the?
> Helas, thy cruellte!
> And wylt thow leve me thus?
>   Say nay, Say nay! (Muir 1949, No. 113, 1–6)

He often gives a characteristically bitter, world-weary turn to the traditional topics and scenes, and to the 'technical' terms of courtly poetry – *crueltie, lyberté, gentilnes* – but we have already seen some premonitions of this in earlier lyrics. And even in his more 'humanist' and Petrarchan poems we can recognise the earlier tradition – in lovers' attitudes of rejection (*farewell Love, and all thy lawes forever*) and in their despair:

> My galy charged with forgetfulness   *galley*
> Thorrough sharpe sees in winter nyghtes doeth pas
> Twene rock and rock . . .
> The starres to be hid that led me to this pain;

Drowned is reason that should me consort,   *escort*
And I remain dispering of the port.   *despairing*

(Muir 1949, No. 28, 1–3, 12–14)

In the following centuries, 'poor Petrarch's long-deceased woes', first introduced to the English lyric by Chaucer, were to echo throughout a tradition of 'courtly lyric' which went from strength to strength. The medieval courtly lyric was a prelude to this, but it was much more than a prelude: in its variety and vitality it was a fine literary monument in its own right.

7

The Middle English Carol

KARL REICHL

Introduction

John Audelay, 'blind Audelay' of Haghmond Abbey in Shropshire, closes one of his poems with the words:

I pray youe al pur charyte	*for the sake of*
Redis this carol reverently,	*read*
Fore I hit mad with wepyng ye;	*weeping eye*
Mi name hit is the blynd Awdlay.	(Whiting 1931, No. 24, 117–20)[1]

The poem Audelay terms a carol is addressed to the Welsh saint Winefride, patron saint of Shrewsbury (Audelay's nearest town), whose intercession the poet implores and some of whose miracles he recounts. This is not the only poem to St Winefride in Audelay's œuvre, a collection of over fifty poems in Bodl. MS Douce 302. This manuscript, which dates from the second quarter of the fifteenth century and is roughly contemporary with the poet, provides the main source of information about Audelay.[2]

Audelay's poem conforms to the modern scholarly definition of the carol as a late Middle English lyric form 'intended, or at least suitable, for singing, made up of uniform stanzas and provided with a burden which begins the piece and is to be repeated after each stanza' (Greene, xi). This insistence on formal criteria is necessary as the term 'carol' has in general use come to mean all types of Christmas songs as well as many types of popular poems. This popular, 'catholic' view of the genre is, for instance, exemplified by the wide range of songs found in the *New Oxford Book of Carols* (Keyte and Parrott, 1992). Few of our

---

1 Audelay's poems are here quoted from Whiting 1931; they may also be found in the standard edition of Middle English carols by R. L. Greene (1977). For carols which have come to light since that edition, see Camargo 1998.
2 On the manuscript and on Audelay, see Whiting 1931, vi–xi and xiv–xvi. For Audeley's role as a poet of carols, see also Chambers and Sidgwick 1910–11. At the end of poem No. 18 there is a note in the manuscript to the effect that the preceding poems were composed by the *capellanus* Johannes Awdely, 'qui fuit secus [caecus] et surdus' [who was blind and deaf], in 1426 (Whiting 1931, 149). At what time the following poems were composed is uncertain, as the note is ambiguous as to whether Audelay was still alive after 1426. Also, Audelay's authorship of two of the later poems (Nos 53 and 54), both heavily alliterating, is disputed; see Whiting 1931, xxiv–xxviii. Arguments against Audelay's authorship are advanced by Putter 2004; however, Stanley 1997, 108–14, supports Audelay's authorship of No. 54. Recent significant light on Audelay's life and work derived from evidence beyond that of Bodl. MS Douce 302 is to be found in Bennett 1981–2.

better-known modern Christmas carols are carols in the medieval sense, although some, like 'Hark, the herald angels sing' or 'Angels, from the realms of glory', have a refrain (but no burden). Here, in Audelay's poem, the burden has two lines written at the beginning of the poem (as it happens, by a second hand):

> Wenefrede, thou swete may,   *maiden*
> Thow pray for us bothe nyght and day.   (Whiting 1931, 171)

The stanzas have four lines, lines one to three having the same rhyme and line four rhyming with the burden. While both the burden and the first three lines of the stanza have four stresses, line four of the stanza tends to have three stresses only.

On the face of it, it looks as if this poem was meant to be read rather than sung (*Redis this carol reverently*). This is possible, although Middle English *reden* does not only mean 'to read' (both silently and aloud), but can in appropriate contexts also mean 'to chant' or even 'to sing'.[3] Preceding the 'carol section' of Audelay's poems (Whiting 1931, Nos 28–52) there is also a note in the manuscript (f. 27v), written in the upper margin by a second hand, to the effect that his carols were meant for singing:

> I pray yow, syrus, boothe moore and las,   *sirs; less*
> Syng these caroles in Cristemas.   (Whiting 1931, 180)

Furthermore, in another carol, on Henry VI (Whiting 1931, No. 39), Audelay uses a similar phrase as in the carol on St Winefride, this time with *syng* instead of *read*:

> I pray youe, seris, of your gentre,   *sirs*
> Syng this carol reverently. (59–60)

That Audelay's carols were probably meant to be sung emerges also from the fact that one of his carols (Whiting 1931, No. 38) has been transmitted with music in other manuscripts (in Bodl. MS Arch. Selden. B.26 and in Cambridge, Trinity College MS O.3.58).[4]

While Audelay's use of the term 'carol' – he also calls two other similarly constructed poems (Whiting 1931, Nos 51 and 52) carols (or *caral*) – conforms to the scholarly definition of the Middle English carol as a specific lyric form, there are other uses of the word *carol* in Middle English. This word occurs no less than five times in *Sir Gawain and the Green Knight*, almost always in contexts that suggest dancing more strongly than singing. What is denoted here is not primarily a lyric form but rather a form of dance or perhaps a combination of dancing and singing. The carol as a dance is clearest in the description of the merrymaking on St John's day at Bertilak's castle:

---

3   See *MED* reden v.(1).
4   Greene doubts that Audelay is the author of this poem: 'The spirited rhythm is so much superior to Audelay's usual metres that his original authorship must be regarded as doubtful' (Greene, 372). See also Greene 1962, 204. A different conclusion is reached by Stanley 1997.

The ioye of sayn Jonez day watz gentyle to here,   *St John's day was*
And watz the last of the layk, leudez ther thoghten.   *entertainment; people*
Ther wer gestes to go vpon the gray morne,   *guests*
Forthy wonderly thay woke, and the wyn dronken,
Daunsed ful dreyly wyth dere carolez.   *unceasingly*

                                    (Tolkien and Gordon 1967, 1022–1026)

The sense of 'danse' is even clearer in Richard Rolle's use of the word *carol*. In his *Form of Living*, Rolle makes a distinction between the sins of the heart, of the mouth and of deed (Chapter Six). Among the sins of the mouth he lists *to syng seculere sanges and lufe tham*, while among the sins of deed he mentions *to lede karols* (Allen 1931, 98). Evidently, the carol is here a dance, something one does, and not a song.

Clearly, there must be a connection between the carol as a lyric form and the carol as a dance form. This connection is best studied by looking at the relationship between the carol and the *carole*. Before discussing this relationship, however, I will first deal with the carol as a late medieval (and early Tudor) lyric and musical form.

The medieval carol: themes

When we look at the twenty-six carols in Audelay's collection of poems and compare them with the corpus of carols as assembled by Greene, we find that Audelay's poems offer a fair reflection of the thematic variety of the genre. Although thematically the carol is by no means limited to the Christmas season, it is nevertheless the preferred vernacular lyric form that is sung, as the couplet in the Audelay manuscript quoted above puts it, *in Cristemas*. Seven of Audelay's carols are explicitly devoted to Christmas, more specifically to the 'Twelve Days of Christmas' from Christmas Day to Epiphany: 'In die natalis Domini' (25 December): *Welcum be thou Heven Kyng*; 'In die Sancti Stephani' (26 December): *Saynt Steven the first martere*; 'In die Sancti Iohannis' (27 December): *Synt Ion is Cristis derlyng dere*; 'In die sanctorum Innocentium' (28 December): *Crist crid in cradil, 'moder baba'*; 'De Sancto Thome archiepiscopo cantuarienci' (29 December): *For on a Tewsday Thomas was borne*; 'In die circumcicionis domini' (1 January): *A Babe is borne of hye natewre*; 'In die epiphanis' (6 January): *Ther is a Babe born of a may* (Whiting 1931, Nos 33–8 and 42). Carols on Christmas and the Christmas season form the central core of the medieval carols extant. In Greene's collection of close to five hundred carols, about two hundred and sixty are devoted to the Christmas season (including carols on Mary). These carols celebrate the events of Christ's annunciation, birth, circumcision and epiphany in a festive and joyful spirit, with exhortations, generally in the burden, to rejoice and be merry. As a typical example I will quote the beginning of Audelay's poem No. 42:[5]

---

5   I have left the faulty Latin of the manuscript text uncorrected.

Nowel! nowel! nowel!

Ther is a Babe born of a may	
In salvacion of us;	
That He be heryd in this day,	*praised*
Vene Creatore Spiritus .	*Come Creator Spirit*
In Bedlem, in that fayre plas,	
This blessid Barne borne he was;	*boy*
Him to serve, God grawnt us grace,	
Tu trinetatis unitas.	*You, unity of Trinity*
The angelis to shepardis songyn and sayd,	
'Pes in erth be mon unto.'	
Ther-with thai were ful sore afrayd,	
Glorea in ex[c]elsis Deo.	*Glory to God in the highest*
The shepardis hard that angel song;	*heard*
Thai heredon God in Trenete;	*praised*
Moche merth was ham among,	*mirth*
Iam lucis ortus sidere.	*now that the light of the sun has risen*
Iij kyngis thai soght Him here-fore,	
Of dyvers lond and fere cuntre,	*far country*
And askidyn were this Barne was borc,	
Hostes Herodes impij. (1–21)	*Herod, cruel tyrant*

The poem has eleven stanzas. In the stanzas omitted here (6–11), the narrative continues with the Three Kings' visit to Herod, their veneration of Jesus, their gifts, an explanation of the gifts' symbolic value, and, after the angel's warning, their return home by a different route. The poem is a good representative of its genre. In content it holds closely to the Christmas story as told in the New Testament (Matthew and Luke), in phrasing and style it is intimately connected to the liturgical texts of the season, and it uses a fairly widespread type of burden. Many burdens are exclamations, as in our example, and many of them have the word *nowel*. Here are some variants (see also Greene, Nos 133, 139, 239, 240, 245, 256, 261):

Nowel, nowel, nowel!	
To us is born owr God Emanuel.	(Greene, No. 18)
Nowel, nowel, nowel,	
Nowel, nowel, nowel!	(Greene, No. 30)
Nowel, el, el, el, el!	
I thank it a maydyn every del.	(Greene, No. 41)
Nowell, nowell, ell, ell:	
Iwys, yt ys a wunder nowell. *certainly*	(Greene, No. 90)

In some cases, *nowel* is given in its Latin form (e.g., Greene, No. 238: *Nova, nova:/ 'Ave' fitt ex 'Eva'* ['Ave' comes from 'Eve']). One-line burdens are comparatively rare; the most frequent case is a burden of two lines, but there are also many occurrences of three-line and especially of four-line burdens. In a second version of our example, found in BL MS Sloane 2593, the burden comprises two lines:

Nowell, el, el, el,
Now is wel that evere was woo. (Greene, No. 122B)

The word *nowel* (from French *noël*) is generally used as 'a cry of joy at the birth of Christ, esp. in carols of the Annunciation and the Nativity' (*MED* nouel n. (1), 2.(a)). The earliest instance of this meaning given in the *MED* comes from Chaucer's *Franklin's Tale*, where Janus, the god of January, is described as sitting by the fire, drinking wine from his bugle horn, and

Biforn hym stant brawen of the tusked swyn,   *meat; boar*
And 'Nowel' crieth every lusty man. (*CT* V, 1254–5)

A second sense of *nowel*, meaning Christmas, is less common; it is first found, according to the *MED*, in *Sir Gawain and the Green Knight* (line 65).

Audelay's poem No. 42 is also typical of the carol genre in its extensive use of Latin, here in the fourth line of every stanza, in most cases a quotation from a liturgical text used in the Christmas (and Advent) season. 'Iam lucis orto sidere', for instance, is the beginning of the hymn sung at Prime for the First Sunday of Advent and 'Hostis Herodes impie' is the beginning of the hymn sung at the First Vesper of the feast of Epiphany. Untypically for a Christmas carol, there are also references to other feasts of the liturgical year such as Whitsun and Trinity Sunday ('Veni, Creator Spiritus' and 'Tu, Trinitatis Unitas').[6] A prime example of this predilection for the inclusion of Latin words and lines in medieval carols is the work of another fifteenth-century poet, the Franciscan James Ryman. Ryman, whose poems have survived in CUL MS Ee.1.12, was younger than Audelay; he lived in the second half of the fifteenth century. According to a colophon in the manuscript, he finished his poems (or part of his poems) in 1492.[7] About 150 poems can be attributed to James Ryman, more than half of which are macaronic (i.e. they systematically incorporate Latin phrases and lines into the English text). Almost all of these macaronic poems are carols (81 out of 88); moreover, the macaronic carols comprise more than two thirds of the 121 carols by Ryman found in Greene's edition.[8]

While the Christmas season can be considered the central theme of the medieval carol, it is by no means the only one, and for the range of other possible topics once again Audelay's poems offer a good example. Three of his carols are devoted to saints – St Winefride, St Francis, and St Anna (Whiting 1931, Nos 24, 52 and 43) – and three to Mary (Whiting 1931, Nos 44, 45 and 46); virginity is specifically praised in a further carol (Whiting 1931, No. 47) and there is also a carol offering advice to virgins (Whiting 1931, No. 48) and one offering advice to married women (Whiting 1931, No. 49). In another of his poems, Audelay admonishes priests to be charitable, friars to be pious and humble, old men to be

---

[6]   According to the use of Sarum the latter is also found in Matins on Friday after the octave of Epiphany.
[7]   Two further poems, both macaronic carols, are transmitted in the so-called Bradshaw Fragments (CUL Additional 7350, Box 1, item 1); cf. Robbins 1966. Ryman's poems are edited in Zupitza 1892. For a recent discussion of Ryman and the Ryman manuscript, see Reichl 2003.
[8]   On the popularity of the macaronic religious lyric in Middle English in general, see Wehrle 1933; on Ryman's macaronic carols, see Jeffrey 1984.

chaste, and knights to fight for a good cause (Whiting 1931, No. 40). In a more doctrinal spirit, moral precepts and instruction are the topics of a group of five carols: on the Ten Commandments, the Seven Deadly Sins, the Seven Acts of Mercy, the Five Senses and the Seven Gifts of the Holy Ghost (Whiting 1931, Nos 28, 29, 30, 31 and 32). Finally, in one poem the poet, in a repentant mood, praises the innocence of childhood (Whiting 1931, No. 41). For all of these themes parallels can be found in other Middle English carols (see Greene, Nos 308 to 412, from carols of saints to carols of marriage and of childhood). A comparatively small subgroup of medieval carols is centred on Christ, some of them on the Passion theme of Christ on the cross (Greene, Nos 263–297); this group is also represented among Audelay's poems by a fervent carol on the love of Christ (Whiting 1931, No. 50).

One carol in particular, *Dred of deth, sorrow of syn* (Whiting 1931, No. 51), merits special mention. It is a macaronic poem, with the refrain: *Passio Christi conforta me!* [May Christ's Passion give me comfort!] Despite this refrain it is not a Passion poem but a poem on mortality and the transitoriness of human affairs. The burden contains the well-known phrase *Timor mortis conturbat me* [The fear of death confounds me], best known perhaps from William Dunbar's *Lament for the Makaris:*[9]

> Lade, helpe! Ihesu, merce!
> Timor mortis conturbat me.
>
> Dred of deth, sorow of syn,
>   Trublls my hert ful grevysly;
> My soule hit nyth with my lust then;   *is harmed*
>   Passio Christi conforta me.
>
> For blyndnes is a heve thyng,
>   And to be def ther-with only,
> To lese my lyght and my heryng;
>   Passio Christi conforta me.
>
> . . .
>
> As I lay seke in my langure,   *sick*
>   With sorow of hert and teere of ye,   *eye*
> This caral I made with gret doloure;   *pain*
>   Passio Christi conforta me.
>
> . . .
>
> Lerne this lesson of blynd Awdlay:
>   When bale is hyest then bot may be;   *remedy*
> Yif thou be nyd nyght or day,   *troubled*
>   Say passio Christi conforta me. (1–10, 31–4, 43–6)

Although the theme of this poem as well as the way it is formulated in conventional phrases and liturgically based quotations are traditional, there is here a

---

[9]   See Bawcutt 1996, 105–10; also MacDonald (below), 258–9. For other poems with this line, see *IMEV* 3743 and 4077.

personal note, a certain authenticity of expression, which no doubt stems from
the fact that Audelay was indeed blind and deaf and is, therefore, neither
speaking metaphorically nor simply of an imagined future as he dwells on the
infirmities of old age which make life a burden. This poem demonstrates that
conventionality in diction or style is no bar to intensity of feeling; it also reminds
us that their religious inspiration endows these poems with a deep sense of the
reality of spiritual life that is often illusive to the modern reader.

While medieval carols are primarily religious poems, also popular were
carols dealing with secular themes. About thirteen per cent of Greene's collection are of the latter kind. They fall mainly into four groups: convivial carols,
political carols, amorous carols and humorous carols (Greene, Nos 413–474).
Audelay's carol on King Henry VI (Whiting 1931, No. 39) belongs to the small
group of political carols; it is an admonition to support King Henry VI, *Fore he is
ful yong, tender of age* (3), and is mostly an encomium of the victories of his father,
Henry V. It is interesting to note that James Ryman also composed a poem on
Henry VI (Robbins *Hist.*, No. 83), in his case, however, after the king had died
and with allusions to several miracles after his death. Perhaps the best-known
political carol is the song praising the English victory at Azincourt (Agincourt)
in 1415, with its triumphant burden: *Deo gracias Anglia / Redde pro victoria!*
[England thank God for the victory!].[10]

Carols of a convivial kind are closely linked to the 'boar's head' carols, carols
which celebrate the bringing in of the boar's head at Christmas dinner, an
ancient custom that still survives in Queen's College, Oxford (Greene, Nos
132–135).[11] Most of the convivial carols are drinking songs, some in a fairly
rumbustious mood. A similar tone of jollity and high spirits characterises some
of the amorous and humorous carols, songs about illicit love affairs, pregnant
maidens and *pastourelle*-type adventures. The connection to Christmas is made
explicit in one of the amorous carols (Greene, No. 457), which offers a humorous
combination of Christmas festivity, liturgical language and light-hearted love
adventure:[12]

> 'Kyrie, so kyrie,'
> Jankyn syngyth merie,   *merrily*
>   With 'aleyson'.
>
> As I went on Yol day in owre prosessyon,   *Yule (Christmas) Day*
> Knew I joly Jankyn be his mery ton.   *note / voice*
>   [Kyrieleyson.]
>
> Jankyn began the Offys on the Yol Day,
> And yyit me thynkyth it dos me good, so merie gan he say,
>   'Kyrieleyson'.

---

10 Greene, No. 426; preserved with its music in Bodl. MS Arch. Selden. B. 26 and Cambridge,
    Trinity College MS O.3.58; for these manuscripts, see below.
11 On the carol sung at Queen's College, Oxford, see Keyte and Parrott 1992, No. 124; see also
    Keyte and Parrott 1992, No. 37, 'The Exeter Boar's Head Carol'. See further, Spears 1974.
12 In the last line the manuscript has *schylde* instead of *chylde*. The metre of this poem varies; see
    Duncan *MEL*, No. 129 and Commentary, 248–9. See also Chambers and Sidgwick 1907, 220–1.

Jankyn red the Pystyl ful fayre and ful wel,
And yyt me thinkyth it dos me good, as evere have I sel.   *bliss*
[Kyrieleyson.]

Jankyn at the Sanctus crakith a merie note,   *divides*
And yyt me thinkyth it dos me good: I payid for his cote.
[Kyrieleyson.]

Jankyn crakith notes, an hunderid on a knot,   *in a phrase*
And yyt he hakkyth hem smallere than wortes to the pot.   *splits; herbs*
K[yrieleyson.]

Jankyn at the Angnus beryth the pax-brede;   *Pax bread* *
He twynkelid, but sayd nowt, and on myn fot he trede.   *trod*
[Kyrieleyson.]

Benedicamus Domino: Cryst fro schame me schylde;
Deo gracias therto: alas, I go with chylde!
K[yrieleyson.]

                            * (to be kissed at the exchanging of the peace)

The tricked girl's perspective gives this poem a deceptive simplicity. Fun here is made not only of her gullibility and of Jankyn's conceited self-assurance, but also of musical styles, in particular the division of notes into small values ('diminution') in the music of the *ars nova* and the later *ars subtilior*, the sophisticated polyphonic styles of the fourteenth century. Among the amorous carols in Greene's edition there are also two earlier poems; these will be discussed below.

The medieval carol: form and music

The thematic survey shows that while poems connected to the Christmas season make up the core of late medieval carols, the carol as a genre cannot be defined by content or relationship to the liturgical year. In order for a poem to qualify as a carol it must have a burden which comes at the beginning of the poem and is repeated after every stanza. This is not just an arbitrary modern definition but accords with the form of the poems that are called 'carol' in medieval sources, such as the self-references in Audelay's carols mentioned above. The term 'burden' in the sense of a refrain is first found in the sixteenth century (also written *burthen*). This is how Ariel uses the word in *The Tempest* (I.ii.380) or a servant in *The Winter's Tale* when he announces a pedlar: 'He hath songs for man or woman, of all sizes: no milliner can so fit his customers with gloves: he has the prettiest love-songs for maids, so without bawdry (which is strange); with such delicate burdens of dildoes and fadings . . .' (IV.iv.193ff.). In Middle English only the term *bordoun* was used, which had the same meaning as the French, from which is was borrowed, i.e. 'drone'.[13] In one of the carol manuscripts (Oxford, Balliol College MS 354 from the beginning of the sixteenth century) a number of burdens are designated by the term 'fote'.[14]

---

[13] See *MED* burdoun n. (2) and Flasdieck 1956.
[14] See Flügel 1903; Middle English *fot* does not have this meaning; cf. *MED* fot n.

It is important to realise that a burden is a special type of refrain, sometimes called an external refrain. An external refrain is defined as a repeated word, group of words, line or group of lines that is independent of the stanza, whereas an internal refrain is part of the stanza, often coming at its end. While poems must have a burden in order to qualify as carols, many carols may also have a refrain, in the sense of an internal refrain. This is, for instance, the case with Ryman's carols, of which the majority also have a refrain.[15]

A second point to make about the form of the carol is that its stanzas are regular, all having the same structure. Many patterns are possible; particularly striking is the variety found among Ryman's carols. Audelay's carols are simpler, restricted to basically two patterns, of which the first is illustrated above (four-line stanzas, here rhyming abab); 'the other is a five-line stanza with the rhyme scheme ababc, also tetrameter except for the last line which is short-ened and which usually consists of some phrase, insignificant in meaning, which serves to introduce the burden' (Whiting 1931, xxi).

There is, however, a third element to take into account. As Greene remarked, a carol is a poem 'intended, or at least suitable, for singing'. A good many carols have been transmitted with their music so that an appreciation of the carol as song is possible. There are about 120 carols with musical settings found in fifteenth-century manuscripts. They are generally set for two or three voices; only in a few cases is the tune alone given. They have all been edited by John Stevens, who, in the introduction to his *Mediaeval Carols*, distinguishes three types of carols:

> We should distinguish at least three kinds of carols – those intended to 'improve' the minds of the congregation, those which reflect the more instructed piety of composers and singers, and those which by their brilliance directly enhance the splendour of their ceremonial setting. These are essentially *musical* categories; they could, if space permitted, be defined in purely musical terms. For now, three examples must suffice to show that the picture of the carol simply as a 're-flection of popular aspiration' is quite one-sided. This 'one side' is amply present in the two settings of *Alma redemptoris mater* (Nos 4 & 23); their vigorous rhyth-mic drive, their warmth and sonority, are signs of a moral 'directness' which might almost be called didactic. On the other hand, the more suspended move-ment, the long interwoven melodies, and the more subtle harmonic progressions of *To many a well* (no. **114**) convey an inward-turning piety for which the proper word is 'meditative'. Lastly, *Nowell: Dieu vous garde* (no. **80**), with its bright, clear texture and its heavily decorated melodies, stresses the ornamental side of carol-music.[16]

A brief look at the simpler kind as exemplified by one of the settings of *Alma redemptoris mater* (Stevens, No. 4, from Cambridge, Trinity College MS O.3.58)

---

[15] For the various patterns in Ryman's poems, see Reichl 2003. Occasionally a burden may be left out at the beginning of a poem, but there is nevertheless an external refrain, existing inde-pendently of the stanza and repeated after each stanza. On the form and sources of burdens see Greene, clx–clxxii.

[16] Stevens 1958, xiv–xv; the carols referred to are, respectively, Greene, Nos 234 A and B, 306, and 6.

may help to clarify the relationship between textual and musical structure. The song has five stanzas, of which the burden and first stanza read:

Alma Redemptoris mater.   *kind Mother of the Redeemer*

As I lay upon a nyght,
My thowgth was on a berde so bright   *maiden*
That men clepyn Marye ful of myght,   *call*
   Redemptoris mater. (Greene, No. 234 A)

All five stanzas have the same refrain, which is textually partially identical with the burden. This type of carol is generally termed a rounded carol.

As to its music, this carol is set for two voices, both burden and stanza. While the music of burden and verse is basically of the same kind – exhibiting, in Stevens' words, a 'vigorous rhythmic drive' – it is interesting to note that the textual correspondence between refrain and burden is not mirrored in the music. There are various modern recordings of medieval English carols; this carol is conveniently found on the compact disc (Naxos 8.550751, band 4) enti-tled *Medieval Carols*, and sung by the Oxford Camerata directed by Jeremey Summerly. A further point to make about the music is that the words *Alma redemptoris mater*, which come from a Marian antiphon, are not set to the litur-gical melody (although there is a general similarity between the melodic contour of the burden and the corresponding section of the antiphon). Manfred Bukofzer, who wrote the first detailed musical analysis of the English carol, has noted that it is characteristic of the genre as a whole that its music is inde-pendent of the melodies to which the texts (in burden and refrain) taken from hymns and other liturgical sources would have been sung in their original contexts (Bukofzer 1950, 151). Bukofzer has also observed that so-called 'rounded carols', carols which show textual correspondences between burden and refrain, as in our example, and/or musical correspondences between burden and refrain ('musical rhyme'), represent by far the most common form. On the basis of these correspondences he distinguishes four types:

> The carol's form allows of a bewildering number of possibilities on account of the criss-crossing of literary and musical factors. For example, a carol without any textual relations between burden and stanza may nevertheless have musical rhyme, and vice versa. Although the number of permutations is high, a rough classification of the four major possibilities may prove helpful. These are (1) rounded text and music, (2) rounded music not paralleled in the text, (3) the re-verse case, rounded text not paralleled in the music and (4) no rounding in either text or music. (Bukofzer 1950, 160)

What Bukofzer's analysis also stresses is the amount of musical sophistication displayed in the polyphonic carols of the fifteenth century. This development is continued into the sixteenth century in the Tudor carols, which are mostly found in the Fayrfax Manuscript (BL MS Additional 5465). From the textual point of view, these carols are characterised by their predilection for the Passion theme; from the musical point of view, the Fayrfax carols present a further elaboration of the variation in musical rhyme between refrain and burden.[17] The musical

---

17 Stevens 1961, 98ff. and Appendix A, *passim*; music edited in Stevens 1975.

elaboration of the polyphonic carol in the fifteenth century to the beginning of the sixteenth has been succinctly summarised by Frank Ll. Harrison, who also noted that the popularity of the carols ceased with the rise of the polyphonic song in the Elizabethan age.[18]

Manuscript transmission

Greene lists almost one hundred manuscripts in his survey of those transmitting English carols.[19] Some contain only one carol, others comprise a substantial collection of poems. Most transmit the text only, but there are also manuscripts that contain text and music. Most of the late medieval and early Tudor polyphonic carols have been transmitted in the following six manuscripts. Cambridge, Trinity College MS O.3.58, a vellum roll from the first half of the fifteenth century consisting of three sections laced together and measuring more than six feet in length, contains thirteen carols.[20] BL MS Egerton 3307 (c.1450), is of disputed provenance; one attribution is to the Cistercian abbey of Meaux in Yorkshire. It contains, in addition to processional music for Holy Week, twelve carols in English (or with English) and nineteen carols in Latin.[21] This manuscript has six concordances with an important musical carol manuscript, Bodl. MS Arch. Selden. B. 26, a composite manuscript which, in its relevant part, dates from the middle of the fifteenth century and contains almost thirty carols, most of which are in English. According to Greene this manuscript comes from Worcester.[22] Another major music manuscript is the 'Ritson Manuscript', BL MS Additional 5665, which dates from the first quarter of the sixteenth century. It contains – apart from Latin masses and motets, a French song and other English songs – over forty carols, most of them in English.[23] Also from around 1500 is the 'Fayrfax Manuscript', BL MS Additional 5465. Once owned by the English composer Robert Fayrfax (1464–1521), it contains (along with some of Fayrfax's own compositions) eight English carols with their music, and, in addition, a number of English songs on religious and secular themes.[24] Finally, five English carols are found in 'Henry VIII's Manuscript', BL MS Additional 31922 (early sixteenth century), an important source for early Tudor music.[25]

Among English carol manuscripts transmitting the texts only, the following can be singled out on account of the number of carols they contain. Two manuscripts preserve the poems of poets known by name: CUL Ee.1.12 (after 1492)

---

[18] Harrison 1963, 416–24. On the development of the Middle English carol, in particular its music, see also under the article 'Carol' in Sadie 2001, vol. 5, 162–70, '1. Origins and Social Setting', and '2. The Pre-Reformation Carol' (J. Stevens).

[19] Greene, 297–337; for printed sources, see Greene, 337–41. The most important sources are also found in Greene 1962, 170–85.

[20] Greene, 327; Stevens 1958, 125.

[21] Greene, 299–301; Stevens 1958, 125; one carol is without words (Stevens 1958, No. 74); Bukofzer 1950.

[22] Greene, 314–15; Stevens 1958, 125.

[23] Greene, 307–8; Stevens 1958, 125; Stevens 1961, 1ff.; Stevens 1975, xvii–xviii.

[24] Greene, 307; Stevens 1961, 1ff.; 351–85; Stevens 1975, xv–xvi.

[25] Greene, 311; Stevens 1961, 1ff.; 386–425; Stevens 1969, Nos 33, 35 and 35A, 41, 50, 65.

contains about one hundred and fifty poems by Ryman, of which about one hundred and twenty are carols;[26] Bodl. MS Douce 302 (second quarter of the fifteenth century) transmits over fifty poems by Audelay, of which twenty-six are carols.[27] Over fifty English carols are found in BL MS Sloane 2593, an important collection of English and Latin songs, unfortunately lacking music, which was put together in Bury St Edmunds in the first half of the fifteenth century.[28] More than seventy English carols are contained in Oxford, Balliol College MS 354 (first half of the sixteenth century). This manuscript is generally known as 'The Commonplace Book of Richard Hill'; it is a miscellany of religious and secular texts, poetic and otherwise, that its compiler, a citizen and grocer of London, found interesting.[29] Bodl. MS eng. poet.e.1 represents a similar collection, with over sixty English carols, a few with musical notation, from the second half of the fifteenth century. In Greene's view 'this excellent and varied collection of carols' comes from Beverley Minster, Yorkshire.[30] Finally, Cambridge, St John's College MS S.54 (259), from the second half of the fifteenth century, should be mentioned. This manuscript, which transmits about twenty English carols, is interesting on account of its format: it is preserved in a 'contemporary wallet-like wrapper' and was obviously a 'pocket-book of carols' (Greene, 325–6).

Carol and carole, carol and processional hymn

The ambiguity of the Middle English word *carol*, which denotes both a song and a dance, has led to the assumption that the carol as a lyrical and musical form had its origin in the dance. Middle English *carol* and *carole(n)* are borrowed from French. The corresponding French words (*carole*, n., and *caroler*, v.) are first recorded in the first half of the twelfth century (also in the forms *querole(r)* and *charole(r)*).[31] The use of these terms in the works of Chrétien de Troyes (fl. c.1160–c.1185) furnishes a first clue as to their meaning in the twelfth and thirteenth centuries. The terms appear in the context of feasts and denote in the first place some kind of dancing. A typical passage is found in the *Chevalier de la Charrete*:

> . . . Lors recomancent
> lor jeus, si querolent et dancent. (1827–28)[32]

[Now they begin their entertainment again / and 'carol' and 'dance'.]

---

[26] Greene, 321; see also above and note 7.
[27] Greene, 317; Brown 1916–20, vol. 1, 113–15; see also above and note 2.
[28] Greene, 306–7; Wright 1847; Fehr 1902.
[29] Greene, 320–1; Dyboski 1908.
[30] Greene, 317–18; see Stevens 1958, Nos 4A and 10A.
[31] 'Les plus anciens exemples connus du mot *carole* se trouvent dans les traductions du Psautier (comm. du XIIe s.) . . .' (Sahlin 1940, 2). On the relationship between the carol, the *carole* and related forms, see also Greene, xliii–lxiv.
[32] Roques 1958, 56. Cf. *Le Chevalier de la Charrete* 1646; *Erec* 2047, *Guillaume d'Angleterre* 1304, *Perceval* 2745, 8254.

However, in one or two contexts, *carole(r)* is also combined with singing, most clearly in *Erec* 5504. When Erec appears, the girls, who are 'carolling', leave off their singing:

> Nes les puceles qui carolent,
> Lor chant an leissent et retardent. (5503–4)[33]
>
> [Even the girls, who were 'carolling', / left off their song and post-poned it for later.]

While *carole(r)* denotes first and foremost a form of dance, there are enough passages in Old French literature, as Margit Sahlin has shown, to warrant an interpretation of *carole* also as a lyric form, a type of song sung together with a dance, as is suggested by the quotation from Chrétien's *Erec*. (In fact, the earliest occurrences of *carole* translate Latin *chorus* as used in the Psalms).[34] Most explicit about the dancing and singing of the *carole* is a passage in Jean Renart's *Roman de Guillaume de Dole*.[35] After a sumptuous meal, the courtly company of Emperor Conrad indulge in various pastimes; some try their luck in different games, others listen to the *viele*-players and again others, young men and women, leave the pavilions and:

> Main a main, em pur lor biau cors,
> devant le tref, en un pré vert,
> les puceles et li vallet
> ront la carole commenciee. (507–10)
>
> [Hand in hand, without outer garments, / in front of the tent, on a green meadow, / the maidens and the young men / started the *carole* again.]

Then a lady steps forward and sings a song (514–19). She is followed by three other persons, who also sing a similar song, i.e. songs about Bele Aelis or Robin and Mariete, songs (*rondets*) that were obviously connected with dancing. This is clear from Jean Renart's text which says that the second song had not lasted three turns when the second person took up the singing (528ff.). This scene is concluded with the following words:

> Que de Robin que d'Aaliz
> tant ont chanté que jusqu'as liz
> ont fetes durer les caroles. (548–50)
>
> [Of Robin as well as of Aaliz / so much did they sing that until bedtime / they made the *caroles* last.]

Although it is clear that in the Middle Ages *carole* denotes both a dance and a dance-song or refrain-song, the textual evidence is not precise and unambig-

---

[33] Foerster 1934, 153. Cf. *Perceval* 8992.
[34] As in Psalms 19:5, 86:6, 149:3; cf. Sahlin 1940, 2–3.
[35] Cf. Sahlin 1940, 9; the following quotations are taken from Lecoy 1963, 16–18; on the dance-songs in Jean Renart's work, see also Butterfield 2002, 45ff.

uous enough to be more specific. Sahlin's conclusion, after a painstaking analysis of the meaning of the Old French terms, is sobering:

> caroler, au moyen âge, avait le sens assez vague de 'chanter, en marchant, des chansons à refrain'. Toutes les particularités, tous les détails concernant la disposition des caroleurs, le rythme des chansons ou des pas, etc., sont des caractères secondaires qui peuvent varier et qui ne font pas partie intégrante de l'idée de carole. (Sahlin 1940, 36)

> [caroller, in the Middle Ages, had the rather vague meaning of 'singing, while walking, refrain songs'. All the specifics, all the details concerning the disposition of the carollers, the rhythm of the songs or of the steps, etc., are secondary features which can vary and which are not an integral part of the idea of carole.]

The ambiguity of the term 'carol' presumably points to an early connection between dance and refrain song. It has long been thought that the carol as dance, the medieval carole, was some kind of round dance, in which the movement of the dancers was regulated according to whether a soloist (or choryphée) was singing the stanzas or the dancers (the choir) were singing the refrain. Although there is no lack of medieval descriptions of the carole (to which illustrations of dancers and singers in medieval manuscripts can be added), its choreography is far from clear. It has been assumed that the singer-dancers formed a circle and that they alternated between going round in a circle (while the stanza was sung by the soloist) and standing still (while they all sang the refrain). As folklorists and ethnomusicologists have shown, the round-dance is a practically universal dance form, found in a great number of variations and confusing multiplicity of forms.[36]

There is no need to doubt that the dance-song, which corresponded by its division into stanza and refrain to the basic structure of the round-dance, might in the course of time have developed into the refrain-song or refrain-poem, performed on its own, independently of dancing. When it comes to the Middle English carols, however, the gap between the carol as dance, as practised in the twelfth and thirteenth centuries, and the carol as lyric and polyphonic song, which flourished in the fifteenth century, has become so wide that a connection is hardly visible any more. Scholars have therefore looked for other origins.

The preponderance of religious themes and the ubiquitous presence of Latin quotations from liturgical texts in the Middle English carol have led to the search for closer parallels in the liturgy itself.[37] The obvious candidates are processional hymns which, like the carol, have a burden. 'Gloria, laus et honor' is one of these hymns, sung during the Palm Sunday procession. The Liber Usualis gives instruction on how to sing this hymn. When the procession returns to the church, two or four singers enter the church and sing the burden:

> Gloria, laus et honor tibi sit,
> Rex Christe Redemptor:
> Cui puerile decus prompsit Hosanna pium. (Liber Usualis, 588–9)

---

36 Sachs 1938, 142–71; see also the article 'Round Dances' in Leach 1972, 957–8.
37 On the sources of the Latin lines, see Greene, lxxxi–cxvii; see in particular his lists, lxxxvi–viii, xcvii–viii and civ–v.

[Glory, praise and honour be to you / Christ the Saviour King, / to
whom the flower of youth offers a pious Hosanna.]

Those outside the church repeat the burden, then the singers inside sing the
various strophes, after each of which the people outside sing the burden. This
manner of performance – the alternation between soloists and the community or
between two choirs in accordance with the alternation between stanza and
burden – basically corresponds to that of dance songs as described above, only
that here we have clear models and are not obliged to have recourse to speculation in absence of unambiguous textual and musical material. M. Sahlin had
already put forward the thesis that the *carole* originated in a Church milieu, and
had drawn attention to the connection between liturgical dance and procession
(Sahlin 1940, 137ff.). Her view was extended to the late medieval polyphonic
carols by Catherine Miller, who argued that these carols often not only have a
clear connection to liturgical feasts but appear in some manuscripts that 'also
contain a high percentage of other processional repertory' (Miller 1950, 63). The
idea that the composition of the carol was not only patterned on processional
hymns but that their use was actually linked to liturgical processions has been
further elaborated by Rossell Hope Robbins. Robbins denied that earlier vernacular traditions of the *carole* had any influence on the English carol and
concluded: 'Its main tradition was not vernacular, secular, and foreign; but
Latin, religious, and native' (Robbins 1959b, 582).

But this only covers a comparatively small subset of the carol corpus. While
Although there is no evidence that Middle English carols were used in
processions, a liturgical connection is certainly possible in the case of the polyphonic religious carols from the late Middle Ages. Frank Ll. Harrison, though
sceptical of their use in processions, has given persuasive reasons for their functioning as *Benedicamus* substitutes on particular feast days. The *Benedicamus* is a
versicle that occurs at the end of the canonical hours; on feast days it is sung to a
somewhat richer melody than is normal at the end of Vespers, Matins and
Lauds. With the rise of polyphony, the *Benedicamus* became a favourite place for
elaboration, insertion and development. Instead of the *Benedicamus*, so-called
Benedicamus substitutes were also used. As polyphonic settings of the
Benedicamus were uncommon in the later Middle Ages in England and as the
conductus, as a *Benedicamus* substitute, had also disappeared in the second half of
the fourteenth century, Harrison proposes a liturgical role for the polyphonic
carols as such *Benedicamus* substitutes.[38]

But this only covers a comparatively small subset of the carol corpus. While
some carols might have fulfilled a liturgical (or possibly para-liturgical) function, and while in the case of religious carols the close connection to the feasts of
the liturgical year, in particular to those of the Christmas season, is clear – both
in topic and more specifically by their frequent quotations from Latin hymns
and similar sources – it must remain doubtful whether the medieval English
carol as a genre can be derived from the liturgy. Evidence against this derivation

---

[38] 'On the other hand, the words of some polyphonic carols, a genre which appeared about the
time the conductus was going out of use, make it likely that the sacred carol of the fifteenth
century took over from the conductus the role of Benedicamus substitute on certain festivals'.
(Harrison 1963, 416–17) See also Harrison 1965.

are carols, in particular secular carols, that were composed before 1400, before the rise of the late medieval polyphonic carol. Robbins counters this objection by pointing out that before 1400 only nine carols have been preserved and that seven of them are religious. Hence, an argument for a secular origin of the carol would have to rest on just two poems. These early Middle English carols must, however, be seen in the context of poems similar in form before their value as evidence (or counter-evidence) can be assessed.

Related medieval forms and the earliest English 'carols'

Poems and songs with refrains belong to the most common lyrical and musical forms of the Middle Ages. It is in particular the *rondeau* which comes to mind – both in the Latin *rondellus* and the vernacular *rondet* or *rondel* in early and in later forms – with its specific use of a verse-internal and a verse-final refrain. It has been argued that these *rondeaux* of the twelfth and thirteenth centuries, as, for instance, inserted into Jean Renart's *Guillaume de Dole* mentioned above, are realizations of the general genre 'carol' as dance-song.[39] Few of the Latin *rondeaux* have an initial refrain comparable to the burden of the carol, but a number of French poems start with the refrain.[40] While then these *rondeaux* begin with a refrain similar to the burden of the carol, there are nevertheless differences, of which the most significant are a refrain in the middle of the stanza (consisting of part of the initial refrain), the identity of initial and verse-final refrain, and the fact that many of these poems comprise only one stanza. An example by the trouvère Guillaume d'Amiens at the end of the thirteenth century will illustrate this:

> C'est la fins, koi que nus die,
> > J'amerai.
> C'est la jus en mi le pré
> – C'est la fins, je veul amer –
> Jus et bais i a levés;
> Bele amie ai.
> C'est la fins koi que nus die,
> > J'amera[i].[41]

> [*It is certain:*
> whatever any one says, I'm going to be in love.
> It's down there in the middle of the meadow –
> *It is certain: I wish to be in love –*
> down there a dance has begun;
> I have a beautiful sweetheart.
> *It is certain:*
> whatever any one says, I'm going to be in love.*]

---

[39] See Stevens 1986, 159–98; see also Bec 1977–8, I, 220–8; for an older and influential (though in some respects superseded) discussion of the *rondeau* in the twelfth and thirteenth centuries, see Gennrich 1963.

[40] On the Latin *rondeau*, see Spanke 1930.

[41] Bec 1977–8, II, 161–2; see also Stevens 1986, 187 for words with music and the translation.

Much closer in form to the English carol are the Italian *lauda* and the Spanish *villancico*. Both lyric genres are interesting, not because they can be assumed to have in any way contributed to the rise and popularity of the English carol, but rather because they represent parallel developments, with similar variations and diversifications. Also, these genres have manifold formal and possibly genetic relationships to other lyrical/musical forms, a fact that underlines both the vitality and the multiformity of the refrain song in medieval Europe. The *lauda* is in form identical with the carol: it has an external refrain (*ripresa*), sung at the beginning and repeated after each stanza; the stanzas do not as a rule have a refrain, but their last line (*volta*) rhymes in general with the last line of the *ripresa*; there is also, as far as we can tell from *laude* transmitted with their music, in most cases a musical relationship between *ripresa* and *volta*. Like the majority of carols, the *lauda* is a religious song, basically non-liturgical but with links to liturgical feasts and ceremonies; it enjoyed a great deal of popularity from the thirteenth century to the nineteenth century; also like the carol, in addition to monophonic songs, the polyphonic *lauda* was developed in the fifteenth century and continued to flourish in the sixteenth century.[42] The rise of the *lauda* is intimately connected to the Franciscan movement of the thirteenth century; in fact one of the few *lauda* poets known by name is the Franciscan Jacopone da Todi (c.1230–1306). In accordance with the Franciscan endeavour to spread the faith as 'God's minstrels' (*ioculatores Dei*), the popularisation of religious ideas with the help of secular forms was part of their programme. It is hence not surprising that the *lauda* is closely modelled on the contemporary Italian dance-song, the *ballata*.[43]

In a similar way, the Latin poems of the fourteenth-century *Red Book of Ossory*, many of them in carol form, were compiled in a Franciscan house as religious imitations (*contrafacta*) of secular songs. There is evidence that 'the Franciscans were directly associated with the development of the carol in England', as Bukofzer points out, only to add, however, that they did not invent the carol but took its form over from secular song.[44]

Very close to the English carol is also the Spanish *villancico*. It has a burden (termed *estribillo*) which is normally repeated after every stanza; the last line of the burden rhymes with the last line of the stanza (*vuelta*); in many songs the *vuelta* is identical to the last line of the burden; furthermore, the music of *estribillo* and that of the *vuelta* are related, with various possibilities of repetition and variation. In this general pattern the *villancico* agrees with the form of other Hispanic poems, in particular that of the *Cantigas de Santa Maria* of King Alfonso X of Castile (1221–1284). It is also generally considered identical in form to the French *virelai*. What is interesting about the *villancico* in connection with the carol is its development. Originally a form of popular poetry, as its name *villancico*, 'little peasant', implies, it flourished in the fifteenth and sixteenth

---

[42] Cf. Liuzzi 1934; Stevens 1990, 433–42.
[43] Cf. 'Ballata', Sadie 2001, vol. 2, 563–5 (K. von Fischer, G. d'Agostino).
[44] Bukofzer 1960, 117–21, quotation on p. 119. The 'Franciscan thesis' has been put forward by R. H. Robbins; see esp. Robbins 1938; on the role of the Franciscans in the development of the carol, see also Greene, cl–clvii.

centuries as polyphonic secular song. From the later sixteenth century onwards the genre began to shift to religious themes, among which the Nativity gradually predominated. In Modern Spanish, the term *villancico* denotes simply a Christmas carol.[45] Although both the *Cantigas de Santa Maria* and the later *villancico* can be seen as genres of religious song, there is agreement among scholars that their source of inspiration is ultimately to be found in secular songs, most probably of the dance-song genre. The question of origins, as researched in detail by Pierre Le Gentil for *villancico* and *virelai*, has revealed the great complexity of the problem; it has also shown that the very ubiquity of similar forms should make us wary of always seeing influences and looking for monogenetic explanations (Le Gentil 1954).

One of the reasons why R. H. Robbins favoured an ecclesiastical origin for the carol was the paucity of secular carols in England before 1400. Two poems in carol-form have been generally considered in discussions of the carol, and it is to these I wish to turn now. One of these poems is found in a legal manuscript of Lincoln's Inn in London and begins with the initial refrain (burden):

> [Nou sprinkes] the sprai,
> Al for love icche am so seek   *I; sick*
> That slepen I ne mai.[46]

The manuscript text is unambiguous as to the form of this poem (unfortunately transmitted without its music): the burden is repeated after every stanza. There is no internal refrain, but the last line of the stanza rhymes with the last line of the burden. Helen Sandison has drawn attention to a close parallel in a French poem with the refrain:

> James n'amerai
> Home de cuer gay.[47]
>
> [Never again will I love / a man with merry heart.]

It is clear both from the contents of the Middle English poem (which is probably fragmentary at the end) and of its French parallel that this lyric belongs to the tradition of the *pastourelle*; in our poem the frame is that of the *chanson d'aventure*: the narrator sets out on a stroll or ride and overhears the words of a young woman who is angry at her lover's change of affection. At this point the English poem breaks off, but in the French poem the narrator offers his love to the girl (a shepherdess) and is successful. The French lyric, which is preserved with its music in the *Chansonnier Cangé*, is a *pastourelle-avec-des-refrains*, in other words one of the many types of refrain songs.

---

45 Cf. 'Villancico', Sadie 2001, vol. 26, 621–8 (I. Pope, P. R. Laird); St Amour 1940; Malkiel and Stern 1984.

46 Lincoln's Inn, MS Hale 135, fol. 137v (beginning of fourteenth century); the manuscript is described in Greene, 313. The poem is found in Brown *XIII*, No. 62; I have transcribed the poem again from the manuscript and interpreted it in the context of the Middle English *pastourelle* in Reichl 1987, 37–8.

47 See Sandison 1913, 47–8; for a discussion of this poem, see also Reichl 1987, 38–40, and Scattergood (above), 42–3.

The second poem is the famous Harley lyric *Ichot a burde in boure bright* (Brown *XIII*, No. 83) with the burden:

> Blow, northerne wynd,
> Sent thou me my suetyng!   *sweetheart*
> Blow, northerne wynd,
> Blou! blou! blou![48]

There can be no doubt that this poem is formally a carol, at least as far as the text is concerned (there is no music transmitted with this lyric). On the other hand, there is little similarity in style and spirit to what otherwise goes under the name of carol. *Blow, northerne wynd* is one of the gems of the early Middle English love lyric, with its elaborate description of the beloved's beauty, both physical and moral, and with its haunting allegorisation of Love and Love's Knights.[49] The burden with its popular tone stands in stark contrast to the tone of the individual stanzas. We are reminded of the use of *refrains* – those short, folksong-like lyrics, whose popular tone cannot be missed – in French refain-poems like the ones inserted in the *Roman de Guillaume de Dole*. There is a deliberate play with popular and courtly modes and styles in these poems.

Both poems then, *Nou sprinkes the sprai* as well as *Blow, northerne wynd*, can be considered carols on formal grounds. On the other hand, they are more clearly linked to the French tradition of refrain-poems than to the later English carol tradition, so that it seems to me more appropriate to call these poems 'carols' only in inverted commas. Despite variation and diversity, the fifteenth-century carols form a group with a comparatively homogeneous core, to which these early poems do not seem to belong. This does not make the fifteenth-century carol into a genre that was derived from liturgical models (such as the processional hymn) in an ecclesiastical milieu (like that of Franciscan activity). The refrain song is such a pervasive lyric form in the Middle Ages that the search for specific origins seems hardly necessary. What defines a genre is its vitality and popularity in particular circles and at particular times. Just as the *lauda* flourished in different forms (as monophonic song and as polyphonic song) in different circles at different times (friars, corporations of *laudesi*, cathedral choirs etc.), the carol found its widest appeal in the fifteenth and early sixteenth centuries, in monophonic and polyphonic form, in a Franciscan context (Audelay, Ryman) as well as in cathedral choirs, as a predominantly (though not exclusively) religious song connected to the great festivals of the Church, in particular those of the Christmas season.

---

[48] For an interpretation, see Spitzer 1962, 193–216; for an attempt to see this poem in the tradition of Middle English amorous carols, see Garner 2000.
[49] See Scattergood (above), 59–60.

Conclusion

R. L. Greene aptly characterised the Middle English carols as poems popular by destination rather than by origin.[50] Although there is enough evidence to point to a popular origin of dance-songs such as the short French songs and lyrics known as *refrains* and although some of the refrain-poems incorporating these *refrains* might still be fairly close to the world of folksong, the English carols as we have them are at several removes from such songs. Individual burdens might hark back to such poems, popular by origin rather than only by destination, but the poems in their entirety, at least as far as the majority of carols is concerned, point by their abundant liturgical references and, in particular in the case of the polyphonic carols, by their rich musical texture, quite unambiguously to a clerical milieu. This does not make the carols into sophisticated lyrics, quite the contrary. As both literary scholars and musicologists have pointed out, some of the most salient stylistic traits of the late medieval carol are its straightforward language, conventional phraseology, imagery of direct appeal, and lively rhythm. The interplay of learned allusion and popular tone in the carol *Of a rose, a lovely rose* (Greene, No. 175) has been highlighted in Leo Spitzer's perceptive interpretation (Spitzer 1962, 216–33). The same interplay of clerical background and overall popular tone has been remarked upon in respect to the music. While, according to Bukofzer, the polyphonic carols 'are not arrangements of pre-existing folksong' but belong rather to the realm of art-music, they are nevertheless 'composed art-music in a popular vein' (Bukofzer 1960, 123).

There is in fact folk poetry which has often been associated with the carol and which has contributed to the confusion about a possible popular origin of the Middle English carol. Among these poems and songs are the so-called ballad carols, poems like *The Cherry Tree Carol*, i.e. ballads on legendary themes connected to the Christmas season, or cumulative poems such as *The Twelve Days of Christmas*, in which the gifts sent by a lover to his lady on each of the days from Christmas to Epiphany are enumerated. These poems or songs have no burdens; their connection to the carol genre is simply one of content.[51]

Together with these songs, poems have also been discussed which clearly are carols in form, the *Coventry Carol* and the *Coventry Shepherds' Carol*, both found in the *Coventry Play* (Greene, Nos 112 and 79B). The first is a lullaby sung by the women of Bethlehem when Herod's knights appear to slay the children; the second belongs to the Nativity scene of the same pageant and is cast in the form of a *chanson d'aventure*. The carol shared the same fate as these medieval mystery cycles: their particular type of religiosity became unfashionable (or undesirable) in the latter part of the sixteenth century, and, apart from isolated later instances,[52] the carol ceased to be a flourishing lyrical and musical genre. It has

---

[50] Greene, cxviii. See his discussion of the carol as popular song, cxviii–cxxxviii.

[51] They are (somewhat confusingly) discussed in Routley 1958, 43–80; these two poems are edited in Keyte and Parrott 1992, No. 128, 'Cherry Tree Carol', and No. 133, 'Twelve Days of Christmas'.

[52] See under the article 'Carol' in Sadie 2001, vol. 5, 170–2, '3. The Post-Reformation Carol' (D. Libby).

only survived as a name in the 'Christmas carol' – songs that can only rarely be classified as carols on formal grounds. Within the context of the Middle English lyric, the importance of the medieval carol can, however, hardly be overestimated. An extensive textual corpus has been preserved that permits the study of a genre in both its homogeneity and diversity; homogeneity on account of basic defining elements and diversity by innumerable variations and modulations of common forms and themes. Equally important, if not more so, is the fact that a comparatively large number of melodies has also been transmitted. While we know that many Middle English lyrics must have been songs, the lack of music allows us to interpret them only as texts. The transmission of music for the carols puts us into the fortunate position of being able to view many of these poems in their entirety, in their union of words and music, and (thanks to modern performances) to experience them as songs rather than as texts only. A carol like *Ther is no rose of swych vertu* (Greene, No. 173), for instance, which has been praised for its exquisite use of the rose image for the Virgin Mary, can also be appreciated as song since the poem is preserved with its music on the Trinity Roll.[53] While the music does not in any direct way relate to the textual meaning of the poem, it does, by adding an additional aesthetic dimension, enhance the poem's imaginative appeal. Our understanding of the Middle English lyric could be much advanced if the other genres were as well documented textually and musically as the carol.

---

[53] See Gray, 77ff. An easily accessible recording of this carol can be found on the CD *Medieval English Music*, performed by the Hilliard Ensemble (Harmonia Mundi France 1901106, band 11).

8

Political Lyrics

THORLAC TURVILLE-PETRE

I

What is a 'political lyric'? The two terms need definition in relation to one another, and I shall explore them each in turn. It is worth stating the obvious at the outset, that whatever a lyric may be, it does not include major poems such as *Wynnere and Wastoure*, Langland's *Piers Plowman* and works by Langland's successors, especially *Mum and the Sothsegger*, Gower's *In Praise of Peace*, Hoccleve's *Regement of Princes*, Lydgate's *Fall of Princes*, and others which would all figure prominently in any wider account of political poetry in Middle English. Though the lyrics cannot be fully understood except in the light of this wider tradition, and indeed in the light of Latin and French political verse, they nevertheless illustrate neatly and on a small scale a number of issues in connection with political poetry.

The term 'political' can be interpreted narrowly or generously. George Kane has argued that the word has been misapplied to fourteenth-century moral satires, and that it is wrong to understand such poems 'as manifesting an increasingly secular concern for political change and reform' (Kane 1986, 82). Kane is undoubtedly right in saying that this is a misinterpretation, but at the same time his contention that 'political' is indistinguishable from 'revolutionary' cannot be maintained. Peter Coss suggests a division that I find helpful, distinguishing three broad categories of medieval political verse: firstly, poems dealing directly with particular current events; secondly, 'verses of social protest' that are 'responses to particular and topical grievances'; and thirdly, 'satires attacking either specific vices or the vices of various social classes and groups' (Coss 1996, xiii). To these I would add a fourth group for consideration: poems on subjects that are not themselves political but have social or political implications.

In the light of these categories I shall first look at some of the famous English lyrics of BL MS Harley 2253, three of which Kane and Coss take up in their discussions.[1] The Harley lyrics provide an excellent starting point for an analysis of the term 'political', for this early collection (c.1340) provides some of the

---

[1] The political lyrics are not included in *The Harley Lyrics*, G. L. Brook's misleadingly titled edition. *Sitteth alle stille ant herkneth to me* is to be found as No. 72 in Brown XIII; the others are in Robbins, *Hist*. There is a good discussion by Scattergood 2000, who also considers the Anglo-Norman lyrics.

finest examples of most of the kinds of political lyric that feature in later manuscripts.

II

In my first category are the five Harley lyrics that engage directly with political events. Taking them in the order in which they appear in the manuscript, the series begins with *Sitteth alle stille ant herkneth to me* (fol. 58v–59r; Brown *XIII*, No. 72), a mocking account of Richard of Cornwall's defeat by Simon de Montfort at the battle of Lewes in 1264. It has the refrain:

> Richard, thah thou be ever trichard,   *though you'll always be a traitor*
> Tricchen shalt thou nevermore! (6–7)   *you'll never be treacherous again*

The poem has considerable specific detail – how Richard of Cornwall, brother of Henry III, was taken prisoner in a mill, how Hugh Bigod and the Earl Warenne, who *hath robbed Engelond*, escaped across the sea. At the end of the poem Prince Edward is rebuked for abandoning the counsel of his uncle Simon de Montfort, a reference to the royal party's failure to maintain the Provisions of Oxford to which his rebellious barons had forced the king to agree – never again will Edward break his agreements. Richard is portrayed as a grasping man who, having demanded £30,000 to make peace, was obliged to take refuge in a windmill, and now, having spent all his treasury on *swiving* [lechery], has not a farthing's worth of his own castle of Wallingford (where he and Edward were imprisoned). It is a clever piece of abusive writing, and is one of several poems, the others in Latin and French, that take the barons' side against King Henry. Indeed the poem on the facing page is an Anglo-Norman lament for Simon de Montfort, killed a year later at the battle of Evesham in 1265.

On the verso of this leaf in the Harley manuscript (fol. 59v–61v) is *Lystneth, lordynges, a newe song ichulle bigynne* (Robbins *Hist.*, No. 4), a description of the execution of Simon Fraser, captured during the Scottish wars at the battle of Methven in 1306 where Robert Bruce had been routed. The retribution was particularly savage since Edward had trusted Bruce, Fraser and the other leaders, until Bruce had seized power and proclaimed himself king at Scone. From beginning to end the poem focuses on the act of execution and the public display of decapitated Scottish heads on London Bridge. It expresses outrage that the Scottish barons could not keep faith with Edward and with their fellow barons in England. From London Bridge, the heads of William Wallace and Fraser send a cautionary message to the Scots:

> To warny alle the gentilmen that bueth in Scotlonde,   *warn; that are*
> The Waleis wos todrawe, seththe he wos anhonge,   *
> Al quic biheveded, ys bowels ybrend,   *beheaded alive; burned*
> The heved to Londone brugge wos send   *head; bridge*
>   To abyde   *wait*
>   After Simond Frysel. (17–22)   *for Simon Fraser*
>   * *Wallace was drawn then hanged*

The Scots thought they were kings, but *betere hem were han ybe barouns ant libbe in godes lawe / wyth love* (12–13). Bruce's regal pretensions are scorned: he was made a *kyng of somere*, referring not only to the shortness of his reign but also to representations in summer games and shows. Fraser is brought to Newgate with his legs fettered under his horse's belly and wearing a garland of periwinkles; the three judges at his trial are named; many Englishmen rushed to see him drawn through Cheapside, garlanded and dressed *in a curtel of burel* [in a tunic of sackcloth]. When his head is set up on London Bridge, many a wife's child came to gaze on it *with gomen and wyth solas* [with mirth and joy].

The huge indignation against the Scots at this time reflects the uncertainties of the relationship with Scotland: were its people part of the nation or not? Could Bruce be forced to be a sort of Englishman and subject of the English crown?

The barouns of Engelond, myhte hue him gripe,	*if they could catch him*
He him wolde techen on Englysshe to pype! (75–6)	*they would teach*

For all its triumphal scorn of the Scots, the last stanza reveals both frustration and fear:

The traytours of Scotlond token hem to rede,	*hit on a plan*
The barouns of Engelond to brynge to dede;	*to death*
Charles of Fraunce, so moni mon tolde,	*said*
With myght and with streynthe hem helpe wolde,	*would aid them*
Hlis thonkes.	*willingly*
Tprot, Scot, for thi strif!	*phooey; fighting*
Hang up thyn hachet ant thi knyf	
Whil him lasteth the lyf	*he remains alive*
With the longe shonkes. (225–33)	*Longshanks (Edward I)*

The Scots had been routed before but regrouped to fight again, and their alliance with France posed a major threat. Over many years of fighting, Longshanks had managed to hold the Scots back, but by the time of Fraser's execution in September 1306 he was obviously dying: he had to be carried on a litter to the great celebration of the knighting of his son on Whitsunday 1306, and after a lengthy illness died in July 1307. The bravado of the poem's last lines is grotesquely misplaced.

Edward's death is recorded in an elegy, *Alle that beoth of huerte* [heart] *trewe* (Robbins *Hist.*, No. 5) later in the manuscript (fol. 73r–v). This is a translation and adaptation of a French poem preserved in an early fourteenth-century manuscript from Ireland. The English version is more nationalistic than the French; it says that all England should know that Edward was honoured throughout the world. On his deathbed Edward charges his people to be faithful to England and to help his son. The French king is condemned for preventing Edward from going on crusade as he had promised, and there is a scene in which the pope laments the death of this flower of Christendom. His son Edward of Carnarvon is now king; may he not be a lesser man than his father, in bringing justice to the poor and heeding good counsel in guiding England; he has no need to be without good knights. Presumably the writer is already aware of Peter Gaveston's malign influence on the king.

The text that follows this (on fol. 73v–74v) is about how the Flemings defeated the French army in 1302, *Lustneth, lordinges, bothe yonge ant olde* (Robbins *Hist.*, No. 3). This might seem an odd topic for an English poem; Edward I's determination to campaign in Flanders in 1297 had provoked very serious opposition from the barons, who set out their complaints in the Remonstrances. The point of the poem, however, is not to express great affection for the Flemings, but to show how a bunch of weavers, *the webbes and the fullaris* (17), could humiliate the flower of French chivalry. The poet exults in the sufferings inflicted on the French, whom he portrays as arrogant and overconfident, and he enjoys the thought of the French ladies *in boure and in halle* (99) waiting in vain for the return of their menfolk. He also emphasises national distinctions linguistically. The French are referred to *dousse pers* (50) and the French barons are accorded a line or two in their own tongue. Likewise, the Flemish *dabbeth* [strike] and *doddeth* [chop], verbs with possible Netherlandish cognates:[2]

The Flemmisshe hem dabbeth o the het bare,	*strike; bare head*
Hue nolden take for huem raunsoun ne ware,	*
Hue doddeth of huere hevedes, fare so hit fare. (85–7)	*they chop off their*
	* they wouldn't; ransom nor goods

For all their arrogance, the pride of the French army is defeated by a few cloth-workers:

Alas thou seli Fraunce, for the may thunche shome	*poor France; it seem a*
That ane fewe fullaris maketh ou so tome;	*bring you so low [disgrace*
Sixti thousent on a day hue maden fot-lome,	*they crippled*
With eorl ant knyht. (121–4)	*including earls and knights*

The implication is, why should anyone be frightened of the French? The poet reckons that if the Prince of Wales survives, the fortunes of the French king will be bitterer than soot. He did indeed survive, but of course things did not turn out as predicted.

With the exception of this poem on the Flemings, the texts referring directly to political events are set out in chronological order in the manuscript. The final political text (on fol. 127r) refers darkly to the disaster at Bannockburn in 1314 (Turville-Petre 1989, 36–7). It is the earliest of the alliterative prophecies, as misty as such prophecies usually are, in which the Countess of Dunbar asks Thomas of Erceldoune when the Scottish war will end. Thomas says this will happen when a king has been made of a madman, when Bannockburn is manured with dead men, when the Scots flee so fast that in the absence of ships they drown themselves, and so on.

Whenne shal this be? Nouther in thine tyme ne in myne,	*neither; nor*
Ah comen ant gon withinne twenty wynter ant on. (17–18)	*but come to pass*

---

2   For possible Dutch and Flemish cognates see *OED* **dab**, *v.*, and *MED* **dodde** *n.*

Thomas flourished in the 1290s, and the poet may have been writing soon after Bannockburn, presumably in the hope of encouraging the English in the depths of their despair. Political prophesy is an important genre throughout the Middle Ages, and its vague, catch-all predictions were often taken so seriously that they had to be proscribed by law.[3]

All the texts in this section, that is, those giving direct accounts of political activities, deal with events that were distant by 1340: the Barons' Wars of 1264–5, the Flemish rising of 1302, the Scottish executions of 1306, the death of Edward I in 1307, and Bannockburn in 1314. Would these historical accounts still interest an audience in 1340? In fact all of them deal with issues that were still current. A number of partisan poems in English, French and Latin depict Simon de Montfort as a martyr to the cause of English freedom, or, to be more precise, to the baronial cause in the unending struggle against absolute royal power. The baronial perspective comes through very clearly in several of the Harley lyrics, perhaps especially in the poem on the execution of Fraser. The Scottish wars remained very much a matter of topical interest in the 1330s, with the decisive defeat of the Scots at Halidon Hill in 1333 and the subsequent concern about a Franco-Scottish alliance. France had now become the centre of attention, with the confiscation of Gascony in 1337 and French raids on southern ports in 1338–9 as the preliminary skirmishes leading to the outbreak of the Hundred Years War, and so the poem ridiculing the French reputation for military prowess offered considerable comfort to those militarily or financially involved in the fighting. These lyrics are the earliest of a long line of attacks on the Scots and the French, as we shall see.

My second group, poems presenting social comment with specific reference to contemporary conditions, is represented in the Harley manuscript by three lyrics, one in French, one in French and Latin, and one in English. The first two can be dated with some confidence. *Talent me prent de rymer* (fol. 113v–114v; Aspin 1953, No. 7), a poem attacking the justices appointed to the commissions of *trailbastons* [armed criminals], names four justices who were appointed to the commission in the south-west counties in 1305. The poet argues that the procedure makes criminals of honest men, particularly clerics who have learning, who will be forced to lie in chains in the bishop's prison, and he presents himself as an outlaw hiding in the woods and falsely accused under the legislation. *Dieu roy de mageste* (fol. 137v–138v; Aspin 1953, No. 10) complains that the annual imposition of the fifteenth does harm to all, so that the *commune gent* must sell all they own, and the wool tax is an even greater burden on *simple gent*. The raising of the fifteenth for war, together with the tax on wool and the reference to the young king point to the preparations for the Hundred Years War from 1337–1340. The English lyric, *Ich herde men upo mold make much mon* (Turville-Petre 1989, 17–20) is well known and has received valuable attention from several scholars.[4] Wright misleadingly titled it 'Song of the Husbandman'; it would more accurately be called 'The Evils of Taxation'. It complains that in

---

3   Many political prophesies are, like the Harley poem, alliterative. For details of the prophesies see Robbins 1975, 1516–36.
4   See Maddicott 1975 and 1986; Kane 1986; Newhauser 2000.

times of poor harvest the heavy and repeated taxation exacted by the officials of both the lord and the king become insupportable. The speaker is a farmer who was once comfortably off, with land and corn, labourers, cattle and a mare, and enough money to bribe the bailiff. There is a detailed description of how the king's officials get to work demanding exorbitant taxes (the *grene wax* was a seal affixed to Exchequer documents containing the names of those to be taxed) and bribes (roast hens or lamprey and salmon on fish days) and of the dire effect all this has on the farmers.

Yet cometh budeles, with ful muche bost:	*come tax-collectors*
'Greythe me selver to the grene wax!	*give me; for this green wax*
Thou art writen y my writ, that thou wel wost'.	*entered in my schedule; know*
Mo then ten sithen told y my tax.	*more than ten times I paid*
Thenne mot ych habbe hennen arost,	*must I produce roast hens*
Feyr on fyhsh-day launprey ant lax.	*excellent; lamprey and salmon*
Forth to the chepyn – geyneth ne chost,	*market; no argument helps*
Thah y sulle mi bil ant mi borstax.	*though I have to sell; axe; pickaxe*
Ich mot legge my wed wel yef y wolle,	*I must put down my deposit*
Other sulle mi corn on gras that is grene. (38–46)	*or sell; while it's still green*

The focus is on the farmer, but the narrator makes the point that society as a whole, *Baroun ant bonde, the clerc ant the knyght* (30), is involved in the effects of excessive taxation and corrupt officials. The poem is certainly not the work of a 'simple peasant', as it was earlier described, but nevertheless it gives a moving picture of rural poverty supposedly at first hand. The poet says that 'the poor man who is of little account is oppressed' (19), and the suffering becomes acute at times of famine, when *Gode yeres ant corn bothe beth agon* (3). The last lines describe the effects of the *wickede wederes* when the corn rots in the fields. J. R. Maddicott has shown how in the years between 1315–17 the effects of famine were compounded by particularly heavy taxation and so the poem would fit well in that period of hardship. Yet the same sort of complaint occurs at other times (e.g. in the Towneley 'Second Shepherds' Play'), and, for all its apparent specificity, it may be unwise to tie it to one date and a single set of conditions.[5] This makes the point that poems of the second and third groups cannot always be distinguished.

This third group consists of the poems of social satire not tied to specific events. How appropriate is it to define these as political? The first of these, *Lord that lenest us lyf* (Turville-Petre 1989, 12–13), which immediately follows the poem on the execution of Simon Fraser on fol. 61v, answers the question rather neatly. It is a wonderfully abusive short poem in English on the vanity of extravagant clothing: 'Every shrew will dress herself up in pride even if she hasn't a smock to hide her foul arse' (13–14). The architectural arrangement of the hair is described in precise technical detail, but rather undermined by the judgement that 'She sits there like a hunted pig that hangs its ears' (23). It is easy to take this

---

5   For the dating in 1315–17, see Maddicott 1975, who however, in a subsequent study, proposes the later date of 1340, though without supporting evidence (Maddicott 1986, 143). See further Newhauser 2000, 210.

simply as a poem of moral exhortation against pride, but its political reverbera-
tions sound more clearly when we understand its context. The earliest of the
sumptuary laws which run on into the sixteenth century was enacted in 1337
(Scattergood 1996, 240–57). They were motivated by a fear that social differen-
tials were being eroded, and gradually the legislation became more far-reaching
and comprehensive than this earliest enactment to restrict the wearing of furs to
the upper ranks. If we look more closely at the poem in this light, we can see
why Wright's title 'Against the Pride of the Ladies' is entirely misleading. The
poet says 'If a lady's clothing is fitted according to fashion, every strumpet about
will play similar tricks' (10–11), and:

Furmest in boure were boses ybroght,	*first in the bower; hair-buns*
Levedis to honoure ichot he were wroght;	*I know they were devised*
Uch gigelot wol loure bote he hem habbe soght.	*every tart will glower unless*
(15–17)	*[she has them*

Here, then, is the distinction between the *levedis*, who rightly doll themselves up,
and the *wymmon unwis*, *strumpets*, *shrews* and *gigelots* who ape their betters. The
poem is a good example of the use of moral exhortation for political ends.

A similar point is to be made about another fine abusive poem in English on
fol. 124v, *Of rybaudz y ryme* (Turville-Petre 1989, 34–5), attacking the retainers
and their attendants who ride across the country living off the land. This later
became a political issue when retainers were the subject of legislation in the statutes of livery and maintenance (Scattergood 2000, 190–1). Retainers are the children of Satan, gluttonous, lousy, proud, covered in scabs. Why didn't God ride
when he was travelling around on earth?

For he nolde no grom to go by ys syde,	*didn't want any attendant*
Ne grucchyng of no gedelyng to chaule ne to chyde	*complaints; any servant*
(35–6)	*[jabbering or quarrelling*

Ne mai no lewed lued libben in londe (fol. 70v; Turville-Petre 1989, 28–31), a witty
poem set in the ecclesiastical court, is more complicated.[6] It is a pretty comprehensive condemnation of the proceedings of a matrimonial case, with fine satirical descriptions of the judge, 'the old churl in a black cap', the clerks recording
names on their parchment, the lying summoners and the ugly screaming
women. But the most scathing satire of the poem is reserved, brilliantly, for the
narrator himself, the proudest, most deceitful, most cowardly character of all of
them, who has plainly committed himself to two women and who fully deserves
his punishment of being whipped round the marketplace like a dog. And yet the
judgement is not so straightforward, for in the first lines of the poem the
narrator attaches both himself and his listeners to the ideological *lewede / lerede*
division: the narrator is the *lewed* man, that is the layman, who is persecuted by
the *lerede*, the clergy, who mislead *us* with their superior knowledge and special
courts. Like the other lyrics in the group, this poem shows a concern for social

---

6   See Turville-Petre 1997.

status, clerical privilege and the corruption of power, and demonstrates how these issues are expressed in the apparatus of the legal system.

The poems in my last category are those for which Harley 2253 is most justly famous, the love lyrics. Here, surely, we are free of politics. After all (one might think) a love lyric is an expression of passion, passion as a private emotion – of misery when unfulfilled, of joy when shared – existing independently of any external context. But this is not the case with the Harley lyrics, in which love and spring are linked in the conventional *reverdie*, and references are made to a world of English towns and villages, of families threatening to kill their daughters' lovers and arranging hasty marriages for pregnant girls. One of the finest of all the lyrics is *When the nyhtegale singes* (Brook, No. 25), in which the bustle of nature in April contrasts with the self-absorption of the lover transfixed with the spear of love that drinks his heart's blood night and day. References to the world about him keep intruding as ironic reminders of the essential silliness of his consuming passion: clearly the lover does not exist in isolation since people say that she loves him; she is the loveliest girl between Lincoln and Lindsey, Northampton and Lound. What a very specific range, like a travelling salesman's round! – or, more exactly, like the round of a son on the marriage market. The girl in *My deth y love my lif ich hate* (Brook, No. 24) warns her clerical lover that her father is on the lookout for him and will kill him if he is caught in her bedroom. In *In a fryth as y con fare fremede* (Brook, No. 8) another girl rejects a bribe (an offer of fine clothes) from a would-be lover. She requires *forwardes faste* [firm undertakings] (19); she is conscious of the danger that, otherwise, should he tire of her, she would find herself deserted, banished by her family and *ycayred from alle that y kneowe* [separated from all I had known] (35). The same contextualisation is characteristic of other love lyrics in the manuscript.[7] So these love poems work within a very specific society, its constraints and practices, and they illustrate the dangers of a passion that threatens to break through the controls within which social life operates. They offer wry reflections on social attitudes in much the same way as the social satires of the third group.

Indeed, the political complexion of Harley 2253 is determined by the complete spectrum of its contents so that, in one way or another, all the poems I have been examining have a political dimension. What sort of society is reflected in the contents of the manuscript? It is predominantly a rural society, in which many issues of baronial and gentry concern are raised. There are, for example, those poems complaining of the effects of harsh taxation on the rural economy, one of which is the desperate poverty of those working on the land, but there is rather more emphasis on the disruption to the finances of the landowner. There is focus on the duties of kingship and especially the need for the king to abide by the provisions of the Great Charter in respecting the rights of his barons. And there is fear of the disruptions caused by wars with the French and the Scots. These issues concerned monastic landowners in the same ways as lay lords, and it is impossible to judge from this whether the manuscript was compiled for a lay or clerical readership.

---

[7]   See Turville-Petre 1996, 203–17; Scattergood 2000, 191–2.

III

The categorisation of the political lyrics in Harley 2253 should provide a useful basis for discussing political lyrics in general, most of which have not received the close attention they merit. For example, the twenty-four early fifteenth-century lyrics of MS Digby 102 (where they accompany a C-text of *Piers Plowman*) were edited in 1904 by Kail as *Twenty-Six Political and Other Poems*. Kail remarks that 'almost all of them have one and the same religious character. They warn against worldly folly, and praise virtue' (Kail 1904, vii). This is accurate enough, but Kail's attempt to date many of the poems by 'allusions to parliamentary transactions and to other affairs' (Kail 1904, x) is unconvincing, though it has never to my knowledge been challenged. There is no reference at all to specific political events in the first poem, which expresses its theme with the refrain *Man knowe thy self, love God, and drede*, though Kail claims to find allusions to the Parliament of 1399 and the conspiracy to kill the king. The third poem, beginning *For drede ofte my lippes y steke* [seal], sets its moral admonitions within the context of a just society, and is one of three Digby lyrics included by Robbins in his anthology. He titles it 'What Profits a Kingdom (1401)' (Robbins *Hist.*, No. 13). The manuscript, however, provides its own, more accurate, heading 'Treuth, reste and pes', and the specific topical allusions suggested by both Kail and Robbins are without justification, based on an anachronistic understanding of the word *comouns*. The poems, says Kail, 'declare the Commons to be the most important of all estates', and he argues that this lyric reflects issues discussed by 'the Commons' in January 1401 (Kail 1904, viii, xi–xiii). The source of his confusion is this stanza which links parliament with the *comouns*, but the word means, as it always does at this time, the common people, the subjects:

To wete yif parlement be wys,	*to know; wise*
The comoun profit wel it preves;	*common good; proves*
A kyngdom in comouns lys,	*resides in the common people*
Alle profytes and alle myscheves.	*benefits; difficulties*
Lordis wet nevere what comouns greves	*realise; troubles the common people*
Til here rentis bigynne to ses.	*their income; cease*
There lordis ere pore, comons releves,	*where; the common people offer relief*
And mayntene hem in werre and pes. (97–104)	*maintain; war; peace*

Robbins boldly entitles the twelfth in the collection 'God Save King Henry V (1413)' (Robbins *Hist.*, No. 14), though its manuscript title, based on the refrain, is 'God save the kyng and kepe the croun'. As this suggests, it is an admonition to support kingship and to avoid dissension, with no mention of any particular king or event.

Twenty-two of the lyrics are in eight-line stanzas; the other two (Kail 1904, Nos 10 and 16) are in more complex stanzas of fourteen lines, the latter with heavy alliteration (see especially No. 16, 99–106). In the whole collection, only this lyric, 'A remembrance of LIJ folyes', makes specific references to political events, as the poet holds up Flanders as an example of the penalties of foolishness:

Flaundres was the richest land and meriest to mynne;   *the most delightful to describe*
   Now is it wrappid in wo and moche welthe raft.   *deprived of much wealth*
For defaute of Justice and singulere to wynne,   *and to gain private profit*
   They were rebell to ryse, craft ayen craft.   *rose in rebellion; force*
Here lord had part of the foly they were wounden ynne; *their lord had a share in*
   Forthy he les his lordshipe and here fraunchise raft.   *and deprived them of their*
      (57–62)   [*freedom*

There is probably a reference here to the assassination in 1419 of John the Fear-less, Duke of Burgundy and ruthless ruler of Flanders, as a result of which his successor was forced into a humiliating treaty with Henry V.[8] But this poem, like all the others in the collection, is actually a general moral reflection on vice, as is made clear in the last stanza with its claim that the only four true folk are Sickness, Sorrow, Death and Dread. It is a mistake to dredge these poems for direct references to current events since they are, with this one exception, poems attacking general abuses of the age and advocating good moral and social behaviour, placing them in my third group rather than my first.

The classification also helps us to appreciate the consequences of a poet reworking a text offering general moral reflection and applying it specifically to particular political events, effectively shifting a poem from one category to another. A good example is provided by the set of four traditional aphorisms, the 'sayings of the four philosophers' that are innocently included in the *Speculum Christiani*, a preaching manual, in which context they have no direct political reference. They are re-used in the Auchinleck manuscript (Robbins *Hist.*, No. 54):[9]

For might is right, the lond is laweles;   *because; without law*
For night is light, the lond is loreles;   *without wisdom*
For fight is flight, the lond is nameles.

  Nu on is two,   *one*
  Wel is wo,
  And frend is fo.

  Nu lust haveth leve,   *will; free reign*
  Thef is reve,   *the thief is magistrate*
  And pride hathe sleve.   *sleeve (fine clothing)*

  Nu wille is red,   *judgement*
  Wit is qued,   *sense; evil*
  And God is dede. (30–2, 39–41, 51–3, 63–5)   *dead*

In the Auchinleck manuscript these sayings are attached to a macaronic French and English poem complaining how the king neglected the charter made by Parliament, and *therefore Engelond is shent* [destroyed]. The earlier version of this macaronic poem, headed 'De Provisione Oxonie' (Aspin 1953, No. 6), makes direct reference to Edward I's refusal in 1306 to maintain the Provisions. In the

---

[8] Scattergood 1971, 47–9; Scattergood 1996, 44–6.
[9] See also Scattergood 1968.

Auchinleck version the lines have been modified so that they may refer to Edward II's breaking of the Ordinances he had signed in 1311.

IV

For the remainder of this chapter I shall concentrate on lyrics of my first group, those that deal directly with political events, because these raise questions about the essential nature of lyric as well as the appeal of political poetry. Even though Middle English political lyrics in general have been neglected and overshadowed by religious and love lyrics, no minor medieval poet has been more often edited than Laurence Minot,[10] who wrote about Edward III's Scottish and continental wars of 1333–52. His eleven poems were first excellently edited by Joseph Ritson in 1795, with a revised edition in 1825. They were again presented in the first volume (1859) of Thomas Wright's classic anthology, *Political Poems and Songs* (1859–61). The standard edition is by Joseph Hall (1914), and among more recent editors are T. B. James and J. Simons (1989), and Richard Osberg (1996). This editorial industriousness has not been matched by critical assessment, which scarcely exists. Perhaps Derek Pearsall gives sufficient reason for this, characterising the poet with withering precision: 'Minot is the first true national propagandist, violent, abusive, narrowly prejudiced, with a repellent glee, very appropriate to the genre, in gloating over the downfall of the enemy' (Pearsall 1977, 122). As this implies, Minot offers a good introduction to the genre of medieval war poetry, which we first encountered in the Harley lyric on the Battle of Lewes. If lyric is essentially a non-narrative form, poems that are essentially narrative descriptions of battles must stretch the definition of lyric. Minot's subject is English victory, and inevitably battles feature prominently in his poems. The seventh poem (on Edward II's French campaign in summer 1346, leading up to the battle of Crécy) gives a lively account, of which this is a representative stanza:

Stedes strong bilevid still	*strong steeds still remained*
Biside Cressy opon the grene;	*on the green beside Crécy*
Sir Philip wanted all his will,	*King Philip was thwarted*
That was wele on his sembland sene.	*plainly seen in his expression*
With spere and schelde and helmis schene	*bright helmets*
The bare than durst thai noght habide;	*the boar (Edward III); encounter*
The king of Beme was cant and kene,	*Bohemia; brave and fierce*
Bot thare he left both play and pride. (101–8)	*gave up both sport and glory*

The narrative is interrupted in the stanza that follows, where Minot pauses for moralisation on those who had failed to support Edward:

Pride in prese ne prais I noght	*I do not praise proud display*
Omang thir princes prowd in pall;	*among these princes in their*
	[proud robes

---

[10] For the suggestion that he is from the family that gave its name to Carlton Miniott in north Yorks, see Hanna 2003, 94.

Princes suld be wele bithoght	*should have thought matters through*
When kinges tham till counsail call.	*call upon them for consultation*
If he be rightwis king thai sall	*just king they must*
Maintene him both night and day,	*support*
Or els to lat his frendschip fall	*give up his friendship*
On faire manere, and fare oway. (109–16)	*with honour and leave him*

If we place the emphasis on Minot's account of the wars, it must be conceded that Minot is neither very informative nor entirely accurate in strictly historical terms. The prose chronicles do it better. Indeed the manuscript presentation invites comparison with the chronicles, since the poems are set out chronologically with rhymed titles, like chapter headings, defining the subject of each lyric, as, for example, the title of the seventh poem, which runs as follows:

| How Edward at Hogges unto land wan | *St Vaast-de-la-Hogue* |
| And rade thurgh France or ever he blan. | *rode; stopped* |

We must look elsewhere to find the lyric impulse in Minot's verses. The stanza forms show close parallels with the Harley lyrics, with some complex arrangements involving iteration within the stanza and concatenation linking one stanza to another, often with heavy alliteration as well. This is how in the tenth poem Minot rebukes the pirate Blackbeard (Barbenoire) in the Spanish fleet attacking the English:

Boy with thi blac berd, I rede that thou blin	*fellow; I advise you to stop*
And sone set the to schrive with sorow of thi syn.	*go to confession*
If thou were on Ingland noght saltou win;	*you'd win nothing*
Cum thou more on that coste, thi bale sall bigin.	*if you come again; shore; misery*
Thare kindels thi care, kene men sall the kepe	*sorrow; seize*
And do the dye on a day, and domp in the depe.	*kill you; plunge*

Ye broght out of Bretayne yowre custom with care,	*Brittany; exactions; misery*
Ye met with the marchandes and made tham ful bare;	*stripped them*
It es gude reson and right that ye evill misfare,	*fare badly*
When ye wald in Ingland lere of a new lare.	*learn a new lesson*
New lare sall ye lere sir Edward to lout,	*to bow to*
For when ye stode in yowre strenkith ye war all to stout.	*strength; haughty*
(19–30)	

Here, too, is another characteristic of lyric: the individual voice with the direct address of the poetic 'I'. Unfortunately, it is not a very interesting or complex voice; it has a single tone and a single, crude message repeated time and again.

One of the most significant events of the wars against the French – at any rate in its long-term implications for national pride – was the capture of Calais in 1347, when its citizens had been starved out by a year's siege. Minot adopts his unvaryingly hostile tone: he accuses the people of Calais of malice and, in his eighth poem, says (mixing his animal metaphors) the boar will hunt them down as the hound does the hare:

Kend it es how ye war kene	*known; fierce*
Al Inglis men with dole to dere,	*to afflict with misery*
Thaire gudes toke ye al bidene,	*all outright*

No man born wald ye forbere.   *would you spare*
Ye spared noght with swerd ne spere
To stik tham and thaire gudes to stele;   *stab; steal their goods*
With wapin and with ded of wer   *weapons; deeds of war*
Thus have ye wonnen werldes wele.   *worldly riches*

Weleful men war ye, iwis,   *rich men; indeed*
Bot fer on fold sall ye noght fare;   *far in the land shall*
A bare sal now abate yowre blis   *boar; lessen your joy*
And wirk yow bale on bankes bare.   *cause you sorrow*
He sall yow hunt als hund dose hare   *as the hound does the hare*
That in no hole sall ye yow hide.
For all yowre speche will he noght spare,   *your words; hesitate*
Bot bigges him right by yowre side. (9–24)   *will set up camp right beside you*

Even the cardinals appointed by the Pope to make peace are accused of plotting
how thai might sir Edward bigile (44). Philip the Bold *fled and faght noght* (48), and
eventually the burgesses were forced to emerge weeping from Calais to sue for
mercy:

The knightes that in Calais were
Come to sir Edward sare wepeand,   *sorely weeping*
In kirtell one and swerd in hand,   *only*
And cried "Sir Edward, thine are.   *have mercy*
Do now, lord, bi law of land
Thi will with us for evermare." (59–64)

In Minot's version, the common citizens of Calais wish to put ropes round the
necks of the burgesses because their leaders have left them without help, so that
they have neither rabbit, nor cat, nor dog, for *all er etin up ful clene* (77). The poem
ends:

All on this wise was Calais won;   *manner*
God save tham that it so-gat wan. (95–6)   *thus*

It is extraordinary how this skates over the famous episode of the Burghers of
Calais, so memorably narrated by Froissart and other chroniclers, so movingly
represented by the sculptor Rodin at the end of the nineteenth century. In
Froissart's account, the burghers come before Edward 'stripped to their shirts
and breeches', with halters round their necks, followed by the common people
in tears. They 'surrender to you the keys of the town and the castle . . . in order
to save the remaining inhabitants of Calais'. All those present weep, except
Edward who orders them to be decapitated immediately, only relenting when
his pregnant queen intercedes for them: 'Your appeal has so touched me that I
cannot refuse it.'[11] This is material out of which really moving lyric poetry might
have been fashioned. It is, though, not to Minot's purpose, whose only concern
throughout is to glorify the warlike deeds of the English and to deride the weakness and wickedness of the French. That war causes appalling suffering which

---

[11] Trans. Brereton 1968, 107–9.

all must regret, and that there are Frenchmen noble enough to sacrifice themselves in order to relieve that suffering is a complication that Minot is not
prepared to explore.

Here and everywhere, Minot's voice misses the pathos of war that we expect
from lyric, particularly since the Romantics. Robert Southey's political poetry is
an interesting example of this. Southey owned a copy of Ritson's 1825 edition of
Minot,[12] and perhaps read the 1795 edition, since it seems to me likely that some
of his poems, such as the much anthologised 'Battle of Bleinheim' and more
especially the little-known poem on the Battle of Poitiers, are written as a
response to Minot's ghastly triumphalism. The poem on Poitiers, called 'The
Victory', published in 1798 (Curry 1984, 97–8), begins very much in Minot's
style:

> Now by my life a glorious day!
>   It warms my English blood;
> Preferring death to infamy,
>   The gallant warriors stood;
> The coward multitudes before
>   Their desperate valour fled,
> And victory and death again
>   Pursu'd where Edward led.

But this glorification of war turns out to be the immature voice of a boy, Henry,
whom the narrator rebukes with the words:

> Look, Henry – what is yonder form
>   Slow moving o'er the plain?
> It is the widow'd wife that comes
>   To search the field of slain.
> Long shall the widow live to mourn,
>   And long her tears shall roll –
> And wouldst thou have at thy death-hour
>   Her curses on thy soul?

Boys (of whatever age) love war, and it is for them that Minot writes. If death
and cruelty are mentioned at all, it is only contemptuously of a defeated enemy.
On first reading, the opening stanza of Minot's tenth poem (on the sea battle
against the Spanish fleet off Winchelsea in 1350) might be a general reflection on
brave men dying in war:

I wald noght spare for to speke, wist I to spede,	*knew I how to do so well*
Of wight men with wapin and worthly in wede	*brave men; weapons; worthily armed*
That now er driven to dale and ded all thaire dede,	*to the grave; all their deeds finished*
Thai sail in the see-gronde fissches to fede.	*to the bottom of the sea*
Fele fissches thai fede, for all thaire grete fare,	*many; noble conduct*
It was in the waniand that thai come thare.	*waning of the moon (i.e. to their*
(1–6)	*misfortune)*

---

[12] See the sale catalogue of Southey's books, Park 1971, 180. I owe this information to my
colleague Lynda Pratt.

But of course the lines are a celebration of the destruction of the Spanish. There is no lack of a personal voice and emotion in Minot; it is the voice of hatred, reinforced by the hammer of the verse-form.

In most respects the hate lyric is less interesting than the love lyric, since it never analyses its emotion. However, Minot does express venom powerfully and inventively, and since hatred is such a universal human phenomenon and frequently leads to bloody conflict, it is worth observing its expression, perhaps especially because it has become unacceptable (not least because of harrowing pictures of the dead and maimed now so immediately present in newspapers and on televisions screens) and in extreme cases illegal today.[13] At least Minot reminds us, and clearly we cannot be reminded often enough, of the blindness and lack of compassion involved in the glorification of war. Froissart invites us to see both the glory and the horror, the heroism and the pathos, and in his account both sides are motivated by the same chivalric ideals. For Minot, however, the French forces are *noght wurth a flye* (Poem 1, 24); the Scottish soldier is a *rughfute riveling* [rough-footed boot] (Poem 2, 19); the French king is a *coward* (Poem 4, 90). In Poem 7 Minot exults in the defeat and humiliation of the enemy:

Oway es all thi wele, iwis,	*gone is all your prosperity, indeed*
Franche man, with all thi fare;	*your splendour*
Of murning may thou never mys,	*sorrow; lack*
For thou ert cumberd all in care.	*mired in misery*
With speche ne moght thou never spare	*could you never desist*
To speke of Ingliss men despite;	*malice*
Now have thai made thi biging bare;	*emptied your building*
Of all thi catel ertou quite. (117–24)	*your possessions; deprived*

If a poet we admire expresses attitudes we abhor, we often call on 'irony' to account for it. So Chaucer's anti-semitism is explained away as the voice of the Prioress and, equally, the xenophobic hatred of the political lyrics can sometimes be made to disappear by the magic of irony. In this way we gloss over aspects characteristic of medieval culture and so miss the opportunity for medieval literature to teach us about cultural difference. A revealing instance of modern attitudes to distasteful features of medieval writings is the critical approach to a clever but disgusting poem written in Ireland, preserved in BL MS Harley 913, and celebrating the exploits of Pers of Bermingham.[14] Pers is praised as a chivalric hero:

Noble werrure he was,	*warrior*
And gode castel in place.	*protector*
On stede ther he wold ride	*wherever*
With his sper and scheld,	
In hard wodde and feld	
No thef him durst abide. (25–30)	

[13] A recent anthology is called *101 Poems Against War*. Can one imagine a companion volume of pro-war poems?
[14] The poems are conveniently available in Lucas 1995. Heuser's edition of 1904 is still valuable. *Pers of Bermingham* has been edited and discussed in detail by Benskin 1989.

As one of the hated English in Ireland, *To Yrismen he was fo* (50), hunting them down *As hunter doth the hare* (54).[15] The Irish chiefs plotted to destroy the English leaders, especially Pers, but the conspiracy became known. Pers invited the conspirators, the O'Connors, to a feast at his castle at Tethmoy, and had hoods made for them all:

Noght on nas forsake,	*not one was left out*
Bot al he did ham grace. (119–20)	*but all were honoured*

This is a playful allusion to the events of Trinity Sunday, 1305, when Pers brutally decapitated twenty-nine O'Connors as they rose from his dinner table, and sold their heads for a ransom of £100. To dispatch a treacherous enemy in this way must have seemed a brilliant ruse to the English in Ireland, one of whom was the poet. However, recent critics have found it impossible to accept the account at face value, with its praise of Pers as a *peruink* [periwinkle] (i.e. 'model of excellence'), and so interpret it as a mock-heroic 'satiric indictment'.[16] Would it were so, but this interpretation flies in the face of the nature of patriotic verse in the Middle Ages, and removes much of the point of this illuminating lyric. We should gasp at the poet's praise of this monster, and shake our heads at his report of the general grief that followed his death:

Al Irlond makith mon,	*laments*
Engelon ek as welle. (14–15)	*England also*

The closer the enemy are, the more they are a threat to English national identity. We have seen that this is true of the Scots, so vehemently attacked in the Harley lyrics and in Minot's poems. We find more examples of this in lyrics incorporated in the vernacular chronicles of Peter Langtoft, Robert Manning, and in the *Brut* chronicle.[17] These provide some powerful invective, as in this example from Langtoft:

And swa may men kenne	*so may one teach*
The Scottes to renne	*the Scots to run*
And werre biginne!	*and begin war*
Somme is left na thing	*some are left nothing*
Bot his rough ryveling	*but their torn boot*
To hippe tharynne.	*to hop in*
Thair kinges sette of Scone	*their royal seat of Scone*
Es driven over done	*has been carried over the downs*
To Lunden iledde.	*taken to London*
In toune herd I telle	*everywhere have I heard tell*
Thair baghel and thaire belle	*their bishop's staff and bell*
Ben filched and fledde.	*have been filched and removed*
	(Wright 1868 II, 264)

15 Cf. Minot No. 8, 21, quoted above.
16 See Lucas 1995, 207–9, following Benskin 1989.
17 The 'tags' in Langtoft and Manning are listed by Robbins 1975, 1400–03. Quotations are from Wright 1868.

But Langtoft's commendation of the English soldiers is double-edged:

The fote folke	*the footsoldiers*
Put the Scottes in the polk	*put the Scots in the puddle*
And nackened thair nages;	*stripped their bums*
Bi waye	*nowhere*
Herd I never saye	*did I ever hear tell*
Of prester pages	*of lads readier*
To pyke	*to rob*
The robes of the rike	*the robes of the rich*
That in the felde felle.	*that fell in the field*
Thay token ay tulke;	*they seized any man*
The roghe raggy sculke	*rough shaggy Skulker*
Rug ham in helle!	*tear them apart in hell*

(Wright 1868 II, 248)

Ironically, the inheritors of this alliterative poetry of invective are the Scots themselves, who make witty literary use of it in their sixteenth-century flytings. Sample, for instance, the following lines from the earliest surviving instance of this genre, Dunbar's celebrated poem, *The Flyting of Dunbar and Kennedie* (Bawcutt 1998a, I, No. 65):

Nyse nagus, nipcaik, with thy schulderis narrow,
Thow lukis lowsy, loun of lownis aw;
Hard hurcheon, hirpland hippit as ane harrow,
Thy rigbane rattillis and thy ribbes on raw. (177–80)

[Idiot scrooge, cake-pincher, with your narrow shoulders, you look lice-ridden, ruffian of all ruffians; rough hedgehog, lurking with hips like an arrow, your backbone and your ribcage rattle.]

The Flemish are given faint praise in the Harley lyrics for their unexpected destruction of the flower of French chivalry, but are more often reviled for their deceitful support of the French. In 1436 they allied with the French in the siege of Calais, and the lyric, *When ye Flemmyng wer fressh* (Robbins *Hist.*, No. 29), inserted into a manuscript of the *Brut* chronicle, scornfully celebrates their defeat. The Flemish are derisively addressed as 'lions of Cotteswold' (8) – a place famous for its sheep! – who fought so mightily against the English *Til of you thre hundrid lay strechid on the sandis* (16). Even their name and language are mocked:

Thus prove I that 'Flemmynges' is but 'a flemed man',	*'an exiled man'*
And 'Flaunders' of 'Flemmynges' the name first began;	
And therfore ye Flemmynges, that flemmynges be named,	*exiles*
To compare with Englisshmen ye aught to be ashamed.	
Ye be nothing elles worth but gret wordes to camp,	*to fight with big words*
Sette ye stille and bith in pees, God gyve you quadenramp!	*'quadenramp'*
(61–6)	*(Flemish for 'misfortune')*

V

The political lyrics are widely scattered in the manuscripts, and almost as widely scattered in printed editions of the last two hundred years. In obvious ways it would be good to have a new, comprehensive anthology with accurate texts and detailed historical notes,[18] even if, in other ways, there are disadvantages in separating them out. To mitigate this disadvantage it would be good to include a small sample of supposedly 'non-political' lyrics and of contemporary lyrics in French and Latin. In such an anthology the Harley lyrics would have pride of place, offering representatives of all the four categories of political lyric distinguished above. The poems from Ireland in MS Harley 913 would illustrate the fraught political rivalries in that situation, and also the perceptions of social life there in poems such as the brilliant 'Satire on the Townsfolk'.[19] Minot would represent the more unpalatable aspects of the genre; while the Vernon manuscript offers a clever and moving lyric on the death of Edward III (Robbins *Hist.*, No. 39). Lyrics from later in the fourteenth century that should be included for their great historical interest are the letters and verses attributed to John Ball during the Peasants' Revolt,[20] and a savage attack that plays on the names of Richard II's disgraced ministers, Bushy, Green and Bagot. This fine poem has been neglected because the manuscript was lost and the only authority for the text has been an obviously faulty transcription printed by William Hamper in 1827. Wright (1859, I, 363–6) relied on Hamper's text, as did Dean (1996, 150–2). The manuscript, a single leaf, has turned up among the Bagot Papers in Staffordshire Record Office, where it is D1721/3/186. Lord Bagot's note dated 1837 records that 'The enclosed <u>original</u> Poem was presented to me by Wm Hamper Esq.', obviously because of its unflattering family connections. The poem should now be re-edited.

Most of the Lydgatian and sub-Lydgatian verses of the fifteenth century are a good deal less interesting than the earlier poems, and it is always difficult to follow what was going on in the Wars of the Roses. However, three of the carols are excellent: the touching carol on the beheading of Archbishop Scrope in 1405,[21] the well-known Agincourt Carol, and John Audelay's misplaced optimism on the accession of Henry VI (Greene, Nos 425, 426, 428). Finally, the memorial inscription for one of the most wicked and unscrupulous lords of the fifteenth century, Ralph, Lord Cromwell (d.1454), is composed by a skilful poet in recognition that *all his castelles and toures hie of stone* will not grant him *pees in perpetuite* (Brown *XV*, No. 154). These poems, it seems to me, would make a good basis for an anthology of political lyrics.

---

[18] A useful recent anthology is Dean 1996, but it is very selective.
[19] See Cartlidge 2003; Turville-Petre 1996, 155–75.
[20] Dean 1996, 135–40; Green, 1992.
[21] See Scattergood 1971, 120–1.

9

The Lyric in the Sermon

ALAN J. FLETCHER

'Only connect'

This leitmotif that E. M. Forster threaded throughout *A Room with a View*
provides one of the handiest watchwords that anyone engaging with medieval
texts could wish for. Again it comes into its own as we broach the subject of the
present chapter and consider an especially productive context for lyric poetry,
yet one which simultaneously connected that poetry so organically to a wider
set of aims and obligations that poetry's existence solely as some self-referential,
literary event was forbidden: this was a context in which poetry as mere
word-game, as literary *jeu de mots* paying no more than incidental heed to the
real world in which its readers lived, moved, and had their being, would never
thrive. Instead, this context recruited poetry precisely in order to bring about a
reorientation of the existential outlook of those who experienced it. This chapter
thus concerns poetry with a collaborative agenda.

The task, then, is to approach the lyric in the sermon, to consider the sorts of
lyric that preaching collected, or indeed, that in many cases it first called into
being in order to further its ends. By adjusting the way we look at this particular
lyric species, choosing to see its examples not in isolation and out of context but
as integral participants in a wider enterprise, a healthier understanding of it may
be possible, and with that an appreciation of the weight of cultural work that
these lyrics were allowed to support. It follows that sermon lyrics must never be
excised from the sermons in which they feature if their essential role as collaborators in preaching's wider project is to be understood. For preaching was a dedicated intervention whose social consequences are hard to overestimate, and in it,
the lyrics examined in this chapter took root. Preaching presented ordinary men
and women with the salvific maps by which they could trace the narrow way to
heaven and avoid the primrose path to the everlasting bonfire. It was one of the
Church's key means for helping them navigate their living and dying, and for
interpreting all of life's experiences in between into one intelligible design.[1] Thus

---

1 The formative modalities of medieval religion were, of course, multiple, and customized
according to the stages of life from cradle to grave. In the schoolroom, for example, the entry
of the child into the symbolic order, the realm of letters, was presided over by religion
(abecedaria were normally accompanied by the *Pater noster* and other prayers), and on the
deathbed, the last sight the dying might expect to see was a crucifix held before their eyes. In
between, the sermon, especially in conjunction with confession, offered repeated opportunities for religion to mould the lives of men and women.

the preacher bore much responsibility, in principle, for purveying personal and social meaning. As he discharged this responsibility, he necessarily explained a sanctioned order and enjoined it upon his congregations. For many preachers (although, as we will see, not for all), lyric utterance could help inscribe and activate that order in the mind.

The category of poetry, while not an entirely a self-evident one, is nevertheless widely agreed to reveal itself in a certain linguistic intensity, contrived by various means, that distinguishes its discourse, marking it off from more routine forms of communication. Through its taut use of language, poetry stands out and becomes arresting, and this in ways often experienced as pleasurable. Poetry may also deliver the delightful shock of the familiar made strangely new. When it comes to medieval vernacular poetry, however, this freshening of the familiar was more usually achieved in local than in wholesale ways. That is, the freshening that poetry might afford was carefully calibrated: more usually it entailed a re-cognition of the familiar than a defamiliarization of the familiar that was so radical that its former truth-claims risked losing their hold.[2] So this poetry, while it might take eye- and brain-catching risks with the presentation of its familiar subject matter, nevertheless finally offered a consoling repetition: familiar subject matter was redelivered fundamentally intact. And in the same moment that poetry emerged colourfully from the grey routine of the everyday, at once arresting and giving pleasure to its receivers, the familiar subject matter which it transformed also acquired memory value, lodging in their heads.

Stating these things about early poetry's mnemonic power is to state little more than the writers on rhetoric and the arts of poetry who were read in the Middle Ages had already appreciated, but, for present purposes, what is to be borne in mind is the extent to which many medieval preachers shared that rhetorical awareness.[3] Making the matter they preached pleasurably memorable was an art that had powerful spiritual endorsement; no frivolous decoration, it was a cultivation warranted in serving a sacred end. Whether or not medieval preachers directly consulted the textbooks for guidance in rhetorical ways for commanding attention, accomplished preachers would have understood, as much from on-the-job instinct as from any written authority, how important it was to make an occasion out of their pulpit performance. Hence it is easy to imagine that the colonization of the congregation's imagination by pleasurable conquest, even were it not the declared primary purpose of preaching, might nevertheless be an important incidental goal for the preacher to aim at.[4] The stakes that the preacher played for were high – winning souls and confirming them in their faith – yet circumstances were often against him.

Given that the lyrics considered in this chapter were so context-sensitive, it

---

2   Sometimes, however, the authority is re-delivered at the cost of a certain audacity, even risk, as, for example, in the lyric *I syng of a mayden* (Duncan *MEL*, No. 79) where the approach of Christ to his mother Mary in the moment of her conception is daringly, if gently, eroticized. See Stanbury (below), 230–1.

3   For a general study, see Carruthers 1990.

4   The doctrine of *docere et delectare*, that teaching should be combined with delighting, was an ancient one. Neither was to be the other's nemesis; both were to be organically fused. By this doctrine, therefore, the most effective preaching would have mixed both.

seems worthwhile, before moving on to examine them, to devote a few pages to evoking the medieval preaching scene, recalling some of the inhospitable circumstances ever likely to thwart even the best attempt of the preacher to get his message across. Some circumstances were intractable, but there were others that he might try to take control of, and in which he might usefully mobilize the power of lyric poetry in his battle for attention.

Wandering minds and the battle for attention

The medieval preacher generally had an uphill task. To begin with, while he urged familiar matter of eternal consequence, he did so through a necessarily ephemeral medium, spoken words, that as soon as uttered vanished on the air. If interest in familiar matter was to be rekindled, and if he was to turn his congregation's recollection of it to salvific effect, the preacher must be memorable both in the moment of utterance and also in a way that outlasted the medium he worked in. The spiritual benefit of his words might only prove durable if they had an afterlife in his congregation's minds. Yet congregations then, no less than ones now, might find their minds fleeing from their pursuer. And understandably. If the preacher were honourable in intent, no mere showman wielding rhetoric for unscrupulous ends,[5] then no matter how favourable an impression he might make, he still in the end came stalking his congregation's souls like a spiritual huntsman. Or, to recall the evangelical simile, he was a fisherman casting to catch souls in his nets. Before he had any hope of success, he had to recognize that those souls inhabited bodies that had to be reckoned with first. And bodies might be recalcitrant for a host of reasons. For example, they might be cold and uncomfortable. One need only recollect the advice given to parish priests by one assiduous late fourteenth-century preacher, John Mirk, about what to do if the wine froze solid in the chalice while they were celebrating Mass, to capture the seasonal chill of many a medieval church.[6] Climate would not always have been on the side of a congregation's attention span. People might also be distracted from listening for all sorts of other reasons: by the children they had brought with them to church, for example. One fifteenth-century English sermon offers a little vignette of exemplary maternal patience in a dialogue that it reports as having taken place between a mother and her son in church. Like all young children, the little boy is inquisitive:

> And upon a certen tyme thei were in there chyrche, and faste this childe behelde ever the rode, and seyde to his moder thus, 'Madame, is that a man or a childe that is so nayled up on yonder tree? What menythe it that he is so arayed?' Sche answerd and seyd, 'Sonne, this is the similitude of Cristis Passion that he

---

5   The outstanding literary paradigm of the abuse of the *officium predicatoris* is found in Chaucer's Pardoner; see Fletcher 1998, 249–65.
6   Mirk's *Manuale sacerdotis* advises: *Si sanguis Christi in calice frigore congelatur, per aspiracionem dissolvatur et gluciatur* [If Christ's blood freezes in the chalice because of the cold, let it be thawed by breathing and swallowed] (Bodl. MS Bodley 549, fol. 157). Mirk's prescription is itself based on earlier canonical precept.

sufferde for us to bryng us to the joyes of heven'. 'And moder, whi stondithe that
woman so by hym?' 'A sonne, that is the moder of Jhesu, his owne modur'. 'And
saw sche tho peynes that he sufferd for us?' 'Yee certen, sonne', seyd sche. Then
seyde the childe to his moder, 'It wolde greve yow right sore at yowre hert, and
case were that ye saw me so farde witheall'. Then seyd sche, 'Yee sonne, the
moste hevynes it were to me that myghte be devised by eny possibil reson'. 'In
certen, moder, then it semythe to my reson that sche was full of hevynes when
sche saw hyr sonne Jhesu suffer so grete tribulacion'.

(Bodl. MS e Museo 180, fol. 85r–v)

The promise that this unnamed child's lively mind shows does not disappoint;
the sermon goes on to relate that he ended up following a distinguished clerical
career in Oxford. Nevertheless, his repeated sleeve-tugging cannot have
improved his mother's concentration. Only transfer his childlike persistence to
the occasion of a sermon being delivered in the same church and, short of
quickly finding a way of keeping him quiet, his mother would have had little
chance of taking everything in.

Churches, too, were full of distractions of other far less edifying kinds, not
least those introduced by people who had gone along precisely for the purpose
of eyeing each other up and gossiping.[7] The same was true outdoors. Many
sermons were preached outside in the open air, in outdoor pulpits, whether
temporary or permanent, or at preaching crosses, or in cemeteries and church-
yards. Here, in addition to distractions of the sort already glanced at, others
might invade. The weather could be the chief enemy, for example. Unless the
preacher had the saintly resources of a St Edmund of Abingdon who, when
preaching outdoors could reprimand any menacing storm clouds and cause
them to scud obediently away, rain might stop play.[8]

No matter how resolute they were, preachers less favoured with divine aid
would have been powerless to hold their congregations in a downpour. But
there was one intangible enemy over which they might seek to develop a greater
degree of direct control, one more insidious than the threat of inclement
weather. Of all the frailties that the flesh is heir to, the one most bedevilling the
preacher's efforts would have been plain boredom, and it was particularly lethal
when mixed with a dash of resistance, of disinclination to listen to what was
uncongenial to hear. Since the path of salvation is trod at a certain fleshly cost,
the flesh is usually reluctant to pay it. Preachers themselves knew the danger
that the unpalatable parts of their message *commeth in at the on ere and goyth oute
at the othur* (Ross 1940, 166, lines 22–3). Furthermore, neither boredom nor disinclination were respecters of class boundaries. Sometimes the loftiest in society,
whom fond hope might fancy would set an example to the rest, simply marched
out if they felt that the sermon was dragging on too long. Alternatively, the
congregation might heckle. Early in the thirteenth century, Stephen Langton,
Archbishop of Canterbury, is related to have suffered this affront, and he,

---

7   Chaucer's Wife of Bath makes a good example of this type; she frankly declares her habit of
    going to sermons in order to see and be seen (*CT* III, 555–9).
8   Matthew Paris relates St Edmund's rain-averting abilities in the Life of him that he wrote (see
    Lawrence 1960, 236).

enjoying no less a nickname than Stephen *de lingua tonante* (Stephen 'of the Thundering Tongue'), was by all accounts no mean preacher (Roberts 1968, 51). On one occasion, the grandee unconcerned about letting his impatience show was King John himself. If King John showed exasperation, there was little hope that those beneath him would behave any better (Douie and Farmer 1985, II, 143). A few centuries later, nothing had changed. According to an early Tudor account of a sermon and the response it provoked, a friar who upbraided a wife in his congregation for chattering while he preached got an impertinent come-uppance when the wife retorted, 'I beshrowe [curse] his harte that babeleth more of us two.' Nor was the congregation embarrassed at this: 'At the which seying the people dyd laughe, because they felte but lytell frute in hys sermonde' (Hazlitt 1881, 85). So sensible preachers knew that they had to get on with it, and not to wear out the patience of their congregations by making need-less demands on them.

Of course, uncongenial subject matter notwithstanding, the force of a preacher's personality and his sheer moral authority, in addition to whatever rhetorical skills he might muster, could go a long way towards holding his audi-ence's attention. The corollary of this is implicit in the frequently reiterated insis-tence of late-medieval clerical authors that, if a preacher's life did not conform to his words, his words would be held in contempt and his preaching scorned. Thus, one sermon writer was moved to apply to the discredited preacher two homely similes: he was like an ass that bears loaves to market, but never tastes one of them; or like a scarecrow set in a field to terrify birds from the corn – at first, this trick works, but when the birds finally realize that the scarecrow is life-less, they simply foul it with their droppings (Bodl. MS Barlow 24, fol. 178v). Such forlorn images of ass and scarecrow picturesquely captured what was self-evident, that, if the preacher's life agreed with his message, he was more likely to be attended to than if it did not.

But apart from burnishing personal moral authority and its concomitant power to command respect (or less demandingly, from simply practising the widely acknowledged virtue of brevity), the astute preacher had other tricks up his sleeve for keeping his audience gripped. These were not always as drastic as those that the sixth-century preacher Caesarius of Arles might employ, who is reputed to have had the church doors locked before starting to preach (Owst 1926, 181). This 'Shut the doors, I'm going to begin' approach seems, however, to have been an exceptional method for securing a captive audience. A more sophisticated tactic was that mentioned earlier, the targeting of the sermon at the imaginations of the congregation. Wooing those might finally prove the best strategy, since less compromising methods were tacit admissions of defeat. If the sermon aspired to being memorable, it might also aspire to being appropriately entertaining, to the extent that entertainment could be made compatible with spreading God's Word and not detracting from it. Many preachers, for example, thought the occasional joke permissible. The tradition of *risus paschalis* (literally, 'Easter laughter') is a case in point, and seems to have been regarded as fair game amongst some for whom it licensed seasonal flickers of fun. Preachers did not have to hold in their sides for the larger part of the year, however; several examples are recorded of the medieval preacher having his little joke, and not just at Eastertide. The fourteenth-century Dominican friar, John Bromyard, for example, whose massive preaching resource, the *Summa predicantium*, still awaits a modern edition, told the tale of a *truffator* [trifler, trickster] who made himself ill by excessive drinking. When the doctor warned him that 'the cup is killing you', he quipped, 'Had I'd known that, I'd have drunk from the saucer.'[9] And another contemporary and equally esteemed Dominican, Robert Holcot, told the tale of an artist who painted superbly, but whose children were startlingly ugly. When the discrepancy was pointed out to him, he replied, 'Ah yes, you see, when I'm producing my paintings I work during daylight hours when I can see what I'm doing . . .'.[10] Neither Bromyard nor Holcot seem to have restricted outings like these to one day in the year, although it seems reasonable to suppose that jokes during the Church's penitential seasons would have been rather less likely for fear of breaching seasonal decorum.

Sterner, Bible-based preachers and reformists would set their faces against such levity as this, condemning it as an adulteration, and lumping it together with the frivolous, vain tales that they claimed certain preachers confected their sermons with merely to curry favour with their audiences and pander to their degenerate tastes. And in this condemnation verse might be included.[11] The position statement issued in the Prologue to the *Mirror*, a late fourteenth-century Middle English translation of an early thirteenth-century French sermon cycle by Robert de Gretham, articulates an important thread of late fourteenth-century English thinking in this respect. In censuring people who wanted to hear romances and heroic tales (*gestes*) read to them, the *Mirror* translator also attacked the composers of these secular *songes and . . . gestes*, accusing them of lying when they said that all things that are written are to be believed:

> Many men it ben that han wille to heren rede romaunce and gestes [tales]. That is more than idilchip, & that Y wil wele that alle men it witen; for hii [they] ben controved [contrived] thurgh mannes wit that setten here [their] hertes to folies and trufles [trifles]. As the leiyer [liar] doth, he maketh his speche queynteliche [artfully] that it may ben delicious to mennes heryng [hearing] for that it schuld be the better listen[d]. . . . And therfor ich have sette myn herte for to drawen out a litel tretice of divinite, that men that han wil for to here swiche [such] trufles, that hii mow tur[n]en her hertes therfro. . . . And for men seyn that al thinges that ben writen it ben for to leven [believe], & hii gabben [lie, prate]; for hii that maken thes songes and thes gestes, hii maken hem after weneinge [idle fancy], & men seit on [it is said in] old englisch that weneinge nis no wisdome. Loke nou to Tristrem, other of Gii of Warwike, other of ani other, & thou ne schalt finde non that ther nis mani lesinges & gret.   (Duncan and Connolly 2003, 3)[12]

---

9   Translated from an entry under 'Mundus', M.XIII, §19, in John Bromyard's *Summa predicantium* (see BL MS Royal 7.E.iv, fol. 361). See also Tubach 1969, No. 5322.

10 Translated from an entry in *lectio* 194A in Robert Holcot's *In Sapientiam* (see Oxford, Balliol College MS 27). The joke circulated widely; see Tubach 1969, No. 3574.

11 The austere, anti-poetic disposition is perhaps most stridently vocal in the criticisms of Wyclif and his fellow travellers, but this criticism, although theirs characteristically, may nevertheless have focused a more general distrust of poetic artifice. See Duncan 1998.

12 It is interesting to note that de Gretham's Middle English translator, censuring those who say that everything that is written is to be believed, claims that they *gabben* [prate], and in so doing, he uses one of the disparaging words favoured in radical Lollard discourse (Hudson 1985, 178, n. 27).

Not surprisingly, the sermons of the Middle English *Mirror* do not come larded with lyrics. Along with those arch-evangelicals and promoters of the vernacular, the Wycliffites, the *Mirror* translator repeatedly affirmed his reliance on Holy Writ, as, indeed, had Robert de Gretham himself over a century earlier. No matter what its ostensible purpose, lyric utterance for such people was too closely associated with reprobate secular taste to warrant any toehold in sacred discourse.

Yet, wiser churchmen knew that just as jokes and tales, provided they were judiciously used and diverted towards a pious end, might earn their place in preaching, so might poetry.[13] Through poetry, a preacher might catch the attention of many a lay man and woman who otherwise might find those main staples of the sermon menu – pastoralia and catechesis – indigestible if served ungarnished. For not only might the syllabus of salvation be rebarbative for reasons explained earlier; as far as it concerned the laity, it was also relatively concise, and by that same token, liable to bore them, so wearily familiar had it become, and thus prone to the sort of audience resistance described earlier. Even if 'Friar John x. commandments', as he got called behind his back, ended up having the last laugh, his case, itself introduced in the context of a joke, shows the perennial truth of the maxim that familiarity breeds contempt. The story goes that Friar John had only one sermon, on the Ten Commandments, and was pilloried for trotting it out on all occasions. His accusers said that everyone knew what he was going to say before he even opened his mouth. But, said he, if it were really true that they knew what he was going to say, they could surely rise to the challenge of telling him what the Ten Commandments were. Put on the spot, one of his accusers triumphantly recited 'pride, covetousness, sloth, envy, wrath, gluttony and lechery' (Hazlitt 1881, 83). Verses to season his Decalogue might have helped the discountenanced fellow remember it better, and so escape his embarrassment; indeed, sermons intercalated with a Decalogue versified can be found.[14] Consequently, many preachers were content to include verse, objectors notwithstanding.[15]

Verses in sermons

Before turning squarely to lyrics and verses in sermons, however, we must first enter a distinction. Sermon verse is broadly classifiable into one of two main categories. I will distinguish these as the 'structural' and the 'non-structural'. By structural, I intend verse which, though sometimes mistaken by modern literary critics as lyric poetry,[16] originally had no existence independent of the structure of the sermon in which it participated (as, conversely, a lyric poem might have); normally, the function of verse of this structural sort was to focus nodal

---

[13] It may be noted that the *Mirror* translator was content to continue the use of *exempla* as found in his early thirteenth-century Anglo-Norman source.

[14] See, for example, Fletcher and Gillespie 2001, 65–6.

[15] It seems almost axiomatic that sermons containing verses are unlikely to be Lollard.

[16] For a classic exposé of this, see Wenzel 1985.

moments in the development of sermons constructed according to rules characteristic of what some theorists called the 'modern' mode of preaching. 'Modern'
sermons – as opposed to 'ancient' ones, the nature of whose (very different) kind
of structure need not detain us here – opened with a theme normally selected
from Scripture, and then, usually after a short introduction or 'protheme', they
proceeded to repeat this theme and announce a division of it into a number of
'principals' or 'members' (often totalling three, less often four, but occasionally
even more).[17] The systematic development and amplification of these 'principals' or 'members' generated the remaining bulk of the sermon. Thus, for
example, the extract given below from an unpublished sermon copied early in
the fourteenth century has an opening theme announced in Latin, *Audi, filia, et
vide* (Psalm 41:11), followed by a short introduction. At the end of the introduction, this theme is repeated and then translated into a Middle English couplet:
My doghter, my derlyngge / Herkne my lore, y-se my techynge. At this point of repetition the theme is made to generate four 'principals' or 'members', rhymed in
English, which are amplified serially until the sermon has run its course. Addi-
tionally, just before the theme's repetition, it might be noted that another
English couplet is used to translate the gospel verse quoted from John 9:11:

> 'Audi, filia, et vide', in Psalmo. Refert Solinus in colectaneis, capitulo de
> mirabilibus Sardinie, quod in regione illa sunt fontes mirabiliter salutares . . .
> sunt tres ille in divinis persone; si possem ab eorum quolibet unam guttam
> inpetrare, a Patre a drope of hys mighty, a Filio a drope of hys wytte, a Spiritu
> Sancto a drope of his milce, possem dicere secure cum ceco nato, 'Lavi oculos
> meos et vide[o]', Iohannis nono capitulo:
>
> > 'Loverd Jhesus, herye the of al thy myghtty.
> > Ich have myn ighe i-wasse and habbe myn syghte'.
>
> Ad istud ergo lumen clare intuendum dat nobis propheta sanum consilium in
> verbis thematis preassumpti, dicens, 'Audi, filia, et vide'. Anglice sic:
>
> > 'My doghter, my derlyngge,
> > Herkne my lore, y-se my techynge'.
>
> Audi et vide: principium a quo processisti; privilegium quale suscepisti;
> preiudicium quantum commisisti; precipicium in quod incedisti. Si
> consideremus sicud prius the busynesse of Cristes godnesse, videlicet, wyth
> what mastrie he hath man y-wrought; wyth what curtaysie he ys to man
> y-brought; wyth what marchandie he hath y-bought; and what seynorie he hath
> to man y-thought, non mirum si querat eum dirigere, wyssy and rede mannes
> sole, tamquam filiam specialissimam, dicens, 'Audi, filia, et vide'.
>
> > 'My doghter, my derlyng,
> > Herkne my lore, y-se my techyng'.
>
> Et hec materia sermonis. Primo dicere potest Deus humano generi, 'Audi et vide
> how mankende furst bygan; in what manschep stow ys man; what wykednesse
> man hath y-do; what joye and blisse man ys y-broght'.

---

[17] 'Ancient' and 'modern' sermon structure is discussed in various places, but for an authoritative study that focuses especially on English practice, see Spencer 1993, 228–68.

'My doghter, my derlyng,
Herkne my lore, y-se my techyng'.[18]

(Bodl. MS Bodley 26, fols 192–3v)

The Latin/English intermixture of this extract is broadly representative of a macaronic style found in a substantial number of late medieval sermons.[19] Vernacular verses are sewn into the Latin prose, as are also occasional English words or phrases (note, for example, the Latin/English alternation in the sentence *non mirum si querat eum dirigere, wyssy and rede mannes sole, tamquam filiam specialissimam*).[20] Flexible though the categories arrived at may be for classifying the Middle English lyric, it is doubtful whether structural verses like these warrant inclusion in any of them.[21]

Conversely, the sermon verses that I have classified as non-structural, like the Decalogue verses referred to earlier, have every reason to be included in the Middle English lyric corpus. Verses of this category, many of which already had independent existence outside the sermons in which they were allowed to make guest appearances, were by that same token unlike the verses mechanically cranked out by the machinery of 'modern' sermon form. The use of non-structural verse in sermons was thus far less predictable, and its functions more flexible and diverse.

In principle, any verse known to the preacher might be recruited for his purposes. This offered him a potential repertoire sufficiently broad to include verses that were bluntly secular. Such lyrics had an attention-catching value and, if corralled within a Christian moral frame, the potentially subversive secular connotations that they imported from their original field of use could be

---

18 'Hear, daughter, and see', in the Psalm. Solinus in his collectanea, in his chapter on the wonders of Sardinia, reports that there are wonderfully health-giving springs in that region . . . there are three persons in divinity; if I might obtain from each of them a drop, from the Father, a drop of his might, from the Son, a drop of his understanding, from the Holy Spirit, a drop of his mercy, I might say with the man born blind, 'I have washed my eyes and see', in the ninth chapter of John: 'Lord Jesu, I praise thee for all thy might / I've washed my eyes and have my sight'. Therefore, the prophet gives us sound advice for seeing that light clearly in the words of the theme taken up earlier, saying, 'Hear, daughter, and see'. In English thus: 'My daughter, my darling, / Hearken to my lore, heed my teaching'. . . . Hear and see: the beginning from which you have issued; what kind of privilege you have received; how great the damage you have committed; the precipice into which you have fallen. If we were to consider as before the activity of Christ's goodness, namely, with what power he has wrought man; with what courtesy he is brought to man; with what merchandise he has redeemed; and what lordship he has intended for man; it would not be surprising were he to seek to guide him, to guide and advise man's soul, like a most cherished daughter, saying, 'Hear, daughter, and see'. 'My daughter, my darling, / Hearken to my lore, heed my teaching'. And this is the matter of the sermon. First, God can say to the human race, 'Hear and see how mankind first began; in what manship set is man; what wickedness man has done; what joy and bliss are brought to man'. 'My daughter, my darling, / Hearken to my lore, heed my teaching'.

19 For surveys, see Wenzel 1994, and Fletcher 1994.

20 'It would not be surprising were he to seek to guide him, to guide and advise man's soul, like a most cherished daughter'. The question of the language in which such sermons were delivered is disputed. Wenzel 1994 suggests that they were delivered in the macaronic language in which they are recorded, while Fletcher 1994 upholds the traditional view, that when preached before the laity, they were largely delivered in the language with which the laity were familiar, that is, in English.

21 Robbins 1938, 243, mistakenly believed that there was an unnoticed, if fragmentary, carol embedded in the *Audi, filia, et vide* sermon.

tamed and harnessed. A famous example is the thirteenth-century *Atte Wrastlinge* sermon, where the preacher, almost certainly a friar, made sermon capital out of a risqué verse detached from what was originally a dance song or 'carole': *Atte wrastlinge my lemman I ches / And atte ston-kasting I him forles;*[22] or again on another occasion when the preacher, possibly this time a Cistercian monk, drafted into his sermon lines from an almost equally bracing poem intended to serve as a lullaby, odd though the appearance of such material in a lullaby today might seem: *Wake* [watch] *wel, Annot, thi mayden boure, / And get* [guard] *the fra Walterot, for he es lichure.*[23] A typical place within the sermon for lyric material of this friskier sort was at or near its beginning, providing the kind of opening gambit still used by preachers for capturing attention before moving on to more solid fare. Whenever the secular material sailed close to the wind, as in the cases just cited, the need to police its application was naturally more pressing. However, even secular poems far less suggestive than these might find themselves being rigorously disciplined before being admitted. Take, for example, the following case of a lyric embedded in a sermon *exemplum*. If we were to excise it from its *exemplum* context, allowing it to return to what in all likelihood was its pristine form before the preacher incorporated it, it would read as follows:

> The dew of Averil
> Haveth y-maked the grene lef to sprynge.
> My sorow is gon.
> My joye is comen.
> Ich herde a fowl synge.

Here, in the lightest and most economical of touches, its speaker sketches nature's revival in springtime (first two lines), declares his/her sorrow to be replaced by joy (second two lines), and ends by merging this now joyful, narrating 'I' with the revived world through remarking on having heard a bird sing. By leaving the speaker faceless and genderless, the experience related becomes all the more readily assimilable by anyone receiving it. Working towards a similar end is the lyric's delicate reticence about how, exactly, it should be that people make connections between signs of natural and personal revival. There is no question but that people do; springtime revival is commonly 'felt under the skin' by any of us. Yet, how is it? The indeterminacy here, which the lyric mimes, leaves the mind free to feel, rather than to understand intellectually, the associational connections in precisely the way people commonly do when they apprehend the unspoken seasonal miracle; having invited the reader's active participation in any connection-making, the lyric draws the

---

22 See Scattergood (above), 44–5.
23 The *Atte Wrastlinge* sermon is published in Förster 1918; for *Wake wel, Annot,* see Fletcher 1998, 32, 20–1. There were also examples of preaching woven around secular songs in French; a famous case, a copy of which also appears in the manuscript that yields the poem *Wan the turuf* discussed below, is found in Cambridge, Trinity College MS B.14.39, fol. 34v. This Latin sermon, attributed in some of its manuscripts, perhaps mistakenly, to Stephen Langton (see Roberts 1968, 24 and note 46, 63 note 160, and 194), discants morally on the song *Bele Alys matyn se leva* [Pretty Alice rose up one morning].

reader into its experience by making him/her responsible for imaginatively completing it.

That may be one way of describing how the lyric works when it existed in its freestanding state, and there is further formal justification for reading it like that when, as the eye scans the manuscript page on which the poem is written, the Middle English vernacular of the lyric seems to surface conspicuously from its surrounding sea of Latin, appearing in the process almost to detach itself linguistically and to insist on respect being accorded to the separate integrity that resides in its sheer vernacularity. In its Latin context, the vernacular seems honoured as a place where certain things not possible in Latin become possible. But in the sermon, the *reverdie* of the vernacular lyric is also anchored down with Latin glosses that aim to bind its vernacular significances to religious meanings imported from the sermon's *exemplum*. As mediated there, the lyric reads somewhat differently:

> The dew of Averil, id est gracia et bonitas Spiritus Sancti; Haveth y-maked the grene lef to sprynge, id est Beatam Virginem; My sorow is gon, id est pena pro meritis; My joye is comen, scilicet per Dei Filium vita beata; Ich herde a foul synge, id est angelum, scilicet, Ave Maria.
>
> (Worcester, Cathedral Library MS F.126, fol. 248) [24]

It is as if the preacher were trying to connect into simultaneity two realms of experience, neither of which was wholly commensurable. The 'secular' experience he located in the vernacular, and the 'religious' in the disciplining Latin. While both areas of experience seem to move towards a certain mutual rapprochement that the Latin initiates as it reaches out to take hold of the vernacular, neither experience seems wholly integrated with the other; but then, whole integration would efface distinctive lineaments of one or the other experience. And so, instead, both manage to exist in a tension, a textual polyphony comparable, if we may apply a contemporary musical analogy, to that heard in certain motets of the musical styles known as the *ars antiqua* and the *ars nova*: in these motets, the tenor line is grounded in a Latin religious text, while above it in the upper voices float secular vernacular verses whose sentiments seem incongruous with that of the voice beneath them even as musically they are supported by it.

Nevertheless, invaluable to preachers though secular lyrics occasionally were, by far the largest number of sermon lyrics of the non-structural sort were, not surprisingly, religious, even when these were robust enough to incorporate secular strains and resonances that set their religious appeal on a more complex basis. Lyrics of such complex internal tonality may epitomize locally within the sermon certain stylistic objectives of the sermon at large. In many cases, non-structural religious lyrics, already suitable for sermon use by virtue of their subject matter, waited in the wings ready against the day of their pulpit appearance. While these sermon lyrics in waiting have not come down to us in actual sermon texts, the reason for this may simply be want of evidence. As it is, they are recorded in the antechamber to preaching, in a group of manuscripts widely produced in the later Middle Ages that were intended to assist preachers. Those

24 See Wenzel 1986, 58, 223–4.

ranged from the informal notebooks that individual preachers made to formal
encyclopædias of preachable material at the other end of the scale, vast quarries
of *predicabilia* like the *Summa predicantium* of John of Bromyard cited earlier, one
of medieval England's most ambitious examples of the genre.[25]

This sense of the 'sermon lyric in waiting', the lyric in the antechamber of
preaching, attends one of the most haunting of the Middle English Passion lyrics
to have survived. It is also one of the earliest. We may turn to it now as an
eloquent witness to the sort of complex simplicity which the religious lyric could
distil. It seems likely that its author was none other than the famous St Edmund
of Abingdon whose rain-banishing skills were mentioned earlier. He was, by all
accounts, a dedicated preacher, and indeed, the contemporary artist and chroni-
cler, Matthew Paris, took the trouble to record one of his sermons, preached to
the monks of Pontigny on the subject of Christ's seven utterances from the cross,
in the *Life of St Edmund* that he composed (Lawrence 1960, 286–9). In fact, St
Edmund's very topic on that occasion, the seven utterances, follows closely
upon the English lyric of present concern in the treatise in which the lyric
appears. This is the *Merure de Seinte Eglise*, a work written by St Edmund in
French, c.1239–40, and dedicated to the Pontigny monks.[26] The *Merure* is a devotional, consultative work, not a sermon, but, as his own practice plainly proves,
his material on the Passion was amphibious, capable of appearing in either treatise or sermon form. So, while the lyric quoted below does not appear in a
sermon proper, it can justly be regarded as belonging to the 'sermon lyric in
waiting' class. Chapter 24 of the *Merure* invites meditation on, among other
things, the sorrow of the Virgin at seeing her crucified son. Momentarily the
chapter modulates into English, focusing this sorrow in a single and, relative to
the French, singleminded, quatrain:

> Ci doit tu penser de la duce Marie
> De quel angusse ele estoit replenie
> Quant estut a son destre
> E receust le disciple pur le mestre;
> Cum ele avoit grant dolur
> Quant le serf receust pur le Seignur –
> Le fiz au peschur
> Pur le fiz al emperor –
> Iohan, le fiz Zebedeu,
> Pur Ihesu, le fiz Deu.
> E pur ceo poeit el dire de soi
> Ceo ke dist Neomi:
> 'Ne me apelez des or ne avant;
> Kar de amerte e dolur grant
> M'ad replenie le tot pussant.'
> Meimes cele tenuire
> Dit ele en le chancon de amur,

---

25 Of the surviving preachers' handbooks, that compiled in 1372 by Friar John of Grimestone
    offers the richest selection of Middle English lyrics preserved in such sources. See Wilson
    1973; also Wenzel 1986, 101–73, Boffey (above), 13, and Gillespie (above), 73.
26 Pontigny is where he died, not long after having left England, in 1240.

'Ne vus amerveillez mie
Que io su brunecte e haslee
Car le solail me ad descoluree.'

E pur ceo dit un Engleis en teu manere de pite:

Now goth sonne under wode,
Me reweth, Marie, thi faire rode.
Now goth sonne under tre,
Me reweth, Marie, thi sone and thee.[27]

Although both Middle English lyric and French text establish a Marian focus, the singlemindedness of the lyric compared with the French accesses a different realm of feeling entirely. Gone are the somewhat learned Biblical references and allusions of the French which tend to scatter attention centrifugally towards the wide hinterlands of Passion exegesis. They make way for an almost exclusively centripetal attention to Mary at the end of the dying day: the sun/son sinks beneath the wood/cross; the speaker pities Mary's fair face; the sun/son sinks beneath the tree/cross; the speaker pities Mary and her son. This coalescence of what could be a timeless sunset with the historical event of the crucifixion blends both in a moment in which, having established the mood of a dying day, the speaker merges that with absolute naturalness into a compassionate pondering of Mary's face, and then, by a small increment, further merges that into a similar pondering of her and her son. Why should the speaker find her face, and her situation with her son, so moving? With an understatement not unlike that already seen in the secular lyric *The dew of Averil*, the reader is again left to supply the connections that frame an answer, is left to infer the precise nature of the scene that the lyric's emotional reasoning suggests: the speaker grieves, we infer, because Mary's face, and her situation with her son, express something that cannot fail to elicit grief. This inferential process set in motion by the poem's reticence prompts the reader's mind to imagine what it will in terms of Mary's grief-touched face and the situation in which she finds herself. Thus the reader assumes responsibility for inventing much of the poem's meaning, bringing it personally to life out of the poem's promptings of his or her prior cultural awareness and understanding of the content of the crucifixion narrative. In completing that experience from his or her own resources, the reader comes to possess that experience uniquely and to identify with it in one of the most closely collaborative of ways: the reader to a point stands in the powerful position of author. As with *The dew of Averil*, the art of the lyric is to be located in the encouragement it gives the reader personally to adopt and inhabit a set of related experiences at which it briefly gestures.

---

[27] 'At this point you must think upon sweet Mary, upon what anguish she was filled with when she was at his right side and received the disciple in the stead of the Master; how great a grief she had when she received the servant in the stead of the Lord, a sinner's son in the stead of the Emperor's son – John, Zebedee's son – in the stead of Jesus, God's son. And because of this, she can say of herself what Naomi says, "Do not call me [Naomi] in the past or from henceforth, for the Almighty has filled me with bitterness and grief." She says a similar matter in the Song of Love, "Be not amazed that I am brown and discoloured for the sun has burnt me." And about this an Englishman says in the following pitying manner: "Nou goth sonne . . .", etc.' (Robbins 1925, 63) The lyric is quoted here as it appears in Duncan *MEL*, No. 84.

Lyrics on the Passion comprise an extremely important subject group among the verses that appear in sermons. They draw extensively on reservoirs of feeling that only the intimacies associated with a mother tongue can most readily access, channelling this feeling into the events of sacred history. Yet the linguistic province of sacred history was chiefly Latin, and thus the mother tongue had the advantage of bringing sacred history's distances emotionally up close: note, too, how in the lyric *Nou goth sonne under wode*, the event is narrated in a timeless, eternal present in which its historical distance tends as a result to be elided. According to the standard affective piety of the age, the feeling of emotional identity with the characters of sacred history was thought to have salvific value, and necessarily, feelings of identity with the past could only be achieved in the surrogacy of the present.

Another group of sermon lyrics, found somewhat less frequently than Passion lyrics but which still form a conspicuous group, are lyrics on old age and dying, and again like Passion lyrics, they typically rehearse emotional repertoires that were thought to work towards salvific ends. This time, it is most frequently sad resignation to mortality, or even mortal fear, that are evoked, and these feelings may be compounded with what some theologians called *timor servilis*, alarm at the prospect of dire eternal consequences for a life lived badly.[28] Here it may be helpful to consider four examples, chosen to illustrate something of the variety that exists within this group.

The first will be relatively unfamiliar, because it has never appeared in any modern anthology of Middle English lyrics. It features within an item in prose found in a manuscript that contains, for the most part, Middle English sermons. (The item may itself have been intended as material from which a sermon could be amplified, or was conceivably deemed preachable even in its own right.) The lyric is given below with its introductory prose context, a discourse on how the life cycle of the rose figures that of man:

> And skylfollich [by reason] mannis lif is tokind to [expressed by] the rose, for thre statis that is in mannis lif: the furst is chyldhede; the secund is manhed; the thryd is held [age]. By the rose, wan he [when it] comith vyrst hout [first out] and sonnyth [suns] furst is [its] red lemys [petals, lit. limbs] in May, his bytoknyd a chyld on is norice [his nurse's] lappe of on yer old othir two that is fayre and lykful, for yong thing is comunlich quemfol [pleasant]. Than he schall be a per-son, a byssoppe, a gret lord. But wel were is modir yiff he mowe boe a god sepherd, for to the sepherdys broght furst the angel tythingys [tidings] of Goddis burthe, aftyr a fewe of Goddis derlingys, Mary and a fewe othir. The secund stat of the ros, is lems [petals] buth [are] sprad abrod [wide] and is in most rode [red-ness], and bytoknith a man in is best stat with ful rode and ful streynthe. And with is long lokkus [locks of hair] and othir joliftese [revelries], a wenith [he thinks] he schal never be feblyr ne foulir than he is than. And tharfor me sayth, he is in is flouris [his flowers, i.e. his prime]. Bote it wol far of hym |fol. 194| as it farith of the rose. Furst he fadith, weltryth [falters], and welouth [turns yellow], and wrynkelith [shrivels], fallyth to the eorthe an rotith [and rots]. So schal man in held [old age] falowyn and weltrin and swyndin [dwindle] away. Wan:

---

28 On the theology of *timor servilis*, see Woolf, 72.

Wan that is wyte waxit falow,	*when what is white grows yellow*
And that is cripse waxit calaw,	*curly hair becomes bald*
Wen thi neb ryvelith as a roket,	*face wrinkles like a rochet*
And thin hein porfilin as scarlet,	*eyes are scarlet rimmed*
And thi nose droppith as a boket,	*drips like a bucket*
Than thou beon y-clipid 'kombir-flet'.	*called 'space-waster'*

(Bodl. MS Hatton 96, fols 193v–4)[29]

The rose is a familiar image in medieval literary texts, as are also narratives in which the rose takes centre stage and which allegorize events in a man's life. The most famous literary example is the thirteenth-century *Roman de la Rose*, where the rose at the heart of the garden stands for the desired woman towards whom the lover steadily makes his way in the course of his wooing, encountering en route various encouragements or obstacles. Thus the rose was well known from the secular literary repertoire for the associations it contracted with mankind. In the sermon, however, the association takes a different turn in a religious and moral direction. The three stages in the rose's life cycle unfold as the three ages of man, beginning in infancy, when the child shows promise of being a valued member of whichever of medieval society's three estates awaits him (traditionally, either the clergy, the aristocracy, or the labouring classes). The next stage is maturity, when man's powers are at their height. But finally and unstoppably come decrepitude and death. It is at this bleak terminus, when the passage is describing the most chilling point of the cycle, that the lyric enters to distil the prose's concluding mood and crystalize its sentiment in a vivid series of pit's-brink images of old age. The lyric thus memorably focuses what the prose has built up towards, and leaves the readers' imagination hesitating at the point where the next inevitable step on the downward path is about to be taken; indeed, where it may just as well be taken, for the old man, bereft of dignity, has been reduced to mere clutter. The last line dismisses him as a *kombir-flet*, a 'space-waster', an encumbering irrelevance.[30] The lyric, then, seems a natural outgrowth and summation of the theme of the prose. Whether it was originally a freestanding poem drafted into the service of its context, or whether composed expressly for its use here, is not clear. What is clear is the way that it works smoothly in a prose-and-poetry ensemble, and its function is the better understood for seeing it in that context.

The second example from the death lyric repertoire will not be familiar to readers at all, since it is published here for the first time. The same fourteenth-century manuscript that gave us *The dew of Averil* also contains in another of its Latin sermons this brief, *ubi sunt* reflection on the great and the good who have passed away in death like a shadow and are seen no more:

---

[29] This text is quoted as found in the manuscript. Its scribal idiosyncrasies (not least the intrusive 'h' in *held* for *eld* and *his* for *is*, etc., and the omission of 'h' in *is* for *his*, etc.) will be immediately apparent to the reader.

[30] For the worthless state to which the aged in medieval extended families were reduced, compare the Harley lyric *Hye Loverd, thou here my bone* (Duncan MEL, No. 51) where an old man laments:

Ther me calleth me 'fille-flet'	*I am called 'floor-filler'*
And 'waynoun wayteglede'. (16–17)	*'good-for-nothing fire-gazer'*

Rogo vos dicatis michi ubi sunt principes gencium, et cetera:
'Where beth thys lordes that holden sted in stall,   *have horses in stables*
Hawkes and houndes in boure and eke in hall,   *also*
That gold and selver leyden op and wenden never adown fall?' *stored up;*
Et statim respondet propheta: [*expected*
'The soules beth in hell, the bodyis stynketh all,   *are*
And other beth up in her sted of wham schoul so byfall'.   *are up*
                        (Worcester, Cathedral Library MS F.126, fol. 29v, col.a)[31]

Readers already familiar with Middle English lyrics will immediately recognize affinities of phrase and sentiment between this lyric and a longer one, whose earliest manuscript, like that of this lyric, also hailed from the West Midlands. The longer poem, *Where ben they before us were* (Duncan *MEL*, No. 47), outstrips *Where beth thys lordes that holden sted in stall* in its ambitious scope, but by that same token, it sacrifices the formal compression that the latter lyric achieves not only in terms of its comparative brevity, but also of its relentless monorhyme. Whereas the pit's-brink symptoms of old age listed in *Wan that is wyte waxit falow* were universal, death in *Where beth thys lordes that holden sted in stall*, as also in the longer poem *Where ben they before us were*, is presented as knocking specifically at the door of society's rich and powerful. Many lyrics in the death repertoire targeted this upper-class audience, and the next to be considered here singles out from the favourite target audience a particular representative.

Sometimes the melancholic, reflective tone of voice assumed by speakers of death lyrics – compare that of the first voice heard in *Where beth thys lordes that holden sted in stall* – is substituted by a voice more stern and unsparing – compare that lyric's second voice, which is clearly distinguished as being a second voice by the intercalated Latin sentence that attributes it to a *propheta*. It is this sterner sort of prophetic voice that may also be heard in another powerful little lyric similarly busy with the death of high-class beauty and status:

Whan the turuf is thy tour,   *turf; tower*
And thy pit is thy bour,   *grave; bower*
Thy fel and thy white throte   *skin; throat*
Shullen wormes to note.   *shall (be) the concern of worms*
What helpeth thee thenne
Al the worilde wenne?   *world's delights*
                        (Duncan *MEL*, No. 45)

This lyric is preserved uniquely in a manuscript of the second half of the thirteenth century, evidently copied for the use of preachers in view of its content, and whose relatively small format and multiplicity of scribes strongly suggest its production amongst the friars.[32] *Whan the turuf is thy tour* colludes with a

---

31 This passage is found in a sermon on the theme *Respicite, et levate capita vestra* [Look up, and raise your heads] (Luke 21: 28).
32 Lerer 1997, 148, dates Cambridge, Trinity College MS B.14.39 too early ('the first half of the thirteenth century'), and perhaps also implies for it a monastic readership (153), whereas the manuscript's use is more likely to have been not monastic but mendicant. Wenzel 1986, 8, agrees with Reichl 1973, 49–58 (though Reichl is not cited by name) in considering the manuscript a preacher's notebook. Reichl's suggestion that the manuscript was a mendicant

traditional medieval preaching theme in choosing to warn the powerful not to be overconfident in their position, since no one, not even the aristocrat, may finally escape unscathed from death. The lyric displays a superb literary compression, again comparable to some of the lyrics already discussed, and also resembles them in its ability to nudge readers into fleshing out for themselves details of a scenario only fleetingly hinted at. It appears in a section of the manuscript in which verses in Latin are rendered by English equivalents:

> Cum sit gleba tibi turris
> Tuus puteus conclavis,
> Pellis et guttur album
> Erit cibus vermium.
> Quid habent tunc de proprio
> Hii monarchie lucro?
>
> Unde anglice sic dicitur:
>
> Whan the turuf . . . etc.[33]

The English achieves a concentration that the Latin does not: note, for example, its accusatory, second-person singular thrust maintained throughout; the Latin, by contrast, disperses its attack in a generality, concluding with a much remoter, third-person plural reference. The implied addressee of the English lyric must also be female – something rather less clear in the Latin – and an aristocratic one into the bargain.[34] The tower and the bower, where she seems to reside, are dedicated architectural places within a castle, for the castle is where towers and bowers coincide, the latter word in medieval English usage also characteristically signifying a lady's bedchamber. Our imagined aristocratic female is challenged by the stern prophetic voice of the lyric speaker to consider what good her present worldly joy will do her when death comes. But that voice does not actually name death as such; instead, life's end is figured obliquely, via a dramatic change of residence and an alternative group of admirers gathered around the skin and the white throat. These two physical endowments, characteristically enjoyed by the ideal medieval mistress and often celebrated in secular love poetry, will come in the fullness of time to the exclusive attention of worms. In this horrid exchange, future worms stand in for present suitors as the stern, prophetic voice wrenches the joys of the present time out of joint. The voice makes the secular 'now' a hostage to the sacred 'then': the ephemeral 'now' has its towers, bowers, (fair) skin and white throats; in the eternal 'then', these will yield to turf, pit and worms, the harbingers of the post-mortem world

---

product has been challenged, though not in my view convincingly, by Frankis 1986, 181–2. Frankis omits to consider codicological possibilities, that the relatively small and portable format of the manuscript, combined with its multiplicity of scribes (some twelve or more different hands have been identified in it), all of whom are engaged in copying material more or less obviously useful to preachers, suggest circumstances typical of mendicant book production.

[33] 'When the glebe is your tower and a pit your chamber, skin and white throat will be worms' food. What will these possess of their own wealth of the kingdom then? Wherefore it is said in English thus: "Whan the turuf . . . etc." '.

[34] Woolf, 82, took the addressee to be a man.

of God's dispensation. The lyric's imagery turns not only on this moral-temporal axis of forward-looking prophecy, but also on a moral-spatial one. Its remorseless, one-way direction, twice repeated, is that of *flattening*: death is inferred metonymically in this lyric in images of falling and levelling, as elevated tower falls into the flatness of turf and eminent bower suffers an even deeper subterranean collapse into a pit. This alliteratively-conjoined alternation, from which this poem derives much of its impact, resembles in its brutality the equally brutal sentiment of a widely circulating sermon *exemplum* with which the sentiment of this poem begs for comparison. In the *exemplum*, a one-time lover, now turned religious, keeps the rotting body of his erstwhile mistress in his cell as a reminder that the charms he so admired in days gone by have been shown by the march of time to be no more than the acceptable face of mere carrion.

Our final example from the death repertoire, *Man mai longe him lives wene* (Duncan *MEL*, No. 39), – picturesquely called 'Death's Wither-Clench' by some editors – also introduces the last dimension of lyrics in sermons that I wish to consider, the possibility of the lyric in the sermon as a *musical* event, whether literally, as the preacher sang lines in the course of his preaching, or at least minimally, by his allusion to the lyric's sung reception. While the earliest text of *Man mai longe him lives wene*, where it is accompanied with a musical setting, does not actually appear in a sermon, its wider manuscript context is nevertheless 'a closely written mass of sermons and pieces useful to a preacher' (Ker 1983, 317), and it is known to have been popular with preachers from certain of its other later appearances and reminiscences:[35]

Man mai longe him lives wene,	*for himself; life; expect*
Ac ofte him lyeth the wrench;	*but; deceives; the quirk of fate*
Fair weder ofte him went to rene,	*turns to rain*
An ferliche maketh is blench.	*and suddenly plays its trick*
Therfore, man, thou thee bi-thench,	*take heed*
Al shal falewi thy grene.	*fade; greenness (i.e. youth)*
Weilaway, nis king ne quene	*alas; queen*
That ne shal drinke of Dethes drench.	*of Death's draught*
Man, er thou falle of thy bench,	*off*
Thy sinne aquench.	*overcome*
Ne mai strong, ne starck, ne kene	*may not prevail; mighty; bold*
Ayein Dethes wither-clench;	*against Death's hostile grip*
Young and old and bright and shene,	*beautiful*
Al he riveth an his strength.	*tears to pieces in his strength*
Fox and ferlich is the wrench,	*crafty and sudden is his twist*
Ne may no man thertoyene,	*no man may prevail against it*
Weylaway, threting ne bene,	*alas, neither threats not entreaty*
Mede, list, ne leches drench.	*bribery, cunning nor doctor's potion*
Man, let sinne and lustes stench,	*abandon sin and the stench of lust*
Wel do, wel thench!	*consider*

---

35   The music of the lyric is published in Dobson and Harrison 1979, 242. Although Wenzel 1986, 204, says of the lyric's earliest manscript, Maidstone Museum A.13, that it cannot 'be definitely shown to have been compiled for use in preaching', Ker's view of its function is surely correct.

Do bi Salomones rede,	*act according to Solomon's advice*
Man, and so thou shalt wel do;	
Do als he thee taught, and hede	*do as; take heed*
What thin ending thee bringth to,	
Ne shaltow never misdo –	
Sore thou might thee adrede!	*sorely you may fear for yourself*
Weylaway, swich wenth wel lede	*such a man fully expects to lead*
Long lyf, and blisse underfo,	*a long life and to enjoy happiness*
There Deth luteth in his sho	*while Death lurks in his shoe*
To him fordo.	*to destroy him*
Man, why niltow thee bi-knowe,	*acknowledge your nature*
Man, why niltow thee bi-se;	*consider yourself*
Of foule filth thou art i-sowe,	*begotten*
Wormes mete thou shalt be.	*food*
Her nastou blisse dayes three,	*here you do not have; three days*
Al thy lif thu drist in wowe;	*you endure in sorrow*
Welaway, Deth thee shal throwe	
Doun ther thou wenst hye ste;	*when you expect; high; to rise*
In wo shal thi wele te,	*into misery will your prosperity pass*
In wop thy gle.	*to weeping your merriment*
World and wele the biswiketh	*prosperity; deceive*
Iwis, they ben thine ifo;	*assuredly; foes*
If thy world mid wele thee sliketh	*with prosperity; flatters you*
That is for to do thee wo.	*cause you harm*
Therfore let lust overgo,	*pass*
Man, and elt it wel the liketh.	*and afterwards it will please you well*
Weylaway, hou sore him wiketh	*how sorely it serves him*
That in one stunde other two	*who in an hour*
Werkth him pine evermo.	*earns himself torment everlasting*
Ne do, Man, swo!	*Man, do not so*

The lyric weaves variations on certain staple motifs of the death tradition in its attempt to bring people to realize their transitoriness and to egg them on to the moral resolutions that that realization encouraged, based on the biblical principle of *Memorare novissima tua, et in eternum non peccabis* [Be mindful of the last things, and you will not sin eternally] (Ecclesiasticus 7:40). The first stanza evokes the sort of reversals in the natural world that are regularly vehicles for medieval death meditation – fair weather turns rainy, greenness grows sere and fallow – and with these may be compared the blossoming and fading rose of the sermon material cited earlier. The first stanza also trades on the familiar idea that no estate is immune, neither king nor queen. But it also introduces a motif not so far encountered, one which, especially after the Black Death crisis of the mid-fourteenth century, would come to loom ever larger: Death personified. The lyric develops this vision of Death stalking a quarry in a steady accumulation of detail through all the remaining stanzas (save the last, by which time the poet is ready to devote his conclusion to exhorting mankind to make an appropriate moral response). The encounter of Life with Death is presented in the lyric as an unequal struggle, a fated contest. Its presentation thus perhaps echoes a medieval conceptualization of the encounter of Life with Death as a duel; for example, the Easter sequence *Victimae paschali laudes* [Praises to the Paschal Sacrifice] projects such an encounter, the ironic difference being that in the Easter sequence, Life triumphs, since it is Christ who is doing the duelling.[36] In mankind's case, however, the victor will always be Death.

It may be fanciful to go as far as imagining some preacher singing the whole of this lyric in the course of his sermon. Yet, since each individual stanza has a self-contained moral, it may have been worth his while to lift stanzas singly for such a purpose. Maybe he lifted and sang snatches briefer still. Many Middle English lyrics were, of course, more heard as song than read on the page, and the prospect of a preacher's sung delivery of at least some non-structural sermon lyrics which are known to have had music does not stretch credibility.[37] Given the battle for the congregation's attention that every preacher waged as soon as he stepped into the pulpit, music might have offered another welcome means of holding attention; we know that the friars, so frequently alluded to in this chapter and whose raison d'être was preaching, were widely known for their musical abilities. St Francis had styled his followers 'God's jesters', by which we should understand not only a taste for wit of the sort illustrated earlier, but also for music, the medieval jester being not just a comedian but an all-round entertainer whose skills might include music. In the century after St Francis, Chaucer would show such a musical ethos alive and well in the person of his Friar Huberd: *And in his harpyng, whan that he hadde songe, / His eyen twynkled in his heed aryght / As doon the sterres in the frosty nyght* (CT, I, 266–8). And in the century after Chaucer, an assiduous Franciscan preacher, Nicholas Philip, who himself incorporated both structural and non-structural verse in his sermon booklets, included within his sermon collection bars of musical notation, revealing himself in the process to be a true heir of a long musical tradition within his Order (Fletcher 1998, 56). One of the most celebrated Middle English lyrics to have survived, *I syng of mayden* (Duncan *MEL*, No. 79), a poem praising the Blessed Virgin Mary (see above, p. 190, and footnote 2), is recorded in a single manuscript copy. Yet, were it not for the industry of a late fourteenth- or possibly early fifteenth-century sermon writer, a man of whom we know nothing save his surname, Selk, we would lack clear external proof that *I syng of mayden* was originally a song, and that it was commonly heard in England. These are things that a single surviving manuscript copy, *prima facie*, might not encourage us to believe. Selk included a reference to *I syng of mayden* in a sermon that he compiled, in Latin, for the feast of the Assumption. Among all the exalted comparisons in Latin that he lavished on Mary, Selk made time to recall a vernacular one. Mary *absque dolore peperit, cum omnes alie in dolore pereant. Unde communiter de eo* [read *ea*] *canitur*: '*Mayde, wyff and moder whas never but ye* [she] / *Well may suche a lady Goddys modyr be.*'[38] Maybe at this point Selk, or whoever

---

36 The line in *Victimae paschali laudes* runs: *Mors et vita duello conflixere mirando; dux vitae mortuus regnat vivus* [Death and life have struggled together in a great battle; the Lord of life who died, now in life reigns].

37 Indeed, this seems more than merely plausible even though there is comparatively little direct evidence of clerics performing music in a preaching context.

38 Mary 'gave birth painlessly, when all other women die of pain. Whence it is commonly sung about her: *Mayde, wyff . . .*' (Bodl. MS Barlow 24, fol. 188v). On the date of the collection, see

else may have preached from his sermon anthology, actually sang a snatch of *I syng of mayden*. We will never know for sure. But what we can certainly know is that some preachers were fully aware of the musical dimension that certain of their non-structural sermon verses accessed. At the very least, we can observe their willingness to allude to that dimension as they sought to hold their congregations.

Conclusion

In the sermon, then, Middle English lyrics found a natural habitat, and we risk restricting our understanding of how some lyrics worked if we persist in isolating them from preaching's wider enterprise; their artistry, some of whose sophistication was glimpsed earlier in this chapter, helped preaching take root in hearts and minds. From structural verses to non-structural ones, the range of sermon lyrics (those on the Passion, on death, and on the Virgin, being only three of the more prominent subject areas) expressed a corresponding range of poeticized experience. The perceived benefits of the reception of this experience in the lives of those who heard or read the lyrics were equally diverse in turn: the lyric might provide aesthetic pleasure that helped memorialize sermon content, or it might move to moral resolve and a better conduct of life according to Christian terms. But fundamentally, the lyric in the sermon helped the preacher to help members of his congregation to nurture the right sort of hopes and fears for themselves as they made their way charily, but also not without a due measure of rejoicing, through the moral landscape of middle earth.

Fletcher 1978. The sermon, found on fols 188–9v, is on the theme *Tu supergressa es universas* [You have surpassed all women] (Proverbs 31: 29).

10

'Cuius Contrarium': Middle English Popular Lyrics

BERNARD O'DONOGHUE

In the most important anthology of the later Middle English secular lyrics, Rossell Hope Robbins's *Secular Lyrics of the XIVth and XVth Centuries*, the opening category, 'Popular Songs', contains a poem headed by Robbins 'Abuse of Women' which has the following epigraph as its burden:

> Of all Creatures women be best:
> Cuius contrarium verum est. (Robbins *Sec.*, No. 38)

It seems strange at first glance to assign this poem in carol form to the 'popular' class; not only does its two-line burden contain a line of Latin but, moreover, this is a line which operates here as what Robbins neatly calls 'the destroying burden'. Surely such features must relate to a learned tradition of satire, of the kind associated with the goliardic Latin poets of the High Middle Ages such as Walter of Châtillon. So what exactly does 'popular' mean in this context?

In the criticism of the Middle English lyrics which followed the pioneering editions by Brown and Robbins and the other canon-forming anthologies listed on the first page of Preston's *Concordance*, a good deal of the scholarly energy was expended on classification along these lines. The fundamental division, which has on the whole proved the most serviceable, is into 'religious' and 'secular'. The second commonest division in those early discussions – one which cut across the religious-secular – was into 'popular' and 'courtly'; indeed, despite the prior assortment of the field into 'religious' and 'secular' in the Oxford anthologies edited by himself and Carleton Brown, Robbins makes this categorisation even more fundamental: 'These are the two big sub-divisions of Middle English poetry, the courtly and the popular – reflecting the stratification of medieval society' (Robbins *Sec.*, xxxiii). The alternative to 'popular' was not always 'courtly'; sometimes it was something like 'literary' or 'artistic' or 'sophisticated' – but a division of which one pole was the 'popular' has come to seem indispensable.

Under scrutiny, however, the term 'popular' proves much more equivocal than might be expected.[1] For one thing, though Robbins's 'stratification of medieval society' is a suggestive idea in this context, it has not been much pursued,

---

[1] I will not go into the wider discussion of the term 'popular' as it has been applied to the Middle Ages, for example, by Bakhtin and Gurevich: see Gurevich 1988; for Bakhtin, see Gurevich, 176ff. This is obviously of crucial relevance here but it is too wide-ranging a matter for the confines of this chapter.

even in his own introduction. Again, a quite different sense of the word had been employed in one of the most influential early discussions, the essay called 'Some Aspects of Mediaeval Lyric' appended by Chambers and Sidgwick to their attractive 1907 anthology, *Early English Lyrics*. They derived the term 'popular' from Gaston Paris's category *chanson populaire*, which represents 'a stock out of which the more developed art-poetry of Provence itself, no less than that of Northern France, had its origin' (Chambers and Sidgwick 1907, 265). Because this sense influenced the way the term 'popular' was used with regard to the English lyrics, Chambers-Sidgwick's elaboration is important: 'What one claims for the *chanson populaire* is, not that it is folk-song, but that it rests upon folk-song, and that the forms and motives which it adapts still inevitably reflect the manners and the sentiments of the folk by whom they were fashioned' (267). This conception of 'the folk', of course, belongs to its time, bringing to mind contemporary collectors like Augusta Gregory and W. B. Yeats; closer to the medieval lyrics, it recalls the employment of the term by E. K. Chambers in *The Medieval Stage* (1903). However, it is a view of popular literary origins that would not now command much assent. Moreover, it is evident that Chambers and Sidgwick themselves employed the term 'popular' somewhat loosely to judge from their own final use of it: 'the vast compilation made by the Franciscan James Ryman about 1494 chiefly serves to show how savourless a thing popular poetry can become in the adapting hands of a pious and unimaginative ecclesiastic' (292). This has little to do either with the strata of medieval society or folk-song. And in what sense is Ryman popular?

Other editors and critics have shown further uncertainty with the term. In the introduction to his canonical edition of the Harley lyrics, G. L. Brook takes some characteristics of the popular lyric for granted. He says of the *pastourelle*, the debate-poem between lovers, that 'these lyrics are more popular in origin than the lyrics written under the influence of the courtly love convention. Signs of their popular origin are the prominence which they give to the woman's point of view and their preoccupation with the possibility of infidelity' (Brook, 7). Concentration on the situation of the woman seems here almost to be definitive as a popular feature: clearly nothing to do with social stratification. Equally significant is the much-used phrase 'popular in origin', dating from a period when critics rather desperately tried to make a distinction between lyrics which were formally founded on folk-songs and dances (which is what 'popular in origin' suggested), and those which were aimed at an unlearned audience, 'popular by destination'.

Peter Dronke, the most authoritative modern commentator on the European medieval lyric, uses the term 'popular' in ways which are useful and clear; it is characteristic of all his definitive discussions of medieval lyric that he does not get bogged down in classification, being always inclined to turn to textual illustration. The terms 'love-lyric' and 'religious lyric' are used in chapter titles in his book *The Medieval Lyric*; either kind can have popular as well as learned forms. Likewise another of his influential essays bears the significant title: 'Learned Lyric and Popular Ballad in the Early Middle Ages' (Dronke 1984): an altogether clearer opposition. Finally, Rosemary Woolf's admirable brief discussion of the lyrics in her essay in the Sphere History expresses salutary doubt about the whole popular-courtly opposition: 'It has long been the custom to make this distinction, though the surviving evidence that would enable this distinction to be safely applied is so scarce that it is hardly usable as a method of classification' (Woolf 1970, 278). Woolf goes on to doubt whether 'so masterly a verse' as *Westron wynde when wyll thow blow?* (Duncan *LMELC*, No. 105) 'ever sprang from the untrained imagination of the common people' (279). Although her scepticism has been largely disregarded by subsequent editors, I will be returning to it here.

Before moving beyond these purely taxonomic matters and deciding which operative sense needs to be borne in mind in discussing the poems themselves, two other distinctions should be noted. In the introduction to the first of his Penguin anthologies, Thomas Duncan reminds us of Deschamps's distinction between the song lyric and the literary lyric (Duncan *MEL*, xxiv). This is a more substantial distinction with wider aesthetic application, but it is also a useful one for the discussion of the 'popular' because the second category is 'literary' by definition while the song lyric tends to be 'popular'. The distinction also makes good sense of the 'destination' category: the literary lyric is clearly addressed to the same audience at which all written literature aims. The standing of the song lyric remains to be considered. And finally, Muscatine's category of the 'bourgeois'/realistic as opposed to 'courtly' has clear implications for the notion of what is newly popular in the later Middle Ages,[2] particularly for secular literature.

It has been generally recognised that the problems which beset newly emergent bourgeois poetry in the vernacular, as well as those particular to the anonymous lyric, both affect the popular secular lyric in extreme form. Whatever categories we use, there is broad agreement that throughout the Middle English period the religious lyric was much more powerfully represented than the secular. The standard view of the medieval lyrics is that, apart from some miniature masterpieces displaying 'the power of the half-stated' – poems like *Foules in the frith* (Duncan *MEL*, No. 16) – the secular lyrics have not attained the status of a confidently achieved category. Although his dating has now been refined (BM MS Harley 2253 is probably half a century later – c.1340 – than he had placed it), Robbins's observation about the fate of the secular lyric remains broadly true: in the years after that Harley manuscript (assigned by Robbins to his category of 'Friar Miscellanies'), 'the continuity of the secular lyric must be inferred from fragments and hints' (Robbins *Sec.*, xxi). The major critical discussions – those by Woolf and Gray (1972) pre-eminently – are on the religious lyrics; there is no modern wide-ranging critical study of the secular lyrics or the love-lyrics of comparable authority, despite the fact that many of the most admired and cherished poems belong to those categories. Moore (1951) and Oliver (1970) are the two most familiar general treatments of the secular lyric. The former, however, is critically unadventurous and inadequate; thus, Moore's observation about poems such as *Westron wynde* and *Foules in the frith* that the nature setting is 'insufficiently articulated with the poet's love-longing' seems rather to miss the

---

2   See Muscatine 1957, especially ch. 2, 'The Courtly Tradition', and ch. 3, 'The Bourgeois Tradition'.

point of a whole European tradition of the unrequited lover's spring-song. In turn, Oliver's method (despite the promising title of his book) is not conducive to a positive assessment of these poems; it is relentlessly formal and hardly considers the poems as having subjects at all. Such judgements as Oliver does pass do not inspire confidence: 'cliché is endemic to such poems' (136), for instance.

There are several explanations for the failure of a sophisticated criticism of the secular lyric to emerge: the most obvious, and the most commonly given, is that many poems were no doubt lost or never recorded, in an era when religion dictated what was to be taken seriously. Some of the categorical treatments of secular lyrics reflect this failure to be fully canonical; it is for instance something of a shock to find a much-loved masterpiece like *Foules in the frith* consigned in Celia Sisam's excellent *Oxford Book of Medieval English Verse* to an appendix headed 'snatches' (Sisam 1970, 549), a relegation which means that it does not feature in her Index of First Lines. Similarly Robbins found difficulty in placing some undoubtedly popular short poems with music such as *Bryd one brere* (Robbins *Sec.*, No. 147) and puts it into his vaguely superior category of 'Courtly Love Lyrics'.

Of course the fate of the secular lyric is only the most marked instance of what happened in the medieval period in England to the anonymous lyric in general – to the 'poems without names' of Oliver's title. Thus some of the most frequently quoted short scraps of secular poetry come in the chapter on 'Lyrical Poetry' in a book called *The Lost Literature of Medieval England*, the source for most modern readers of such familiar anecdotes as the priest singing *'Swete Lemman, thin are!'* ['Mercy, sweet love!'] presumably because of a tune shared with a more liturgical text (Wilson 1970, ch. 9). We are said to come up against what R. T. Davies memorably calls 'a wall of silence cutting us off from what was doubtless a whole world of song' (Davies 1963, 31). And some of the more canonical poems occur in the oeuvres of major writers such as Chaucer and Dunbar, where they tend to remain as authorial products rather than part of a body of works called 'medieval lyric'.

This precariousness of survival is very unfortunate, given Robbins's conclusions at the end of his introduction. There he takes issue with H. J. Chaytor's view (see Chaytor 1923) that the best – and the majority – of the Middle English secular lyrics were ultimately descended from French and Provençal. Robbins dissents, claiming that there is little French influence in the period after the Black Death when English had a new literary prominence, and concluding that subsequently 'English poetry shows its continuity much more in the secular than in the religious poems' (Robbins *Sec.*, lv). And there is indeed one clear category of indisputably popular poetry which will be the main subject of this essay, a category of poems which has been prominently available since Robbins's edition was completed in 1950 and which is the principal evidence for his claim for the secular lyrics of the fourteenth and fifteenth centuries, that 'the best of these poems have a natural and unaffected charm, a quality which much of the poetry of later centuries has lost' (Robbins *Sec.*, lv). Persuasive as I think this is, it is a case that has been very little argued in criticism of the lyrics. Robbins's first category is headed 'Popular Songs' (a title which, oddly, he also assigns to a sub-section of that category). The full section comprises 60 poems, taking up the anthology's first 57 pages. There is a good brief account of poems of this kind in the introduction to Duncan's second Penguin volume (*LMELC*, xlix–liv), and they are generously represented in his 'Part IV: Popular and Miscellaneous Lyrics' (*LMELC*, Nos 105–150). Duncan raises the question of what popular means for these poems, seeing 'uncourtly' as the primary element (*LMELC*, xlix), a criterion I will return to later. They form a new category in the later Middle Ages in England, according to the traditional account (challenged by Chaytor) quite cut off from the serious tradition of great lyric poetry which prevailed in all the major literary languages of Europe in the *Blütezeit* around 1200, the era of the troubadours, minnesänger and goliards. Robbins's poems are gathered under the headings 'Rhymes of the Minstrels', 'Drinking Songs', 'Love Songs' and 'Popular Songs' (Robbins *Sec.*, vii–viii) – categories which hardly seem mutually exclusive, though they do give a good indication of their popular nature and provenance. Duncan, as I have said, includes them with some other types of poem under the heading 'Popular and Miscellaneous Lyrics' (*LMELC*, x–xi).

There are two crucial ways in which the failure of these poems to find their way into the critical mainstream is unfortunate. First, they at least raise the possibility of incorporating vernacular poems in English into the great traditions of European lyric because they have obvious links with goliardic poetry in metrical expertise and in impropriety of subject matter, both very prominent features. I will argue later that the insistent use of parody is a further link with the Latin goliards. Second, and more important, to ignore these popular poems gives a skewed impression of the tradition of the short poem in English at the beginnings of the Early Modern English period. They meet all the definitive requirements of a formal genre, employing the same patterns, diction and topics across a substantial corpus. This, within its limits, is a whole world of song, in the terms of Wilson or Davies, which is decidedly *not* lost. These poems are also very foreign in temper to what C. S. Lewis devastatingly called 'Drab Age Verse' (Lewis 1954, 222ff.), as Robbins's later category 'Practical Verse' clearly is not, although they have not been invoked to counter that generalisation. It could be claimed that these lively poems are a victim of the recent domination of the criticism of Middle English by religious approaches. They certainly might suggest a world of a rather different temper and spirit as the local background to the Elizabethan lyric-poets and dramatists, as well as making the appearance of goliardic elements in writers such as Dunbar and Skelton less miraculously unprecedented in English.

Often the material of these poems is cheerfully indecent: what Robbins calls 'lewd'. As has always been noted, it is the same indecency which the critical world has happily embraced in Chaucer's *Miller's Tale* and other fabliaux (I will note the similarities in more detail later on). Robbins himself seems rather coy with the material, not commenting for instance on the cheerful description of the fate of 'Old Hogyn' who, in Duncan's words, 'is made the victim of the same prank as that suffered by Absolon in Chaucer's *Miller's Tale*' (*LMELC*, liv):

She torned owt her ars & that he kyst. (Duncan *LMELC*, No. 121, 27)

There has been strikingly little critical consideration of such material, long after even a poet like Rochester has found acceptance in the canon. Such 'lewdness' is obviously not equivalent to 'unlearned'; as Woolf says of the word 'fart' in *The Miller's Tale* and the lyric *Somer is y-comen in* (Duncan MEL, No. 110), 'the belief that "low" words, whether of a lavatorial or sexual meaning, were ever used with innocent seriousness is probably a romantic fantasy of the [twentieth] century' (Woolf 1970, 280). A further revealing parallel to the outrageous events in *The Miller's Tale* is found in '*Alas, good man, most yow be kyst?*' (Robbins *Sec.*, No. 32), a carol Robbins called 'Little Pretty Mopsy' after a line in its burden. There the pleading lover appears to ask as a sexual favour for precisely the liberty that is thrust out of the window by Chaucer's Alison, though it is possible that the line is a dismissal formula, related to the Host's rebuff to the Pardoner that he is asking him to *kisse thyn olde breech* [breeches] (*CT* VI, 948):

> I pray yow, let me kyss yow.
> If that I shall not kyss yow,
> Let me kyss yore karchos nocke. (17–19)   *your body's cleft*

One way and another, it becomes apparent that the implications of the scatological horseplay in *The Miller's Tale* are rather more complex than they have traditionally been thought to be, making even more horrifying, for instance, Absolon's design to burn with a red-hot brand what he expects to be Alison's backside.

In reconsidering then the grounds on which poems were assigned to popular categories or not in the light of their relations with more canonical texts, we might take note of what Robbins says of the love poems which are his Nos 15–32. These are led by the beautiful poems which have been impressively expanded by editors from the packed lines on the flyleaf of Bodl. MS Rawlinson D.913 – *Ich am of Irlaunde*, *Of everykune tre* [Of every kind of tree], *Al night by the rose, rose*, and *Maiden in the mor lay* (Robbins *Sec.*, Nos. 15–18). Having described them as 'among the freshest and most charming of all early English compositions', Robbins adds:

> They are genuinely popular, as is shown by their realistic content, their simple form, and their casual manner of preservation. Many of them have come down only by hazard, being scribbled on the blank leaves of learned books. This group forms a counterpart to the more sophisticated group of lyrics (many with the music preserved). (Robbins *Sec.*, 233)

Once again, this is surely a dubious means of categorization. It seems to compound the misfortune of marginal survival to say that this in itself consigns the poems to the non-sophisticated. It is true that the casual survival of these poems is an important fact; but that is bad luck rather than an index of 'popularity' or otherwise. Their simplicity of form is open to question, their language as we will see, if not their attitudes, is often French-influenced, and, to take one example, Duncan's analysis of the abbreviated Rawlinson text of *Maiden in the mor lay* to establish this lyric's stanzaic structure makes a strong plea for its musical sophistication (see Duncan, above, 32–5). It is even odder to claim 'realistic content' for those poems which are so cryptic that it is not at all clear what their content is. Who is the Irish Dancer? And *Al night by the rose, rose* has the tantalising inexplicitness of Marvell's Mower poems, the quality which often commended short medieval poems in Old and Middle English to the early twentieth-century modernists for manifesting the power of the half-stated. Moreover, as I have been arguing, where elements are shared with Chaucer or (as I will note shortly) *Sir Gawain and the Green Knight*, we should be cautious about assigning these poems to the category of the lesser literary.

To justify, and bring to a close, this necessarily protracted consideration of what exactly might count as 'courtly' or 'popular', I want to quote in full the poem *Of all Creatures women be best* (Robbins *Sec.*, No. 38) from which I have taken the title of this chapter. It is a fairly representative example of the most fully achieved of these poems, and I want to draw on Robbins's discussion of its status in his notes (often his notes remain the most useful criticism of this poetry). It is of interest for many reasons: it occurs in two manuscripts from both of which it has frequently been printed; like many of these poems of light-hearted misogyny it is in the form of a carol and, accordingly, appears in Greene's authoritative collection of carols (Greene, No. 399). Robbins entitles the poem 'Abuse of Women', basing his text on Oxford, Balliol College MS 354, Richard Hill's commonplace book, which is also the source of the improper Old Hogyn poem mentioned above.

> *Of all Creatures women be best:*
> *Cuius contrarium verum est.*

> In every place ye may well see,
> That women be trewe as tirtyll on tree,   *turtle-dove*
> Not lyberall in langage, but ever in secree,   *ever discrete*
> And gret joye amonge them ys for to be.

> The stedfastnes of women will never be don,
> So jentyll, so curtes they be everychon,
> Meke as a lambe, still as a stone,
> Croked nor crabbed fynd ye none!   *perverse*

> Men be more cumbers a thowsand fold,   *trouble*
> And I mervayll how they dare be so bold,
> Agaynst women for to hold,
> Seyng them so pascyent, softe and cold.   *cool*

> For tell a woman all your cownsayle,
> And she can kepe it wonderly well;
> She had lever go quyk to hell,   *rather go alive*
> Than to her neyghbowr she wold it tell!

> For by women men be reconsiled,
> For by women was never man begiled,
> For they be of the condicion of curtes Gryzell   *courteous Griselda*
> For they be so meke and mylde.

> Now say well by women or elles be still,
> For they never displesed man by ther will;
> To be angry or wroth they can no skill,
> For I dare say they think non yll.

Trow ye that women list to smater,   *chatter*
Or agaynst ther husbondes for to clater?
Nay, they had lever fast bred and water   *fast on*
Then for to dele in suche a mater.

Thowgh all the paciens in the world were drownd,
And non were lefte here on the growd,
Agayn in a woman it myght be fownd,
Suche vertu in them dothe abownd!

To the tavern they will not goo,
Nor to the ale-hows never the moo,
For, God wot, ther hartes wold be woo,
To spende ther husbondes money soo.

Yf here were a woman or a mayd,
That lyst for to go fresshely arayd,
Or with fyne kyrchers to go displayed,   *scarves*
Ye wold say, 'they be prowde:' it is yll said.
                         Explicit

What is immediately striking here for the reader of Middle English is the Chaucer resonances, as in many of these poems which have been assigned to minstrels' Autolycan stock-in-trade. There is the explicit reference to the Clerk's patient Griselda (interestingly given the courtly epithet 'courteous' here). Most instructive though are the gender implications of the relation between the function here of 'the destroying burden' (as Robbins aptly dubbed it) with its undercutting line in Latin and *Mulier est hominis confusio* [Woman is man's ruination] (*CT* VII, 3164) in Chaucer's *Nun's Priest's Tale*. This Latin insult is glossed by Chauntecleer for the benefit of his wife as 'Womman is mannes joye and al his blis' (*CT* VII, 3166). Clearly Chauntecleer's procedure is the mirror image of what happens in the burden of the later carol where the praise of woman is announced only to be undermined by a Latin gloss as a kind of conspiracy of the learned.

It does not particularly matter whether the poem helps us to decide who is the butt of Chaucer's joke, Pertelote or Chauntecleer: whether it is the cock's pretentious vanity that is being exposed by the learned conspiracy, rather than the female's lack of Latin – or whether it is even a joke at the audience's expense. The crucial point is that poems like this provide a potentially widening context in which to place the exchange in Chaucer's tale, so it is important that they should be known as a canonical category. In addition this poem, like several others in Robbins's 'minstrel' group, also links instructively to the hilariously bitter marital passage at the start of *The Merchant's Tale*, especially the lines which have always been thought the funniest part of that brilliant diatribe. Here are the words of the starry-eyed ancient January about the joys of marriage:

A wyf! a, Seinte Marie, benedicite!   *blessings!*
How myghte a man han any adversitee
That hath a wyf? Certes, I kan nat seye.
The blisse which that is bitwixe hem tweye
Ther may no tonge telle, or herte thynke.

> If he be povre, she helpeth hym to swynke;   *work*
> She kepeth his good, and wasteth never a deel;   *goods; a bit*
> Al that her housbonde lust, hire liketh weel;   *wishes*
> She seith nat ones 'nay', whan he seith 'ye'.
> 'Do this,' seith he; 'Al redy, sire,' seith she. (*CT* IV, 1337–46)

We can easily supply our lyric's *'cuius contrarium'* to any of these propositions: indeed there may be a hint of this learned superiority in the 'benedicite!'.

Passages like this one from *The Merchant's Tale* could be seen as a dramatisation of an ironic theme which is widely prominent in the lyrics, both popular and courtly. Amongst the later medieval lyrics it is vigorously argued through in the two incomplete Clerk-Nightingale disputations (Robbins *Sec.*, Nos 179 and 180) in which the Clerk, representative of officialdom, is pro-woman while a fiercely ironic version of the conventional anti-feminist case is argued by the Nightingale, the traditional voice of courtly and sexual love. At the extreme point of its impossibility formulae the Nightingale's argument is chilling:

> Clerk, ylk trew woman hath upon,   *wears*
>   Withowt any lesyng,   *lying*
> A robbe of grey marbyl ston   *robe*
>   And of gret compasyng.   *great size*
> (Robbins *Sec.*, No. 180, 39–42)

'Every woman who is faithful wears a tomb of grey marble and of great size': she is only faithful when dead. These poems, of course, are in a learned tradition in which even the non-clerical Nightingale cites Solomon and David in support of its case. But I mention them here, not only to extend the Chaucer lyrics parallel, but also to suggest again that their themes and materials are at root the same as in the popular poems. The popularity is, so to speak, no more than skin deep. It does not belong to a different world, as we found with Robbins's 'Little Pretty Mopsy' discussed above. In short, I believe there is no point in fundamentally dividing up the goliardic category they both belong to.

In considering the question of the generic separability of such categories, we might also examine the overall context of these popular poems with their Chaucer parallels which are unmissable by the modern reader of Middle English. Several are found in Oxford, Balliol MS 354, the contents of which are summarised by Douglas Gray as follows:

> A livelier taste is found in the commonplace book of the grocer Richard Hill, which contains that marvellously evocative and mysterious poem the 'Corpus Christi Carol', and has a remarkable range of English poetry, as well as puzzles, riddles, useful information, family records, and a chronicle of public events. (Gray 1988, xviii)

This breadth of content – especially the occurrence of the 'Corpus Christi Carol', one of the greatest early English poems – should lead us to be prepared for sophistication in the poems, whether categorised as popular or not.

We may likewise be led to take issue with the classification Robbins offers of such poems in his note to *Of all Creatures women be best*:

As with the poems attacking marriage and poems treating of love in a mocking fashion, so here in poems of attacks on womankind, there are two main classes: popular poems and sophisticated poems. In the minstrel collection, Bodl. MS. Eng. poet. e.1 [the other manuscript containing this poem], a MS. containing the popular songs of the day, collected to meet a genuine popular demand, and not collected because they appealed to the interests of a single literate poetaster, there are many attacks on women . . . Then there are the literary attacks . . . These poems quickly developed stereotyped conventions, and the sophisticated attacks parallel the set descriptions of the beloved and of the routine love epistles. (Robbins *Sec.*, 238–9)

This follows the traditional opposition between the popular and the sophisticated, but it is hard to see what purpose this speculation serves, or how to reconcile it with Gray's description of the parallel manuscript's contents quoted above. And who is the undistinguished-sounding absent 'single literate poetaster'? Amongst the poems in his anthology that Robbins assigns to the 'sophisticated' category are three 'pseudo' items: one each of 'pseudo-Chaucer', 'pseudo-Lydgate' and 'pseudo-Hoccleve'. No doubt the non-attributions here are correct. But the only categorical purpose this pseudo-poet/poetaster category serves, is to suggest a second-class quality in their work, that – by contrast with the 'popular' minstrels' songs – these are 'routine' love epistles and that they feature 'set descriptions'. On the other hand, there is much to be said for abandoning such authorial distinctions and for simply seeing the popular poems as similar works whose authors are unknown, in the same way that the beautiful anonymous courtly-love poem *O Mestres, whye* (Robbins *Sec.*, No. 137) – called by Davies 'My mistress of Savoy' – belongs to precisely the same category as Wyatt's *My Lute and I* with which it shares a tune. As a parallel, there wouldn't seem to be much point in expending energy in deciding whether Dowland is popular or sophisticated. It seems to me that, beyond noting that they are anonymous, there is likewise no reason to separate off these popular poems from the literary world of Chaucer, Lydgate and Hoccleve to which they are related – as they are to the poems of Dunbar, Skelton and the Elizabethans. The more important conclusion to this discussion, though, is that the separation of categories has worked to the disadvantage of both: the 'popular' came not to be taken seriously, and the more ambitious 'literary' efforts were assigned to 'literate poetasters'.

Our objective then must be to establish these late medieval popular poems, preserved in many commonplace books and what are somewhat circularly called 'minstrels' collections', as a serious presence in the canon of short poems in English. For the rest of this essay I shall describe them in some detail. For convenience we can still concentrate on the sixty poems of Robbins's opening two sections of which 21 come from what he calls the 'Minstrel Collections'; the other 39 are from various places – Commonplace Books, scraps of English poetry interleaved in Latin manuscripts and elsewhere. The only difference, it seems, between 'Minstrel Collections' and 'Commonplace Books' is that the former term seems to apply only to manuscripts whose contents were confined to poetry though there is an interesting hint in Robbins's note to his No. 56, entitled 'A Boar's Head Carol, III', that the term 'Commonplace' carries some of its pejorative connotations:

The next two stanzas are merely versified quatrains of the dishes at a medieval banquet. At this point the versifier apparently lost interest in his song, and added the remainder of the catalogue in three rhymed couplets. This approach is what might be expected in a commonplace book such as Porkington MS.10.

(Robbins *Sec.*, 243)

This, again, is rather strange: is the compiler of this commonplace book a scribe or is he also the 'versifier' – what in a more exalted literary context might be called the 'poet'? Moreover, this 'approach' is certainly not that of Richard Hill, citizen of London, who compiled his commonplace book, Balliol MS 354, over a period of some thirty years up to 1536. In a similarly cavalier spirit Robbins confidently identifies the whole section as 'the poems circulated among the "lewd" ', and warms to the theme of their popularity: they are 'the songs which would be sung at popular gatherings in the hall, in the inn, on the green, on the road' (Robbins *Sec.*, xxxiv). We have come to be suspicious of these subjunctive assertions of what must have prevailed in the roadside hostelries of medieval England; but this characterisation is broadly workable. We might see such poems – whether learned in origin or not – as literature of the profane world as opposed to the shared writing of the religious and courtly world. Again this is broadly the same distinction as Duncan makes in his opening attempt, noted already, to decide in what sense these poems might be called 'popular': 'Some may be said to be un-courtly' (*LMELC*, xlix).

This opposition, also proposed with reference to the language of Middle English literature by David Burnley, is arguably the most enlightening way of placing these 'minstrel' poems. Burnley, like many critical predecessors, draws attention to 'the mutuality of language and concepts enjoyed by the religious and secular love lyrics' which 'allowed the poet to combine in the same poem a frank appreciation of the lady's physical beauty with a confident prayer for Christ's approval of his true love for her' (Burnley 1998b, 193). It is precisely this mutuality, especially of concepts, that the 'popular' poems do not share. They are not respecters of persons, in the way that the religious and courtly-secular both are; their version of 'the lady's physical beauty', to begin with, is couched very differently. What separates them is their attitude: one might call it their manners. Thus Robbins's first poem, which he entitles 'A Minstrel's Greeting', is in the form of a carol with a half-French macaronic burden beginning *Bon jowre, bon jowre a vous* and has an imprecation *by Mary myld* before concluding *Explicit* (Robbins, *Sec.*, No. 1). Yet this is a brilliantly accessible poem of a drunkard, made belligerent and insulting by drink. Chaucer's Miller concedes *I am dronke, I knowe it by my soun* (*CT* I, 3138); and we can tell just as certainly by this lyric's voice that the speaker is drunk, like that of Robbins No. 14 from the same manuscript (Balliol 354) who starts off bawling at the butler – the barman – for more drink: *Jentill butler, bell amy*. Robbins's title, 'A Minstrel's Greeting', euphemises the voice nicely:

Loo, this is he that will do the dede!	*get something done*
He tempereth his mowth, therefore take hede.	*is restraining (with difficulty)*
. . .	
Sir, what say ye with your face so lene?	

. . .
Sir, what say ye with your fat face?
. . .

    Nay, be nat ashamed;
    Ye shall not be blamed,
    For ye have ben famed   *reputed*
The worst in this Contrey!
    Bon jowr.
        Explicit (18–19, 25, 33, 45–8)

If literary sophistication is the achievement of its aim, then this qualifies as well as the Miller. Furthermore it links to the classic mincing drunkard's monologue from Rawlinson D.913 in which the speaker is trying to stay on his feet: *Stondet alle stille* – / *stille, stille, stille* (Robbins *Sec.*, No. 117, 7–8), a highly sophisticated piece of comic writing, included by Robbins as 'Occasional Verse'.[3]

Here we might repeat Woolf's acute observation quoted already, that 'innocent seriousness' in the deployment of low language is a romantic invention. We might return too to a striking link here with another cornerstone of the Ricardian canon. It seems in keeping with the assignment of these poems to 'popular gatherings in the inn, the green, the road' that in the poem called by Robbins 'The Serving Maid's Holiday' the heroine should predict (or male-fantasise?) that Jacke will

    . . . take me be the hand
    And he wolle legge me on the lond,   *lay*
    That al my buttockus ben of sond
        Opon this hye holyday. (Robbins *Sec.*, No. 29, 29–32)

To see how this is popular as opposed to courtly we have only to recall the expectations and sense of ceremony associated with the *hye holyday* in the opening sections of *Sir Gawain and the Green Knight*. One might of course complicate the generic discussion by recalling that there is at least one poem in the Richard Hill commonplace book which is much closer to the requirements of the ceremonial spirit of the opening of *Sir Gawain*:

    Lett no man cum into this hall –
    Grome, page, nor yet marshall,
    But that sum sport he bryng with-all
        For now ys the tyme of Crystmas. (Robbins *Sec.*, No. 2, 1–4)

However, the comparison between *Gawain* and Robbins's popular serving-maid can be intriguingly extended by a consideration of the cheerfully crude term 'buttocks' here. One might have thought that it would occur more naturally in this popular context than in the courtly context of *Gawain* where famously it occurs rather shockingly in the description of the ugly old woman who accompanies Bercilak's beautiful wife. The old woman, in contrast to her young

---

[3] A different understanding of this poem is offered by Burrow (1984, 11–12) who argues that it is a dance song. See also Duncan *MEL*, 243–4.

companion with *hir brest and hir bright throte bare displayed*, has lips which *were soure to se and sellyly blered*:

> Hir body was short and thik,
> Hir buttokez baly and brode.   *bulbous*
>
> (*Sir Gawain and the Green Knight*, 955–67)

The striking point though is that the word 'buttocks' is unique to its genre in both contexts: that is, according to Preston's *Concordance* to 1,328 poems, 'The Serving Maid's Holiday' is the only short poem in Middle English to use it; and according to Kottler and Markham's *Concordance* to the four poems of the *Gawain*-poet and *St Erkenwald*, this – perhaps less surprisingly – is the only occurrence of the term in those five poems.

I have dwelt on the lexical case of buttocks because it again focuses interestingly the matter of 'lewdness' in these poems. The poems in this popular category *are* often rude, but within a narrow conventionalised compass. For one thing, the various sexual encounters – seductions, flings and fantasies – end in pregnancy with rather tedious and moralising inevitability. They are dictated by precedents that are essentially literary, even if one of the conventional literary topics is the sexual or lavatorial matter that Woolf notes. Even at the start of the twenty-first century, in an age that often feels itself to have moved dramatically towards permissiveness in sexual mores and reference, we can still be relatively prudish in our response to some of these poems – or at least find them tediously protracted by lewd convention. So Robbins says of poems such as *At the northe ende of selver white* and *May no man slepe in youre halle* (Robbins *Sec.*, Nos 30 and 31, both from CUL MS Additional 5043) that in them 'the double entendre is marked' and that 'although these songs are apparently sophisticated, nevertheless the tone of these two poems suggests a popular usage' (Robbins *Sec.*, 236). The second poem, which he entitles 'In My Lady's Chamber', urges *madame* not to allow any man to *slepe* in her *halle* for fear of dogs, rats and flies between her legs, laps or thighs – proceeding, Oliver claims rather puzzlingly, 'with inscrutable logic' (Oliver 1970, 105). Even Duncan, who is not prudishly inclined, concedes that some of these poems are 'rather crude' (*LMELC*, liii).

However, Duncan also places them in the right context I think: they are all essays in a well-trodden literary tradition of satire and parody. This tradition might be – and has traditionally been – called anti-feminist; it certainly centres on representations of women in a way that the modern consumer recognises as male fantasy, and it is of course the world of Chaucer's Wife of Bath or Jean de Meun's Vieille in *The Romance of the Rose*. But it can be linked to another extensive set of poems within the series and another important context whose undeveloped critical treatment has contributed to the under-representation of these poems. It has long been a commonplace of observation that there is little study or understanding of the function of parody in medieval English literature. More widely, indeed, we are rather uncomprehending of the precise operation of parody in medieval culture as a whole. Why exactly was the parodic treatment of sacred subjects – in medieval drama for instance – tolerated in an era when the sacred was all-important? Why were the Latin goliards of the twelfth century allowed to compose parodies of the most sacred texts: for example the address to alcohol which parodied the 'Our Father', beginning *'Potus noster qui es in cypho'* ['Our drink who art in cup']?

Medieval parody has only been much studied in relation to Latin literature: to the goliards and the wide traditions of constructing formal parodies of the most central religious texts. The understanding of these traditions for the English reader was greatly advanced by the recent appearance of Martha Bayless's substantial study *Parody in the Middle Ages. The Latin Tradition.* Two things in Bayless's discussion are particularly significant for a discussion of the lyrics. First she notes that the highly developed Latin practice of parody is widely reflected in vernacular medieval literature, though that is not the concern of her book. Secondly, she makes this important observation:

> Parody was a popular form in all senses of the word: in its quotidian concerns, continuously adapted versions, and *low status in the literary hierarchy*; and in its widespread appeal to audiences. (Bayless 1996, 10: my italics)

(She might have added lewdness: on her first page she notes that medieval humour 'may still alarm those who, like Chaucer's Absolon, are "squeamish of farting" '.) But parody has hardly been mentioned in the context of the Middle English lyric, despite its clear bearing on the relations between secular and religious forms. A carol in praise of ivy (Robbins *Sec.*, No. 52) has a macaronic burden, the Latin line of which is repeated at the end of each stanza as a refrain:

> Ivy, chefe off treis it is;
> Veni, coronaberis.   *Come: you shall be crowned*
>
> The most worthye she is in towne –
> He that seyth other do amysse –
> And worthy to ber the crowne.
> Veni, coronaberis. (1–4)

In his notes Robbins comments:

> 'Veni, coronaberis' (*Song of Songs*, iv. 8) is more properly found as the burden and refrain of a carol to the Blessed Virgin by James Ryman (*Index*, No. 641); and as the refrain of a Song on the Assumption (*Index*, No. 3225). This parodying of a poem in honour of the Virgin is continued by the phraseology (especially in lines 3 and 6). In *Index*, No. 2735, the popular praise of Ivy is given a religious interpretation by the acronym I (Ihesus), V (Virgin), and E (Emmanuel).
> (Robbins *Sec.*, 242)

These parallels are clearly of great interest, and of course the exploration of the 'twilight area' between the religious and the secular has been the most sustained and successful critical approach to the lyrics; but as long as poems like the one just quoted remain confined to a setting amongst the Holly and Ivy, and Boar's Head Songs in the loose category of 'Popular Songs' they will fail to be given the attention that has been accorded to works in the more official, clerical tradition. What I am suggesting in general is that this whole category of poems is simply the transfer of the goliardic, with all its learning, mock-learning, anti-feminism and wit, into the English vernacular. In the case in question, indeed, the parody element can be taken further; in her closing section Bayless shows the acronym to be a staple both of religious poems and prayers, and of the goliardic parodying of them. Of the Holly-and-Ivy carols Duncan says 'they are closely related to folk-song' (*LMELC*, li), a proposition which raises the taxonomic issues discussed in the early section of this essay. While there is doubtless some connexion with folk-song in theme and vocabulary, the parodic connexions with the religious lyric are of at least equal significance, as it was for the Latin goliards. But we are less likely to see that link because it is a genre that has hardly been touched in the medieval secular lyric.[4]

To ignore this context is not simply a matter of failing to establish a genre; it is also a consequence of the limited kinds of criticism the secular lyrics have been subject to. So, finally, I want to suggest briefly what an active criticism of these poems might find, once they have been recognised as representing a significant presence of parody within the canon of early English poetry. Although much productive scholarly energy has been expended in the establishment of texts, date and geographical provenance, these lyrics have tended to remain what Burrow, with reference to the lyrics in Bodl. MS Rawlinson D.913, felicitously called 'Poems without Contexts' (Burrow 1984, 1–26). As an example of the kind of criticism which these poems have tended to lack, we might look briefly, for contrast, at a non-popular area, to the discussion of one of the linguistically intricate Harley lyrics, *Weping haveth myn wonges wet* (Brook, No. 6), one of those which certainly do have links with the learned traditions of European lyric of the high Middle Ages. In a very incisive, but brief and almost apologetic, foray into critical reading, Bennett and Gray comment as follows on this enigmatic Harley lyric of ostensible love-longing:

> There is occasionally . . . rhetorical decoration – the phrase 'bruches broken' nicely plays with two etymologically related, as well as alliterating, words. This writer can be allusive (in the second stanza he refers, successively, to Eve, to the story of Aristotle – a wise man made a fool by love – being ridden by a girl, the Virgin Mary, and to the common image of Christ entering her womb like light through glass – this last being boldly and imaginatively treated), but the argument is not complex, nor the thought profound. (Bennett and Gray 1986, 400)

It is rare to find criticism of this 'metaphysical' awareness applied to the lyrics at all, even to the highly sophisticated Harley poems.

But what might such linguistically alert criticism find in the popular secular lyrics, a category which has been defined as less sophisticated and which is almost never read in these ways? What kind of closer verbal analysis might be applicable to them, to establish perhaps the lines along which their parody works? It is a crucial critical question, if only in explaining why we like what we like. What is the spirit of the popular song which stays in the mind of everyone who encounters it?

---

[4] For an extended sample of the Latin poems, we can still turn profitably to Helen Waddell's *The Wandering Scholars* (described by its author as 'a kind of imperfect history of medieval lyric') and her *Medieval Latin Lyrics*, as well as to F. J. E. Raby's *Oxford Book of Medieval Latin Verse*.

> A woman ys a worthy thyng –
> They do the wash and do the wrynge;
> 'Lullay, lullay,' she doth the sing,   *thee*
> And yet she hath but care and woo. (Robbins *Sec.*, No. 34, 5–8)

Is this a genuine praise of woman, as Robbins entitles it: or at least sympathetic to the hardship and exploitation of women, in a way that the cruder sarcasm of my title-poem 'Abuse of Women' is not?

> The stedfastnes of women will never be don,
> So jentyll, so curtes they be everychon,
> Meke as a lambe, still as a stone,
> Croked nor crabbed fynd ye none!   *perverse*
> (Robbins *Sec.*, No. 38, 5–8)

Clearly an analysis of *A woman ys a worthy thyng* is unlikely to yield the etymological depth of the linked senses in the Harley lyrics; but a certain characteristic strength is to be found in the simplicity and – often claimed – directness of these poems. It tempts us to invoke the dangerous concept of sincerity, a quality which can only be suggested by artful rhetorical skill. And a related strength can be found in another poem from Robbins's first category, *The man that I loved altherbest* (Robbins *Sec.*, No. 22), entitled (I think rather inappropriately) 'Careless love'. This poem begins as a conventional love-lament by the estranged or unrequited lover – *to me he ys a strange gest* (3) – though already it is a surprise in this spring-poem that the unseasonal unfulfilment is in a female voice. The female voice in the popular lyrics is traditionally coquettish rather than lovelorn. The end approaches, however, with an even more daring inversion of the experience of the lover in spring:

> I am i-comfertyd in every syde,
> The colures wexeth both fres and newe; *fresh*
> When he ys come and wyl abyde
> I wott ful wel that he ys trywe. (17–20)   *know; true*

To appreciate this poem's achievement we have to see it as a sophisticated variation on a literary theme rather than an unschooled effusion, as a reversal of the norm of the *reverdie* which customarily contrasts the natural colours of spring, 'fresh and new', with the lover's despair – classically in a poem like *Foules in the frith* where the libidinous activity of birds and fishes makes the unrequited lover *waxe wod* [go mad].

As a final example of a salutary critical process from which the lyric has mostly not benefited, we might recall the essential issue of *New Literary History* in Winter 1979, in which our relations with the 'alterity and modernity' of medieval literature were debated by many of the era's leading medievalists, both theoretical and New Critical (Zumthor, Jauss, Burrow and others). When Jauss itemises the set of medieval genres with which we have to become familiar in order to close the hermeneutic gap between us and the Middle Ages, the lyric is not even mentioned. And we have been even less successful in closing the gap between us and medieval popular lyrics, even when their materials were patently shared with Chaucer and his contemporaries.

Of course nobody would argue that this body of late medieval popular English poems is a major genre. These poems, however, are a major presence in the developing world of medieval and renaissance English poetry: an element without which it is not seen whole. Standard accounts of the history of English literature have represented Chaucer as making the courageous decision to write in unfashionable English and to hew out of it a new literary language, turning his back on French and the other dominant languages of medieval literature. The testimony of the lyrics is not only that there was a 'whole world of song' in English all around him but also that it was an established and confident corpus with its own themes and practices to which his writing links widely. This large body also extends across genres, into parody of form and situation. It has never been doubted that this was true of the religious lyric, as reflected in the successful studies by Gray and Woolf; the same may also be claimed for the secular lyric, not just the expressive scraps like *Foules in the frith* and *Westron wynde* which are eloquent but marginal relatives of the great European love-tradition of the Latin and Provençal poets, but just as much the popular carolling tradition of the 'minstrels', whoever or whatever they were. It is particularly important to establish that genre because of its close links to Chaucerian stories and episodes, particularly in *The Canterbury Tales*. And of course it should not surprise us that a crucial definitive feature of this Chaucer-linked form is parody.

One of the universal co-options to the popular cause is *Westron wynde* with which Duncan starts the popular section of his second volume (Duncan *LMELC*, 135). Despite Woolf's persuasive (if somewhat patrician) argument quoted already that 'there is no evidence that so masterly a verse ever sprang from the untrained imagination of the common people' (Woolf 1970, 279), one can understand the wish to co-opt it (just as its origins in a sixteenth-century song-book has enabled editors to claim it for the courtly category). In particular the imprecation in 'Christ! if my love were in my arms' seems to link it with the modern popular lyric: Dylan seems to quote it. While there has been a readiness to recognise the works of named poets like Charles d'Orléans, there has been less of a critical urge to hail the anonymous lewd songs of sandy buttocks or the expert literary variations on the themes of anti-feminism: the charms of *A woman ys a worthy thyng*. One may readily go along with Robbins's claim (already quoted above) that 'the best of these poems have a natural and unaffected charm, a quality which much of the poetry of later centuries has lost' (Robbins *Sec.*, lv). But there is much more to be said: these poems are also to be seen both as the mediators of some important aspects of the European literary tradition (and not least of the lyrics within that tradition) and as a vigorous, well-defined body of lyric at the start of Early Modern English literature.

11

Gender and Voice in
Middle English Religious Lyrics

SARAH STANBURY

In Middle English lyric poetry, most of which is anonymous, only a few fragments and poems can be can be identified as the work of named women poets. One of these is a *Hymn to Venus*, attributed in its single manuscript to 'Queen Elizabeth', probably Elizabeth Woodville, the wife of Edward IV. Another is a hymn to the Virgin described by the scribe John Shirley as being *by an holy Ankaresse of Maunsffeld*. Yet another is also a poem in praise of the Virgin described in its manuscript as the prayer (*oratio*) of Eleanor Percy (Barratt 1992, 262–3; 275–81). Thus, of the sizable corpus of Middle English lyrics extant today, only three poems, all from the fifteenth and early sixteenth centuries, have been identified as the work of specific female writers.[1] With other lyrics, assumptions we might make about the gender of the poet rest with voicing, subject matter, or the cluster of inferences and implications we might call attitude. As Sarah McNamer has convincingly argued, some of the poems in the late fifteenth-century Findern manuscript may be the work of female poets. This judgment is based on evidence in the manuscript that women from prominent local families copied the poems, on the large number of unique poems in this manuscript, on the voicing of some of the lyrics from a woman's point of view, and on the approach taken to the subject of these lyrics which, in all cases, is love (McNamer 1991, 279–302). It is also possible that women may have written a number of the extant devotional poems. Alexandra Barratt suggests that some lyrics in which the Virgin laments the death of her son and lyrics of the Passion might have been the work of female poets (Barratt 1992, 262). In the case of these devotional poems, as with the love lyrics of the Findern manuscript, speculations about the gender of the poet are based on style, subject matter, and point of view: there is no hard evidence to tell us whether they were written by men or women.[2]

In a search for the poet behind the words in the manuscript, we might expect the point of view of the poem's speaker to give us the best evidence. Although

---

1 For, in addition, a carol praising King Henry VIII, possibly by Queen Catherine, see Gray (above), 146, note 57.
2 The possibility of a poem by a woman written in the voice of a man or *vice versa* is not to be discounted. An excellent example of the latter is found in Lydgate's 'balade sayde by a gentil-womman whiche loved a man of gret estate' – see Gray (above), 133.

theories of 'the persona' and 'the speaker' as propounded by modernist critics such as Booth and Eliot have given rise to generations of critics trained to be suspicious of any simple equation between the voice of the narrator and the voice of the writer, lyric has always resisted this divorce.[3] Lyric is the autobiographical genre above all others. Whereas we expect the 'I' in narrative to be an imaginative construction, we expect the lyric 'I' to be speaking for the poet. Why lyric resists the splitting of persona from poet is a complicated question; but it may be, in part, that lyric is housed in isolation: as Helen Vendler puts it, 'lyric is the genre of private life; it is what we say to ourselves when we are alone' (Vendler 2002, xlii). Narrative gives a history, tells a story that takes place in linear time, and moves through places; narratives often require houses peopled by characters along with their friends and enemies. Lyric poems, on the other hand, lack these accoutrements. Lyrics take place outside of history and out of time. If a lyric has characters, they are typically only the speaker and one other, his or her love. Lyrics are utterances, not stories. Without a house to live in, the only space for the lyric persona is in the being of the poet.

Such assumptions and expectations about an autobiographical lyric 'I' may not, however, apply so neatly to Middle English lyrics. The term 'lyric' first appeared in the late sixteenth century, and only in the late nineteenth century did it come to mean a poem of private emotion, 'the expression by the poet of his own feelings' as Ruskin defined it in 1873.[4] In medieval England the short vernacular poems we now call lyrics were referred to in their manuscripts as prayers, meditations, or treatises (Woolf, 1). Some were performed as songs, and a few appeared in the dramatic mystery cycles. Thus while many Middle English lyrics appear to speak for the life of an individual, that private life, as Vendler says, also has a public dimension through performance. Sung or performed aloud and live, the lyric 'I' takes on a visible persona, one that may be many degrees of separation from its original creator. Performance slips in new characters to break up the intimate rapport between the reader and the poet/narrator. In the many lyrics that adopt the voice of Jesus speaking from the cross, the lyric 'I' might well have been performed as part of a Crucifixion play. Christ speaking from the cross often takes the persona of the Man of Sorrows, an immensely popular subject in fifteenth-century art.[5] The single and private utterance in these lyrics thus has a distinctly public, and even narrative, dimension. The speaking 'I' reaches out verbally to a community of believers, or even to a congregation. Through their ventriloquized voicing and rehearsal of a well-known devotional episode, 'Man of Sorrows' lyrics articulate the ritual life of the community.

---

3   The modernist bible on narrative voicing is no doubt Wayne Booth's *Rhetoric of Fiction* (1961). On lyric voicing see Eliot 1954; here the term 'persona', attributed to Ezra Pound (22), is used to describe the imaginary voice adopted in a dramatic monologue. For Eliot on lyric, which he also calls 'meditative verse' (27), see 25–31.

4   See *OED* under **Lyric** A. *adj.* 1., where Ruskin is quoted. See also Woolf, 1, fn. 1, and McNamer 1991, 299.

5   For an excellent discussion of the links between the Man of Sorrows in devotional art and the theme in lyrics of the Passion, see Woolf, 183–238, and her brief Appendix on the history of the *imago pietatis*, 389–91.

Performance also complicates assumptions we might make about the relationship between the voice of the speaker and the actual gender of the poet. John Plummer has convincingly argued that lyrics which he calls 'woman's songs', those in which the narrator adopts the persona of a woman who has been betrayed in love, actually belong to the genre of anti-feminist satire rather than to the lament, and are probably the work of male writers (Plummer 1981, 150–1). Depicting situations of betrayal and humiliation, and artfully fulfilling misogynist stereotypes even as they purport to be authentic emotional outpourings of lovelorn and betrayed women, these poems reveal bedroom secrets and work to paint their speakers as libidinous, dependent and wrathful. In such poems the narrative 'I', Plummer argues, sits in inverse relation to the gender of the poet. If these poems had been read aloud by a male reader, as they probably were, one can well imagine how the cross-gendered performance could have furthered their satiric edge.

Yet play with categories of gender in Middle English lyrics is not only a function of aspects of performance. In many lyrics, particularly laments and dialogues at the cross, point of view, articulated both through the voices as well as through the gazes of the reader and internal viewers, repeatedly unsettles expectations we might have about male/female relationships. Middle English religious lyrics often use the family as a framework for exploring devotional relationships, but will transform familial relationships, sometimes in dramatic ways, to imagine not only new forms of devotion but also new forms of family. The redemptive promise and, indeed, the 'passion' of many Passion lyrics derives in part from their re-imagining of domestic affiliations and feelings. When the speaker adopts a female voice, often it will be as the Virgin, addressing her son on the cross or speaking to the reader as she describes her grief. Although she speaks within a pre-defined familial role, she adopts an extraordinarily wide range of emotional personae: mother, lover, intimate friend. To imagine life *in extremis* is to imagine how one might act in that situation, and the laments at the cross are no exception: What would you do? What would you feel? What would you say? Through their voicing, the dialogues at the cross quite literally give women a speaking part, and one that gives dramatic rhetorical range to heroic sacrifice.

The flexible uses of categories of family, sexuality, gender, and the body are a marked feature of late medieval devotional language and imagery generally, appearing throughout Middle English religious lyrics as well as in meditative guides and treatises. In a fifteenth-century lament, *As reson rywlyde my rechyles mynde* (Brown *XV*, No. 6), the Virgin speaks of Jesus as *my fadur, my brother, my spouse* (52), imagining him as close to her in multiple permutations of male intimacy. This cross-category troping, particularly in the narrator's relationship to Christ, takes other forms as well. Christ in lyrics of the Passion is often described as a chivalric knight; he is also repeatedly desired and mourned in the language of courtly love. While these category-crossings are typical of devotional writings in general, they appear with particular urgency in the spiritual writings of medieval women, with perhaps the most striking example being the image of Jesus as a mother, nurturing and nourishing us with his milk, a trope brilliantly elaborated by Julian of Norwich in her *Revelations* (Crampton 1994, chapters 57–62).

As recent work by Caroline Walker Bynum, Karma Lochrie, Amy Hollywood and others has demonstrated, female spirituality in the late Middle Ages was characterized by a drive to experience an embodied spirituality that fused body and spirit. Women's bodies could even become the site of spiritual mystery and revelation.[6] Miraculous pregnancies and lactations, uncontrolled weeping, preservation of the body after death, and the five wounds of the stigmata are just some examples of the ways the divine could be seen to show itself in a woman's body (Bynum 1991, 194). Through its most prosaic capacities – bleeding, weeping, or lactating – the female body could itself articulate God's special grace.

Perhaps the best-known Middle English lyric to use the paradoxes of familial category-crossing as a central feature of its devotional plan is *I syng of a mayden* (Duncan *MEL*, No. 79). In this poem the *mayden . . . makeles* of the opening lines, identified in the final stanza as the Virgin Mary, is presented throughout as a courtly maiden, in tryst with her lover/son.

I syng of a mayden
    that is makeles,   *peerless*
King of alle kinges
    to here sone she ches.   *as her son she chose*

He cam also stylle   *as silently*
    ther his moder was,   *where his mother was*
As dew in Aprylle
    that falleth on the gras.

He cam also stylle
    to his moderes bowr,   *bower*
As dew in Aprille
    that falleth on the flour.   *flower*

He cam also stille
    ther his moder lay,   *where*
As dew in Aprille
    that falleth on the spray.   *leafy branch*

Moder and mayden
    was never non but she –   *was never anyone*
Wel may swych a lady   *such*
    Godes moder be!   *mother*

The shock of this poem lies in its eroticizing of incest as a trope for the holy. The son comes as still *as dew in Aprylle* (7, 11, 15) to his mother's bower, an extraordinarily rich simile that conveys, at once, both sexuality and vernal purity. The approach as dew represents, of course, the Incarnation;[7] but this poem plays the son as lover, incarnating himself. Where is the father? If we can speak of 'the

---

6   Bynum 1991; Lochrie 1991, esp. 'The Body as Text and the Semiotics of Suffering', 13–55; Hollywood 2002.

7   The Biblical story of the dew which fell on Gideon's fleece (see Judges 6) was allegorically understood in the Middle Ages as representing the descent of the Holy Ghost upon Mary at the Incarnation.

work' of this lyric, it would be to explain the paradox of Mary's virginal maternity. How can virginity and maternity coexist? How can Mary be both *Moder and mayden* (17)? That paradox, itself a disruption of categories, is, uniquely in this poem, expressed in an act of desire transcending taboo. This is not to suggest that this lyric is a celebration of incest, but to argue that it celebrates desire, even in its sexual form, as a powerfully transformative force, what Georges Bataille calls 'sanctified transgression' (Bataille 1986, 90). Here the paradox of virgin maternity is all the more astonishing because of the absence of an inseminating God the father. Maternal love is not so far from erotic love; and in this lyric, which effaces the agency of the father, the relationship between a mother and her son imagines a new kind of family as well as a hybrid spirituality that seems to acknowledge female sexuality and bodiliness.

Another well-known lyric that uses an erotic relationship between Christ and its central character as the basis for transfigured devotion and transformed family violence is the fourteenth-century poem *Undo thi dore, my spuse dere* (Brown *XIV*, No. 68).[8] This lyric makes brilliant use of the mystery of ambiguous voicing; the first speaker, whom we learn only later is Christ, takes the persona of a wife or husband locked outside. The poem sets up a story immediately to reconfigure its terms. It appears to start as a domestic squabble, or even as a picture of domestic violence. One spouse, bloodied 'for thy sake', stands outside, moaning at the keyhole:

Undo thi dore, my spuse dere,	*spouse*
Allas! why stond I loken out here?	*locked*
Fre am I thi make.	*noble; male*
Loke mi lokkes and ek myn heved	*locks, head*
And al my bodi with blod be-weved	*covered*
For thi sake. (1–6)	

The speaker of the opening lines implores a *spuse dere* to open the door. The term 'spouse' immediately implies a marriage, but it is uncertain whether the voice outside the door is male or female. Since the speaker is covered with blood, the voice could be that of a battered wife; but since the speaker bears wounds gained 'for thy sake', the voice might just as well be that of a husband who has just defended his wife's honour. This ambiguity, I believe, is important for the shift in voicing that comes following the lament of the banished lover. In the third stanza, where the point of view moves to the spouse inside, behind the door, the spouse outside is identified as Jesus. Here, however, there occurs a significant modulation in the affinity of the speakers.

'Alas! Alas! evel have I sped,	*badly have I fared*
For senne Jesu is fro me fled,	*sin*
Mi trewe fere'. (7–9)	*companion*

---

8   Brown prints this lyric as it appears in NLS MS Advocates 18.7.21, John of Grimestone's preaching book. A different version is found in London, Lambeth Palace Library MS 557, on the evidence of which it would appear that in Grimestone's text the order of lines 1–6 and 7–12 has been reversed and lines 13–22 (which depart from the stanza form of lines 1–16) have been added. Needless to say, the different versions of this lyric invite different interpretations. See, for instance, Whitehead (above), 104–5.

In the shift from *spuse dere* of line 1 to *trewe fere* in line 9, explicit spousal and heterosexual gendering appears to give way to a more companionate relationship;[9] this shift also makes for a redefinition of the persona of lines 7–9 as sinful humanity in general. And gender now seems to evaporate as a significant category. The speaker's longing, expressed in the poem's last couplet, mimics Christ's desire and demand at the outset: desiring to be pierced with Christ's love, as if with the spear of Longinus, and begging for a place of residence, he or she will also be bloodied, but this time with love.

> Perce myn herte with thi lovengge,
> That in the I have my dwellingge. (21–2)   *in thee I may have*

That act of piercing will also open the door so that the 'I' of the final line can have a place to live. Following a dramatic beginning that locates its personae on two sides of a door playing out a domestic scene, the act of transcendence performed by the shift in voice in the third stanza is all the more marked. In this transformation of love and reconciliation, gender is indeterminate and, the lyric seems to say, unimportant. Men and women can both experience contrition, and in much the same way.

The central metaphor in this lyric is the house, and the desire it voices is for domestic intimacy: opening the door, living with Jesus. This drive to fracture distance, a desire that often crosses or blurs lines of gender, is characteristic generally of lyrics of the Passion. An early fourteenth-century lyric of the Passion, *Man and wyman, loketh to me* (Brown *XIV*, No. 4), also works to elide visual distance through meditation, and in terms that place both the man and woman addressed in exactly the same relationship to the speaking Christ. In this poem the speaking body on the cross commands both men and women to stop and study his wounds, setting in motion a move towards physical intimacy. Christ invites us to use the verbal image, the poem, as a crucifix, and commands us to use vision as a way to share pain:

> Man and wyman, loketh to me,
> Hu michel pine ich tholede for the;   *how much pain; suffered*
> Loke up-one mi rig, hu sore ich was i-biten;   *back*
> Loke to mi side, what blode ich have i-leten.
> Mine vet an mine honden nailed beth to the rode; *feet; hands*
> Of the thornes prikung min hived urnth a blode. *head runs with blood*
> Fram side to side, fro hived to the fot
> Turn mi bodi abuten, overal thu findest blod.
> Man, thin hurte, thin hurte thu turne to me,   *thy heart / hurt*[10]
> For the vif wndes the ich tholede for the.   *five wounds which*

---

9 Although in Middle English *fere* may mean 'spouse', it commonly meant 'companion'. See *MED* **fere** n.(1).
10 The usual reaction invited in Middle English lyrics presenting Christ crucified or Christ as the Man of Sorrows is that of a penitential 'turning of the heart' stimulated by love in response to Christ's sufferings. Here, however, *hurte* (9), may be the 'hurt', the spiritual sorrow or injury of soul of the addressee – cf. *MED* **hurt** n. 1. (c) – or, as suggested here, an empathetic entering into Christ's 'hurt' on the part of the addressee.

The speaking Christ from the cross invokes the reader's gaze (*loketh to me*) and then takes him or her through a visual tour of his tortured body, ending in a moment of integration where Christ and the viewer come to suffer the same pain. After demanding that the reader look at his side, feet, hands and head pierced with thorns, Christ asks the viewer/reader to perform two turns; one of them is a physical 'turn', an inspection of the body on the cross; and the other, which follows from the first, is an emotional 'turn' of his or her own empathy toward that suffering body. The pierced 'side' of his body in line 4 invites, a few lines later, the reader's 'side to side' scrutiny; the 'pain' (line 2) Christ suffers activates and redeems the *hurte* (9) in the viewer, who turns his or her own heart or pain toward Christ in the penultimate line. While this Man of Sorrows initially addresses us from a distance, stopping us as passers-by and commanding us to stop and look, he then asks us, both men and women, to touch him. In giving Christ a tactile form that also is suggestive of a devotional object that can be held and turned in the hand, the lyric positions both its addressees, man and woman, within church space, demanding that its readers participate as members of a congregation, touching not only Christ's body but also the crucifix that represents it. Christ's command, *turn mi bodi abuten*, to see its blood, invites an extraordinary physical intimacy that dissolves taboos on touch. Men and women, in just the same way, can handle this body.

In many Middle English devotional lyrics, the voice of Christ on the cross engages in direct dialogue with a passer-by, with the Virgin, or with an implied witness. Middle English lyrics of the Passion are remarkable for their dramatic voicing and uses of dialogue. The demand that we look on his body, voiced by the speaking Christ on the cross, is one of the most pervasive and dramatically riveting principles organizing Middle English lyrics of the Passion. It is in these lyrics that we find not only the most systematic use of verbal commands, but also commands to gaze. Christ commands us to look at his body on the cross; his mother watches and describes how she responds to that experience, internalizing his suffering in a dynamically charged display of shared or transferred pain. Laments at the cross, describing a mother's witnessing of her son's execution, make dramatic use of visual transgression. In some respects, the voicing of these dramatic lyrics allows gendered identities traditional expression: Christ, embodied and suffering, speaks to his mother, and his mother responds to him in maternal pain and sorrow. Although lyrics dramatizing the dialogue between the Man of Sorrows and the Virgin achieved wide popularity in the fifteenth century, articulating a theme that was also widely represented in the visual arts of the time, they themselves appear as early as the thirteenth century.[11] Inasmuch as the Man of Sorrows is itself something of a hybrid or transitional form, speaking in the voice of the living dead, the voices in the lyrics themselves shift positions, trading voices and affect. Explicit voicing in dialogue or direct address requires that the addressee take up a persona and hence the mark of gender; but the dynamic of responsive voicing and mutual gazing also allows

---

[11] For the historical development of the theme see Woolf, 239–54.

these lyrics to articulate a wide range of possibilities in their pictures of intersubjectivity.

It is to these laments at the Cross that I would like to turn, for in these lyrics we find an extraordinarily rich domestic drama, particularly as expressed through strategic uses of Mary's gaze on Christ's body. From her first appearances at the Crucifixion scene in thirteenth-century Middle English lyrics – appearances that are marked by an attention to Christ's body and the emotional engagement of a narrator (Bennett 1982, 35) – to her fifteenth-century presence within distinct tableaux (such as the complaint of the Virgin, the lamentation of the Three Marys, and the pietà) that share iconographic features with developments in drama and the visual arts, Mary comes to occupy an increasingly important place in Middle English passional verse.[12] Her gaze on Christ's dying or dead body, correspondingly, takes on an increasingly strategic role in the meditative process as the focus of the speaking Christ, of a narrative passer-by, or of her own discourse. Christ focuses on her gaze, for instance, when he commands her to come and look – *Maiden and moder, cum and se, / Thi child is nailed to a tre* (Brown *XIV*, No. 67, 1–2) – or when he tells her, in a macabre lullaby, what it will be like for her to see his bloody body (Brown *XV*, No. 1, 21–4). In a large group of lyrics a narrator, textually present either as voice-over or as direct witness at the scene, describes Mary's gaze on Christ's body, as in the lyric *Ihesu that hast me dere i-boght* (Brown *XIV*, No. 91), a version of the *Orison of the Passion*: [13]

> Ihesu that art so myche of myght,   *great*
> Write in my hert that reuthful syght,   *pitiful*
> To loken on thy modyr fre   *noble*
> When thou were honget on roode tre.
>
> Write thy swete moderes woo
> Whan sho saw the to [the] deth goo. (53–8) *she*

When the Virgin herself describes the mutilated body of her son in the laments, it is often with particular attention to her gaze on his body (Brown *XIV*, No. 64; Brown *XV*, Nos 6–9). In the fourteenth-century *Suete sone, reu on me* (Brown *XIV*, No. 64) for example, her gaze and voice centre a descriptive and emotive framework:

---

[12] For the development of the pietà and the complaint in Middle English religious lyrics see Woolf, 139–73; see also her discussion of the development of the Virgin's role in Passion lyrics (193). Bennett 1982, 39 notes the relation between the development of the *respice* theme in poetry and the appearance of Crucifixion scenes in missals, books of hours, psalters, and churches. For a history of the complaint of the Virgin in medieval Latin literature see Sticca 1988, 71–117.

[13] The *Orison* is incorporated, almost in entirety, into the text of the fourteenth-century poem from BL MS Additional 11307, *Meditations on the Life and Passion of Christ*. As a separate poem, the *Orison* survives (sometimes incomplete) in ten other manuscripts from the fourteenth and fifteenth centuries – see Brown *XIV*, 274. D'Evelyn 1921, vii, describes the *Meditations* as a 'compendium of the lyric themes of Middle English religious poetry' and prints the *Orison* from Bodl. MS Additional E.4 in an Appendix (60–4). For other examples of meditations framed by a narrative voice that also include accounts of the Virgin's gaze, see Brown *XIV*, Nos 69 and 125, 56–57, and Brown *XV*, Nos 11, 93, and 94.

Suete sone, reu on me, and brest out of thi bondis;   *take pity; burst*
For nou me thinketh that I se, thoru bothen thu hondes,   *through*
Nailes dreven in-to the tre, so reufuliche thu honge[s]. (1–3)   *pitifully*

The Virgin's gaze in the Passion lyrics and laments at the cross is not, of course, the only gaze invoked. In many lyrics the dialectic of looking occurs between Christ and the reader: 'behold my body, behold my hands, behold my crown of thorns', Christ orders the reader or spectator, identified most often as 'man', as in *Thow synfull man that by me gais* [goes] (Brown XV, No. 102, 8). Middle English lyrics of the Passion are profoundly visual, not only in their use of literalizing and graphic metaphors but also in their concern with the process of visual empathy, a development from Cistercian meditation and the common-place *Respice in faciem Christi tui* [Look into the face of thy Christ].[14] When the Virgin looks – as she is begged or observed to do by numerous, chiefly male, voices, including those of the poet, an anonymous wayfarer at the site of the Crucifixion, or even the speaking body of Christ – she does so within a complex viewing enterprise. The reader looks not only at Christ's suffering and mutilated body but also at the Virgin gazing on that body, a spectacle that is further mediated by the poet, often in the persona of an actual witness at the scene. Her role in the Crucifixion drama is shaped by the intersected trajectories of multiple lines of sight, both those of viewers within the narrative space of the lyric and those of a culture that regulates and politicizes the act of looking. In their commands to look on the other and descriptions of what they see, laments at the cross fully exploit tensions and taboos governing the social gaze, and particularly those that work to limit a woman's gaze as an extension of her body, in the late Middle Ages as in subsequent centuries. As I have detailed more fully elsewhere, rules of decorum circumscribing how and when women should use their eyes were well defined in the Middle Ages.[15] For upper-class women to stare at or ogle men was, as it is today, impolite or worse – trashy, cheap, or crude. To stare is to send an invitation.

Yet while rules of decorum governing how women should or should not gaze seem similar to codes of female modesty still practised and taught in many places in the world today, the mechanics of vision were believed to operate rather differently; and while gazing may have been circumscribed along the lines of gender in some instances, in others it was sanctioned and even invited. Central to medieval optical theory were beliefs about mechanical linkages between the viewer and object of his or her gaze. Vision was believed to be accomplished through the blending or meeting of visual 'species', or rays emitted by the eye, a mingling that one recent scholar has called 'ocular communion' (Biernoff 2002, 140–9). As Grosseteste (c.1168–1253) writes, the visual species was a substance that joined with an emanation from the object to complete vision:

Nor is it to be thought that the emission of visual rays [from the eye] is only imagined and without reality, as those think who consider the part and not the whole.

14 See Woolf, 30–31; Bennett 1982, 37–40.
15 Stanbury 1991, 1083–85. The discussion of the laments in this chapter draws upon the 1991 article.

But it should be understood that the visual species [issuing from the eye] is a substance, shining and radiating like the sun, the radiation of which, when coupled
with the radiation from the exterior shining body, entirely completes vision . . .
Therefore true perspective is concerned with rays emitted [by the eye].[16]

Up until Kepler, who developed the theory of the retinal image, the workings of
species continued to be debated at great length by optical theorists, but most
agreed that species were real and operative. Bacon, writing in the mid-thirteenth
century, sheds light on the nature of the debate through his defence of
extramission and visible species:

But many have denied that something issues from the eye to complete the act of
sight, positing that vision is completed only by intromission and not by
extramission . . . However . . . this opinion is false . . .[17]

Species emanating from things 'must be aided and excited by the species of the
eye', which alters the eye to allow it to receive the entering visual impression.
Gazing is a direct kind of physical sensation, altering the eye and also altering
the object seen. Vision is a form of touch.[18]

How beliefs about visual species as debated and taught in the universities
might have affected the representation of vision in medieval literature and art is
a complex topic, and one that has only recently begun to be addressed.[19] How
are the directives to gaze on Christ's body, as voiced in Middle English laments
and lyrics of the Passion, underwritten by scientific beliefs that vision operates
as touch? Ocular communion is one of the organizing drives in Christian ritual
theatre, especially after the late twelfth century when the elevation of the host
became an important part of the mass (Rubin 1991, 55–63). The gaze on the body
of Christ on the cross participates in this central eucharistic drama; and in fact
gazing on the eucharistic wafer during the ritual elevation during the mass can
only be a cool imitation of the drama of love and death at the cross. The workings of visual union and communion were articulated not only academically by
optical theorists, but also dramatized through practices of devotion. When
Christ demands that men and women stop and gaze on his body on the Cross in
Ihesu that hast me dere i-boght (Brown XIV, No. 91) and then shifts to demand we
turn and touch his body, that drive to fracture distance joins our gaze and our
touch. This lyric, as do many others, seems to enact the workings of species
through ocular communion, naturalizing or essentializing ritual practices
through the science of visual rays. We look, we touch, and we are then 'turned'
or changed in our own hearts. And looking in this way is available to both men
and women.

When the Virgin looks on Christ's body on the cross in the laments, her gaze

---

[16] Grosseteste, *De iride*, in Grant 1974, 389; see the discussion in Stanbury 1992, 225.

[17] Bacon *De multiplicatione specierum*, in Lindberg 1983, 33.

[18] For a fuller discussion see Stanbury 1997, 269–71; also Biernoff 2002, 90.

[19] See Camille 2000, 207; Stanbury 1997; Collette 2001, 13–20. For a recent study that considers
medieval optical theory and visual metaphor in relation to later visual theorists, see Biernoff
2002, 96–103. As Biernoff puts it: 'whether carnal or scientific, vision was a dynamic extension
of the subject into the world and at the same time a penetration and alteration of the viewer's
body by the object' (102).

and Christ's responsive gaze when he looks back at her are both structured, at least in part, by a regime of the visual based on principles of species and visual rays. Through looking, they each touch each other and respond immediately and emotionally. At the same time, however, visual gestures are also orchestrated by rules of conduct, as I discussed above, that equate gazing with mastery and power; Mary's gaze, in particular, takes its dramatic edge through the transgressions inherent in witnessing a scene of terror and pathos, but even more directly through its transgressions of rules of decorum defined by gender – as the fixed stare, on a male body, of a woman. Category crossing and sanctified transgression, as we see in *Undo thi dore, my spuse dere* (Brown *XIV*, No. 68) and *I syng of a mayden* (Brown *XV*, No. 81), is characteristic generally of Middle English devotional lyrics, which often elide boundaries between sacred and sexual. When the Virgin looks in laments and lyrics of the Passion, and indeed, in Marian poems in general, it is also to participate in a system of sanctified transgression. Freed from the domestic sphere (on a hill, outside a cave, or at the gates of the city), she gazes unencumbered on the naked male body, that swoons in her arms or sags on the cross, nailed down in forced passivity. The repeated attention paid to her gaze on Christ's body derives, I believe, from the excitation, both erotic and maternal, adhering to this formal tableau. In a thirteenth-century lyric praising Mary's maternity, for instance, the speaker begs the Virgin for her gaze – *Moder, loke one me / With thine swete eyen* (Brown *XIII*, No. 27, 13–14) – as if her look could bestow the reassuring benefice of nurturing. A fifteenth-century 'Salve regina', *Hayl! oure patron and lady of erthe* (Brown *XV*, No. 26), explicitly yokes the looks of mother and lover, for in pleading for the Virgin's gaze, the narrator suggests that it offers several kinds of pleasure or *disporte*:

> Thi mercyful eene and lufly loke
> Cast opon us for oure disporte.
> And Ihu, thi babe, that thi flesche toke,   *Jesus*
> So blyssed a lord, make us supporte. (25–8)

Praying to be held by Mary's gaze, the speaker immediately turns to Jesus, allowing us to identify with the infant in a drama of courtly desire. Loving as well as infantilizing, the Virgin's gaze in these lyrics, as in Passion lyrics in which she looks on Christ's body, is defined by the privileges and prohibitions affecting her sex; it is legitimized by maternity and eroticized by its transgressive sexuality. In both lyrics, however, the speaker begs not only to be granted her gaze but also to be governed by it, thereby implicitly defining the look as an assertion of power.

The Virgin's assumption of power by fixing her eyes on the cross is often at the centre of the devotional process, for it sets in motion a complex and often uneasy dialectic that reshapes the relationships among the narrator and the mother and son. Her gaze seems to oscillate between its assertive command of Christ's body and an objectified deferral in which her own act of looking turns her into a spectacle. The potent and even galvanizing effect on the dying Christ of her visual assertiveness, assertiveness socially legitimized as a gesture of mourning or grief, is brilliantly dramatized in *Stond wel, moder, under rode*, a frequently anthologized lyric in which the mother-son debate is an expression of the Latin sequence *Stabat iuxta Christi crucem*.[20] In this lyric, which begins with Christ's response to the Virgin's gaze, an aggressive rhetoric dictates a number of reversals and inversions; the body speaks from the cross, the son commands his mother, he even orders her to look at him cheerfully, *with glade mode*:

> 'Stond wel, moder, under rode,
> byholt thy sone with glade mode.   *with gladsome heart*
>   blythe, moder, myght thou be!'   *happy*
> 'Sone, hou shulde y blithe stonde?
> Y se thin fet, y se thin honde
>   nayled to the harde tre.' (Brook No. 20, 1–6)

The scene's physical arrangement, however, is itself the most coercive feature of the debate, for until the last two stanzas the lyric progresses as a dialogue between the son dying on the cross and the mother mourning below, gazing on his body, and describing what she sees: his feet and hands nailed to the *harde tree* (6); blood flowing from his wounds: *Y se the blody stremes erne* [flow] */ from thin herte to my fet* (23–4); and then his body scourged: *Sone, y se thi bodi byswngen* [beaten], */ fet ant honden thourhout stongen* [pierced] (28–9). What Roland Barthes calls the 'haptic' function of the gaze (Barthes 1985, 283) – its power to seize, to take – is here dramatized through the process of visual meditation and, even more emphatically, through the mother's arrested gaze. The scene fixes her, transfixes her, in place, not simply as a spectator, but as a spectator whose very act of looking controls the linear drama of Christ's suffering.

Yet although she is the only one who looks, she does not entirely control her own gaze. In speaking to her from the cross, Christ is implicitly recognizing the power of her look. It is as if her gaze of maternal pity had impaled and infantilized his body, trapping him in immanence; thus his response to her anguished look is, in fact, equally agonized. Her gaze, that is, exists first as it is recognized and resisted by the speaking Christ; and it is only through his response to its haptic, impassioned plea that the lyric ultimately rewrites its own stern admonitions. In a convention repeated in medieval Passion plays, as Woolf points out, Christ is stern and restrained, whereas the Virgin speaks her grief (Woolf, 246). Yet this positioning also sets up a volatile balance of power between mother and son. The lyric should be read as drama or even as melodrama; the voices of mother and son are pitched in impassioned exchange, and the dialogue develops as a sequence of declarations and deflections that enact a family history, one initiated by the Virgin's grieving gaze.

For it is the Virgin's gaze rather than Christ's body that is the centre of pain and redemption in this lyric. Suffering resides not so much with Christ on the cross as with the mother, and it is focused and articulated through the

---

[20] *Stond wel, moder* is quoted here from Brook's edition of the version as found in BL MS Harley 2253. Like the Latin *Stabat iuxta Christi crucem*, this Middle English poem is in the form of a sequence. It first appears in Bodl. MS Digby 86; it also occurs in other thirteenth- and fourteenth-century manuscripts, in some with music (see Dobson and Harrison 1979, 153–4). For evidence suggesting that these verses were used in preaching, see Brown *XIII*, 204.

transformative power of her look. Even though Christ's body is broken on the cross, he seems somehow intact, able to command and attempt to silence his mother; but her directed and grieving gaze enables the empathetic fracture of the single body. Her continued stare forces him into a series of confessions about the complicitous cycle of suffering that extends or even displaces pain from him to her and ultimately into a dyad of grief and love that includes all women. He cannot bear her pain, he says; he cannot die if she suffers so, and if he does not die, she will go to hell. To her continued refrain that she sees his pain and that it is her nature, her *kynde* (35), to suffer, he reveals to her, stanza by stanza, how it is that she (and by extension, the reader), participates in his agony: *nou y may the seye* [now I can tell you] (25), *now y shal the telle* (31) how my death saves you and all humankind from damnation. The series of revelations – she says she sees his pain, he then tells her more of the story of salvation – culminates in his extraordinary acknowledgment of the special pain women experience. Finally he tells her that she, miraculously exempt from the pain of childbirth, now understands women's pain; she now knows the destiny of women:

> Moder, nou thou might wel leren   *learn*
> whet sorewe haveth that children beren,   *they have*
>   whet sorewe hit is with childe gon. (37–9)

She counters by imploring him to help those that turn to her. Until this point in the lament her part of the dialogue has been solipsistically centred on her own pain and grief, but here she frames a specific request, one that emphatically yokes mother and son with all women:

> Sone, help at alle need   *in every necessity*
> alle tho that to me grede   *all those who; cry out*
>   maiden, wif, ant fol wymmon. (46–8)   *foolish*

Their shared acknowledgment of her pain, that is, transfers the narrow filial-maternal circle of suffering onto the community of women, to whom both Christ and the Virgin are now accessible.

The lyric's ocular plot thus develops through a mirroring in which the Virgin's grieving gaze is as potent and transformative as the spectacle of the body in pain. Although her directed gaze on Christ's body, shaped by the conventions of the Passion, transfixes her with grief, it also entitles her to a subtle control: a system of complex role reversals, similar to the positionings of the pietà, both infantilize and eroticize the male body in forced passivity and locate the woman as spectator, looking on. The drama of the lyric – and its progress through a series of acknowledgments, promises, and revelations – is shaped through these reversals, for throughout the lyric, from the son's first cry that his mother look on him not with sorrow but with *glade mode* to his statement that she now knows what it is to suffer, the voice from the cross is a voice of resistance to Mary's grieving gaze. Initially empowered by its implicit transgressiveness, her gaze explicitly realizes its ascendancy through a fracture of boundaries, one that re-establishes the primal order of mother and infant; and the mother's final request that Christ help all women who turn to him, the request that forecloses private suffering, has been enabled by their joint admission of empathetic pain and love.

Among the many emotions that this mother-son debate expresses, one of the most subtle but perhaps most important to the process of the poem is Christ's ambivalence toward maternal power, power that is chiefly invested in the Virgin's anguished look. His attempts to assuage and deflect her grief describe, of course, a fully human response: what else could he do? Yet the dramatic appeal of this moment, a moment favoured for representation in poetry and late-medieval painting, may arise in part because of the inherent tension, even the inherent threat, that her look involves. And while the series of responses to the visual and verbal dialogue of suffering allows the two figures, facing death, to reconfigure themselves as mother and child, facing eternal life, the dialogue also allows pain to reside with the mother, and with all women, as if the consequence of looking were to suffer, transfixed by the pain of revelation.

'When the woman looks,' Linda Williams writes of twentieth-century horror films, it is to become a victim: 'the woman's look of horror paralyzes her in such a way that distance is overcome; the monster or the freak's own spectacular appearance holds her originally active, curious look in a trancelike passivity that allows him to master her through *her* look' (Williams 1984, 86). In Marian laments the Virgin's fixed and horrified gaze on her son on the cross or in her lap collapses space and arrests time in ways similar to the scenes Linda Williams describes. She becomes a victim. Her victimization is explicit in *Stond wel, moder*: watching her son's death on the cross, she finally learns what it is to feel pain.

This is also a story that has a long future. In Mel Gibson's 2004 film, *The Passion of the Christ*, the primary witness and visual filter for the film's horrific spectacle of suffering is the Virgin, effectively played by Maia Morganstern. As in *Stond wel, moder*, pain is literally transferred to her through her act of gazing. Yet unlike Middle English laments, Gibson's Mary is a silent witness to her son's pain. In the film they almost never speak: she stands in the crowd during the scourging, follows him on the road to Calvary, and watches, horrified, as he is nailed to the cross. With a few exceptions, Jesus does not look back to meet her gaze. Mary's presence as witness in all of these scenes follows the medieval tradition, but her language, or lack of it, is modelled on the accounts in the Gospels. Gibson's interpretation of the Passion, a celebration of masculine heroic martyrdom, gives women only one role, and that is as the bearers of emotional pain. Mary's angry and silent stare out at the audience in her final scene, where she holds Jesus in her lap just as in a pietà, communicates rage as well as powerlessness.

Middle English lyrics of the Passion, in contrast, give the Virgin, and by extension, their female readers, a far more participatory role. In Marian laments the gazes of the Virgin and of Christ on the cross are articulated through dialogue, and dialogue about shared or even transfused pain that makes full use of the optics of ocular communion: *Stond wel, moder* brilliantly tropes intersubjectivity, male and female gazes mingling in a shared and transformative touch. Taboos and conventions surrounding female gazing may work to victimize the female watcher in *Stond wel, moder* as well as in other laments at the cross, but that is far from the whole story. Her gaze meets his; she addresses him, or in some lyrics, addresses the reader as well. Compassionate, desiring, infantalizing, moralizing, her gaze, articulated through dialogue, jockeys with and even at times resists textual strategies for controlling her lines of sight. Even if point of view can never give definitive information about the identity of the poet, it can tell us a great deal about desires for authority and voice. In the laments where the Virgin speaks at the cross and addresses, in second person, the second person of the Trinity, dialogue brilliantly articulates physical intimacy with Christ in his human form. These poems, enacting Christianity's central trauma, place a woman at the scene and in some cases even give her the final word.

12

Lyrics in Middle Scots

A. A. MACDONALD

The medieval vernacular lyric in Scotland exhibits many points of similarity with its English counterpart; this is only to be expected, given the many points of contact in the history of the two countries, the mutual intelligibility of the two languages, and the fact that English and Scottish poets were receptive to the same external cultural influences – from (Anglo-) French and, especially, Latin. Furthermore, the two countries had in common several institutional factors which significantly facilitated literary production: these included a court culture open to influences from France and Burgundy, a church-led educational system, and a network of mendicant houses with a programme of evangelisation directed towards the population at large. On the other hand, many differences between the two traditions are also evident, the most obvious being the fact that Middle Scots literature is so late in starting (c.1375).[1] Moreover, it is not only in its smaller comparative total volume that the corpus of Middle Scots lyrics differs from that of England, but also in its range of topics, the nature of its textual preservation, and its literary character. As will be argued below, the most notable Scottish specimens display a level of stylistic sophistication which transcends what is normally considered most characteristic of the medieval English lyric. Consequently, it is better to consider the Middle Scots lyrics not so much as a tardy, northern extension of the Middle English tradition, but rather as an independent and parallel development from a common cultural base.

Textual intertraffic

There were many opportunities for texts to be passed between the two kingdoms. This might happen, for example, on the occasion of diplomatic and ecclesiastical contacts, whether occurring at home, in the capital cities of neighbouring countries, or at the papal court at Rome. Moreover, in an age addicted to the tournament, knights often travelled widely between centres of chivalry, expanding their acquaintance among the members of the francophone social elite, and helping in the transmission of courtly literature. Students, with their command of the international language of learning, Latin, were also active trav-

---

[1] The earliest surviving literary text is John Barbour's historical romance celebrating the heroic deeds of Robert I (the Bruce) at the time of the War of Independence. See McDiarmid and Stevenson 1980–85.

ellers with literary interests. Dynastic marriages, such as those between James I and Joan Beaufort (1424) and James IV and Margaret Tudor (1503), had important implications for cultural contact. Visitors from abroad might take in both the English and the Scottish courts in the course of the same journey, and thus help to promote cultural cross-fertilisation: one thinks of Jean Froissart at the courts of Edward III and David II, Jörg von Ehingen at the courts of Henry VI and James II, and Giacomo Passarella at the courts of Henry VII and James III.[2] Kings and their courts might encounter each other during periods of expulsion from their own countries: at one stage of the Wars of the Roses, in 1461 and 1462, Henry VI and Margaret of Anjou were refugees in Edinburgh, and the exile of Edward IV in Bruges (1470–71) coincided with that of Mary, sister of James III, and her family in the same city.[3]

Such varied cultural contacts at the personal level have still not, perhaps, been accorded either the kind or the degree of attention that they deserve. Instead, if we confine ourselves to the case of the medieval Scottish poets, we find that the latter have generally been considered under the single, traditional label of 'Scottish Chaucerians'.[4] This blanket term is unfortunate in more than one way. First, it suggests (wrongly) that there was only one significant cultural influence at work in medieval Scotland, though it does not specify just what constitutes the essence of 'Chaucerianness' as such; second, it is clearly inappropriate for Scottish poetic productions unaffected by Chaucerian influence; and third, it does not discriminate between works which, while Chaucerian in one way or other, may be so to different degrees, and to different ends. However, even if, for the sake of simplicity, one grant the general Chaucerian influence, the reality is yet more complicated. For a start, there is the need to distinguish between authentic and apocryphal Chaucerian material: while several genuine lyrics by Chaucer are found in Scottish manuscripts, the latter include several other lyrics that – whether in hope or in ignorance – have been erroneously ascribed to the English master. For example, the manuscript containing the *Kingis Quair* (Bodl. MS Selden. B. 24) is outstanding in the Chaucerian emphasis of its contents, which, indeed, extends to a Middle Scots translation of *Troilus and Criseyde*; however, this manuscript also contains several specimens of English post-Chaucerian verse (e.g., by Thomas Hoccleve, John Lydgate and John Walton).[5] The same goes for the Bannatyne MS, NLS MS Advocates 1.1.6 (Ritchie 1928–34; Fox and Ringler 1980). This great collection includes among the genuine Chaucerian items a text of the 'Song of Troyelus', *Gife no luve is, O God, quhat feill I so?*; this lyric, excerpted from *Troilus and Criseyde*, is a reworking in English of a sonnet by Petrarch.[6] Bannatyne's source here was no manuscript

---

2   On Froissart see Hume Brown 1978, 7–15; on von Ehingen, Letts 1929; on Passarella, MacDonald 2000, 38.

3   See Macdougall 1982, 58–61; MacDonald 2000, 41–2.

4   E.g. Harvey Wood 1967; Rossi 1964. John MacQueen was among the first to impugn the unfortunate implications of the term: MacQueen 1971, 235.

5   Boffey and Edwards 1997; Boffey 2000a; Edwards 2000a. The manuscript is hereafter referred to as the Selden MS.

6   Ritchie 1928–34, III, 304–5; Windeatt 1984, 112–13. The Bannatyne MS was intended to be a collection of lyrics in four sections; however, much non-lyric material was later inserted into the third section, and a new, fifth, section was added: MacDonald 2003.

but one of the editions of Chaucer printed at London by William Thynne (c.1545–50) – a volume which includes many works of the Chaucer Apocrypha.[7] In Bannatyne's section of moral poems, one finds poems by Chaucer, e.g. *Lak of Stedfastnesse*, juxtaposed with others by pseudo-Chaucer, e.g. *Quhylome in Grece, that nobill regioun* (Ritchie 1928–34, II, 164–5, 113–15). The same holds true for Bannatyne's texts of such English Chaucerians as John Lydgate, of whom one finds the genuine work, *Ryght as a Rammes Horne*, and the doubtfully attributed *Thingis in kynd desyris thingis lyke*.[8] Indeed, one important aspect of the reception of Chaucerian influence in late-medieval Scotland was this very indirect influence transmitted through the works of Chaucer's English followers. The Hoccleve lyric in the Selden MS (*Mother of God*, *IMEV* 2221), for example, also appears (again attributed to Chaucer) in the manuscript of John Ireland's *Meroure of Wysdome*.[9] Likewise, in addition to the poems by Lydgate (or pseudo-Lydgate) already mentioned, one may note the (now repudiated) attribution to Lydgate of a Complaint of Christ in the Bannatyne MS, and the version of part V of the same poet's *Testament* (*IMEV* 2464) in the Arundel MS, BL MS Arundel 285 (Ritchie 1928–34, II, 105–8; Bennett 1955, 270–4). However, despite the existence of such texts, which testify to a considerable northern interest in Chaucerian material (whether genuine or supposed), there is surprisingly little in the original Middle Scots lyric corpus that is explicitly reminiscent of Chaucer. It is worth recalling that the memorable tribute to Chaucer (and to Gower and Lydgate) paid by William Dunbar at the end of *The Goldyn Targe* (Bawcutt 1998a, I, 192) was not concerned with any specific point of connection at the level either of genre or form, but only with the general issue of the rhetorical possibilities of vernacular verse.[10]

Scottish awareness of non-Chaucerian English lyric verse is also well attested. The Arundel MS contains a Scottish version of Richard de Caistre's lyric on the Holy Name, *Iesu Lord, that maid me*, *IMEV* 1727, immediately followed by another (anonymous) on the same subject, *IMEV* 1703 (Bennett 1955, 277–8). The Arundel MS contains a Complaint of Christ from the Cross (*Now herkynnis wordis wunder gude*), and this item is found in another Scottish manuscript, the Makculloch MS (EUL MS 205 (= La.III.149)). The lyric in question (*IMEV* 1119), however, is English in origin, and occurs in the so-called Towneley Plays and in the famous devotional collection, BL MS Additional 37049 (Bennett 1955, 261–5). Where there was a musical dimension to vernacular lyrics, transmission of influence from one country to the other was particularly easy. Thus one English song, *Alas, departyng ys ground of woo!* (*IMEV* 146), lends its opening line to a new Scottish lyric in the Bannatyne MS.[11] Similarly, the song attributed to Henry VIII, *Passetyme with good cumpanye*, was imitated by Sir Richard Maitland in his *contrafactum*, *Pastyme with godlie companie* (Stevens 1961, 344–5; Craigie 1920,

---

7   Fox and Ringler 1980, xxxiv. Thynne's first edition appeared in 1532: Brewer 1969; Blodgett 1984, 41–2.
8   Ritchie 1928–34, II, 201–2, 199–201. There are yet more lyrics by Lydgate in the manuscript.
9   Macpherson 1926, 166–70; Boffey and Edwards 1997, 2 and fols 130–131v. The manuscript colophons both identify the lyric as 'Oracio Galfredi Chauceir'.
10 See further: Kratzmann 1980; MacDonald 1991a; Bawcutt (2005).
11 For the English song see Robbins *Sec.*, No. 156; Ritchie 1928–34, III, 284–5.

63–4). Another interesting case is Alexander Scott's poem, *Lo, quhat it is to luve*, which would appear to be an emulatory response to a lyric by Sir Thomas Wyatt.[12] In addition – though this might take us rather too far away from the Middle English lyric – there is a large number of short (and eminently forgettable) versifications copied into the Bannatyne MS from Tudor printed books: for example, the frequently reprinted *Treatise of Morall Philosophye* by William Baldwin and Francis Paulfreyman has supplied some two dozen items (Fox and Ringler 1980, xv–xvi, xli.). The Scottish versions of English Protestant poems of the Reformation age also deserve mention: one thinks of the lyrics by Myles Coverdale, Bishop of Exeter, in the *Gude and Godlie Ballatis* (1565 and later).[13] The same collection has a lyric excerpted from the late fifteenth-century English poem, *The Court of Sapience*, and it contains many *contrafacta* of English lyrics – such as the poem *Grevous is my sorrow*, which is based on *IMEV* 1018.[14]

Complementing the Scottish awareness of English lyric verse, there was also transmission in the opposite direction. A long verse meditation, the *Contem placioun of Synnaris*, by the Scottish Observant Franciscan William of Touris, was taken south, and rendered (as far as possible) into English; in 1499 it was printed by Wynkyn de Worde at Westminster. This work enjoyed a long popularity, and adaptations from it were still being read in the later sixteenth century: one extract appears as a Scottish religious lyric on the Passion in the Bannatyne MS (1565–68), and a version of the whole text was printed in 1578 at London by Hugh Singleton, this time as a book of Anglican devotions (MacDonald 1984). A second example is the Scottish lyric on Our Lady, *Ros Mary, most of vertewe virginale*, found in the Asloan MS (NLS MS 16500), in part in the Makculloch MS, in NLS MS Advocates 18.5.14, and in BL MS Harley 1703, which latter belonged to William Forrest, the confessor of Mary Tudor.[15] Most apposite of all in this context is the well-known Scottish poem celebrating the city of London, *London, thou art of townes A per se*; this lyric was by earlier critics attributed to Dunbar and is found in as many as five manuscripts (*IMEV* 1933.5).[16] It is likely that this poem arises from a Scottish embassy to London connected with the negotiations for the marriage between James IV and Margaret Tudor. Diplomatic contact may well have facilitated the printing of the *Contemplacioun of Synnaris*, while reporting of Scottish politics by the English ambassador, Thomas Randolph, was certainly responsible for the preservation of the text of the lyric welcoming Mary Queen of Scots on her royal entry to Edinburgh in 1561.[17] From all this evidence

[12] For the view that the direction of borrowing went from Scott to Wyatt, see MacQueen 1983, 50–8.

[13] Mitchell 1897, lxvi–lxxii. Henceforth referred to as *GGB*. The present writer is preparing a new edition.

[14] MacDonald 1990; Mitchell 1897, 151–7, 275–6; for the complete text of the English lyric see Robbins *Sec.*, No. 206.

[15] Craigie 1923–25, II, 271–2; Stevenson 1918, 24–5; Cunningham 1985–86, 86–7, 32–40. On Forrest see Guiney 1938, 137–45.

[16] Perhaps most easily consulted in Mackay Mackenzie 1960, 177–8. See also Bawcutt 1998b, 68; Mapstone 2001b, 27.

[17] MacDonald 1991b; *Calendar of State Papers Scotland*, 174. See also Davidson 1995; MacDonald 1997; Gray 1998, 26–8; Kipling 1998, 352–6.

it is clear that quite a number of English lyrics circulated in late-medieval and early-modern Scotland, and that the converse was also true.

The manuscript witnesses

The great majority of Scottish lyrics have been preserved in a small number of miscellanies and anthologies, nearly all of which date from the sixteenth century or even later: Selden (c.1490–1500); Asloan (c.1515–25); Arundel (c.1540–55); Bannatyne (1565–68).[18] To this list may be added the Maitland Folio MS, Cambridge, Magdalene College, Pepysian Library MS 2553 (c.1570), and the Maitland Quarto MS, Cambridge, Magdalene College, Pepysian Library MS 1408 (c.1586).[19] These Maitland manuscripts were further transcribed in, respectively, the Reidpeth MS, CUL MS Ll.5.10 (c.1623), and the Drummond MS, EUL MS De.3.71 (before 1627); the Reidpeth MS is of particular value in preserving texts of poems by Dunbar now lost from the Maitland Folio.[20] In addition to this list of manuscripts, there exist a few others of lesser importance for the lyric: CUL MS Kk.1.5 No.6 (late fifteenth century), and the Gray MS, NLS MS Advocates 34.7.3 (c.1520–30).[21] Several lyrics are preserved in the booklets printed at Edinburgh by Walter Chepman and Andro Myllar in 1508, and there are sporadic survivals scribbled on the empty pages of manuscripts of a non-literary nature, such as the Makculloch MS, which comprises principally the lecture notes on philosophy and theology made in 1477 by a Scottish student at the university of Leuven (Beattie 1950; Stevenson 1918, xiv).

Almost wholly absent, however, are certain kinds of manuscript which provide much of the English corpus of lyrics. The solitary Scottish specimen of a prayer book containing vernacular religious lyrics is the Arundel MS. Collections made by friars, which might be expected to contain lyrics useful in illustrating sermons, are altogether lacking in Scotland; this has particular implications for such a genre as the carol, which was especially cultivated by the friars (Greene, cl–clix). As a result, while a large number of carols survive from England, medieval Scottish specimens are extremely rare. Yet, in view of the plethora of injunctions levied by the post-Reformation Kirk, it seems safe to assume that this kind of poem was indeed once popular in Scotland.[22] We also lack manuscripts from Scottish monastic or collegiate libraries which might have contained vernacular lyrics. Scottish commonplace books are uncommon, and those which do survive, such as John Maxwell's MS, EUL MS Laing III.467, are late, 1584–89 (Bawcutt 1990).

The textual preservation of the Middle Scots lyrics is thus radically different from what one encounters with the Middle English lyrics. Since, as has been said above, the cultures of the two countries in the later Middle Ages had so much in

---

18 For a recent discussion of these and other Scottish manuscripts see MacDonald 2003.
19 Craigie 1919–27; Craigie 1920; Boffey 2001.
20 On these manuscripts see MacDonald 2001b; Bawcutt (2005).
21 Girvan 1939; Stevenson 1918, xvi–xvii, 39–56.
22 For a non-religious specimen see Bawcutt 1986. For the outlawing of carols see Mill 1924, 10; Todd 2002, 188–9, 221.

common, there clearly must be particular reasons for the disparity. In this connection the factor most frequently invoked is, of course, the Reformation, which is generally agreed to have been carried out more rigorously in Scotland than in England. Another possibility is that at the time of the Scottish Reformation (c.1559–67) there may have been little organised attempt to collect and rescue medieval manuscripts: one thinks by contrast of the antiquarian activities in England of John Bale and John Leland.[23] Certainly, in Scotland there were fewer academic collegiate and aristocratic libraries into which manuscripts might have been gathered for safety. Lowland Scotland also suffered from its proximity to England. When, in the 1540s, Henry VIII, on behalf of his son, launched the 'Rough Wooing' of the infant Mary Stewart, the town of Edinburgh was sacked: among the goods purloined was a manuscript of John Bellenden's translation of the *Scotorum historiae* of Hector Boece, now in the library of the Marquess of Bath; it is likely that the Longleat manuscript of Gavin Douglas's translation of the *Aeneid* was acquired at the same time (Chambers, Batho and Husbands 1938–41; Coldwell 1957–64, I, 100).

The consequence of all of this is that the student of the medieval Scots lyric is dependent upon post-medieval, and often post-Reformation, sources, with the consequent possibility – even probability – of distortions in the medieval record. All things being equal, Protestant scribes were unlikely to have shown much enthusiasm for lyrics with a markedly Catholic content: hence, no doubt, the paucity of surviving Scottish medieval lyrics on the Virgin Mary (MacDonald 1983 and 1988). More subtly, however, the largest anthologies (the manuscripts of Asloan, Bannatyne, and Maitland, with their derivatives) can be shown to have made their own very specific selections from the literary material available: it is somewhat alarming to realise how much the modern notion of the Middle Scots literary corpus has been conditioned by the preferences of just three families of Edinburgh lawyers (MacDonald 2003).

It is thus an intriguing fact that the medieval Scottish lyric can today only be viewed through the filter of early-modern anthologies. In this regard a comparison may be made with the widespread use of anthologies of English literature in many university courses at the present time: no matter how discriminating the editors or how generous the selection, what is on offer can hardly rise above a mere sampling. Furthermore, the sixteenth-century Scottish anthologies resemble their modern counterparts in at least one other important respect: their inevitable promotion of the sense of a canon. On the basis of frequency of transcription, a basic canon of Middle Scots lyrics would certainly contain poems by Robert Henryson (d. c.1490), William Dunbar (d. c.1513) and Gavin Douglas (d.1522). There are also a few less famous poets who deserve to be considered along with this celebrated trio: these would include Walter Kennedy (d.1518), mentioned in Dunbar's so-called *Lament for the Makaris*, and William of Touris (d. c.1500?), who is absent from Dunbar's literary catalogue. In the great anthologies of Middle Scots lyric verse, however, this short list of poets is augmented with a secondary canon, a sixteenth-century list, dominated by such figures as

---

[23] Hudson 1997; Simpson 2002, 8–33. The earliest equivalent in Scotland is Thomas Dempster, from the following century: Morét 2000; Durkan 2003.

William Stewart (d.1548), David Lindsay (d.1555), Alexander Scott (d.1582/3) and Sir Richard Maitland of Lethington (d.1586). The perspective of the present volume, however, dictates that the discussion below will be restricted to the earlier, and more properly medieval, of these groups.

Classifications and terminology

From medieval Scotland no critical discussion at the meta-level survives, and it is perhaps unlikely that it ever existed. However, the headings and colophons used by the scribes in the manuscripts furnish some indication of the kinds of lyric possible in the early-modern period. Thus one observes that John Asloan uses the terms 'tretis' or 'buke' for substantial works of poetry. In the Bannatyne MS, the scribe's practice is somewhat different. There, poems longer than 100 lines (on average) are usually equipped with an individual title – such as the *Benner of Peetie* [Banner of Mercy], on the Incarnation of Christ, by John Bellenden (Ritchie 1928–34, II, 3–8). Occasionally, moreover, the scribe's title may rather serve to indicate the original context of the lyric – as with the immediately following work, Bellenden's *Proheme of the Cosmographe* (Ritchie 1928–34, II, 9–20). The latter poem was written to introduce the cosmographical chapter which, with its description of the land of Scotland in all its richness of climate and of animal, bird and fish life, prefaces Bellenden's translation of Boece's history.[24] Sometimes it behoves the reader to be suspicious, since a fragment chiselled out of a longer work may be passed off as a lyric of sorts: this is true of the stanzas, mentioned above, excerpted from the Friday part of Touris's *Contemplacioun of Synnaris*, which Bannatyne terms a *cantilena*. On the whole, the usual Middle Scots designation of a shortish lyric is 'ballat': thus the Bannatyne MS, of which the first four divisions consist entirely of lyrics, is said by the scribe to be a 'ballat buke'.[25] As regards formal features, most Middle Scots lyrics contain more than ten and fewer than 120 lines; they are composed in regularly metrical stanzas, in which the pentameter is the line of preference; the stanzas are linked by the use of a regular and recurring rhyme-scheme, and they normally exhibit a refrain line encapsulating the main theme of the whole poem.

In the Asloan MS the term 'a ballat of Our Lady' occurs; this generic label is unsurprisingly absent from the post-Reformation Bannatyne MS (Craigie 1923–25, II, 270). The latter text, however, is justly famous for its profusion of classifications.[26] For example, in his division of religious lyrics, Bannatyne has 'ballatis of the Nativity', 'cantilenae de passione' [i.e., ballatis of the Crucifixion], 'ballatis of the Resurrection', and 'Complaints of Christ from the Cross'. In his division of lyrics on the theme of love, Bannatyne recognises (i) songs of love, (ii) ballatis in praise of women, (iii) ballatis in reproach of false, vicious men, and

---

24 For the printed text: Bellenden 1977.
25 Ritchie 1928–34, IV, 107. As already mentioned in note 6, above, the inclusion of comic interludes in the third section, and that of the entire fifth section (fables), were afterthoughts: MacDonald 1986.
26 Shire 1969, 11–23; Ramson 1977; Hughes and Ramson 1982, 22–39; MacDonald 1986; MacDonald 1994a; Bawcutt (2005); MacDonald 2003.

(iv) ballatis in contempt of love and lechery. Within the second of these categories the scribe employs the term 'ballat of impossibilities' for a subspecies of
love-lyric constructed on the principle of the 'world upside down' (Ritchie
1928–34, IV, 42, 44). Bannatyne's generic labels have been much discussed:
suffice it here to note that they are more than abstractly taxonomic, but require
to be understood against the background of the cultural, religious and political
circumstances obtaining at the time of the compilation of the manuscript
(1565–68). After the downfall of Queen Mary in 1567, with the consequent
triumph of the Protestant party in Lowland Scotland, lyric verse of the courtly
and erotic kinds was suddenly at a discount, and this would seem to be reflected
in Bannatyne's classifications. However, such a revaluation, made from hind-
sight, is clearly irrelevant to the years of Mary's personal reign (1561–67), and *a
fortiori* to the lyric production of the courts of her grandfather and father (James
IV and James V).[27] What Bannatyne has done is to impose the generic termi-
nology of 1568 onto the Scottish lyric production of the late Middle Ages and the
Renaissance. The appropriateness of this procedure is debatable: while it is
certainly of great interest, it can also be (sometimes deliberately) confusing.[28] To
give but one illustration: Bannatyne includes, as his final lyric in detestation of
love and lechery, the prologue to Gavin Douglas's fourth book of *Eneados*
(completed in 1513).[29] The original function of this poem was to introduce the
main thematic concerns of this famous part of the *Aeneid*, which contains the
story of Dido; appropriately, Douglas gives many examples of lovers who have
come to grief through love, and he distinguishes between virtuous love and
sensuality. Bannatyne's understanding, however, is inextricably bound in with
the contemporary politics of his country, with the result that he wrenches
Douglas's poem out of context, and applies it in a way that the poet could not
possibly have imagined.

It will be clear that the critic who comes to the Middle Scots lyrics directly
from a study of the Middle English corpus has to make several readjustments in
his or her expectations. On the one hand, the ready system of generic classifications which is found in the Bannatyne MS, for all its fascination, may actually be
an obstacle to the proper historical contextualisation of the late-medieval lyrics.
On the other, when considered *en masse*, the Middle Scots lyrics are typically
different from those of medieval England. For one thing, most of the Scottish
lyrics are appreciably longer than the English norm. Moreover, the preference
for the pentameter line is not shared by most Middle English lyrics – except for
those emanating from courtly circles, or modelled upon courtly verse styles. The
English and Scottish lyric corpora also differ markedly in the proportion of
authored lyrics to anonymous ones, with the Scottish results being noticeably
higher. There is in Scotland a striking preference for the eight-line stanza (the
so-called 'ballat royal'[30]) – so much so, that any apparently 'Scottish' lyric with
shorter stanzas (such as several of those in the Arundel MS) has a good chance

[27] On the poetry of Mary's reign see MacDonald 2001a.
[28] This is developed in MacDonald 2003.
[29] Ritchie 1928–34, IV, 108–16. See Ross 1986, 396–7.
[30] For this term see Craigie 1955–58, I, 80.

of being an English import, which may have been composed at a date long before that of the Scottish manuscript in which it is preserved. Furthermore, whereas the balance of the total corpus of lyric verse in England is greatly skewed in favour of religious poetry (Robbins *Sec.*, xvii), this is not the case with the Middle Scots corpus. Corroboration hereof may be deduced from the relative size of the sections within the Bannatyne MS. In this all-important collection, the religious lyrics are but one of the four original divisions (of which the others are comprised of moral, comic and amatory verse). Moreover, even if – given that moral and religious verse is often hard to distinguish – one were to take the religious and moral lyrics as a single, combined group, they would still not exceed the space given by the scribe to the amatory lyrics alone: and this in the age of Reformation!

In truth, a direct comparison between the total lyric corpus of Scotland and that of England is fundamentally misleading. Rather than compare the works of the canonical Middle Scots lyric poets with the mostly anonymous English productions of the thirteenth and fourteenth centuries – which, after all, were written in very different circumstances – one might do better to seek to make comparisons with the works of English contemporaries of the allegedly 'drab' Tudor age.[31] Thus the still all too common use of the facile label of 'Scottish Chaucerians' is unfortunate in its potential to suggest synchronicity and affinity. The Middle Scots lyric poets are not great writers because they are Chaucerians: they are great by virtue of their own talents, and in their reaction to the English master and his followers they exhibit a proper measure of discrimination.

Religious and moral lyrics

Perhaps the humblest kind of religious lyric, from the rhetorical point of view at least, is that which consists of little more than the versification of known and formulaic texts, such as prayers. Examples are the Scots texts of the *Pater noster*, the *Ave Maria*, and the *Credo* scribbled on one folio of the Makculloch MS (Stevenson 1918, 17–19). In such compositions the metre and rhyme have a lightly decorative but mainly mnemonic function. Several poems are based on contemporary devotional practices, even though no standard formulas of prayer may be involved: this applies to the two lyrics on the Holy Name in the Arundel MS – though, as mentioned above, these are actually English poems in Scottish guise (Bennett 1955, 277–8). Another is the lyric 'In honour of the Seven Words that our Saviour spoke upon the Cross', *O Lord God, O Crist Iesu* (*IMEV* 2486). A Scots verse translation from a Latin prose prayer is *I pray yow, lady, Mary deir* (*IMEV* 1343), of which the original Latin text, *Obsecro te, domina sacra Maria*, is common in Books of Hours; also based on Latin verse prayers are *Haill, Mary, quhais concepcioun* (*IMEV* 1070.3), from *Ave, cuius concepcio*, and *Haill, glaid and glorius* (*IMEV* 1044), for which the editor was able to identify no precise source.[32]

---

31 For the term 'drab' see Lewis 1954, 64.
32 The Scots lyric is in fact an expansion of a Latin text set to music in the Carver Choirbook (formerly known as the 'Scone Antiphonary'): NLS MS Advocates 5.1.15, fols 178v–180. On Carver and his manuscript see Ross 1993; Woods Preece 2000, 129–68.

There is an acephalous Scots versification of the 'Fifteen Oes' (*IMEV* 3777.5), a widely disseminated devotion, of which English versions exist in manuscript and print, in prose and verse.[33] Much more elaborated is William Dunbar's *Tabill of Confessioun*, which has a prominent place at the beginning of the Arundel MS (Bennett 1955, 1–6; Bawcutt 1998a, I, 267–73). The poem catalogues all the sins that an individual might possibly commit in the course of a life, and ranges *inter alia* over the five senses, the seven deadly sins, the seven deeds of corporal mercy, the seven deeds of spiritual mercy, the seven sacraments, the ten commandments, the twelve articles of the faith, the three theological and four moral virtues, and the seven commands of the Church. This work has not found much favour with critics, one of whom found it necessary to explain that Dunbar was actually incapable of having committed some of the sins to which he confesses (Scott 1966, 292)! In reality, of course, this poem, like others mentioned in this paragraph, exists as an impersonal formula of words, designed to channel the penitential awareness of any reader (not excluding the poet himself). As such, the poem is entirely compatible with the many prose devotional exercises included in the Arundel MS (MacDonald 1988 and 1998).

Probably more interesting for the modern reader are lyrics which are not so narrowly constrained by any pre-existing devotional source. The following deserves to be quoted in its entirety:

Haill, quene of hevin and sterne of blis,	*star*
Sen that thi sone thi fader is,	*since*
How suld he ony thing the warn,	*refuse*
And thou his mother and he thi barne?	*child*
Haill, fresche fontane that springis new,	
The rute and crope of all vertu,	
Thou polist gem without offence,	
Thou bair the lambe of innocence.	*bore* (Bennett 1955, 298)

Originality of thought is not the strong point of this lyric, and the ideas and images can be paralleled in many other medieval poems. However, what is admirable is the economy and dexterity of the poet's allusions to the miraculous: in the first stanza, it is the mystery of the relationships linking the Father and Son to Mary, at a moment subsequent to the Coronation of the Virgin; in the second, images from the world of external nature communicate the inexhaustibility (fountain) of Mary's love, in all its fresh cleanness (water), plenitude (root and crop), pure beauty (jewel), and innocence (lamb).

Also worthy of notice is *O farest lady, O swetast lady, O blisful lady, hewynnis quheyne* (Stevenson 1918, 9; Brown *XV*, No. 20). The infelicitous way in which this lyric was first published obscures the fact that it is actually a carol, with the ostensible opening line actually functioning as a burden, to be repeated at the end of each of four stanzas. The first stanza runs as follows:

O sterne so brycht, that gyfys lycht,	*star*
Til hewyne and haly kyrk,	*to heaven*

---

[33] For the poems mentioned here see, respectively, Bennett 1955, 259–61, 290–3, 287, 294–8, 170–81.

Thi help, thi mycht, grant ws ful rycht,
    Raik throw thar clowdis dirk;   *reach*
Fra hel sa fel, conwoy ws clene,   *from hell so terrible*
On the, Mare, thus most I meyne: *cry*
    O farest lady, O swetast lady,
    O blisful lady, hewynnis quheyne.

The metrical scheme, with its abundant internal rhyme, is skilfully maintained throughout the poem, which is a work of true merit. In these last two poems one glimpses a trace of the now well nigh vanished corpus of anonymous Middle Scots religious lyrics written in lines shorter than the pentameter.

Considerably more numerous, however, are the poems in a more expansive mode, which on occasion verges on rhetorical floridity. Here belong several of the most celebrated lyrics by Dunbar: on the Annunciation and Nativity, *Rorate celi desuper*; on the Passion, *Amang thir freiris within ane cloister*; on the Resurrection, *Done is a battell on the dragon blak*; and on Our Lady, *Hale, sterne superne!* (Bawcutt 1998a, I, 182–3, 34–8, 69–70, 83–5, respectively). Not incompatible with these are Henryson's poem on the Annunciation, *Forcy as deith is likand lufe*, his penitential lyric *O eterne God, of power infinyt*, and Douglas's lyric on the Trinity, *He plasmatour of thingis universall.*[34] Many, though not all, of these lyrics are incorporated into the Bannatyne MS, alongside a number of anonymous lyrics on similar topics; the fact that not a few of the latter have at various times been printed in editions of poems by Dunbar may be taken as a testimony to the authoritative example of this greatest of all medieval Scottish lyricists.

Many critics have commented favourably on the sheer verbal energy of Dunbar's poems on the Nativity and the Resurrection. In *Rorate celi desuper* – the Biblical text comes from Isaiah 45:8, and was used in Christian tradition to express the Incarnation in terms of the metaphor of vivifying dew – the poet generates an irresistible sense of exultation, as he imagines the whole of creation as musically telling the glory of God. *Done is a battell on the dragon blak* works in quite another style of rhetoric: here the basic image is that of the battle, and the suggestion of violence is communicated through the ostentatious use of plosive consonants, in combination with the cumulative effect of parataxis.

The fo is chasit, the battell is done ceis,
The presone brokin, the ievellouris fleit and flemit,   *gaolers scared and put to flight*
The weir is gon, confermit is the peis,   *war is over; confirmed*
The fetteris lowsit and the dungeon temit,   *fetters loosened; emptied*
The ransoun maid, the presoneris redemit,
The feild is win, ourcumin is the fo,
Dispulit of the tresur that he yemit: *despoiled, guarded*
Surrexit dominus de sepulchro. (33–40)   *the Lord is risen from the tomb*

For its part, Dunbar's Marian lyric, *Hale sterne superne*, is perhaps the *locus classicus* of extreme aureation in English vernacular verse (Bawcutt 1992, 354–8). Essentially, the performative language of the lyric advances no argument

---

[34] Fox 1981, 154–6, 167–9; on the first of these see MacDonald 1994b. For Douglas's poem: Ritchie 1928–34, II, 20–6.

beyond what is inherent in its lexically coruscating eulogy. Unlike some other poets indulging in aureation, however, Dunbar retains complete control of his subject through the tight discipline of a virtuoso stanza-form, which, though it has only two end-rhymes in its twelve lines, exploits to the full the chiming harmonies of internal rhyme. The reiterated use of the first words of the Angelic Salutation *Ave Maria, gracia plena* (St Luke 1:28) further unites the poem, and prompts the linkage of these seven stanzas with the devotion based on the Seven Joys of Our Lady (of which the Annunciation is the first).

Hale, sterne superne, hale, in eterne	*hail, star supernal*
In Godis sicht to schyne,	
Lucerne in derne for to discerne,	*lamp in darkness by which to see*
Be glory and grace devyne.	
Hodiern, modern, sempitern,	*for the present, for now and for ever*
Angelicall regyne,	*queen*
Our tern Inferne for to dispern,	*hellish gloom, drive away*
Helpe, rialest rosyne.	*most royal rose*
Aue, Maria, gracia plena.	*Hail Mary, full of grace*
Haile, fresche flour femynyne,	
Yerne, ws guberne, wirgin matern,	*diligently guide us; maternal*
Of reuth baith rute and ryne. (1–12)	*compassion; root and bark*

This lyric, consequently, is unsurpassed in the way in which its shimmering rhetoric perfectly celebrates the initial, mysterious moment in the soteriological programme (Gray 2001). It is possible that Dunbar may have been emulating Henryson's excellent Annunciation lyric, *Forcy as deith is likand lufe,* which likewise consists of twelve-line stanzas in short lines, but, if so, he surpasses the earlier poet. Aureation, of course, is a rhetorical trick by no means unknown to Henryson, as one sees towards the end of the penitential lyric, *O eterne God, of power infinyt,* when, after confession of sins and imploration of mercy, the poet, at line 65, requests that God listen to the people's prayer: *Superne lucerne, guberne this pestilence.* A quite different sort of aureation, however, is found in Douglas's Prologue to the tenth book of his *Eneados*: as befits the subject (the Trinity), Douglas employs the special, learned vocabulary of theology: *He plasmatour of thingis universall.*[35]

A lengthy work which, as one critic has observed, takes one to the outer limits of the lyric, is Walter Kennedy's *Passioun of Crist.*[36] Kennedy gives a detailed and expansive account of the last days of Christ on earth, and he identifies a prose work, the enormous *Vita Christi* of the Carthusian Ludolphus of Saxony, as an important influence. As a distinct part of Kennedy's treatment of the Crucifixion, however, one finds a remarkably powerful lyrical passage (lines 974–1190) in which the meditating narrator enters into a dialogue with the Cross. At such a moment, narration passes over into meditation, and through such a passage the reader can actively participate in the poem, just as he or she might do when confronted with a lyric of more modest proportions. By contrast,

---

[35] On aureation in Middle Scots verse see Ellenberger 1977; Corbett 2001.
[36] Woolf, 237; MacDonald 1998, 125–30. For the text: Bennett 1955, 7–63.

Dunbar's lyric on the Passion, *Amang thir freiris within ane cloister*, is much more economical, though it is also couched in the narrative mode. Here the account of the Crucifixion is contained within the frame-story of a personal meditation putatively performed by the poet himself, genuflecting before a crucifix. By a further sophistication, Dunbar's story of the Passion is immediately followed by a complementary allegorical narrative, the function of which is to instruct the reader in the proper emotional and psychological effects that the Passion ought already to have induced – especially when this event is recounted with a brutality of visual detail that betrays the empathising aesthetic of the *Meditationes vitae Christi*.[37] It will have become clear from the foregoing that the Middle Scots religious lyrics contain several poems of the very highest literary quality. Equally, however, one will appreciate the extent to which the spectacular artistry of such poems renders them untypical of the medieval English vernacular lyric genre if considered as a whole. As we shall see, this observation is also pertinent to Middle Scots lyrics on non-religious subjects.

The appeal of poems on moral themes is more to the reason than to either the spirit or the emotions. They deal, characteristically, in such fundamental and universal matters as the human condition, the imperfections of human society, and the contrast between fleeting pleasures and eternal joys. Though such topics may not be immediately gratifying to some modern tastes, it must be conceded that there are many Middle Scots moral lyrics which are impressive within the terms of their various sub-genres. With this class of lyric, however, the universality of thematics does permit one to perceive parallels between the Middle Scots specimens and their English predecessors.

Of essential importance is the establishment of a poetic voice of incontrovertible moral authority. Sometimes the poet speaks in his own voice, as in the pseudo-Henrysonian lyric, *Me mervellis of this grit confusioun*, in the genuinely Henrysonian *Fals titlaris now growis up full rank*,[38] and – most importantly – in many lyrics by Dunbar. The voice of authority is not infrequently assigned to a prophet-bird, as, for example, in Dunbar's *Off lentren in the first mornyng*, and in such anonymous lyrics as *Furth throw ane forrest as I fure*, *Walking allone amang thir levis grene*, and *Doun by ane rever as I red* (Bawcutt 1998a, I, 159–60; Ritchie 1928–34, II, 109–12, 132–6, 122–4). Another strategy is to assign the message to a man of venerable age, as in Henryson's *Within ane garth, undir ane reid rosier* and Kennedy's *At matyne houre in midis of the nicht* (Fox 1981, 165–7; Ritchie 1928–34, II, 131–2), or to one who may be the articulator of some authoritative verse from the Bible or the liturgy, for instance, Dunbar's *Memento, homo, quod cinis es*, a text which is also used as the refrain in Lichtoun's *O mortall man, remembir nycht and day* (Bawcutt 1998a, I, 120–1; Ritchie 1928–34, II, 119–20). A variant of this is found in lyrics where the narrator is suddenly confronted with an admonitory inscription (Henryson, *Allone as I went up and doun*; Walter Broun, *Lettres of gold writtin I fand*), or with a speaking emblem, such as the three skulls in

---

[37] Bawcutt 1998a, I, 34–8; Woolf, 233–4; Bawcutt 1992, 167–71; MacDonald 1998, 123–4.

[38] The first of these, traditionally known as 'The Want of Wysemen', is ejected from the Henrysonian canon by Fox 1981, cxvi–cxvii; it is perhaps most easily consulted in Harvey Wood 1958, 189–91. For the second of these poems: Fox 1981, 163–5.

Henryson's, *O sinfull man, in to this mortall se* (Fox 1981, 156–8; Ritchie 1928–34, II, 127–31; Fox 1981, 182–4). In still other lyrics the message may be communicated in a revelatory dream, for instance, Dunbar's *Doverrit with dreme, devysing in my slummer*; alternatively, it may emerge from a debate as in Henryson's *Quhen fair Flora, the godes of the flouris*, and *O mortall man, behald, tak tent to me* (Bawcutt 1998a, I, 71–4; Fox 1981, 170–3, 173–5). Such variant strategies for the establishment of a normative voice tend to cast the author of moral lyrics in one or more of the following roles: teacher, priest, prophet, exhorter, satirist, scourge, and spokesman for values inherited from the past.

Dunbar's Ash Wednesday poem is particularly effective and typical of the genre, in its review of human mortality:

Memento, homo, quod cinis es:	*Remember, man, that thou art ash*
Think, man, thow art bot erd and as.	*earth and ashes*
Lang heir to dwell na thing thow pres,	*in no way strive*
For as thow come sa sall thow pas.	*came*
Lyk as ane schaddow in ane glas,	*reflection in a mirror*
Hyne glydis all thy tyme that heir is.	*hence*
Think, thocht thy bodye ware of bras,	*though*
Quod tu in cinerem reuerteris.	*that thou must return to ash*

(Bawcutt 1998a, I, 120–1, lines 1–8)

The standard technique here, as in so many other such compositions, is for the poet to present a brutal juxtaposition of conflicting perspectives on human existence: for the reader, the intended effect is one of surprise, and even of shock, as he or she is manœuvred into conceding the truth of the uncomfortable message. This may be triggered by eschatological terror, as in a lyric by Walter Broun:

Fra hevin to hell, throw erd and air,	
That hiddeous trump sa lowid sall sound,	
That throw the blast, I yow declair,	
The stanis sall cleive, erd sall redound.	*shudder*
Sall no man respect get, that stound,	*hour*
For gold, for riches, or for rent,	
For all mon cum ouir see and sound	*must*
And present thame to iugement.	

(Ritchie 1928–34, II, 127–31, lines 17–24)

Poems which use personifications (Age and Youth, Death and Life, etc.) to dramatise the opposing views are often neatly efficient in their communication. In Henryson's *Ressoning betuix Deth and Man*, for example, the dialectic is, in miniature, that which animates such a work as the medieval play of *Everyman* (Fox 1981, 173–5). In Walter Kennedy's *At matyne houre, in midis of the nicht* the clash of values leaves only one party as a realistic option:

O bittir yowith, that semis delitious,	
O haly aige, that sumtyme semit soure,	
O restles yowth, hie, hait and vicious,	*contemptuous; impulsive*
O honest aige, fulfillit with honoure.	

(Ritchie 1928–34, II, 131–2, lines 17–20)

In Henryson's *Ressoning betuix Aige and Yowth*, however, the poet concludes
with a bare recapitulation of the two irreconcilable views of life:

> O yowth, be glaid in to thy flowris grene;
> O yowth, thy flowris faidis fellone sone.   *extremely*
>
> (Fox 1981, 170–3, lines 71–2)

In this last case, the poet's readiness to give vent to both attitudes is untypical,
but is perhaps none the less effective for that.

Moral lyrics attacking the evils of society were as widely cultivated in Scotland as in England; indeed, this is one of the central themes of the *œuvre* of
William Dunbar. It is perhaps more interesting, however, to observe certain
innovations of the late Middle Ages. One new subject seems to be the praise of
measure:

> Be nocht our mad attour mesure,   *too passionate beyond*
> Nor yit our meik in thy moving;
> Be nocht our rad for no dreddure,   *too fearful; dread*
> Nor yit our derf in thy doing.   *bold*
> As Cato sayis in his teiching,
> In al thingis knaw the quantetie,
> As all tyme askis of every thing,
> In alkyn materis mesur the.   *all kinds*
>
> (Ritchie 1928–34, II, 109–12, lines 49–56)

This anonymous poem is the very first item in the section of moral poems in the
Bannatyne MS. Although the date of the poem cannot be fixed with certainty, it
seems to stand at the meeting point of the medieval and early modern worlds: on
the one hand, the poet relies on such standard texts as the Bible and 'Cato'; on the
other, the lyric seems almost humanistic in its praise of the middle way in religion
and morality. Another subject offering novel possibilities is the discussion of vice
at court. In the period with which we are dealing, this means not so much the
age-old censure of life within the palace, but rather Renaissance satire on the
operation of the judicial system. Bannatyne even has a generic label for such
compositions: 'ballattis again[s] the vyce in sessioun court and all estaitis' (Ritchie
1928–34, II, 145). In Dunbar's handling of this subject, acute observation of the
detail of corrupt behaviour goes hand in hand with a sharply ironic humour:

> Sum withe his fallow rownys him to pleis,   *whispers*
> That wald for anger byt of his neis.   *nose*
> His fa sum be the oxtar leidis.   *enemy; arm*
> Sum pattiris with his mouthe on beidis   *prayers*
> That hes his mynd all on oppressioun.
> Sum bekis full laich and schawis bair heidis, *bows; low*
> Wald luke full heich war not the Sessioun.
>
> (Bawcutt 1998a, I, 39–40, lines 15–21)

Half a century later, such lines were doubtless to inspire Sir Richard Maitland,
who was a judge as well as a poet.[39] One of the most interesting of these new

---

[39] On whom see MacDonald 1972; MacDonald 2001b.

lyric themes consists of the poet's difficulty of assessing his own place in the society in which he finds himself. Once again, William Dunbar stands out in his exploration of this topic, in which one seems to hear the voice of the early modern personal subject:

> How sowld I rewill me or quhat wyis,
> I wald sum wyisman wald dewyis.   *devise*
> I can not leif in no degre,   *live*
> Bot sum my maneris will dispyis.
> Lord God, how sall I governe me?   *shall*
>
> (Bawcutt 1998a, I, 87–8, lines 1–5)

In this poem, as in quite a number of others, Dunbar engages with the problems of his own role at the court of James IV; the venerable theme of estates satire is made consonant with an articulation of the personal moral and psychological integrity of the observing poet. As a consequence, Dunbar emerges as one of the subtlest, if also one of the less representative, writers of medieval lyric verse. In the present context, however, space does not permit further discussion of his many remarkably versatile and brilliant lyrics dealing with *mores* at the Scottish court.

Comic and amatory lyrics

The largest collection of Middle Scots lyrics on these two subjects is that preserved in respectively the third and fourth sections of the Bannatyne MS. As with the religious and moral poems, so too here the manuscript corpus is comprised of lyrics from around or before 1500 together with others written in the following six decades. Once again, English poems make an appearance in Scottish guise: these include both Chaucerian material and more modern work, such as several poems by John Heywood.[40] Although it is difficult to say much about the origin and date of the large number of anonymous lyrics preserved by Bannatyne, certain general trends can be discerned. Just as Bannatyne's manuscript evinces the dominating position of William Dunbar among the Scottish lyricists at the opening of the century, so does it testify to the equivalent prestige of Alexander Scott in the age of Mary Stewart – albeit that, as one moves through the sixty years that separate the main production of the two men, the medieval pattern of poets who are priests gives way to the Renaissance norm of the secular poet (van Heijnsbergen 2001 and 1996). Thus, while one finds some, but not many, love-lyrics written (presumably to commission) by churchmen at the court of James IV, such poems become common in the reigns of the latter's successors; a concomitant development is the visible decline in the courtly-style religious lyric, which in the age of the Reformation is eclipsed by translations, adaptations and original compositions variously proclaiming and responding to

---

[40] For details: Fox and Ringler 1980, xli; Bawcutt (2005).

new dogma.[41] The discussion offered here, however, once again restricts itself to lyrics from no later than the age of James IV.

As with so many kinds of lyric, William Dunbar is also a master of the comic, and in his poems this element is regularly linked with court life. Examples would be the macaronic *I maister Andro Kennedy*, which seems to be a parodic piece of self-dramatisation on the part of the shamelessly inebriated speaker. Other memorable poems have recourse to narrative – such as *Lucina schyning in silence of the nicht*, in which the poet tells of a dream in which a devil disguised as St Francis tempted him to assume the habit of a grey friar, and *As yung Awrora with cristall haile*, in which Dunbar speaks of an attempt at flight made by a parasitical mountebank; needless to say, the foolish enterprise is ludicrously unsuccessful (Bawcutt 1998a, I, 89–92, 114–15, 56–9). The modern reader, however, may be surprised by certain poems, which George Bannatyne classed as comic. One of these is *This nycht in my sleip I wes agast*, a poem in which the devil claims the souls of all kinds of men guilty of swearing thoughtless oaths:

> Me thocht, as he went throw the way,
> Ane preist sweirit be God verey,
> Quhilk at the alter ressauit he.   *which; received*
> 'Thow art my clerk,' the devill can say,
> 'Renunce thy God and cum to me.'   (Bawcutt 1998a, I, 250–7, lines 6–10)

It would therefore seem as if this devil – the Tutivillus of tradition – is for Dunbar a figure inspiring more amusement than terror. A comparable uncertainty as to the appropriate response arises in the case of the famous catalogue generally known as the *Lament for the Makaris* which likewise is contained in the comic section of the Bannatyne MS (Bawcutt 1998a, I, 94–7). Interestingly, the same poem also appears in the company of three indubitably comic works in an early printed booklet, now bound with the productions of Chepman and Myllar. The refrain line, *Timor mortis conturbat me* [the fear of death distresses me], is found in a number of Middle English lyrics and carols on the theme of death, and the easiest interpretation has always been to see Dunbar's poem as belonging within the same plangent tradition. Indeed, the critical consensus holds that this poem expresses a particularly late-medieval sense of melancholy *angst*, in its evocation of the dance of death.[42] However, in view of the evidence from the contexts in which this poem is preserved, the possibility ought not automatically to be excluded that this lyric may in fact be an ironically *humorous* meditation on the longevity of poetic reputation.[43] Such an innovative interpretation, of course, depends upon discovering here a wittily incongruous manipulation of generic expectations. However, is not precisely this one of the things for which Dunbar is especially notable among late-medieval lyricists? In this context, one recalls the colophon (only in the Maitland Folio MS) to one of

---

[41] MacDonald 1978, 384–466. Not surprisingly, there is some degree of connection at the level of *contrafactum*: MacDonald 1996.

[42] For this tradition of interpretation see Woolf, 335; Gray 1972, 216–17; Bawcutt 1992, 153–8.

[43] MacDonald 1994c. Hughes and Ramson go so far as to allow for the possibility of 'savage but salutory' comedy in such a work: 1982, 111–12, 115.

Dunbar's most comical love lyrics (*My hartis tresure and swete assured fo*) in its use of overblown rhetoric: the poet is said to have written this work 'quhone he list to feyne' [when he chose to pretend]. It is unfortunate that we have no knowledge of the performance aspect of such lyrics, since this might be expected to provide a clue to the true meaning.[44]

This delight in the exploitation of rhetoric also marks Dunbar's treatment of love, as is clearly seen in the following:

In secreit place this hyndir nycht	*last*
I hard ane beyrne say till ane bricht:	*hero; lady*
'My hwny, my hart, my hoip, my heill,	*honey; health*
I haue bene lang your luifar leill	*loyal*
And can of yow get confort nane.	
How lang will ye with danger deill?	*show disdain*
Ye brek my hart, my bony ane.'	*pretty one*

(Bawcutt 1990a, 106–8, lines 1–8)

What is admirable here is the way in which Dunbar brilliantly subverts the clichés of courtly love: *your luifar leill, get confort nane, with danger deill*, etc. This also involves using some archaic vocabulary (*ane beyrne, ane bricht*), and, in the third line, an absurd quadrupling of vapid terms of endearment, aurally suggestive of the rustic lover's heavy breathing. The ensuing stanzas continue the strain of fantastic wordplay, showing that Dunbar is interested not so much in love, as in the rhetorical representation of love as a comical game of social and literary conventions.

An equivalent attitude is seen in the English and Scottish lyrics which treat love in terms of impossibilities. A charming English specimen is found in Richard Hill's MS (*IMEV* 3999):

Whan netilles in wynter bere rosis rede,
And thornys bere figges naturally . . . (Robbins *Sec.*, No. 114, 1–2)

Such tropes can be exactly paralleled in certain lines by William Stewart on the loyalty of women (Ritchie 1928–34, IV, 41–2; Hadley Williams 2001, 98), and in two anonymous lyrics in the Bannatyne MS, which introduce Scottish details in order to accentuate the absurdity of the premiss:

Quhen the Ochellis ar flittit over the Ferry,	*removed*
And Loch Levin rynnis over the Eist Lowmond,	*runs*
And gud wyne growis on the brwmill berry,	*broom*
And Tay and Tweid ar temit to the grund,	*run dry*
And bellis quhen thay ar rungin hes no sound,	
And quhen the wind is stable and still standis so:	
Than sall my lady luve me and no mo.[45]	

---

44 Bawcutt reads this lyric 'straight': 1992, 299–301.
45 Ritchie 1928–34, IV, 42–3, 44–5, lines 15–21. In the latter passage the references are topographical: the Ochil Hills (between Stirling and Kinross) are imagined as being transported across the river Forth, at Queensferry; likewise Loch Leven (in Kinross-shire) is to overflow the neighbouring hill of Easter Lomond, near Falkland (in Fife).

Although at first blush such lines may appear anti-feminist, they in fact belong within a tradition of intellectual game, in which the superficial and jejune 'message' pales into insignificance beside the witty inventiveness of the poet in the specification of riddling conditions (Utley 1944, 133–4).

Most of the best Scottish poems that seem sincere in the expression of love come from the middle of the sixteenth century, the period of the great lyricist Alexander Scott. However, certain of the lyrics which may have seemed new to George Bannatyne are actually recyclings of much older material. One of the longest, entitled *The Lettre of Cupeid*, consists in fact of Thomas Hoccleve's adaptation of *L'Epistre au dieu d'amours*, by Christine de Pisan. Bannatyne took this poem, however, from Thynne's edition of Chaucer of c.1545–50. The same book provided him with his next love-lyric, *All tho that list of wemen evill to speik*, which, though here attributed to Chaucer, is elsewhere often ascribed to Lydgate.[46] It was in this rather wordy style that Dunbar composed his lyric, *My hartis tresure and swete assured fo*, which is rhetorically correct in venting the lover's formulas of erotic reproach. For its part, another courtly poem, *Sweit rois of vertew and of gentilnes*, is technically perfect – despite the somewhat artificial message of planting anew the flower of rue within the garden of the lady's emotions (Bawcutt 1998a, I, 125–6, 235). It is interesting that such poems were still thought worthy of transcription in the age of Mary Stewart.

It is, however, among the lyrics which Bannatyne labels as being 'in contempt of blinded love' that Dunbar really comes into his own, with his voice of the priest-poet observing the phenomenon of love from the sidelines. To some extent one is reminded of the monk Lydgate, and it is altogether congruous that this same section of the manuscript contains a lyric with a listing of unfortunate lovers, excerpted from Lydgate's *Complaint of the Black Knight*, here ascribed to Chaucer (Ritchie 1928–34, IV, 82–7; Fox and Ringler 1980, xxxviii). One must admire the deftly economic skill with which Dunbar can communicate the sardonic mood of the man weary of the stale rigmarole of courtly love:

> It is ane pount of ignorance
> To lufe in sic distemperance,   *such*
> Sen tyme mispendit may avance   *since*
>   No creature.
> In luve to keip allegance,
> It war als nys an ordinance   *foolish*
> As quha wald bid ane deid man dance
>   In sepulture.   *grave*
>   (Bawcutt 1998a, I, 161, lines 17–24)

In other poems, Dunbar opposes the love of God to that of an earthly mistress, as in *In May as that Aurora did upspring*, or waxes lyrical at the way in which his love for Christ is able to expel all thoughts of sexual attraction in *Now culit is Dame Venus' brand* (Bawcutt 1998a, I, 101–5, 130–2). Dunbar's lyrics in this vein lend themselves well to being associated with the more disillusioned writings of Alexander Scott.[47] They are a world away from the Harley lyrics.

[46] Ritchie 1928–34, IV, 49–64, 64–70; Fox and Ringler 1980, xxxvii.
[47] Cranstoun 1896; MacQueen 1970; van Heijnsbergen 1991; Dunnigan 2002.

Conclusion

The corpus of Middle Scots lyric verse is rich, varied, subtle and rewarding; it is also large enough to prevent more than selective commentary in this chapter. As has been demonstrated above, there are many contacts with the equivalent English corpus, but there is also a need to make clear distinctions between the two traditions. The best Scottish lyrics are sophisticated productions, and are of comparatively late date. They seem to assume a knowledge of earlier work, which they then set out to transcend. It is important that one appreciate how, for Scottish readers in the mid-sixteenth century, Chaucer's works might still possess the attraction of novelty, and this was doubtless the reason why such poems were so often copied from printed books into manuscript anthologies. It is regrettable, however, that there is now no trace in the Middle Scots lyrics of the activities of the friars. Those lyrics which we do have doubtless emanate, in the main, from court circles, and they are commensurately artful and decorative. Among many great writers of lyric verse, William Dunbar is outstanding. One of the most interesting features of the literary culture of early modern Scotland is the way in which the lyrics of the Middle Ages were repackaged to make them acceptable in the post-Reformation climate. The transmission and reception history of the Middle Scots lyric is thus very different from that of England, and George Bannatyne's skilful and innovative generic classifications have the oddly dislocating effect of making a medieval poet such as Dunbar seem the putative contemporary of a Renaissance poet such as Alexander Scott. It may be that the waning of the Middle Ages continued in Scotland somewhat longer than it did in England, but as far as the lyric is concerned, the resulting cross-fertilisation with the Renaissance was well worth the wait.[48]

[48] This chapter has benefited from the scrutiny of Mr Theo van Heijnsbergen and Dr Sally Mapstone; any errors are my own responsibility.

Bibliography of Works Cited

Aers, D., ed. 1992. *Culture and History, 1350–1600*. Hemel Hempstead.

Aers, D. and Staley, L., eds. 1996. *The Powers of the Holy: Religion, Politics, and Gender in Late Medieval English Culture*. University Park, Pennsylvania.

Aitken, A. J., McDiarmid, M. P. and Thomson, D. S., eds. 1977. *Bards and Makars*. Glasgow.

Aitken, A. J., McIntosh, A. and Pálsson, H., eds. 1971. *Edinburgh Studies in English and Scots*. London.

Allen, H. E. 1927. *Writings Ascribed to Richard Rolle, Hermit of Hampole, and Materials for his Biography*. New York and London.

Allen, H. E., ed. 1931. *The English Writings of Richard Rolle, Hermit of Hampole*. Oxford. Repr. 1988. Gloucester.

Anderson, J. J. 1980. 'Two Difficulties in *The Meeting in The Wood*'. *Medium Ævum* 49. 258–9.

Archibald, E. 1992. 'Tradition and Innovation in the Macaronic Poetry of Dunbar and Skelton'. *Modern Language Quarterly* 53. 126–49.

Arn, M.-J., ed. 1994. *Fortunes Stabilnes, Charles of Orleans's English Book of Love*. Medieval and Renaissance Texts and Studies, Vol. 138. Binghampton, New York.

Arn, M.-J., ed. 2000. *Charles d'Orléans in England 1415–1440*. Cambridge.

Aspin, I. S. T., ed. 1953. *Anglo-Norman Political Songs*. Anglo Norman Text Society 11.

Astell, A. W. 1990. *The Song of Songs in the Middle Ages*. Ithaca, New York and London.

Audiau, J. and Lavaud, R., eds. 1928. *Nouvelle Anthologie des Troubadours*. Paris.

Ayto, J. and Barratt, A., eds. 1984. *Aelred of Rievaulx: De Institutione Inclusarum*. EETS OS 287.

Backhouse, J. 1995. 'Illuminated manuscripts Associated with Henry VII and Members of his Immediate Family'. In B. Thompson. 175–87.

Barbour, John. See McDiarmid and Stevenson.

Barney, S. 1993. *Studies in 'Troilus': Chaucer's Text, Meter, and Diction*. East Lansing.

Barnum, P. H., ed. 1976, 1980. *Dives et Pauper*. EETS OS 275, 280.

Barr, H., ed. 1993. *The 'Piers Plowman' Tradition: A Critical Edition of 'Pierce the Ploughman's Creed','Richard the Redeless', 'Mum and the Sothesegger' and 'The Crowned King'*. London.

Barr, H. 1994. *Signes and Sothe: Language in the Piers Plowman Tradition*. Cambridge.

Barr, H. 2001. *Socioliterary Practice in Late Medieval England*. Oxford.

Barratt, A. 1975. 'The Prymer and its Influence on Fifteenth-Century Passion Lyrics'. *Medium Ævum* 44. 264–79.

Barratt, A., ed. 1992. *Women's Writing in Middle English*. London and New York.

Barratt, A., ed. 1995. *A Commentary on The Penitential Psalms translated by Dame Eleanor Hull*. EETS OS 307.

Barthes, R. 1985. *The Responsibility of Forms: Critical Essays on Music, Art, and Representation*. Trans. R. Howard. New York.

Bartsch, K., ed. 1870. *Altfranzösischen Romanzen und Pastourellen*. Leipzig.

Baswell, C. 1999. 'Latinitas'. In Wallace 1999. 122–151.

Bataille, G. 1986. *Erotisme: Death and Sensuality*. Trans. M. Dalwood. San Francisco.

Bawcutt, P. 1981. 'Source-hunting: some reulis and cautelis'. In Lyall and Riddy. 85–105.

Bawcutt, P. 1986. 'Dunbar's Christmas Carol'. In Strauss and Drescher. 381–92.

Bawcutt, P. 1990. 'The Commonplace Book of John Maxwell'. In Gardner-Medwin and Hadley Williams. 59–68.

Bawcutt, P. 1991. 'The Earliest Texts of Dunbar'. In *Regionalism in Medieval Manuscripts and Texts*. Ed. F. Riddy. Cambridge. 183–98.

Bawcutt, P. 1992. *Dunbar the Makar*. Oxford.

Bawcutt, P., ed. 1996. William Dunbar. *Selected Poems*. London.

Bawcutt, P., ed. 1998a. *The Poems of William Dunbar*, 2 vols. Glasgow.

Bawcutt, P. 1998b. 'Crossing the Border: Scottish poetry and English Readers in the Sixteenth Century'. In Mapstone and Wood. 59–76 (68).

Bawcutt, P. 2005. 'Scottish manuscript miscellanies from the fifteenth to the seventeenth century'. *English Manuscript Studies* 12. 46–73.

Bayless, M. 1996. *Parody in the Middle Ages. The Latin Tradition*. Ann Arbor.

Bazire, J. 1982. 'Mercy and Justice'. *Neuphilologische Mitteilungen* 83. 178–91.

Beadle R. and Owen A. E. B., intro. 1977. *The Findern Manuscript: Cambridge University Library, MS Ff.1.6*. Facsimile. London.

Beattie, W., ed. 1950. *The Chepman and Myllar Prints*. Edinburgh Bibliographical Society. Edinburgh.

Bec, P. 1977–78. *La Lyrique française au moyen-age (XIIe–XIIIe siècles). Contribution à une typologie des genres poétiques médiévaux. I. Études. II. Textes*. Paris.

Beckwith, S. 1992. 'Ritual, Church and Theatre: Medieval Dramas of the Sacramental Body'. In Aers. 65–89.

Beckwith, S. 1993. *Christ's Body: Identity, Culture and Society in Late Medieval Writings*. London and New York.

Bellenden, J. 1540? *The Hystory and Croniklis of Scotland*. Trans. Hector Boece. Edinburgh.

Bellenden, J. 1977. *Chronicle of Scotland*. Trans. Hector Boethius. Amsterdam. Facsimile of Bellenden 1540?

Bellenden, J. See Chambers, Batho and Husbands.

Bennett, J. A. W., ed. 1955. *Devotional Pieces in Verse and Prose*. STS. Edinburgh and London.

Bennett, J. A. W. 1981. 'Scottish pre-Reformation devotion: some notes on British Library MS Arundel 285'. In Benskin and Samuels. 299–308.

Bennett, J. A. W. 1982. *The Poetry of the Passion: Studies in Twelve Centuries of English Verse*. Oxford.

Bennett, J. A. W. 1986. *Middle English Literature*. Ed. and completed by D. Gray. The Oxford History of English Literature, Vol. 1, Part 2. Oxford.

Bennett, J. A. W. and Smithers, G. V., eds. 1968. *Early Middle English Verse and Prose*. 2nd edn. Oxford.

Bennett, M. J. 1981–82. 'John Audley: some new Evidence on his Life and Work'. *Chaucer Review* 16. 344–55.

Bennett, M. J. 1992. 'Conviviality and Charity in Medieval and Early Modern England'. *Past and Present* 134. 19–41.

Benskin, M. J. 1989. 'The Style and Authorship of the Kildare Poems – (I) *Pers of Bermingham*'. In *In Other Words. Transcultural Studies in Philology, Translation and Lexicology Presented to H. H. Meier*. Eds J. Lachlan Mackenzie and R. Todd. Dordrecht. 57–75.

Benskin, M. and Samuels, M. L., eds. 1981. *So meny people longages and tonges: Philolog-

ical Essays in Scots and Medieval English Presented to Angus McIntosh. Edinburgh.

Benson, L. D., ed. 1988. *The Riverside Chaucer*. 3rd edn. Oxford.

Bent, M. 1973. 'The Transmission of English Music, 1300–1500: Some Aspects of Repertory and Presentation'. In *Studien zur Tradition in der Musik: Kurt von Fischer zum 60. Geburtstag*. Eds. H. H. Eggebrecht and M. Lütolf. Munich. 65–83.

Biernoff, S. 2002. *Sight and Embodiment in the Middle Age*. Houndsmills, Hampshire and New York.

Blodgett, J. E. 1984. 'William Thynne (d. 1546)'. In Ruggiers. 35–52.

Blume, C. and Bannister, H. M., eds. 1915. *Analecta Hymnica Medii Aevi* 54. Leipzig.

Blunt, J. H., ed. 1873. *The Myroure of Oure Ladye*. EETS ES 19.

Boece, H. (Boethius). See Bellenden, J.; Chambers, Batho and Husbands.

Boffey, J. 1983. 'The Manuscripts of English Courtly Love Lyrics in the Fifteenth Century'. In *Manuscripts and Readers in Fifteenth-Century England*. Ed. D. Pearsall. Cambridge. 3–15.

Boffey, J. 1985. *Manuscripts of English Courtly Love Lyrics in the Later Middle Ages*. Woodbridge.

Boffey, J. 1988. 'French Lyrics and English Manuscripts: the transmission of some poems in Trinity College, Cambridge, MS R.3.20, and British Library MS Harley 7333'. *Text* 4. 135–46.

Boffey, J. 1993. 'The Reputation and Circulation of Chaucer's Lyrics in the Fifteenth Century'. *Chaucer Review* 28. 23–40.

Boffey, J. 1996. 'Short texts in Manuscript Anthologies: the Minor Poems of John Lydgate in two Fifteenth-Century Collections'. In *The Whole Book: Cultural Perspectives on the Medieval Miscellany*. Eds. S. G. Nichols and S. Wenzel. Ann Arbor. 69–82.

Boffey, J. 1997. ' "Loke on þis wrytyng, man, for þi devocion": Focal Texts in Some Late Middle English Religious Lyrics'. In Pickering. 129–46.

Boffey, J. 2000a. 'Bodleian Library, MS Arch. Selden. B. 24 and Definitions of the "Household Book" '. In Edwards, Gillespie and Hanna. 125–34.

Boffey, J. 2000b. 'Prospecting in the Archives: Middle English Verse in Record Repositories'. In *New Directions in Later Medieval Manuscript Studies*. Ed. D. Pearsall. York. 41–51.

Boffey, J. 2001. 'The Maitland Folio Manuscript as a Verse Anthology'. In Mapstone 2001a. 40–50.

Boffey, J. and Edwards, A. S. G., intro. 1997. *The Works of Geoffrey Chaucer and 'The Kingis Quair': A Facsimile of Bodleian Library, Oxford, MS Arch. Selden. B.24*. Cambridge.

Boffey, J. and Edwards, A. S. G. 1999. 'Bodleian MS Arch. Selden. B. 24 and the "Scotticization" of Middle English Verse'. In Prendergast and Kline. 166–185.

Boffey, J. and Edwards, A. S. G. 2000. 'Middle English Verse in Chronicles'. In *New Perspectives on Middle English Texts. A Festschrift for R.A. Waldron*. Eds. S. Powell and J. J. Smith. Cambridge. 119–28.

Boffey, J. and Edwards, A. S. G. 2001. 'An Unpublished Middle English Lyric and a Chaucer Allusion'. *Archiv für das Studium der neueren Sprachen und Literaturen* 238. 327–30.

Boffey, J. and Edwards, A. S. G. 2003. 'Unrecorded Middle English Verse Texts in a Canterbury Cathedral Library manuscript'. *Medium Ævum* 72. 49–62.

Boffey, J. and Thompson, J. J. 1989. 'Anthologies and Miscellanies'. In *Book Production and Publishing in Britain 1375–1475*. Eds. J. Griffiths and D. Pearsall. Cambridge. 279–315.

Boklund-Lagopoulou, K. 2000. '*Yate of Heven*: Conceptions of the Female Body in the Religious Lyrics'. In Renevey and Whitehead. 133–54.

Boklund-Lagopoulou, K. 2002. '*I have a yong suster*': *Popular Song and the Middle English Lyric*. Dublin.

Bonaventure, Bro. 1961. 'The Teaching of Latin in Later Medieval England'. *Mediaeval Studies* 23. 1–20.

Booth, W. 1961. *The Rhetoric of Fiction*. Chicago.

Bowers, J. M. 1989. 'Hoccleve's Huntington Holographs: the First "Collected Poems" in English'. *Fifteenth-Century Studies* 15. 27–51.

Bowers, R. 1995. 'Early Tudor Courtly Song: An Evaluation of the Fayrfax Book (BL, Additional MS 5465)'. In B. Thompson. 188–212.

Breeze, A. 1989. 'The Three Sorrowful Tidings'. *Zeitschrift für Celtische Philologie* 43. 141–50.

Brereton, G., trans. 1968. *Froissart: Chronicles*. Harmondsworth.

Brewer, D. S. 1955. 'The Ideal of Feminine Beauty in Medieval Literature, Especially "Harley Lyrics", Chaucer and Some Elizabethans'. *Modern Language Review* 50. 257–69.

Brewer, D. S., ed. 1969. Geoffrey Chaucer, *The Works 1532*. Facsimile. Menston.

Brewer, D. S. and Owen, A. E. B., intro. 1977. *The Thornton Manuscript (Lincoln Cathedral MS. 91)*. 2nd edn. London.

Brook, G. L. 1933. 'The Original Dialects of the Harley Lyrics'. *Leeds Studies in English* 2. 38–61.

Brook, G. L., ed. 1968. *The Harley Lyrics*. 4th edn. Manchester.

Brown, C. 1916–20. *A Register of Middle English Religious and Didactic Verse*. 2 vols. Oxford.

Brown, C. 1928. 'A Thirteenth-Century MS from Llanthony Priory'. *Speculum* 3. 587–95.

Brown, C., ed. 1932. *English Lyrics of the Thirteenth Century*. Oxford.

Brown, C., ed. 1939. *Religious Lyrics of the Fifteenth Century*. Oxford.

Brown, C., ed. 1952. *Religious Lyrics of the Fourteenth Century*. 2nd edn revised by G. V. Smithers. Oxford.

Brown, C. and Robbins, R. H. 1943. *The Index of Middle English Verse*. New York.

Bukofzer, M. 1950. 'Holy-Week Music and Carols at Meaux Abbey'. In *Studies in Medieval and Renaissance Music*. New York. 113–75.

Bukofzer, M. 1960. 'Popular and Secular Music in England (to c.1470)'. In *Ars Nova and the Renaissance 1300–1540*. Eds. Dom A. Hughes and G. Abraham. New Oxford History of Music 3. London. 107–33.

Burnley, J. D. 1998a. *Courtliness and Literature in Medieval England*. London and New York.

Burnley, J. D. 1998b. *Chaucer's Language and the Philosophers' Tradition*. Cambridge.

Burrow, J. A. 1979. 'Poems Without Contexts'. *Essays in Criticism* 29. 6–32.

Burrow, J. A. 1984. *Essays on Medieval Literature*. Oxford.

Burrow, J. A. 1990. 'The Shape of the Vernon Refrain Lyrics'. In Pearsall 1990. 187–99.

Burrow, J. A., ed. 1999. *Thomas Hoccleve's 'Complaint' and 'Dialogue'*. EETS OS 313.

Burrow, J. A. and Doyle, A. I., intro. 2002. *Thomas Hoccleve: A Facsimile of the Autograph Verse Manuscripts*. EETS SS 19.

Butterfield, A. 2002. *Poetry and Music in Medieval France: From Jean Renart to Guillaume de Machaut*. Cambridge.

Bynum, C. 1991. *Fragmentation and Redemption: Essays on Gender and the Human Body in Medieval Religion*. New York and Cambridge.

Caie, G., Lyall, R. J., Mapstone, S. and Simpson, K., eds. 2001. *The European Sun*. East Linton.

Calendar of State Papers Scotland, 1509–89. 1858. London.

Camargo, M. 1998. 'Two Middle English Carols from an Exeter Manuscript'. *Medium Ævum* 67. 104–11.

Camille, M. 2000. 'Before the Gaze: The Internal Senses and Late Medieval Practices of Seeing'. In *Visuality Before and Beyond the Renaissance*. Ed. R. S. Nelson. Cambridge. 197–223.

Carruthers, M. J. 1990. *The Book of Memory: A Study of Memory in Medieval Culture*. Cambridge.

Cartlidge, N. 1997. 'The Composition and Social Context of MSS Jesus College Oxford 29 (II) and BL Cotton Caligula A. ix'. *Medium Aevum* 6. 250–69.

Cartlidge, N. 2003. 'Festivity, Order, and Community in Fourteenth-Century Ireland: The Composition and Contexts of BL MS Harley 913'. *Yearbook of English Studies* 33. 33–52.

Chambers, E. K. and Sidgwick, F., eds. 1907. *Early English Lyrics: Amorous, Divine, Moral and Trivial*. Repr. 1966. London.

Chambers, E. K. and Sidgwick, F. 1910–11. 'Fifteenth Century Carols by John Audelay'. *Modern Language Review* 5 (1910). 473–491; 6 (1911). 68–84.

Chambers, R.W., Batho, E. C. and Husbands, H. W. 1938–41. John Bellenden, *The Chronicles of Scotland by Hector Boece*. STS, 2 vols. Edinburgh and London.

Champion, P., ed. 1923. *Charles D'Orléans Poésies*. Vol. 1. Paris.

Chaucer, G. See Benson; Boffey and Edwards; Brewer.

Chaytor, H. J. 1923. *The Troubadours and England*. Cambridge.

Clark, A., ed. 1911. *The English Register of Godstow Nunnery*. EETS OS 129.

Clayton, M. 1990. *The Cult of the Virgin Mary in Anglo-Saxon England*. Cambridge.

Coldwell, D. F. C., ed. 1957–64. Gavin Douglas, *Virgil's 'Aeneid' Translated into Scottish Verse*. STS, 4 vols. Edinburgh and London.

Coleman, J. 1992. *Ancient and Medieval Memories*. Cambridge.

Colledge, E., ed. 1974. *The Latin Poems of Richard Ledrede OFM*. Toronto.

Collette, C. P. 2002. *Species, Phantasms, and Images: Vision and Medieval Psychology in The Canterbury Tales*. Ann Arbor.

Collier, H. 1997. 'Richard Hill – a London Compiler'. In *The Court and Cultural Diversity; Selected Papers from the Eighth Triennial Congress of the International Courtly Literature Society, The Queen's University of Belfast, 26 July – 1 August 1995*. Eds. E. Mullally and J. Thompson. Cambridge. 319–29.

Connolly, M. 1998. *John Shirley: Book Production and the Noble Household in Fifteenth-Century England*. Aldershot.

Cooper, H. and Mapstone, S., eds. 1997. *The Long Fifteenth Century: Essays for Douglas Gray*. Oxford.

Coote, L. 2000. *Prophecy and Public Affairs in Later Medieval England*. Woodbridge.

Copeland, R. 1984. 'The Middle English "Candet Nudatum Pectus" and Norms of Early Vernacular Translation Practice'. *Leeds Studies in English* NS 15. 57–81.

Corbett, J. 2001. 'Aureation Revisited: The Latinate Vocabulary of Dunbar's High and Plain Styles'. In Mapstone 2001a. 183–97.

Corrie, M. 1997. 'The Compilation of Oxford, Bodleian Library, MS Digby 86'. *Medium Aevum* 66. 236–49.

Corrie, M. 2000. 'Harley 2253, Digby 86, and the Circulation of Literature in Pre-Chaucerian England'. In Fein 2000. 427–43.

Corrie, M. 2003. 'Kings and Kingship in British Library MS Harley 2253'. *Yearbook of English Studies* 33. 64–79.

Coss, P., ed. 1996. *Thomas Wright's Political Songs of England*. Cambridge.

Courcelle, P. 1974–75. *Connais toi-même de Socrate à Saint Bernard*. Études Augustinienne. Paris.

Craigie, J., ed. 1955–58. *The Poems of James VI of Scotland*. STS, 2 vols. Edinburgh and London.

Craigie, W. A., ed. 1919–27. *The Maitland Folio Manuscript*. STS, 2 vols. Edinburgh and London.

Craigie, W. A., ed. 1920. *The Maitland Quarto Manuscript*. STS. Edinburgh and London.

Craigie, W. A., ed. 1923–25. *The Asloan Manuscript*. STS, 2 vols. Edinburgh and London.

Crampton, G. R., ed. 1994. *The Shewings of Julian of Norwich*. Medieval Institute Publications. Kalamazoo, Michigan.

Cranstoun, J., ed. 1896. *The Poems of Alexander Scott*. STS. Edinburgh and London.

Cressy, D. 1980. *Literacy and the Social Order: Reading and Writing in Tudor and Stuart England*. Cambridge.

Cunningham, I. C. 1985–86, 1986–87. 'Two Poems on the Virgin (National Library of Scotland, Advocates MS 18.5.14)'. *Edinburgh Bibliographical Society Transactions* 5, Part 5. 32–40.

Curry, K., ed. 1984. *The Contributions of Robert Southey to the Morning Post*. Alabama.

Curtius, E. R. 1953. *European Literature and the Latin Middle Ages*. Trans. from the German edition of 1948 by W. R. Trask. New York.

D'Evelyn, C., ed. 1921. *Meditations on the Life and Passion of Christ*. EETS OS 158. London.

Davidson, P. 1995. 'The entry of Mary Stewart into Edinburgh, 1561, and other ambiguities'. *Renaissance Studies* 9. 416–25.

Davies, R. T., ed. 1963. *Medieval English Lyrics: A Critical Anthology*. London.

Davis, N. 1965. 'The *Litera Troili* and English Letters'. *Review of English Studies* NS 16. 233–44.

Davis, N., ed. 1971. *Paston Letters and Papers of the Fifteenth Century*. Oxford.

Dean, J. M., ed. 1996. *Medieval English Political Writings*. Kalamazoo, Michigan.

Degginger, S. H. L. 1954. ' "A Wayle Whyt ase Whalles Bon" Reconstructed'. *Journal of English and Germanic Philology* 53. 84–90.

Dobson, E. J. and Harrison, F. Ll., eds. 1979. *Medieval English Songs*. London and Boston.

Donaldson, E. T. 1970. *Speaking of Chaucer*. London and New York.

Donaldson, E. T. 1974. 'The Manuscripts of Chaucer's Works and Their Use'. In *Geoffrey Chaucer*. Ed. D. Brewer. London. 85–108.

Dorleijn, G. J. and Vanstiphout, H. L. J., eds. 2003. *Cultural Repertoires: Structure, Function and Dynamics*. Leuven.

Douglas, G. See Coldwell.

Douie, D. L. and Farmer, D. H., eds. 1985. *Magna Vita Sancti Hugonis*. 2 vols. Oxford.

Dove, M. 2000. 'Evading Textual Intimacy: The French Secular Verse'. In Fein. 329–49.

Doyle, A. I. 1958. 'Books Connected with the Vere Family and Barking Abbey'. *Transactions of the Essex Archaeological Society* NS 25. 222–43.

Doyle, A. I., intro. 1987. *The Vernon Manuscript: A Facsimile of Bodleian Library, Oxford, MS Eng. Poet. a. 1*. Cambridge.

Doyle, A. J. 1990. 'The Shaping of the Vernon and Simeon Manuscripts'. In Pearsall 1990. 1–13.

Dronke, P. 1968a. *Medieval Latin and the Rise of the European Love-Lyric*. 2 vols. Oxford.

Dronke, P. 1968b. *The Medieval Lyric*. London.

Dronke, P. 1984. *The Medieval Poet and his World*. Edizioni di Storia e Letteratura. Roma. 167–207. Repr. of Dronke, P. 1976. 'Learned Lyric and Popular Ballad in the Early Middle Ages'. *Studi Medievali* 3rd Series 17. 1–40.

Duffy, E. 1992. *The Stripping of the Altars*. New Haven and London.

Duggan, H. N. 1997. 'Meter, Stanza, Vocabulary, Dialect'. In *A Companion to the Gawain Poet*. Eds D. Brewer and J. Gibson. Arthurian Studies 38. Cambridge. 221–42.

Duncan, T. G. 1987. 'The Text and Verse-Form of "Adam lay i-bowndyn" '. *The Review of English Studies* 38. 215–21.

Duncan, T. G. 1992. 'Textual Notes on Two Early Middle English Lyrics'. *Neuphilologische Mitteilungen* 93. 109–20.

Duncan, T. G. 1994. 'Two Middle English Penitential Lyrics: Sound and Scansion'. In *Late-Medieval Religious Texts and Their Transmission*. Ed. A. J. Minnis. Cambridge. 55–65.

Duncan, T. G., ed. 1995. *Medieval English Lyrics 1200–1400*. Harmondsworth.

Duncan, T. G. 1996. 'The Maid in the Moor and the Rawlinson Text'. *The Review of English Studies* NS 47. 151–62.

Duncan, T. G. 1998. 'The Middle English Translator of Robert de Gretham's Anglo-Norman *Miroir*'. In *The Medieval Translator* 6. Eds R. Ellis, R. Tixier, and B. Weitemeier. Turnhout. 221–31.

Duncan, T. G., ed. 2000. *Late Medieval English Lyrics and Carols 1400–1530*. Harmondsworth.

Duncan, T. G. and Connolly, M., eds. 2003. *The Middle English 'Mirror': Sermons from Advent to Sexagesima*. Middle English Texts 34. Heidelberg.

Dunnigan, S. M. 2002. *Eros and Poetry at the Courts of Mary Queen of Scots and James VI*. Basingstoke.

Durkan, J. 2003. 'Thomas Dempster: a Scottish Baronius'. *Innes Review* 54. 69–78.

Dyboski, R., ed. 1908. *Songs, Carols, and other Miscellaneous Poems from Balliol MS 354, Richard Hill's Commonplace Book*. EETS ES 101.

Edden, V., ed. 1990. *Richard Maidstone's Penitential Psalms*. Middle English Texts 22. Heidelberg.

Edwards, A. S. G. 1985. 'Additions and Corrections to the Bibliography of John Lydgate'. *Notes and Queries* 230. 450–2.

Edwards, A. S. G. 1997. 'Middle English Inscriptional Verse Texts'. In *Texts and their Contexts: Papers from the Early Book Society*. Eds. J. Scattergood and J. Boffey. Dublin. 26–43.

Edwards, A. S. G. 2000a. 'Fifteenth-Century Middle English Verse Author Collections'. In Edwards, Gillespie, and Hanna. 101–12.

Edwards, A. S. G. 2000b. 'Editing and Manuscript Form: Middle English Verse Written as Prose'. *English Studies in Canada* 22. 1–18.

Edwards, A. S. G., Gillespie, V. and Hanna R, eds. 2000. *The English Medieval Book: Studies in Memory of Jeremy Griffiths*. London.

Eliot, T. S. 1954. *The Three Voices of Poetry*. New York.

Ellenberger, B. 1977. *The Latin Element in the Vocabulary of the Earlier Makars Henryson and Dunbar*. Lund.

Ellis, R., ed. 2001. *Thomas Hoccleve: 'My Compleinte' and Other Poems*. Exeter Medieval Texts and Studies. Exeter.

Empson, W. 1930. *Seven Types of Ambiguity*. London.

Erbe, T., ed. 1905. *John Mirk: Festial*, Part I. EETS ES 96.

Evans, J. 1931. *English Poesies and Posy Rings*. London.

Fallows, D. 1977. 'Words and Music in Two English Songs of the Mid-Fifteenth Century'. *Early Music* 5. 38–43.

Fehr, B. 1902. 'Die Lieder der Hs. Sloane 2593'. *Archiv für das Studium der neueren Sprachen und Literaturen* 109. 33–70.

Fein, S. 1988–89. '*Haue mercy of me* (Psalm 51): An Unedited Alliterative Poem from the London Thornton Manuscript'. *Modern Philology* 86. 223–41.

Fein, S. 1997. 'Twelve-Line Stanza Forms in Middle English and the Date of *Pearl*'. *Speculum* 72. 367–98.

Fein, S., ed. 1998. *Moral Love Songs and Laments*. Medieval Institute Publications. Kalamazoo, Michigan.

Fein, S. 1999. 'Quatrefoil and Quatrefolia: The Devotional Layout of an Alliterative Poem'. *Journal of the Early Book Society* 2. 26–45.

Fein, S., ed. 2000. *Studies in the Harley Manuscript: The Scribes, Contents, and Social Contexts of British Library MS Harley 2253*. Kalamazoo, Michigan.

Fein, S. 2003. 'Good Ends in the Audelay Manuscript'. *Yearbook of English Studies* 33. 97–119.

Flasdieck, H. M. 1956. 'Elisab. *faburden* "Fauxbourdon" und ne. *burden* "Refrain" '. *Anglia* 74. 188–238.

Fletcher, A. J. 1978. ' "I Sing of a Maiden": A Fifteenth-Century Sermon Reminiscence'. *Notes and Queries*, NS. 25. 107–8.

Fletcher, A. J. 1981. ' "In Die Sepulture seu Trigintali": The Late-Medieval Funeral and Memorial Sermon'. *Leeds Studies in English* NS 12. 195–228. Reptd in Fletcher 1998. 170–97.

Fletcher, A. J. 1986. 'The Sermon Booklets of Friar Nicholas Philip'. *Medium Aevum* 54. 188–202. Reptd in Fletcher 1998. 41–57.

Fletcher, A. J. 1994. 'Benedictus qui venit in nomine Domini: A Thirteenth-Century Sermon for Advent and the Macaronic Style in England'. *Mediaeval Studies* 56. 217–45.

Fletcher, A. J. 1998. *Preaching, Politics and Poetry in Late-Medieval England*. Dublin.

Fletcher, A. J. and Gillespie, R., eds. 2001. *Irish Preaching 700–1700*. Dublin.

Fletcher, B. Y, intro. 1987. *Trinity R. 3. 19, Trinity College, Cambridge*. Norman, Oklahoma.

Flügel, E. 1903. 'Liedersammlungen des XVI. jahrhunderts, besonders aus der Zeit Heinrichs VIII. III'. *Anglia* 26. 94–285.

Förster, M. 1918. 'Kleinere Mittelenglischen Texte'. *Anglia* 42. 145–224.

Förster, W., ed. 1934. Kristian von Troyes. *Erec und Enide*. Romanische Bibliothek 13. Halle an der Saale.

Fox, D., ed. 1981. *The Poems of Robert Henryson*. Oxford.

Fox, D. and Ringler, W. A., eds. 1980. *The Bannatyne Manuscript*. Facsimile. London.

Fox, J., ed. 1973. *Charles d'Orléans: Choix de poésies. Ed. d'après le MS Royal 16.F.ii du British Museum*. Exeter.

Francis, W. N., ed. 1942. *The Book of Vices and Virtues*. EETS OS 217.

Frankis, J. 1986. 'The Social Context of Vernacular Writing in Thirteenth Century England: the Evidence of the Manuscripts'. In *Thirteenth Century England, I. Proceedings of the Newcastle upon Tyne Conference,1985*. Eds P. R. Coss and S. D. Lloyd. Woodbridge. 175–84.

Furnivall, F. J., ed. 1886. *Political, Religious and Love Poems from Lambeth MS. 306 and other sources*. EETS OS 15.

Furnivall, F. J., ed. 1901. *The Minor Poems of the Vernon MS*, Part II. EETS OS 117.

Gardner-Medwin, A. and Hadley Williams, J., eds. 1990. *A Day Estivall*. Aberdeen.

Garner, L. A. 2000. 'Contexts of Interpretation in the Burdens of Middle English'. *Neophilologus* 84. 467–83.

Gaunt, S. and Kay, S. 1999. *The Troubadours: An Introduction*. Cambridge.

Gennrich, F. 1963. *Das altfranzösische Rondeau und Virelai im 12 und 13 Jahrhundert. Band III der 'Rondeaux, Virelais und Balladen'*. Langen bei Frankfurt am Main.

Gibson, J. A. 1914. 'The Lyrics of MS. Harley 2253'. London University M.A. Dissertation, unpublished typescript.

Gibson McMurray, G. 1989. *The Theater of Devotion: East Anglian Drama and Society in the Late Middle Ages*. Chicago and London.

Gillespie, V. 1989. 'Vernacular Books of Religion'. In Griffiths and Pearsall. 317–344.

Gillespie, V. 2004. 'Anonymous Devotional Prose'. In *A Companion to Middle English Prose*. Ed. A. S. G. Edwards. Cambridge. 127–49.

Gillespie, V. 2005. 'Commentary on Classical and Secular Authors 1200–1500'. In Minnis and Johnson.

Girvan, R., ed. 1939. *Ratis Raving and other Early Scots Poems on Morals*. STS. Edinburgh and London.

Glasscoe, M., ed. 1993, repr. 1996. *Julian of Norwich: A Revelation of Love*. Revised edn. Exeter.

Graef, H. 1963. *Mary: A History of Doctrine and Devotion*. 2 vols. London and New York.

Grant, E. 1974. *A Source Book in Medieval Science*. Cambridge, Massachusetts.

Gray, D. 1963. 'Two Songs of Death'. *Neuphilologische Mitteilungen* 64. 52–74.

Gray, D. 1972. *Themes and Images in the Medieval English Religious Lyric*. London and Boston.

Gray, D., ed. 1975. *A Selection of Religious Lyrics*. Oxford.

Gray, D. 1983. 'Songs and Lyrics'. In *Literature of Fourteenth-Century England*. Eds P. Boitani and A. Torti. Cambridge. 83–98.

Gray, D. 1984. 'The Robin Hood Poems'. *Poetica* 18. 1 39.

Gray, D. 1986. 'Lyrics'. In Bennett 1986. 364–406.

Gray, D., ed. 1988. *The Oxford Book of Late Medieval Verse and Prose*. Oxford.

Gray, D. 1989. 'Medieval English Ballads'. In *Actas del Primer Congreso Internacional de la Sociedad Española de Lengua y Literatura Inglesa Medieval*. Eds P. Shaw Fairman et al. Oviedo. 129–53.

Gray, D. 1997. 'Medieval English Mystical Lyrics'. In W. F. Pollard and R. Boenig. 203–18.

Gray, D. 1998. 'The Royal Entry in Sixteenth-Century Scotland'. In Mapstone and Wood. 10–37.

Gray, D. 2001. ' "Hale Sterne Superne" and its Literary Background'. In Mapstone. 198–210.

Green, R. F. 1992. 'John Ball's Letters: Literary History and Historical Literature'. In *Chaucer's England: Literature in Historical Context*. Ed. B. Hanawalt. Minneapolis, Minnesota. 176–200.

Green, R. F. 1997. 'The Ballad in the Middle Ages'. In Cooper and Mapstone. 163–84.

Green, R. F. 1999. *A Crisis of Truth: Literature and Law in Ricardian England*. Philadelphia, Pennsylvania.

Greene, R. L. 1933, 'A Middle English "Timor Mortis" Poem'. *Modern Language Review* 28. 234–8.

Greene, R. L. 1952. ' "The Maid of the Moor" in the Red Book of Ossory'. *Speculum* 27. 504–6.

Greene, R. L., ed. 1962. *A Selection of English Carols*. Clarendon Medieval and Tudor Series. Oxford.

Greene, R. L., ed. 1974. *The Lyrics of the Red Book of Ossory*. Medium Ævum Monographs, NS 5. Oxford.

Greene, R. L., ed. 1977. *The Early English Carols*. 2nd edn, revised and enlarged. Oxford.

Greentree, R. 2001. *The Middle English Lyric and Short Poem*. Annotated Bibliographies of Old and Middle English Literature 7. Cambridge.

Griffiths, J. J. 1995. 'Unrecorded Middle English Verse in the Library of Holkham Hall, Norfolk'. *Medium Ævum* 64. 278–84.

Griffiths J. J. and Pearsall, D., eds. 1989. *Book Production and Publishing in Britain 1375–1475*. Cambridge Studies in Publishing and Printing History. Cambridge.

Grisdale, D. M., ed. 1939. *Three Middle English Sermons from the Worcester Chapter Manuscript F. 10*. Leeds School of English Language Texts and Monographs 5.

Guddat-Figge, G. 1976. *Catalogue of Manuscripts Containing Middle English Romances*. Munich.

Guiney, L. I. 1938. *Recusant Poets*. London and New York.

Gurevich, G. 1988. *Medieval Popular Culture. Problems of Belief and Perception*. Trans. J. M. Bak and P. A. Hollingsworth. Cambridge.

Hadley Williams, J. 2001. 'Dunbar and his Immediate Heirs'. In Mapstone 2001a. 85–107.

Hall, J., ed. 1914. *The Poems of Laurence Minot*. 3rd edn. Oxford.

Hanna, R., intro. 1997. *The Index of Middle English Prose. Fascicle 12: Shorter Bodleian Collections*. Cambridge.

Hanna, R. 2000. 'Humphrey Newton and Bodleian Library MS Lat. Misc. c. 66'. *Medium Aevum* 69. 279–91.

Hanna, R. 2003. 'Yorkshire Writers'. *Proceedings of the British Academy* 121. 91–109.

Hardman, P. 1978. 'A Medieval "Library *in Parvo*" '. *Medium Aevum* 47. 262–73.

Hardman, P., intro. 2000. *The Heege Manuscript: A Facsimile of National Library of Scotland MS Advocates 19. 3. 1*. Leeds Texts and Monographs NS 16.

Harrison, F. Ll. 1963. *Music in Medieval Britain*. 2nd edn. London.

Harrison, F. Ll. 1965. 'Benedicamus, Conductus, Carol: A Newly Discovered Source'. *Acta Musicologica* 37. 35–48.

Hartung, A., ed. 1993. *A Manual of the Writings in Middle English 1050–1500*. Vol. 9. New Haven, Connecticut.

Harvey Wood, H., ed. 1958. *The Poems and Fables of Robert Henryson*. 2nd edition. Edinburgh and London.

Harvey Wood, H. 1967. *Two Scots Chaucerians*. London.

Harvey, P. D. A. 1996. *Mappa Mundi: The Hereford World Map*. London.

Hazleton, R. 1957. 'The Christianisation of "Cato": The *Disticha Catonis* in the Light of Late Medieval Commentaries'. *Mediaeval Studies* 19. 157–73.

Hazlitt, W. C., ed. 1881. *Shakespeare Jest-Books, I. A Hundred Mery Talys, II. Mery Tales and Quicke Answeres*. London.

Heffernan, T. J. 1981. 'Four Middle English Religious Lyrics from the Thirteenth Century'. *Mediaeval Studies* 43. 131–50.

Heffernan, T. J. 1982. 'Unpublished Middle English Verses on the Three Sorrowful Things'. *Neuphilologische Mitteilungen* 83. 31–2.

Heffernan, T. J., ed. 1985. *The Popular Literature of Medieval England*, Tennessee Studies in Literature 28. Knoxville, Tennessee.

Henryson, R. See Fox.

Hermans, J. M. M. and van der Hoek, K., eds. 1994. *Boeken in de late Middeleeuwen*. Groningen.

Heuser, W., ed. 1904. *Die Kildare-Gedichte*. Bonner Beiträge zur Anglistik 14. Repr. Darmstadt, 1965.

Heuser, W. 1907. 'Fragmente von unbekannten Spielmannsliedern des 14. Jahrhunderts, aus MS. Rawl[inson] D.913'. *Anglia* 30. 173–9.

Hill, B. 1963. 'The History of Jesus College, Oxford, MS 29'. *Medium Aevum* 32. 203–13.

Hill, B. 1975. 'Jesus College, Oxford, MS 29, Addenda'. *Notes and Queries* 220. 98–105.

Hirsh, J. C. 1968. 'Two English Devotional Poems of the Fifteenth Century'. *Notes and Queries* 213. 4–10.

Hogg, J., ed. 1981. *An Illustrated Yorkshire Carthusian Religious Miscellany. British Library London Additional MS. 37049 Vol. 3. Illustrations*. Analecta Cartusiana 95.

Hollywood, A. 2002. *Sensible Ecstasy: Mysticism, Sexual Difference, and the Demands of History*. Chicago and London.

Holmstedt, G., ed. 1933 for 1929. *Speculum Christiani*. EETS OS 182.

Horgan, F., trans. 1994. *The Romance of the Rose*. Oxford.

Horrall, S. M. 1983. 'Latin and Middle English Proverbs in an Manuscript at St. George's Chapel, Windsor Castle'. *Mediaeval Studies* 45. 343–84.

Horrall, S. M. 1986. 'Thomas of Hales, O.F.M.: His Life and Works'. *Traditio* 42. 287–98.

Horstmann, C., ed. 1892. *The Minor Poems of the Vernon MS*, Part I. EETS OS 98.

Horstmann, C., ed. 1895–96. *Yorkshire Writers: Richard Rolle of Hampole and his followers*. 2 vols. London and New York.

Houwen, L. A. J. R. and MacDonald, A. A., eds. 1994. *Loyal Letters: Studies on Mediaeval Alliterative Poetry and Prose*. Groningen.

Houwen, L. A. J. R., MacDonald, A. A. and Mapstone, S. L., eds. 2000. *A Palace in the Wild: Essays on Vernacular Culture and Humanism in Late-Medieval and Renaissance Scotland*. Leuven.

Howell, A. J. 1980. 'Reading the Harley Lyrics. A Master Poet and the Language of Conventions'. *English Literary History* 47. 619–45.

Hubbell, H. M., ed. and trans. 1949. *Cicero: De inventione*. Loeb Classical Library.

Hudson, A. 1985. *Lollards and their Books*. London and Ronceverte.

Hudson, A. 1997. 'Visio Baleii: An Early Literary Historian'. In Cooper and Mapstone. 313–29.

Hughes, J. and Ramson, W. S. 1982. *Poetry of the Stewart Court*. Canberra.

Hume Brown, P., ed. 1978. *Early Travellers in Scotland*. Edinburgh. Repr. of Edinburgh, 1891.

Hunt, T. 1991. *Teaching and Learning Latin in 13th-Century England*. Cambridge.

Huws, D. 1996. 'MS Porkington 10 and its Scribes'. In *Romance Reading on the Book: Essays on Medieval Narrative*. Eds. J. Fellows, R. Field, G. Rogers and J. Weiss. Cardiff. 188–207.

Ireland, J. (Johannes de Irlandia). See Macpherson.

Jack, R. D. S., ed. 1988. *The History of Scottish Literature*, Vol. I. Aberdeen.

James VI. See Craigie, J.

James, T. B. and Simons J., eds. 1989. *The Poems of Laurence Minot 1333–1352*. Exeter.

Jansen, J. P. M. 1989. 'Charles d'Orléans and the Fairfax Poems'. *English Studies* 70. 206–24.

Jauss, H. R., Zumthor, P., Burrow, J. A., et al. 1979. 'Medieval Literature and Contemporary Theory'. *New Literary History: A Journal of Theory and Interpretation* 10, No. 2. 181–416.

Jeffrey, D. L. 1975. *The Early English Lyric and Franciscan Spirituality*. Lincoln, Nebraska.

Jeffrey, D. L. 1984. 'James Ryman and the Fifteenth-Century Carol'. In *Fifteenth-Century Studies: Recent Essays*. Ed. R. F. Yeager. Hamden, Connecticut. 303–20.

Jeffrey, D. L. 2000. 'Authors, Anthologists, and Franciscan Spirituality'. In Fein. 261–70.

Kail, J., ed. 1904. *Twenty-Six Political and Other Poems*. EETS OS 124.

Kane, G. 1986. 'Some Fourteenth-Century "Political" Poems'. In *Medieval English Religious and Ethical Literature*. Eds. G. Kratzmann and J. Simpson. Cambridge. 82–91.

Kane, H., ed. 1983. *The Prickynge of Love*. Elizabethan and Renaissance Studies 92:10. 2 vols. Salzburg.

Keiser, G. R. 1979. 'Lincoln Cathedral Library MS 91: Life and Milieu of the Scribe'. *Studies in Bibliography* 32. 158–79.

Keiser, G. R. 1983. 'More Light on the Life and Milieu of Robert Thornton'. *Studies in Bibliography* 36. 111–19.

Keiser, G. R. 1984. ' "To Knawe God Almyghtyn": Robert Thornton's Devotional Book'. In *Spätmittelalterliche Geistliche Literatur in der Nationalsprache*. Ed. J. Hogg. Analecta Cartusiana 106. 2103–29.

Keiser, G. R. 1985. 'The Middle English *Planctus Mariae* and the Rhetoric of Pathos'. In Heffernan.167–93.

Ker, N. R. 1949–53. 'Medieval Manuscripts from Norwich Cathedral Priory'. *Transactions of the Cambridge Bibliographical Society*, Part I. 1–28.

Ker, N. R., intro. 1963. *The Owl and the Nightingale: Facsimile of the Jesus and Cotton Manuscripts*. EETS OS 251.

Ker, N. R. 1964. *Medieval Libraries of Great Britain. A List of Surviving Books*. 2nd edn. London.

Ker, N. R., intro. 1965. *Facsimile of British Museum MS. Harley 2253*. EETS OS 255.

Ker, N. R. 1983. *Medieval Manuscripts in British Libraries III: Lampeter-Oxford*. Oxford.

Keyte, H., and Parrott, A., eds (Bartlett, C., associate ed.). 1992. *The New Oxford Book of Carols*. Oxford.

King, P. M. 1981. 'Eight English *Memento Mori* Verses from Cadaver Tombs'. *Notes and Queries* 226. 494–6.

Kinsley, J., ed. 1958. *William Dunbar: Poems*. Oxford.

Kinsley, J., ed. 1979. *The Poems of William Dunbar*. Oxford.

Kinsman, R. S. and Yonge, T. 1967. *Skelton: Canon and Census*. Renaissance Society of America, Bibliographies and Indexes 4 .

Kipling, G. 1998. *Enter the King: Theatre, Liturgy and Ritual in the Medieval Civic Triumph*. Oxford.

Klibansky, R., Panofsky, E. and Saxl, F. 1965. *Saturn and Melancholy*. London.

Knapp, E. 1999. 'Bureaucratic Identity and the Construction of the Self in Hoccleve's *Formulary* and La Male Regle'. *Speculum* 74. 357–76.

Knapp, E. 2001. *The Bureaucratic Muse: Thomas Hoccleve and the Literature of Late Medieval England*. Philadelphia.

Knight, I. K., ed. 1967. *Wimbledon's Sermon, Redde rationem villicationis tue*. Duquesne Studies, Philological Series 9.

Kottler, B. and Markham, A. M. 1966. *A Concordance to Five Middle English Poems*. Pittsburg.

Krapp, G. F. and Dobbie, E. V. K., eds. 1936. *Anglo-Saxon Poetic Records III: The Exeter Book*. New York and London.

Kratzmann, G. 1980. *Anglo-Scottish Literary Relations 1430–1550*. Cambridge.

Kuczynski, M. P. 1995. *Prophetic Song: The Psalms as Moral Discourse in Late Medieval England*. Philadelphia.

Kuczynski, M. P. 2000. 'An "Electric Stream": The Religious Contents'. In Fein. 123–61.

Kurath, H., Kuhn, S. M., Lewis, R. E., et al., eds. 1956–2001. *Middle English Dictionary*. Ann Arbor, Michigan.

Kurvinen, A. 1953. 'MS Porkington 10'. *Neuphilologische Mitteilungen* 54. 33–67.

Langland. See Schmidt 1978.

Larrington, C. 1993. *A Store of Common Sense: Gnomic Theme and Style in Old Icelandic and Old English Wisdom Poetry*. Oxford.

Lawrence, C. H. 1960. *St. Edmund of Abingdon*. Oxford.

Lawson, A., ed. 1910. *The Kingis Quair and the Quare of Jelusy*. London.

Le Gentil, P. 1954. *Le Virelai et le villancico. Le Problème des origines Arabes*. Paris.

Leach, M., ed. 1972. *Funk & Wagnalls Standard Dictionary of Folklore Mythology, and Legend*. Revised ed. San Francisco.

Lecoy, F., ed. 1963. Jean Renart. *Le Roman de la Rose ou de Guillaume de Dole*. Les Classiques Français du Moyen Age 91. Paris.

Lerer, S. 1997. 'The Genre of the Grave and the Origins of the Middle English Lyric'. *Modern Language Quarterly* 58. 127–61.

Letts, M., ed. 1929. *The Diary of Jörg von Ehingen*. London.

Lewis, C. S. 1936. *The Allegory of Love*. Oxford.

Lewis, C. S. 1938. 'The Fifteenth-Century Heroic Line'. *Essays and Studies* 24. 28–41.

Lewis, C. S. 1954. *English Literature in the Sixteenth Century, Excluding Drama*. Oxford.

Lewis, R. E., ed. 1978. *Lotario dei Segni (Pope Innocent III), De miseria condicionis humane*. The Chaucer Library. Athens, Georgia.

Liber Usualis. Liber Usualis Missae et Officii pro Dominicis et Festis. Ed. by the Monks of Solesmes. Paris, Tournai, Rome. 1950.

Lindberg, D. C. 1976. *Theories of Vision from Al-Kindi to Kepler*. Chicago and London.

Lindberg, D. C., ed. 1983. *Roger Bacon's Philosophy of Nature: A Critical Edition, with English Translation, Introduction, and Notes, of 'De multiplicatione specierum' and 'De speculis comburentibus'*. Oxford.

Liuzzi, F., ed. 1934. *La lauda e i primordi della melodia italiana*. 2 vols. Rome.

Lochrie, K. 1991. *Margery Kempe and Translations of the Flesh*. Philadelphia.

Loomis, R. S. 1965. *A Mirror of Chaucer's World*. Princeton.

Louis, C., ed. 1980. *The Commonplace Book of Robert Reynes of Acle: An Edition of Tanner MS 407*. Garland Medieval Texts 1. New York.

Louis, C. 1993. 'Proverbs, Precepts and Monitory Pieces'. In Hartung 1993. 2957–3048.

Lucas, A. M., ed. 1995. *Anglo-Irish Poems of the Middle Ages*. Blackrock, County Dublin.

Lucas, A. M. and Lucas, P. J. 1990. 'Reconstructing a Disarranged Manuscript: The case of MS Harley 913, a Medieval Hiberno-English Miscellany'. *Scriptorium* 14. 286–99.

Luick, K. 1914–. *Historische Grammatik der englischen Sprache*. Leipzig.

Lyall, R. J. and Riddy, F., eds. 1981. *Proceedings of the Third International Conference on Scottish Language and Literature (Medieval and Renaissance)*. Stirling and Glasgow.

Macaulay, G. C., ed. 1901 *The English Works of John Gower*, Vol. 2. EETS ES 82.

MacCracken, H. N. 1907. 'The Earl of Warwick's Virelai'. *Publications of the Modern Language Association of America* 22. 597–607.

MacCracken, H. N., ed. 1908–09. 'Quixley's Ballades Royal (?1402)'. *Yorkshire Archeological Journal* 20. 33–50.

MacCracken, H. N., ed. 1911a. *The Minor Poems of John Lydgate*, Part I. EETS ES 107.

MacCraken, H. N. 1911b. 'An English Friend of Charles d'Orléans'. *Publications of the Modern Language Association of America* 26. 142–80.

MacCracken, H. N., ed. 1934. *John Lydgate: The Minor Poems*, Part II. EETS OS 192.

MacDonald, A. A. 1972. 'The Poetry of Sir Richard Maitland of Lethington'. *Transactions of the East Lothian Antiquarian and Field Naturalists' Society* 13. 7–19.

MacDonald, A. A. 1978. *The Middle Scots Religious Lyrics*. PhD dissertation. University of Edinburgh.

MacDonald, A. A. 1983. 'Poetry, Politics and Reformation Censorship in Sixteenth-Century Scotland'. *English Studies* 64. 410–21.

MacDonald, A. A. 1984. 'Catholic Devotion into Protestant Lyric: The Case of the *Contemplacioun of Synnaris*'. *Innes Review* 35. 58–87.

MacDonald, A. A. 1986. 'The Bannatyne Manuscript – A Marian Anthology'. *Innes Review* 37. 36–47.

MacDonald, A. A. 1988. 'Religious Poetry in Middle Scots'. In Jack. 91–104.

MacDonald, A. A. 1990. 'The *Court of Sapience* and *The Gude and Godlie Ballatis*'. *Neophilologus* 74. 608–11.

MacDonald, A. A. 1991a. 'Anglo-Scottish Literary Relations: Problems and Possibilities'. *Studies in Scottish Literature* 26. 172–184.

MacDonald, A. A. 1991b. 'Mary Stewart's Entry to Edinburgh: an Ambiguous Triumph'. *Innes Review* 42. 101–10.

MacDonald, A. A. 1994a. 'The printed book that never was: George Bannatyne's poetic anthology (1568)'. In Hermans and van der Hoek. 101–10.

MacDonald, A. A. 1994b. 'The Latin Original of Robert Henryson's Annunciation Lyric'. In MacDonald, Lynch and Cowan. 45–65.

MacDonald, A. A. 1994c. 'Alliterative Poetry and its Context: The Case of William Dunbar'. In Houwen and MacDonald. 261–79.

MacDonald, A. A. 1996. 'Contrafacta and the *Gude and Godlie Ballatis*'. In Wilcox, Todd and MacDonald. 33–44.

MacDonald, A. A. 1998. 'Passion Devotion in Late-Medieval Scotland'. In MacDonald, Ridderbos and Schlusemann. 109–31.

MacDonald, A. A. 2000. 'The Chapel of Restalrig: Royal Folly or Venerable Shrine?'. In Houwen, MacDonald and Mapstone. 27–59.

MacDonald, A. A. 2001a. 'Scottish Poetry of the Reign of Mary Stewart'. In Caie, Lyall, Mapstone and Simpson. 44–61.

MacDonald, A. A. 2001b. 'Sir Richard Maitland and William Dunbar: Textual Symbiosis and Poetic Individuality'. In Mapstone. 134–49.

MacDonald, A. A. 2003. 'The Cultural Repertory of Middle Scots Lyric Verse'. In Dorleijn and Vanstiphout.

MacDonald, A. A., Lynch, M. and Cowan, I. B., eds. 1994. *The Renaissance in Scotland: Studies in Literature, Religion, History and Culture Offered to John Durkan*. Leiden.

MacDonald, A. A., Ridderbos, H. N. B. and Schlusemann, R. M., eds. 1998. *The Broken Body: Passion Devotion in Late-Medieval Culture*. Groningen.

MacDonald, A. R. 1997. 'The Triumph of Protestantism: the Burgh Council of Edinburgh and the Entry of Mary Queen of Scots, 2 September 1561'. *Innes Review* 48. 73–82.

Macdougall, N. 1982. *James III: A Political Study*. Edinburgh.

Mackay Mackenzie, W., ed., revised by B. Dickins. 1960. *The Poems of William Dunbar*. London.

Macpherson, C., ed. 1926. Johannes de Irlandia, *The Meroure of Wysdome*. STS, Vol. I. Edinburgh and London.

MacQueen, J., ed. 1970. *Ballattis of Luve*. Edinburgh.

MacQueen, J. 1971. 'The case for early Scottish literature'. In Aitken, McIntosh and Pálsson. 234–247.

MacQueen, J. 1983. 'The Biography of Alexander Scott and the Authorship of *Lo, quhat it is to lufe*'. In McClure. 50–8.

Macrae-Gibson, O. D., ed. 1973–79. *Of Arthour and of Merlin*. EETS 268, 279.

Maddicott, J. R. 1975. *The English Peasantry and the Demands of the Crown, 1294–1341*. Past and Present Society Supplement 1. Oxford.

Maddicott, J. R. 1986. 'Poems of Social Protest in Early Fourteenth-Century England'. In *England in the Fourteenth Century*. Ed. W. M. Ormrod. Woodbridge. 130–44.

Maggioni, G. P., ed. 1998. *Jacopo da Varazze: Legenda aurea*. Florence.

Malkiel, Y. and Stern, C. 1984. 'The Etymology of Spanish villancico "Carol": Certain Literary Implications of This Etymology'. *Bulletin of Hispanic Studies* 61. 137–50.

Manning, S. 1962. *Wisdom and Number: Toward a Critical Appraisal of the Middle English Religious Lyric*. Lincoln, Nebraska.

Mapstone, S., ed. 2001a. *William Dunbar, 'The Nobill Poyet': Essays in Honour of Priscilla Bawcutt*. East Linton.

Mapstone, S. 2001b. 'Dunbar's Disappearance'. *London Review of Books*. 27–9.

Mapstone, S. and Wood, J., eds. 1998. *The Rose and the Thistle: Essays on the Culture of Late Medieval and Renaissance Scotland*. East Linton.

Marsh, D. 1996. ' "I see by sizt of evidence": Information Gathering in Late Medieval Cheshire'. In *Court, Courtiers and the Capital in the Late Middle Ages*. Ed. D. E. S. Dunn. Stroud. 71–92.

Matsuda, T. 1989. 'Death and Transience in the Vernon Refrain Series'. *English Studies* 70. 193–205.

Matsuda, T. 1997. *Death and Purgatory in Middle English Didactic Poetry*. Cambridge.

McClure, J. D., ed. 1983. *Scotland and the Lowland Tongue: Studies in the language and literature of Lowland Scotland in honour of David D. Murison*. Aberdeen.

McDiarmid, M. P. and Stevenson, J. A. C., eds. 1980–85. *Barbour's Bruce*. STS, 3 vols. Edinburgh.

McGovern-Mouron, A. 1996. 'An Edition of *The Desert of Religion* and its Theological Background'. 2 vols. University of Oxford D. Phil. dissertation.

McNamer, S. 1991. 'Female Authors, Provincial Setting: the re-versing of Courtly Love in the Findern Manuscript'. *Viator* 22. 279–310.

McSparren, F. 2000. 'The Language of the English Poems'. In Fein. 391–426.

McSparran, F. and Robinson, P. R., intro. 1979. *Cambridge University Library MS Ff. 2. 38*. London.

Meale, C. M. 1982. 'Wynkyn de Worde's Setting Copy for *Ipomydon*'. *Studies in Bibliography* 35. 156–72.

Meale, C. M. 1983. 'The Compiler at Work: John Colyns and BL MS Harley 2252'. In *Manuscripts and Readers in Fifteenth-Century England: The Literary Implications of Manuscript Study*. Ed. D. Pearsall. Cambridge. 82–103.

Meale, C. M. 1990. 'The Miracles of Our Lady: Context and Interpretation'. In Pearsall 1990. 115–36.

Meale, C. M., ed. 1993. *Women and Literature in Britain 1150–1500*. Cambridge.

Migne, J. P., ed. 1842–80. *Patrologiae Cursus Completus . . . Series Latina [Patrologia Latina]*. 221 vols. Paris.

Mill, A. J. 1924. *Medieval Plays in Scotland*. Edinburgh and London. Repr. New York, 1969.

Miller, B. D. H. 1963. 'The Early History of Bodleian MS Digby 86'. *Annuale Medievale* 4. 23–56.

Miller, C. K. 1950. 'The Early English Carol'. *Renaissance News* 3. 61–4.

Minnis, A. J. and Johnson, I., eds. 2005. *The Cambridge History of Literary Criticism.* Vol. 2. The Middle Ages. Cambridge.

Mitchell, A. F., ed. 1897. *The Gude and Godlie Ballatis.* STS. Edinburgh and London.

Mitchell, B. and Robinson, F. C., eds. 2001. *A Guide to Old English.* 6th edn. Oxford.

Mitchell, J. and Doyle, A. I. 1970. Revised combined reprint of Furnivall, F. J., ed. 1892. *Hoccleve's Works: The Minor Poems.* Vol. 1. EETS ES 61, and Gollancz, I., ed., 1897. *Hoccleve's Minor Poems.* Vol. 2. EETS ES 73.

Mooney, L. R. 1989. 'Lydgate's "Kings of England" and Another Verse Chronicle of the Kings'. *Viator* 20. 255–90.

Mooney, L. R. 2000. 'A New Manuscript by the Hammond Scribe Discovered by Jeremy Griffiths'. In Edwards, Gillespie and Hanna. 113–23.

Mooney, L. R. 2001. 'Scribes and Booklets of Trinity College, Cambridge, Manuscripts R. 3. 19 and R. 3. 21'. In *Middle English Poetry: Texts and Traditions. Essays in Honour of Derek Pearsall.* Ed. A. J. Minnis. York. 241–66.

Mooney, L. R. 2003. 'John Shirley's Heirs'. *Yearbook of English Studies* 33. 182–98.

Moore, A. K. 1951. *The Secular Lyric in Middle English.* Lexington, Kentucky.

Moran, M. J. H. 1985. *The Growth of English Schooling, 1340–1548: Learning, Literacy and Laicization in the Pre-Reformation York Diocese.* Princeton.

Morét, U. 2000. 'An Early Scottish National Biography: Thomas Dempster's *Historia ecclesiastica gentis Scotorum* (1627)'. In Houwen, MacDonald and Mapstone. 249–69.

Morrill, G. L., ed. 1898. *Speculum Gy de Warewyke.* EETS ES 75.

Morris, C. 1972. *The Discovery of the Individual 1050–1200.* London.

Morton, J., ed. 1853. *Ancrene Riwle.* Camden Society 57. London.

Muir, K., ed. 1949. *Collected Poems of Sir Thomas Wyatt.* London.

Murray, H. M. R., ed. 1911. *The Middle English Poem 'Erthe upon Erthe'.* EETS OS 141.

Muscatine, C. 1957. *Chaucer and the French Tradition.* London.

Newhauser, R. 1993. *The Treatise on Vices and Virtues in Latin and the Vernacular.* Typlogies des sources du Moyen Age occidental. Fascicule. 68. Turnhout.

Newhauser, R. 2000. 'Historicity and Complaint in *Song of the Husbandman*'. In Fein. 203–17.

Newman, F. X., ed. 1968. *The Meaning of Courtly Love.* Albany, New York.

Norton-Smith, J. 1966a. 'Chaucer's Epistolary Style'. In *Essays in Style and Language.* Ed. R. Fowler. London. 157–65.

Norton-Smith, J., ed. 1966b. John Lydgate *Poems.* Oxford.

Norton-Smith, J. 1974. *Geoffrey Chaucer.* London.

Norton-Smith, J., intro. 1979. *Bodleian MS Fairfax 16.* Facsimile. London.

O'Donnell, J. J., ed. 1992. *St Augustine: Confessions.* 3 vols. Oxford.

O'Donoghue, B. 1982. *The Courtly Love Tradition.* Manchester.

Ogilvie-Thompson, S. J., ed. 1988. *Richard Rolle: Prose and Verse from MS. Longleat 29 and related manuscripts.* EETS OS 293.

Oliver, R. 1970. *Poems Without Names: the English Lyric 1200–1500.* Berkeley, California.

Osberg, R. H., ed. 1996. *The Poems of Laurence Minot 1333–1352.* Kalamazoo, Michigan.

Oulmont, C., ed. 1911. *Les Débats du Clerc et du Chevalier dans la Littérature Poétique du Moyen Age.* Paris.

Owst, G. R. 1926. *Preaching in Medieval England.* Cambridge.

Pace, G. B. 1961. 'The True Text of "The Former Age" '. *Medieval Studies* 23. 363–7.

Padelford, F. M., ed. 1908. 'The Songs in MS Rawlinson C.813'. *Anglia* 31. 309–97.

Park, R., ed. 1971. *Sale Catalogues of Libraries of Eminent Persons*, Vol. 9. *Poets and Men of Letters*. London.

Parkes, M. B. 1973. 'The Literacy of the Laity'. In *The Medieval World. Literature and Western Civilization, Vol. 1*. Eds. D. Daiches and A. Thorlby. 555–77.

Patterson, F. A. 1911. *The Middle English Penitential Lyric: A Study and Collection of Early Religious Verse*. New York.

Patterson, L. 1991. 'The Subject of Confession: The Pardoner and the Rhetoric of Penance'. In his collected papers *Chaucer and the Subject of History*. London. 367–421.

Pearsall, D. 1977. *Old English and Middle English Poetry*. London.

Pearsall, D., ed. 1990. *Studies in the Vernon Manuscript*. Cambridge.

Pearsall, D. 2000. 'The Literary Milieu of Charles of Orléans and the Duke of Suffolk, and the Authorship of the Fairfax Sequence'. In Arn 2000. 145–56.

Phillips, H. 2000. ' "Almighty and al merciable Queene": Marian titles and Marian lyrics'. In Wogan-Browne. 83–100.

Piaget, A. 1891. 'La cour amoureuse dite de Charles VI'. *Romania* 20. 417–454.

Piaget, A. 1902. 'La cour amoureuse dite de Charles VI'. *Romania* 31. 597–602.

Pickering, O. S., ed. 1997. *Individuality and Achievement in Middle English Poetry*. Cambridge.

Plummer, J. F. 1981. 'The Woman's Song in Middle English and its European Backgrounds'. In *Vox Feminae: Studies in Medieval Women's Song*. Ed. J. F. Plummer. *Studies in Medieval Culture* 15. Kalamazoo, Michigan. 135–54.

Pollard, W. F. 1997. 'Richard Rolle and the "Eye of the Heart" '. In Pollard and Boenig. 85–105.

Pollard, W. F. and Boenig, R., eds. 1997. *Mysticism and Spirituality in Medieval England*. Cambridge.

Prendergast, T. A. and Kline, B., eds. 1999. *Rewriting Chaucer: Culture, Authority, and the Idea of the Authentic Text 1400–1602*. Columbus.

Preston, M. J. 1975. *A Concordance to the Middle English Shorter Poem*. Leeds.

Pritchard, V. 1967. *Medieval Graffiti*. Cambridge.

Pseudo-Anselm. *Dialogus beatae Mariae et Anselmi de passione Domini*. PL 159. 271–90.

Pseudo-Bernard. *Liber de passione Christi et doloribus et planctibus matris eius*. PL 182. 1133–42.

Putter, A. 2004. 'The Language and Metre of *Pater Noster* and *Three Dead Kings*'. *The Review of English Studies* 55. 498–526.

Putter, A. and Stokes, M. 2000. 'Spelling, Grammar and Metre in the Works of the *Gawain*-Poet'. In *Medieval English Measures: Studies in Metre and Versification*. Ed. R. Kennedy. *Parergon* 18. 77–95.

Raby, F. J. E., ed. 1959. *The Oxford Book of Medieval Latin Verse*. Oxford.

Ramson, W. 1977. 'On Bannatyne's Editing'. In Aitken, McIntosh and Pálsson. 172–83.

Reichl, K. 1973. *Religiöse Dichtung im englischen Hochmittelalter. Untersuchungen und Edition der Handschrift B.14.39 des Trinity College in Cambridge*. Munich.

Reichl, K. 1987. 'Popular Poetry and Courtly Lyric: The Middle English Pastourelle'. *The Yearbook of Research in English and American Literature* 5. 33–61.

Reichl, K. 2000. 'Debate Verse'. In Fein. 219–39.

Reichl, K. 2003. 'James Ryman's Lyrics and the Ryman Manuscript: A Reappraisal'. In *Bookmarks from the Past. Studies in Early English Language and Literature in Honour of Helmut Gneuss*. Eds L. Kornexl and U. Lenker. Texte und Untersuchungen zur Englischen Philologie. Frankfurt am Main. 195–227.

Reimer, S. R., ed. 1987. *The Works of William Herebert, OFM*. Studies and Texts 81. Toronto.

Reiss, E. 1972. *The Art of the Middle English Lyric: Essays in Criticism*. Athens, Georgia.

Renevey, D. 2000. 'Margery's Performing Body: The Translation of Late Medieval Discursive Religious Practices'. In Renevey and Whitehead. 197–216.

Renevey, D. 2001. *Language, Self and Love: Hermeneutics in the Writings of Richard Rolle and the Commentaries on the Song of Songs*. Cardiff.

Renevey, D. and Whitehead, C., eds. 2000. *Writing Religious Women: Female Spiritual and Textual Practices in Late Medieval England*. Cardiff.

Renoir, A. and Benson C. D. 1980. 'John Lydgate'. In *A Manual of the Writings in Middle English, 1050–1500* Vol. 6. Ed. A. E. Hartung. New Haven.

Revard, C. 2000. 'Scribe and Provenance'. In Fein. 21–109.

Richmond, C. 1994. 'Margins and Marginality: English Devotion in the Later Middle Ages'. In *England in the Fifteenth Century: Proceedings of the 1992 Harlaxton Symposium*. Ed. N. Rogers. Harlaxton Medieval Studies 4. Stamford, Lincolnshire. 242–52.

Rickert, E. 1932. 'Chaucer at School'. *Modern Philology* 29. 257–74.

Riddy, F. 1993. 'Women Talking about the Things of God: A Late Medieval Sub-Culture'. In Meale. 104–37.

Rigg, A. G. 1968. *A Glastonbury Miscellany of the Fifteenth Century*. Oxford.

Ritchie, W. T., ed. 1928–34. *The Bannatyne Manuscript*. STS, 4 vols. Edinburgh and London.

Ritson, J., ed. 1825. *Poems Written Anno MCCCLII. by Laurence Minot*. London.

Robbins, H. W. 1925. *Le Merure de Seinte Eglise by Saint Edmund of Pontigny*. Lewisburg, Pennsylvania.

Robbins, R. H. 1935. 'The Earliest English Carols and the Franciscans'. *Modern Language Notes* 53. 239–45.

Robbins, R. H. 1939a. 'The Arma Christi Rolls'. *Modern Language Review* 34. 415–21.

Robbins, R. H. 1939b. 'The *Speculum Misericordie*'. *Publications of the Modern Language Association of America* 54. 935–66.

Robbins, R. H. 1940. 'The Authors of the Middle English Religious Lyrics'. *Journal of English and Germanic Philology* 39. 230–8.

Robbins, R. H. 1950. 'The Poems of Humfrey Newton, Esquire, 1466–1536'. *Publications of the Modern Language Association of America* 65. 249–81.

Robbins, R. H., ed. 1952. *Secular Lyrics of the Fourteenth and Fifteenth Centuries*. Revised edn. Oxford.

Robbins, R. H. 1954. 'The Findern Anthology'. *Publications of the Modern Language Association of America* 69. 610–42.

Robbins, R. H., ed. 1955. *Secular Lyrics of the Fourteenth and Fifteenth Centuries*. 2nd edn. Oxford.

Robbins, R. H., ed. 1959a. *Historical Poems of the Fourteenth and Fifteenth Centuries*. New York.

Robbins, R. H. 1959b. 'Middle English Carols as Processional Hymns'. *Studies in Philology* 56. 559–582.

Robbins, R. H. 1966. 'The Bradshaw Carols'. *Publications of the Modern Language Association of America* 81. 308–310.

Robbins, R. H. 1968. 'Mirth in Manuscripts'. *Essays and Studies* NS 21. 1–28.

Robbins, R. H. 1969. 'A refrain-poem from N.L.W. Peniarth MS. 395'. *Trivium* 4. 43–9.

Robbins, R. H. 1972. ' "Conuertimini": A Middle English Refrain Poem'. *Neuphilologische Mitteilungen* 73. 353–61.

Robbins, R. H. 1975. In *A Manual of the Writings in Middle English*, Vol. 5. Ed. A. E. Hartung. Hamden, Connecticut.

Robbins, R. H. and Cutler, J. L. 1965. *Supplement to the Index of Middle English Verse*. Lexington, Kentucky.

Roberts, P. B. 1968. *Stephanus de Lingua-Tonante: Studies in the Sermons of Stephen Langton*. Toronto.

Robertson, D. W. Jnr. 1951. 'Historical Criticism'. In *English Institute Essays*. Ed. A. Downer. New York.

Robinson, P. R. 1990. 'The Vernon Manuscript as a "Coucher Book" '. In Pearsall 1990. 15–28.

Roques, M., ed. 1958. *Les Romans de Chrétien de Troyes. III. Le Chevalier de la Charrete*. Les Classiques Français du Moyen Age 86. Paris.

Ross, D. J. 1993. *Musick Fyne: Robert Carver and the Art of Music in Sixteenth Century Scotland*. Edinburgh.

Ross, I. S. 1986. ' "Prologue" and "Buke" in the *Eneados* of Gavin Douglas'. In Strauss and Drescher. 393–407.

Ross, W. O., ed. 1940. *Middle English Sermons*. EETS OS 209.

Rossi, S. 1964. *I Chauceriani Scozzesi*. Naples.

Routley, E. 1958. *The English Carol*. London.

Rubin, M. 1991. *Corpus Christi: The Eucharist in Late Medieval Culture*. Cambridge.

Ruggiers, P. G., ed. 1984. *Editing Chaucer: The Great Tradition*. Norman, Oklahoma.

Russell, G. H. 1962–63. 'Vernacular Instruction of the Laity in the Later Middle Ages in England: Some Texts and Notes'. *Journal of Religious History* 2. 98–119.

Ruud, J. 1992. *'Many a Song and Many a Lecherous Lay': Tradition and Individuality in Chaucer's Lyric Poetry*. New York and London.

Ryan, W. G., trans. 1993. *Jacobus de Voragine: Legenda aurea*. 2 vols. Princeton.

Sachs, C. 1938. *World History of the Dance*. Trans. B. Schönberg. London.

Sadie, S., ed. 2001. *The New Grove Dictionary of Music and Musicians*. 2nd edn. 29 vols. London.

Sahlin, M. 1940. *Étude sur la carole médiévale. L'origine du mot et ses rapports avec l'église*. Thèse pour le doctorat. Uppsala.

Saintsbury, G. 1907. 'The Prosody of Old and Middle English'. In *The Cambridge History of English Literature*, Vol. 1. Eds A. W. Ward and A. R. Waller. Cambridge. 372–8.

Salter, E. 1979. 'A Complaint against Blacksmiths'. *Literature and History* 5. 194–215. Reptd in *English and International: Studies in the Literature, Art and Patronage of Medieval England*. 1988. Eds. D. Pearsall and N. Zeeman. Cambridge. 199–214.

Samuels, M. L. 1972. 'Chaucerian Final "-e" '. *Notes and Queries* 217. 445–8.

Sandison, H. E. 1913. *The 'Chanson d'Aventure' in Middle English*. Bryn Mawr College Monographs 12. Bryn Mawr, Pennsylvania.

Sandler, L. F. 1983. *The Psalter of Robert de Lisle*. Oxford and New York.

Sargent, M. D., ed. 1992. *Nicholas Love's Mirror of the Blessed Life of Jesus Christ*. London and New York.

Saupe, K., ed. 1998. *Middle English Marian Lyrics*. Medieval Institute Publications. Kalamazoo, Michigan.

Scahill, J. 2003. 'Trilingualism in Early Middle English Miscellanies: Languages and Literature'. *Yearbook of English Studies* 33. 18–32.

Scattergood, V. J. 1968. 'Political Context, Date and Composition of *The Sayings of the Four Philosophers*'. *Medium Ævum* 37. 157–65.

Scattergood, V. J. 1971. *Politics and Poetry in the Fifteenth Century*. London.

Scattergood, V. J., ed. 1983a. *John Skelton: The Complete English Poems*. Harmondsworth.

Scattergood, V. J., ed. 1983b. *John Skelton: The Complete English Poems*. New Haven and London.

Scattergood, V. J. 1987a. 'Two Unrecorded Poems from Trinity College, Dublin, MS 490'. *Review of English Studies* NS 38. 46–9.

Scattergood, V. J. 1987b. 'The "Bisynesse" of Love in Chaucer's Dawn Songs'. *Essays in Criticism* 37 ii. 110–20.

Scattergood, V. J. 1995. 'The Short Poems'. In A. J. Minnis, with V. J. Scattergood and J. J. Smith. *Oxford Guides to Chaucer: The Shorter Poems*. Oxford. 455–512.

Scattergood, V. J. 1996. *Reading the Past. Essays on Medieval and Renaissance Literature*. Blackrock, County Dublin.

Scattergood, V. J. 2000. 'Authority and Resistance: The Political Verse'. In Fein. 163–201.

Schmidt, A. V. C., ed. 1978. *William Langland: The Vision of Piers Plowman, A Complete Edition of the B-Text*. London.

Schulz, H. C. 1939–40. 'Middle English Texts from the "Bement" MS'. *Huntington Library Quarterly* 3. 443–65.

Scott, A. See Cranstoun.

Scott, K. L. 1996. *Later Gothic Manuscripts, 1390–1490*. 2 vols. London.

Scott, T. 1966. *Dunbar: A Critical Exposition of the Poems*. Edinburgh and London.

Seymour, M. C., ed. 1967. *Mandeville's Travels*. Oxford.

Shippey, T. A. 1976. *Poems of Wisdom and Learning in Old English*. Cambridge.

Shire, H. M. 1969. *Song, Dance and Poetry of the Court of Scotland under King James VI*. Cambridge.

Silverstein, T., ed. 1971. *Medieval English Lyrics*. London.

Simpson, J. 2002. *Reform and Cultural Revolution*. Oxford.

Sisam, C. and Sisam, K., eds. 1970. *The Oxford Book of Medieval English Verse*. Oxford.

Sisam, K., ed. 1921. *Fourteenth Century Verse and Prose*. Oxford.

Sitwell, G. 1950. 'A Fourteenth-Century English Poem on *Ecclesiastes*'. *Dominican Studies* 3. 284–90.

Skeat, W. W., ed. 1897. *The Complete Works of Geoffrey Chaucer*, Vol. 7: *Chaucerian and Other Pieces*. Oxford.

Smithers, G. V., ed. 1952–57. *Kyng Alisaunder*. 2 vols. EETS OS 227, 237.

Smithers, G. V. 1983. 'The Scansion of *Havelok* and the Use of ME *–en* and *–e* in *Havelok* and Chaucer'. In *Middle English Studies Presented to Norman Davis in Honour of his Seventieth Birthday*. Eds D. Gray and E. G. Stanley. Oxford. 195–234.

Southworth, J. G. 1962. *The Prosody of Chaucer*. Oxford.

Spanke, H. 1930. 'Das lateinische Rondeau'. *Zeitschrift für französische Sprache und Literatur* 53. 113–148.

Spears, J. E. 1974. 'The "Boar's Head Carol" and Folk Tradition'. *Folklore* 85. 194–8.

Spencer, H. L. 1993. *English Preaching in the Late Middle Ages*. Oxford.

Spitzer, L. 1951. '*Explication de Texte* Applied to Three Great Middle English Poems'. *Archivum Linguisticum* 3. 1–22.

Spitzer, L. 1962. *Essays on English and American Literature*. Princeton, New Jersey. 193–247. Repr. of Spitzer, L. 1951. '*Explication de Texte* Applied to Three Great Middle English Poems'. *Archivum Linguisticum* 3. 1–22, 157–65.

St Amour, Sister M. P. 1940. *A Study of the Villancico up to Lope De Vega: Its Evolution from Profane to Sacred themes, and Specifically to the Christmas Carol*. Washington, District of Columbia.

Stanbury, S. 1991. 'The Virgin's Gaze: Spectacle and Transgression in Middle English

Lyrics of the Passion'. *Publications of the Modern Language Association of America* 106. 1083–93.

Stanbury, S. 1992. 'The Lover's Gaze in Troilus and Criseyde'. In *'Subgit to alle Poesye': Essays in Criticism*. Ed. R. A. Shoaf. Binghamton, New York.

Stanbury, S. 1997. 'Regimes of the Visual in Premodern England: Gaze, Body, and Chaucer's *Clerk's Tale*'. *New Literary History* 28. 261–89.

Stanley, E. G. 1997. 'The Verse Forms of Jon the Blynde Awdelay'. In Cooper and Mapstone. 99–121.

Statutes of the Realm: Printed by the command of his Majesty King George the Third. 2 vols. London, 1810–28.

Steele, R. and Day, M., eds. 1941–46. *The English Poems of Charles of Orleans*. EETS OS 215, 220.

Steele, R., ed. 1941. *The English Poems of Charles of Orleans*. EETS OS 215.

Stemmler, T. 1962. *Die englischen Liebesgedichte des MS. Harley 2253*. Bonn.

Stemmler, T., ed. 1975. *The Latin Poems of Richard Ledrede*. Mannheim.

Stevens, J., ed. 1958. *Mediaeval Carols*. Musica Britannica 4. 2nd revised edn. London.

Stevens, J. 1961. *Music and Poetry in the Early Tudor Court*. London and Lincoln, Nebraska.

Stevens, J. 1962. *Music at the Court of Henry VIII*. Musica Britannica 18. London.

Stevens, J., ed. 1975. *Early Tudor Songs and Carols*. Musica Britannica 36. London.

Stevens, J. 1979. *Music and Poetry at the Early Tudor Court*. Cambridge.

Stevens, J. 1982. *The Old Sound and the New: An inaugural lecture*. Cambridge.

Stevens, J. 1986. *Words and Music in the Middle Ages: Song, Narrative, Dance and Drama, 1050–1350*. Cambridge.

Stevens, J. 1990. 'Medieval Song'. In *The Early Middle Ages to 1300*. Eds R. Crocker and D. Hiley. The New Oxford History of Music 2. Oxford. 357–451.

Stevenson, G., ed. 1918. *Pieces from the Makculloch and the Gray MSS. Together with The Chepman and Myllar Prints*. STS. Edinburgh and London.

Sticca, S. 1988. *The Planctus Mariae in the Dramatic Tradition of the Middle Ages*. Trans. J. R. Berrigan. Athens, Georgia.

Strauss, D. and Drescher, H. W., eds. 1986. *Scottish Language and Literature, Medieval and Renaissance*. Frankfurt am Main.

Strohm, P. 1989. *Social Chaucer*. Cambridge, Massachusetts.

Strohm, P. 1992. *Hochon's Arrow: The Social Imagination of Fourteenth-Century Texts*. Princeton.

Strohm, P. 1998. *England's Empty Throne: Usurpation and the Language of Legitimation 1399–1422*. New Haven.

Taylor, A. 2002. *Textual Situations: Three Medieval Manuscripts and their Readers*. Philadelphia.

Thompson, B., ed. 1995. *The Reign of Henry VII*. Harlaxton Medieval Studies 5. Stamford, Lincolnshire.

Thompson, J. J. 1987. *Robert Thornton and the London Thornton Manuscript: British Library Additional 31042*. Cambridge.

Thompson, J. J. 1988. 'Literary Associations of an Anonymous Middle English Paraphrase of Vulgate Psalm L'. *Medium Ævum* 67. 38–55.

Thompson, J. J. 1990. 'The Textual Background and Reputation of the Vernon Lyrics'. In Pearsall 1990. 201–24.

Thornley, E. M. 1967. 'The Middle English Penitential Lyric and Hoccleve's Penitential Poetry'. *Neuphilologische Mitteilungen* 68. 295–321.

Tilley, M. P. 1950. *A Dictionary of the Proverbs of England in the Sixteenth and Seventeenth Centuries*. Ann Arbor.

Todd, M. 2002. *The Culture of Protestantism in Early Modern Scotland*. New Haven and London.

Tolkien, J. R. R. and Gordon, E. V., eds. 1967. *Sir Gawain and the Green Knight*. 2nd edn revised by N. Davis. Oxford.

Toscani, B., ed. 1990. *Lorenzo de' Medici, Laude*. Florence.

Trapp, J. B., Gray, D. and Boffey, J., eds. 2002. *Medieval English Literature*. 2nd edn. The Oxford Anthology of English Literature. New York and Oxford.

Trigg, S., ed. 1990. *Wynnere and Wastoure*. EETS OS 297.

Tschann, J. and Parkes, M. B., intro. 1996. *Facsimile of Oxford, Bodlian Library MS Digby 86*. EETS SS 16.

Tubach, F. C. 1969. *Index Exemplorum: A Handbook of Medieval Religious Tales*. Folklore Fellows' Communications 204. Helsinki.

Turville-Petre, T., ed. 1989. *Alliterative Poetry of the Later Middle Ages*. London.

Turville-Petre, T. 1996. *England the Nation: Language, Literature, and National Identity, 1290–1340*. Oxford.

Turville-Petre, T. 1997. 'English Quaint and Strange in "Ne mai no lewed lued" '. In *Individuality and Achievement in Middle English Poetry*. Ed. O. S. Pickering. Cambridge.

Utley, F. L. 1944. *The Crooked Rib: An Analytical Index to the Argument about Women in English and Scots Literature to the End of the Year 1568*. Columbus, Ohio.

van Heijnsbergen, Th. 1991. 'The Love Lyrics of Alexander Scott'. *Studies in Scottish Literature* 26. 366–79.

van Heijnsbergen, Th. 1996. 'The Sixteenth-Century Scottish Love Lyric'. In Wilcox, Todd and MacDonald. 45–61.

van Heijnsbergen, Th. 2001. 'Dunbar, Scott and the Making of Poetry'. In Mapstone 2001a. 108–33.

van Zutphen, J. P. W. M., ed. 1956. *Richard Lavynham: A Litil Tretys on the Seven Deadly Sins*. Rome.

Vendler, H. 2002. *Poems, Poets, Poetry: An Introduction and Anthology*. 2nd edn. Boston and New York.

von Ehingen. See Letts.

Wack, M. 1990. *Lovesickness in the Middle Ages: The 'Viaticum' and its Commentaries*. Philadelphia.

Waddell, H. 1930. *Medieval Latin Lyrics*. London.

Waddell, H. 1938. *The Wandering Scholars*. London.

Wallace, D. 1997. *Chaucerian Polity: Absolutist Lineages and Associational Forms in England and Italy*. Stanford.

Wallace, D., ed. 1999. *The Cambridge History of Medieval English Literature*. Cambridge.

Walsh, P. G., ed. and trans. 1982. *Andreas Capellanus on Love*. London.

Watson, N. 1995. 'Censorship and Cultural Change in Late-Medieval England: Vernacular Theology, the Oxford Translation Debate, and Arundel's Constitutions of 1409'. *Speculum* 70. 822–64.

Watson, N. 1999. 'The Politics of Middle English Writing'. In Wogan-Browne, Watson, Taylor and Evans. 331–52.

Wehrle, W. O. 1933. 'The Macaronic Hymn Tradition in Medieval English Literature'. Ph. D. Dissertation Catholic University of America. Washington, District of Columbia.

Wenzel, S. 1974. 'The Moor Maiden: A Contemporary View'. *Speculum* 49. 67–74.

Wenzel, S. 1978. *Verses in Sermons: 'Fasciculus Morum' and its Middle English Poems*. The Medieval Academy of America Publication No. 87. Cambridge, Massachusetts.

Wenzel, S. 1983. 'A New Occurrence of an English Poem from the Red Book of Ossory'. *Notes and Queries* 228. 105–8.

Wenzel, S. 1985. 'Poets, Preachers, and the Plight of Literary Critics'. *Speculum* 60. 343–63.

Wenzel, S. 1986. *Preachers, Poets, and the Early English Lyric*. Princeton, New Jersey.

Wenzel, S., ed. and trans. 1989. *Fasciculus Morum: A Fourteenth-Century Preacher's Handbook*. University Park, Pennsylvania and London.

Wenzel, S. 1994. *Macaronic Sermons: Bilingualism and Preaching in Late-Medieval England*. Ann Arbor.

Whitehead, C. 2000. 'A Fortress and a Shield: The Representation of the Virgin in the *Château d'Amour* of Robert Grosseteste'. In Renevey and Whitehead. 109–32.

Whiting, B. J. and Whiting, H. W. 1968. *Proverbs, Sentences and Proverbial Phrases from English Writings Mainly Before 1500*. Cambridge, Massachusetts.

Whiting, E. K., ed. 1931. *The Poems of John Audelay*. EETS OS 184 .

Wilcox, H. E., Todd, R. M. and MacDonald, A. A., eds. 1996. *Sacred and Profane: Secular and Devotional Interplay in Early Modern British Literature*. Amsterdam.

Williams, L. 1984. 'When the Woman Looks'. In *Re-Vision: Essays in Feminist Film Criticism*. Ed. M. A. Doane, P. Mellencamp, and L. Williams. Frederick, Maryland and Los Angeles. 83–99.

Wilson, E. 1973. *A Descriptive Index of the English Lyrics in John of Grimestone's Preaching Book*. Medium Ævum Monographs NS 2. Oxford.

Wilson, E., intro. 1981. *The Winchester Anthology: A Facsimile of British Library Additional Manuscript 60577*. Cambridge.

Wilson, E. 1983. 'A Poem Presented to William Waynflete as Bishop of Winchester'. In *Middle English Studies presented to Norman Davis in Honour of his Seventieth Birthday*. Eds. D. Gray and E. G. Stanley. Oxford. 127–151.

Wilson, R. M. 1952. *The Lost Literature of Medieval England*. London.

Wilson, R. M. 1968. *Early Middle English Literature*. 3rd edn. London.

Wilson, R. M. 1970. *The Lost Literature of Medieval England*. 2nd revised edn. London.

Wimsatt, J. I. 1982. *Chaucer and the Poems of 'Ch'*. Cambridge.

Windeatt, B., ed. 1984. Geoffrey Chaucer, *Troilus and Criseyde: A new edition of 'The Book of Troilus'*. London and New York.

Wogan-Browne, J., Watson, N., Taylor, A. and Evans, R. 1999. *The Idea of the Vernacular: An Anthology of Middle English Literary Theory 1280–1520*. Philadelphia and Exeter.

Wogan-Browne, J., Voaden, R., Diamond, A., Hutchison, A., Meale, C. M. and Johnson, L., eds. 2000. *Medieval Women: Texts and Contexts in Late Medieval Britain*. Turnhout.

Woods Preece, I. W. 2000. *Music in the Scottish Church up to 1603*. Glasgow and Aberdeen.

Woods, M. C. and Copeland, R. 1999. 'Classroom and confession'. In Wallace. 376–406.

Woolf, R. 1968. *The English Religious Lyric in the Middle Ages*. Oxford.

Woolf, R. 1969. 'The Construction of "In a fryght as y con fere fremede" '. *Medium Aevum* 38. 55–9.

Woolf, R. 1970. 'Later Poetry: the Popular Tradition'. In W. F. Bolton, ed. *The Sphere History of Literature in the English Language*. Vol. 1: *The Middle Ages*. London. 263–311.

Wright, T., ed. 1842. *Specimens of Lyric Poetry*. Percy Society 4. London.

Wright, T., ed. 1847. *Songs and Carols, Now First Printed, From a Manuscript of the Fifteenth Century*. Percy Society 23. London.

Wright, T., ed. 1859–61. *Political Poems and Songs Relating to English History*. Rolls ser. 14. 2 vols.

Wright, T., ed. 1868. *The Chronicle of Pierre de Langtoft*, Vol. 2. Rolls ser. 47.

Wynnere and Wastoure. See Trigg 1990.

Yates, F. 1966. *The Art of Memory*. London.

Yeats, W. B. 1973. *Collected Poems*. London.

Zink, M. 1972. *La Pastourelle: Poésie et Folklore au Moyen Age*. Paris.

Zinn, G. A., trans. and intro. 1979. *Richard of St-Victor: The Twelve Patriarchs. The Mystical Ark. Book Three of the Trinity*. Classics of Western Spirituality. New York.

Zupitza, J. 1892. 'Die Gedichte des Franziskaners Jakob Ryman'. *Archiv für das Studium der neueren Sprachen und Literaturen* 89. 167–338.

Index of Manuscripts Cited

General Index

Recent (twentieth-century) and contemporary lyric scholars and critics are not listed.

Index of Lyrics

In this index are listed the Middle English and macaronic lyrics named, quoted or discussed in this volume. Lyrics cited without title, quotation or discussion (i.e. as passing references by IMEV or edition numbers) are not included. The lyrics are mostly identified by first lines (and/or by the first lines of burdens in the case of carols), but sometimes by titles, and occasionally by refrains. Only one form of each line is used in this index though variant forms of such lines may occur throughout the volume depending on the sources cited. First lines of burdens, traditional titles and refrains are given in italics. Titles adopted by Brown or Robbins are given in inverted commas. Substantial quotations from the body of lyric texts are also indexed by first lines or titles even where not so identified in the text.

Printed in the United States
98525LV00003B/7-12/A

9 781843 840657